# Motorcycle Basics Manual

by Pete Shoemark

(1083-8Q3)

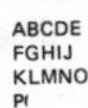

**Haynes Publishing Group**
Sparkford Nr Yeovil
Somerset BA22 7JJ England

**Haynes Publications, Inc**
861 Lawrence Drive
Newbury Park
California 91320 USA

## Acknowledgements

Our thanks are due to the following companies who provided many of the illustrations used throughout this book:

The Avon Rubber Company, Burmah Castrol Ltd, Ducati Meccanica SpA, Dwek International Ltd, Heron Suzuki (GB) Ltd, Kawasaki (UK) Ltd, Mitsui Machinery Sales (UK) Ltd, NVT Motorcycles Ltd, Robin Chan of Contact Developments and Vespa (UK) Ltd.

We would also like to thank Bruce Main-Smith for his permission to reproduce extracts from his book, the *Motorcyclists Encyclopedia,* which is now out of print; and also Tony Tranter who gave permission to use line drawings from his book, *The Motorcycle Electrical Manual.*

The cutaway Yamaha XV750 engine featured on the front cover was kindly supplied by Mitsui Machinery Sales (UK) Ltd.

---



---

A book in the **Haynes Owners Workshop Manual Series**

---

**Printed by J.H. Haynes & Co. Ltd, Sparkford, Nr Yeovil, Somerset BA22 7JJ, England**

---



---

**ISBN 1 85010 083 7**

---

**Library of Congress Catalog Card Number 85-80285**

---

**British Library Cataloguing in Publication Data**
Shoemark, Pete
Motorcycle basics manual.
1. Motorcycles
I. Title
629.2'275 TL440
ISBN 1-85010-083-7

---

# Contents

# Introduction

Quite a large proportion of motorcycles, mopeds and scooters in everyday use are ridden by owners who have little understanding of how their machine works. Many are quite content to remain in this state of blissful ignorance, having their machine serviced at regular intervals as and when the need occurs, or repairs carried out when problems necessitate taking the machine off the road. Not everyone has the ability or inclination to look after these matters themselves and it is as well that they are aware of their own limitations.

Unfortunately, roadside breakdowns are likely to occur without warning, often at times that prove particularly inconvenient. They can range from something mildly irritating, such as the refusal to start one morning to a complete breakdown in some remote spot, miles from home on a dark, wet winter's night. It is on occasions like these that most people begin to have some regret at not having even a basic understanding of how their machine works so that they could, perhaps, have taken precautionary measures to prevent such a happening, or, at the very least, have an idea of where the fault lies. No book, however well written, can turn an unskilled amateur into a skilled mechanic. What it can do is to explain in simple terms how each major component of a motorcycle functions and the role it plays in ensuring the machine remains in good running order. With just this basic knowledge it should be possible to pinpoint what has gone wrong when a machine fails to start or stops running – and if it is only a simple fault, how to get going again without having to seek outside help.

There are two ways in which to approach the subject of motorcycle mechanics, the easiest and most comfortable of which is to sit by the fireside with this and as many other books as can be found and absorb their content. This is fine if only theoretical knowledge is required. But as is so often the case, it is first-hand practical experience that counts, and this can only be acquired by actually examining and, if needs be, working on the machine itself. Today's two wheelers are the end product of many years' continual development work, becoming both complicated and sophisticated particularly in the larger capacity range. Unlike television or Hi-Fi equipment, their function is essentially mechanical, so that it is possible to observe what is going on in most cases. Except in extreme cases, expensive diagnostic equipment is not required, most repairs and overhauls being feasible with the tools usually available in the home garage or workshop. If the correct mental approach is adopted, it will often be found that a quite complicated-looking assembly is nothing more than a number of relatively simple basic units bolted together to make up a single, compact unit.

It is strongly recommended that this book should be used in conjunction with either the appropriate Owners Handbook provided with the machine, or with a Haynes Owners Workshop Manual when starting with simple maintenance tasks. As confidence builds up, more detailed tasks can be undertaken, by which time the use of a workshop manual as a source of reference will have become an essential requirement. It will be possible to compare the different components and assemblies on the machine with those illustrated in this book, even if their appearance differs according to the make and model of machine. Even so, they will be recognisable and if difficulty is experienced in obtaining a firm grasp of their function or mode of operation, a knowledgeable friend or even a local dealer or mechanic will be willing to explain in even greater detail. Never be afraid to ask when in doubt; it can save some expensive mistakes later.

Eventually, it will be possible to build up a complete mental picture of exactly what is happening to keep your machine running as you ride. With this newly-acquired knowledge you will be better equipped to know what has gone wrong with your machine when it ceases to run, even if you do not have the confidence and ability to tackle its repair. If you use this book in conjunction with the Haynes Owners Workshop Manual pertinent to your machine, the probability is that you will be able to tackle the repair with confidence too by following the easy-to-read text and the many photographs and line drawings that make even the most complicated repair tasks well within the capabilities of the average D-I-Y mechanic. Perhaps even of more importance, it will save you time and money too.

It has been our objective to present the information given in this book in as simple a form as possible, using line drawings wherever possible to illustrate components and systems in their most basic form. Technical terms have been kept to a minimum and used only where considered necessary, but to help readers even further, a basic glossary of terms will be found immediately before the index, with a simple explanation in a few lines.

# Chapter 1 Engine

## Contents



## 1 Introduction

All powered two-wheelers share a number of similarities, even though at first glance a 50cc Japanese scooter seems far removed from a large-capacity sports motorcycle. Each has two wheels, an engine and some form of transmission, these being held in position by a frame. In this chapter we will be looking at various types of engine to try to establish how they work and why they come in so many diverse shapes and sizes. Before we go any further we should be clear on exactly which part of the machine we mean by the engine. On almost every modern design, the engine components are housed in cast alloy cases together with the transmission components. These cases are almost universally called crankcases, even though they contain rather more than the crankshaft, because this stems from earlier designs where the engine was entirely separate from the transmission. Modern designs are normally referred to as being of 'unit construction' whilst the earlier arrangement, found mainly on older British-built bikes, has been dubbed 'pre-unit', for obvious reasons.

We are concerned here with the cylinder head, the cylinder barrel(s) and piston(s) and the crankshaft assembly. The last is housed inside the crankcase, usually near the front and always just below the barrel. All engines have these components, (with one exception which is described below), the main difference being in the number of cylinders and pistons, and their arrangement.

## 2 Which engine?

The purpose of an engine is to convert fuel into work, and in motorcycles, all engines are of the 'internal combustion' type. All this means is that the fuel is burnt inside the engine, rather than outside it as is the case with steam engines. Steam has never been a popular choice of motive power in the two-wheel world, so we can ignore that particular type of engine.

Just about every machine you are likely to encounter will have a two-stroke engine or a four-stroke engine, and these have much in common. In both types, a mixture of fuel and air is compressed inside the cylinder and then ignited by a spark. The mixture burns very quickly, and in doing so it expands, pushing the piston down the cylinder bore. The piston is connected to the crankshaft by a connecting rod, and its up and down (or reciprocating) movement is converted at the crankshaft into the rotary motion required to turn the rear wheel and thus drive the machine.

The exception to the above is the Wankel or rotary engine. This is also an internal combustion engine, but it works on a rather different principle to conventional two- and four-stroke designs. There have to date been only two commercially-produced rotary-engined motorcycles, the ill-fated Suzuki RE5 and the Hercules. Though technically advanced, a combination of unreliability and poor public acceptance meant a short production life, and few examples remain on the road. Norton have been working on their own rotary design for some years now, but it has yet to go into full production. For the present, suffice it to say that two- and four-stroke engines are collectively known as reciprocating engines, to distinguish them from the rotary type.

Having set aside the Wankel, there remains the choice of two-stroke or four-stroke units. Each has its own advantages and disadvantages, and this is why neither has ever managed to oust the other. In its simplest form the two-stroke unit is by far the less complicated of the two, and is thus cheaper to manufacture. In the past this has been the main reason for its almost exclusive use in mopeds, scooters and lightweight motorcycles. The simple two-stroke does have its drawbacks, though, and at one stage the disappearance of the two-stroke seemed inevitable because of the insurmountable problems of high noise and air pollution levels. In recent years the two-stroke engine has become an altogether more sophisticated device, and the advances are such that it remains a popular choice for many applications. The 'low-cost' aspect has largely disappeared though, and the modern two-stroke is now employed primarily in the interests of light weight and power output.

The four-stroke engine was traditionally chosen for larger machines because of its superior spread of power and fuel economy. Its main drawback was the higher manufacturing cost and relative complexity, and this made it a bad choice for smaller capacity engines. Just as the two-stroke became more refined, however, so did the four-stroke, and over the years the distinction between the role of each type blurred; small four-strokes became just as good a proposition as large two-strokes.

In the end, two-stroke and four-stroke engines can be viewed as two means to the same end, namely a way of propelling a vehicle. Each has its supporters and detractors and this is reflected in manufacturers' catalogues which often offer very similar models with two- and four-stroke engines, leaving the choice in the hands of the prospective owner. Until recently it was quite easy to look at a particular engine type and see clearly its good and bad points. The level of technology now applied to engine design and manufacture has led to a situation where almost any drawback can be engineered out of the design, though often at the expense of simplicity. Later in this Chapter we will examine the two-stroke and four-stroke engines in greater detail, but before looking at the differences between them, let us deal with their similarities.

## 3 Basic principles

### The cylinder and piston

All 'reciprocating' engines have in common a number of basic parts, and these are recognisably similar even between the extreme examples of a model aircraft engine and a large diesel truck engine. To convert the fuel/air mixture into useful work it must be burnt in a carefully

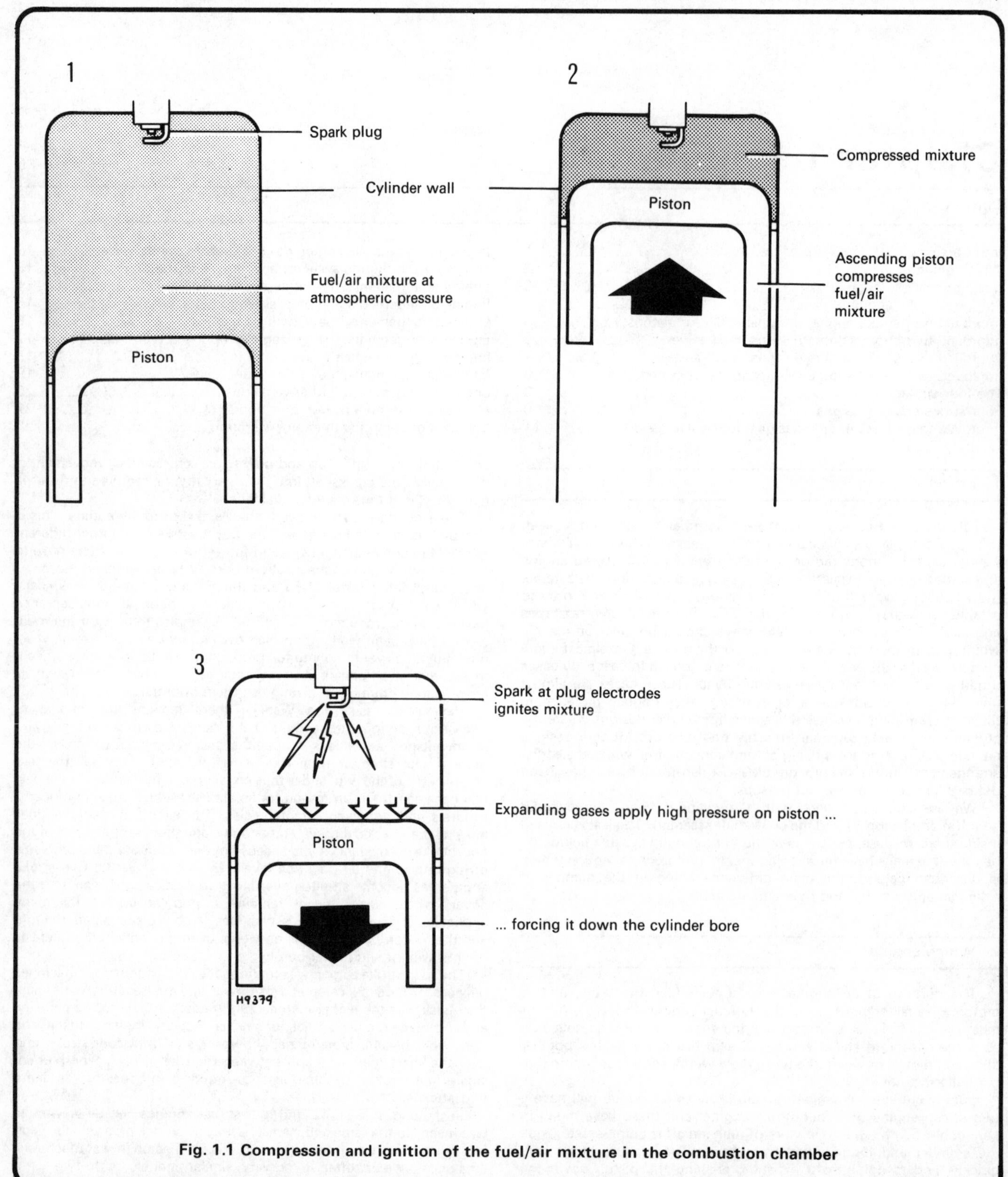


Fig. 1.1 Compression and ignition of the fuel/air mixture in the combustion chamber

controlled manner and the resulting energy changed into movement. This takes place in a closed cylinder, and the process is illustrated in Fig. 1.1.

(1) A mixture of fuel together with the necessary amount of air is introduced into the cylinder, above the piston. The piston, which is a tight fit in the cylinder bore to prevent leakage, is pushed upwards and the mixture is compressed.
(2) The fuel air mixture now occupies a much smaller space than it did at atmospheric pressure. This effectively concentrates the energy contained in the fuel, allowing the maximum amount of power to be extracted when it is burnt.
(3) At the appropriate moment a spark jumps across the spark plug electrodes, igniting the mixture. This burns very quickly, and can be considered almost a controlled explosion. The resulting hot gases rapidly increase the pressure in the cylinder, forcing the piston down with far more energy than was required to compress the mixture originally.

**The crankshaft**

In the above example we have seen how the controlled combustion of fuel in air can be used to produce useful work, and in practice this cycle is repeated many times every minute to produce a relatively continuous source of motive power. In the present form, however, it is of little use in driving a motorcycle; we must first convert it to rotary motion.

The principle of the crankshaft is well known and is employed by most people every day. Each time you ride a bicycle, wind down a car window or operate a can opener you are converting a more or less linear movement into a rotary one. In Fig. 1.2 we can see the comparison between a hand-operated flywheel and a similar engine-powered version. The flywheel performs a very important role; as the piston is pushed down the cylinder bore, part of the energy is 'stored' in the flywheel and is used to carry the piston back up to the next power stroke and to compress the next mixture charge. Similarly, if in the hand-operated version we assume that the wheel is turned only by pushing in one direction, momentum will keep the flywheel turning until it is in the right position to be pushed round again.

To allow our example crankshaft to work, one or two refinements are needed. Firstly, there has to be some sort of bearing between the lower bearing or big-end of the rod that connects the piston and the flywheel. This can be a bush or a ball or roller bearing fitted into the big-end eye and engaging over the crankpin. Similarly, at the upper bearing of the connecting rod or small-end, it will be necessary to allow the piston to rock in relation to the connecting rod. Again, a bush or bearing is used and the piston is located by a short pin, known as a gudgeon pin in the UK or more descriptively as a wrist pin in the US.

In a working example of an engine there are normally two flywheels connected by a short crankpin, and the connecting rod runs between the two, on this crankpin. The flywheels are carried in bearings at each side, these being fitted into a light alloy casing, or crankcase. The cylinder is held in the correct position by being bolted to the crankcase in which the crankshaft runs.

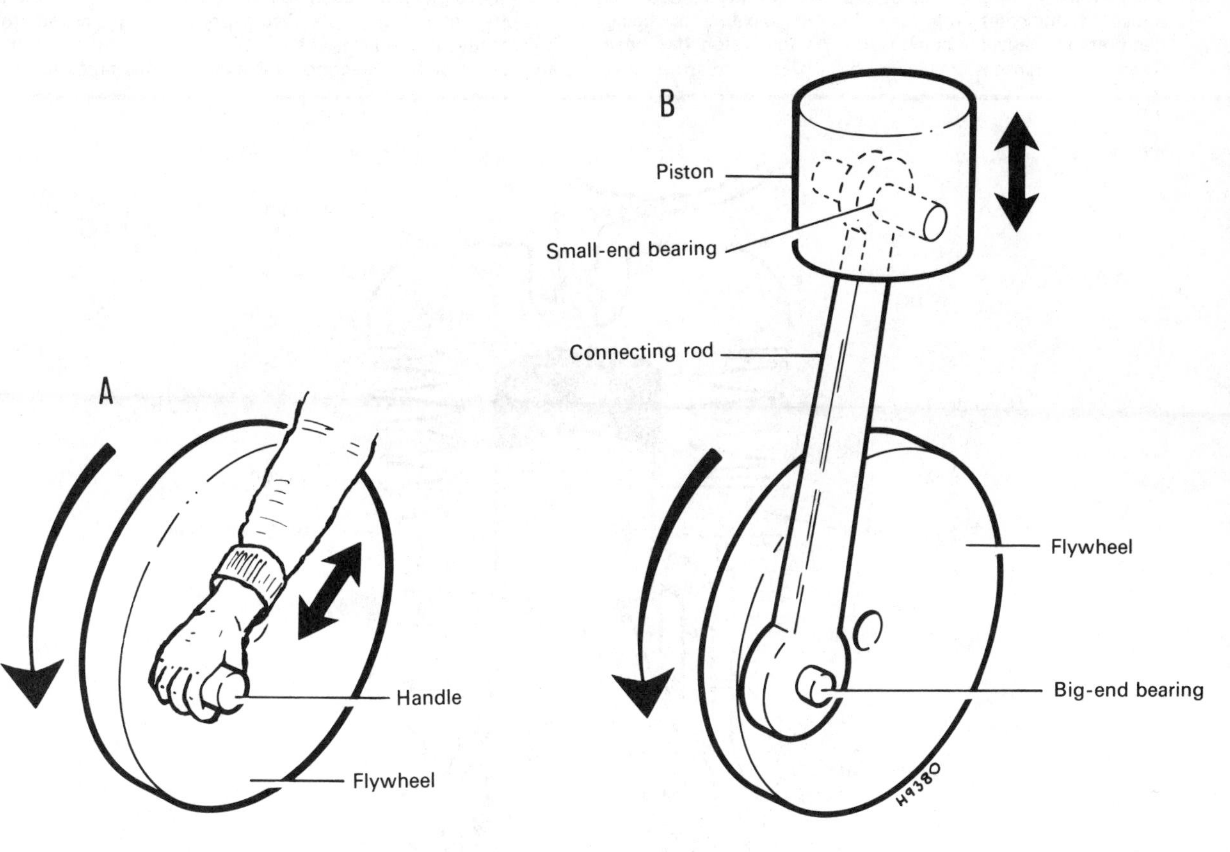


**Fig. 1.2 How the crankshaft converts linear motion into the rotary motion required to turn the rear wheel**

**A** By alternately pushing and pulling on the handle, the flywheel can be made to revolve. At the two extremes of the stroke there will be no significant force applied to the flywheel, but stored energy, or momentum. will carry it through these dead points.

**B** Compare this with (A). The force applied by hand through the handle has been replaced by the connecting rod assembly and big-end bearing.

## 4 The two-stroke engine

Having established the mechanical requirements of a simple internal combustion engine we can now look at ways of making it run as a suitable power source for a motorcycle. The simplest of these in mechanical terms is the piston-ported two-stroke, and this is described in Fig. 1.3. The drawing shows the engine in section, and you should be able to identify the engine components shown in the previous illustrations.

You may have noticed that the cylinder bore has gained a few holes in its surface. These are known as ports and are fundamental to two-stroke operation. The inlet and exhaust ports are obvious enough, their purpose being to allow the fuel/air mixture into the engine (inlet) and to allow the exhaust gases to be expelled (exhaust). The function of the transfer port is to allow the mixture to be passed from the crankcase to the combustion chamber, and this raises the question of what the mixture is doing below the piston.

To understand this it should be noted that the crankcase fulfils an important secondary role in a two-stroke engine, acting as a sort of pump for the mixture. It forms a sealed chamber, closed at the top by the piston, and it follows that the volume of this chamber varies as the piston rises and falls in the cylinder. The inlet port in the cylinder wall is kept closed for much of the time, but is uncovered as the piston nears the top of its stroke. The resulting partial vacuum draws a fresh charge of mixture into the cylinder, and this is then pushed into the combustion chamber through the transfer port. The sequence is described below in conjunction with Figs. 1.4 and 1.5.

(A) The piston is nearing the top of its stroke, and the shaded area above it indicates that the fuel/air mixture is being compressed ready for combustion. As the piston has been rising the crankcase volume has been increasing, but since it is sealed a partial vacuum has been created. The piston has now passed the inlet port and a fresh charge is drawn into the crankcase from the carburettor, indicated by the arrows.

(B) The spark plug ignites the compressed mixture and the expanding gases force the piston downwards. The piston has now covered the inlet port and has begun to compress the fresh mixture trapped below it. At about the same time, the top of the piston passes the exhaust port and transfer port. Though most of the useful power has been extracted, the gases in the combustion chamber are still under pressure, and rush out through the exhaust port. The fresh mixture charge is now able to escape from the crankcase into the combustion chamber. Note that the transfer port directs the incoming mixture upwards, where it helps to displace the burnt gases. If this were not done, the incoming mixture would tend to rush straight out of the exhaust port, wasting fuel and leaving some of the spent mixture from the last power stroke in the cylinder. The piston has now passed the bottom of its stroke and begins to ascend. The exhaust and transfer ports are closed and the mixture in the combustion chamber is compressed. As the piston continues to rise, the inlet port is uncovered and thus the cycle is completed.

The above design, known as a 'piston-ported' two-stroke for obvious reasons, is the simplest form of two-stroke engine, and has very few moving parts. Whilst this is a considerable advantage in many respects, it leaves a lot to be desired in terms of efficiency. At one time almost every two-stroke engine was of the piston-ported type, but on current designs it has been abandoned in favour of more sophisticated and efficient arrangements. Piston-ported designs are still to be found, but mostly on mopeds where a high power output is not necessary, and where poor fuel economy is a less serious problem.

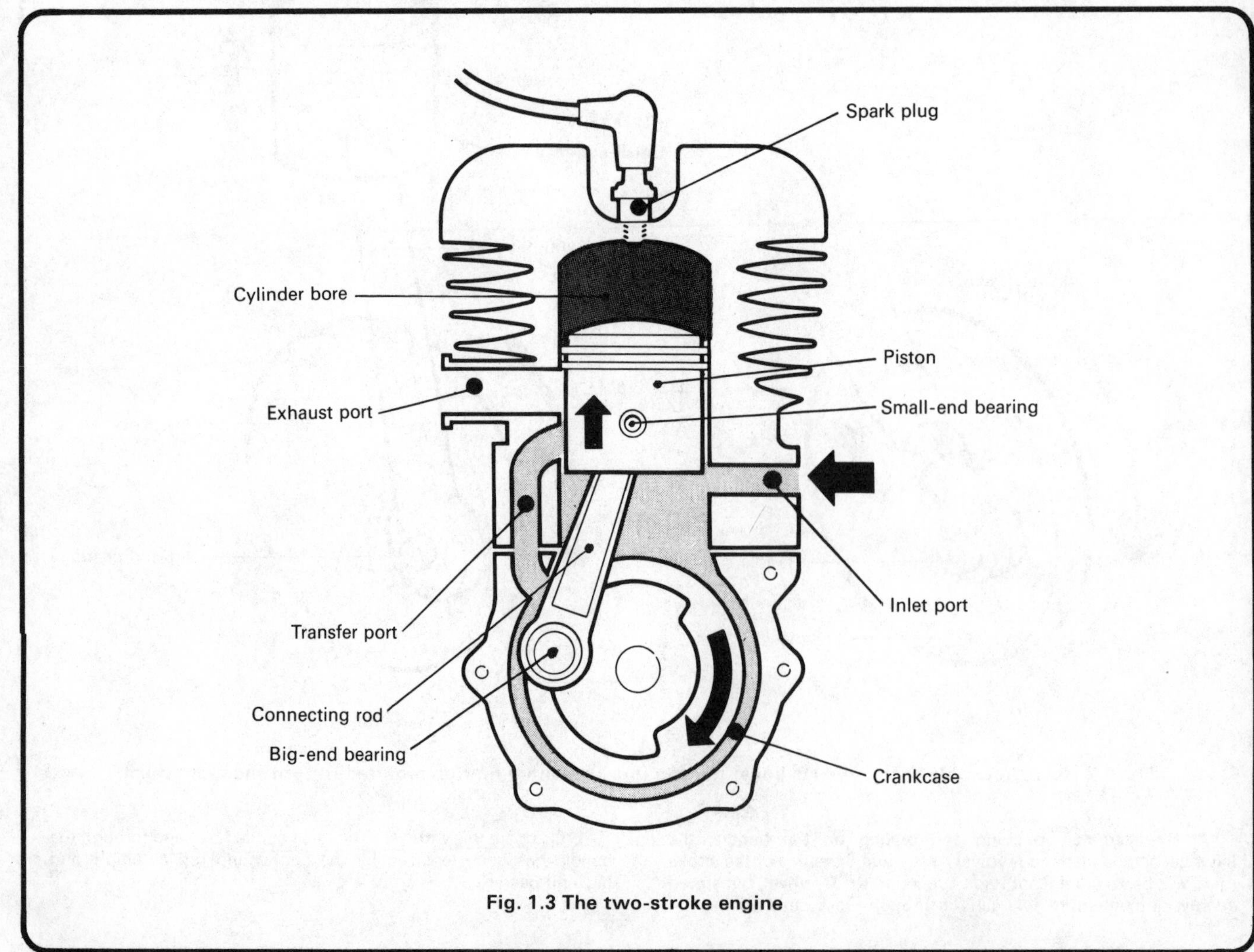


Fig. 1.3 The two-stroke engine

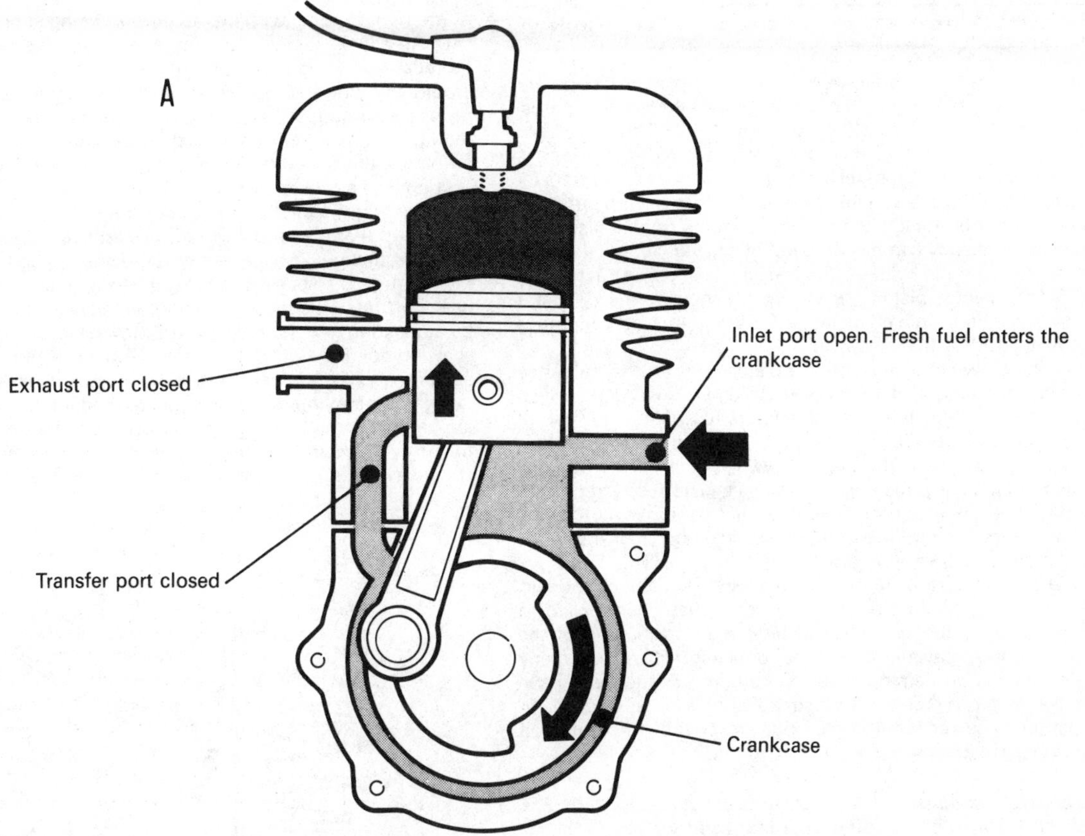


Fig. 1.4 Induction and compression

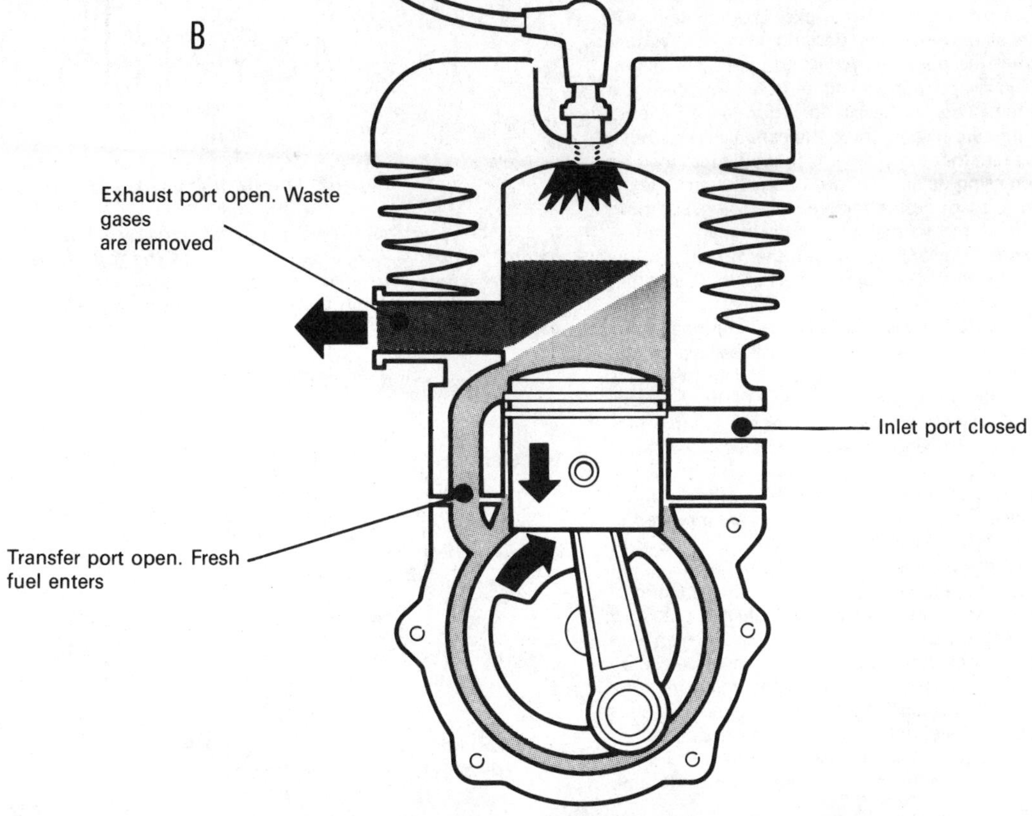


Fig. 1.5 Ignition and exhaust

## 5 Improved two-stroke engine designs: deflector pistons

The main cause of inefficiency in the simple piston-ported two-stroke engine is the incomplete scavenging of the exhaust gases. If these remain in the cylinder they prevent a full charge of fresh mixture from entering and thus the power output is reduced. There is also the related problem of the fresh charge passing from the transfer port and straight out of the exhaust port, and as has been mentioned above, the transfer port directs the mixture upwards to minimise this.

Scavenging efficiency can be improved by paying careful attention to the gas flow inside the cylinder, and the simplest way of achieving this is to fit a deflector piston. As its name suggests, the deflector piston helps to create a more efficient gas flow, and thus scavenging is more complete and less fuel is wasted.

The rounded crown of a conventional piston does little to influence the flow of the incoming mixture of the escaping exhaust gases, whilst the deflector design helps to direct the mixture up towards the top of the cylinder and away from the exhaust port. This in turn helps displace the exhaust gases more thoroughly. Whilst this offers a real improvement in efficiency, the engine remains a piston-ported design. Deflector pistons were once used extensively in two-stroke motorcycle engines, but in more recent times the undesirable effects of the offset weight at the piston crown have discouraged their use. This drawback has become much more evident with the development of modern high-speed engines. As an alternative, attention has been turned to improved gas-flow in the cylinder, and by careful positioning of the transfer ports good scavenging can be obtained. There are many variations of transfer port arrangements in current use, and these have increased the efficiency of the two-stroke engine a great deal. To improve performance further it is necessary to control the induction timing more precisely.

## 6 Improved two-stroke engine designs: reed valves

With any two-stroke design, improving performance and fuel economy requires the engine to do its job more efficiently, and that entails burning the maximum amount of fuel (and thus extracting the maximum amount of power) on each power stroke. There remains the problem, of trying to expel all of the exhaust gas and filling the cylinder with as much fresh mixture as possible. Whilst the deflector piston helps to improve the basic piston-ported engine it cannot prevent a little of the exhaust gas remaining in the cylinder, nor can it increase the volume of incoming mixture to help force the exhaust gases out.

At first sight it would seem that the answer is to draw more mixture into the crankcase by increasing its volume, but in practice this means that the pumping action is made less effective. Increasing pumping efficiency, on the other hand, means reducing the crankcase volume, and thus restricting the space available to contain the mixture. In this way a compromise is soon arrived at, and we must look at other methods of improving efficiency.

In the case of a piston-ported two-stroke it is inevitable that some of the fuel/air mixture drawn into the crankcase will be lost as the piston begins to move downwards during combustion. This mixture is pushed back out of the inlet port and is wasted. To prevent this happening, a more efficient way of controlling the incoming mixture is required. This can be achieved by using either a reed valve or a disc (or rotary) valve.

A reed valve consists of a metal valve case with a synthetic rubber sealing lip bonded to its face. Two or more valve petals are attached to the valve case and are normally closed. Also fitted are stopper plates, one for each valve petal, whose purpose is to limit the petal movement and thus prevent breakage. The thin valve petals are normally made of flexible steel, though more exotic materials such as phenolic resin or glass reinforced epoxy resin are becoming popular, and are able to open by bending out against the stopper plates. The valve petals are designed to open readily under pressure from the incoming mixture, but will close rapidly once the pressure inside the crankcase reaches that of the surrounding atmosphere. In this way, the maximum amount of mixture is admitted and any back-leakage is prevented. The additional mixture fills the cylinder much more completely and scavenging is more effective.

To start with, reed valves were adapted for use on existing piston-ported engines, and they made a significant improvement to engine efficiency. In some cases manufacturers chose a combination of the two designs, with piston porting being supplemented by a reed valve to allow induction to continue when reed valves had proved to be reliable in production designs. The dire warnings that reed petals would fracture and be drawn into the engine proved to be largely groundless, and since it was no longer necessary to control the induction timing with the piston, because it was now controlled automatically by the reed valve, the position of the valve and the inlet port could be moved to the crankcase.

Re-siting the inlet port provides a number of advantages, the main one being that the gas flow into the crankcase area is more direct, and so more mixture can be drawn in. This is aided to some extent by momentum; the speed and weight of the incoming mixture. With the inlet port removed from the barrel, efficiency can be further improved by relocating the transfer port(s) to the best possible position for scavenging. Inevitably, the basic reed valve arrangement has been subjected to a good deal of research in recent years, and sophisticated designs employing two-stage petals and multi-reed cages are now appearing. Though outside the scope of this book it is worth noting that now the reed valve has become part of most modern two-strokes it shows every sign of further development in the future.

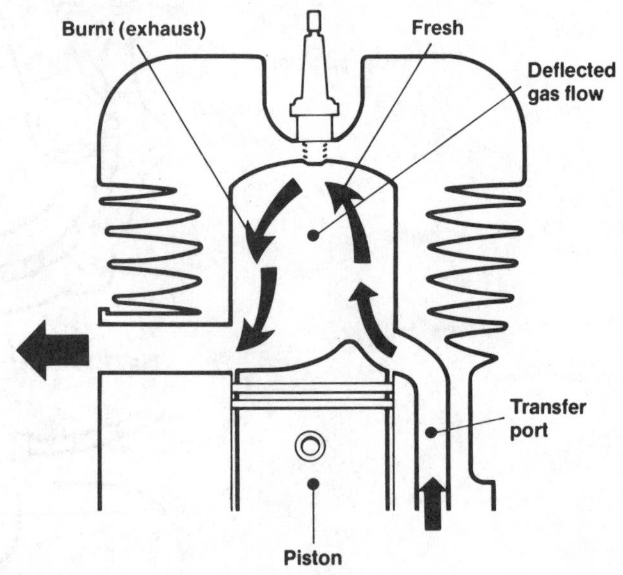


**Fig. 1.6 The deflector piston**

*In this drawing the effect of the deflector piston is illustrated. The incoming mixture is directed up towards the top of the combustion chamber where it helps to displace the exhaust gases from the previous power stroke. This helps to prevent the incoming mixture and the burnt gases from mixing.*

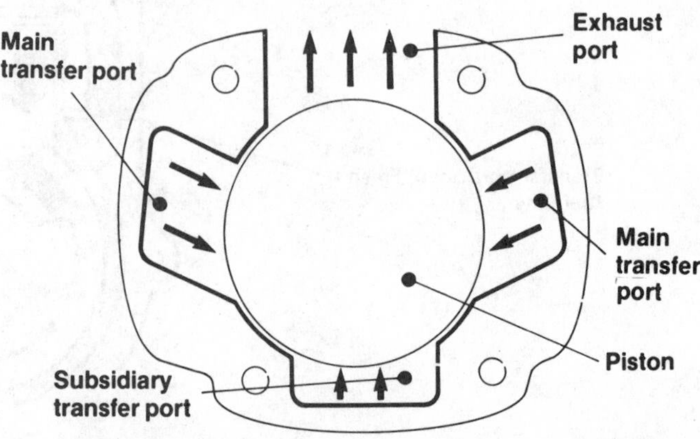


**Fig. 1.7 Transfer port positions on a modern two-stroke engine**

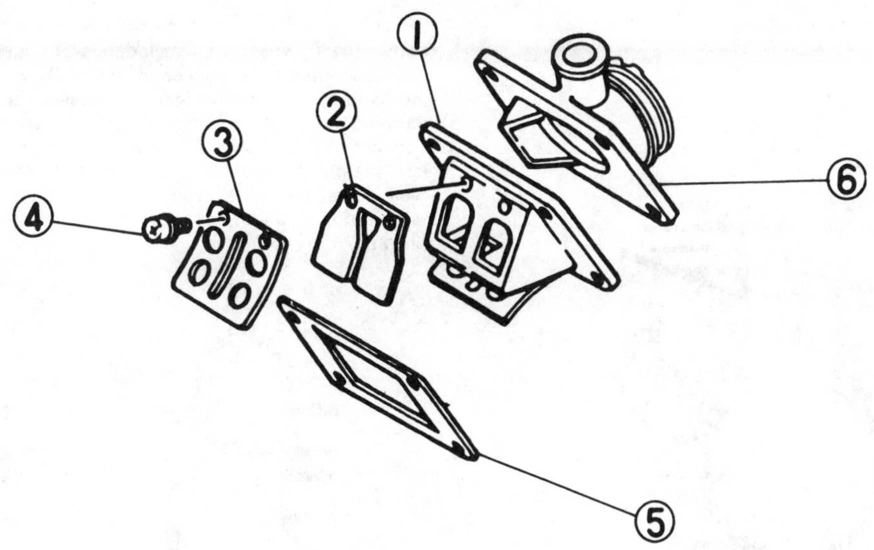


**Fig. 1.8 A typical reed valve unit**

*1 Reed valve body*
*2 Valve petal*
*3 Stopper plate*
*4 Screw*
*5 Gasket*
*6 Mounting stub*

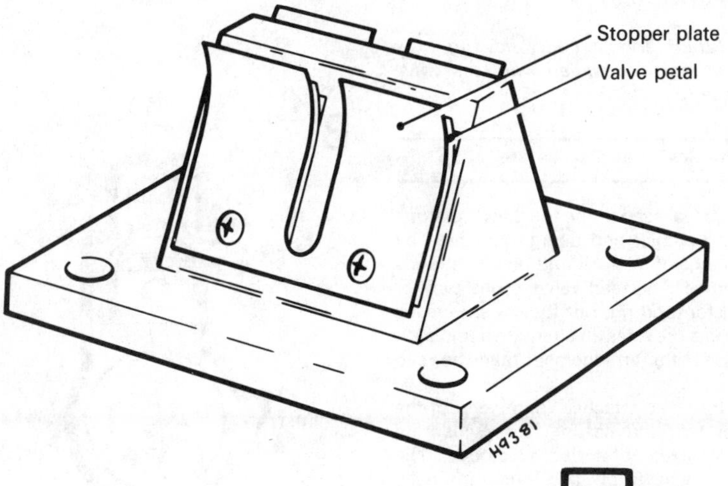

Stopper plate
Valve petal
H9381

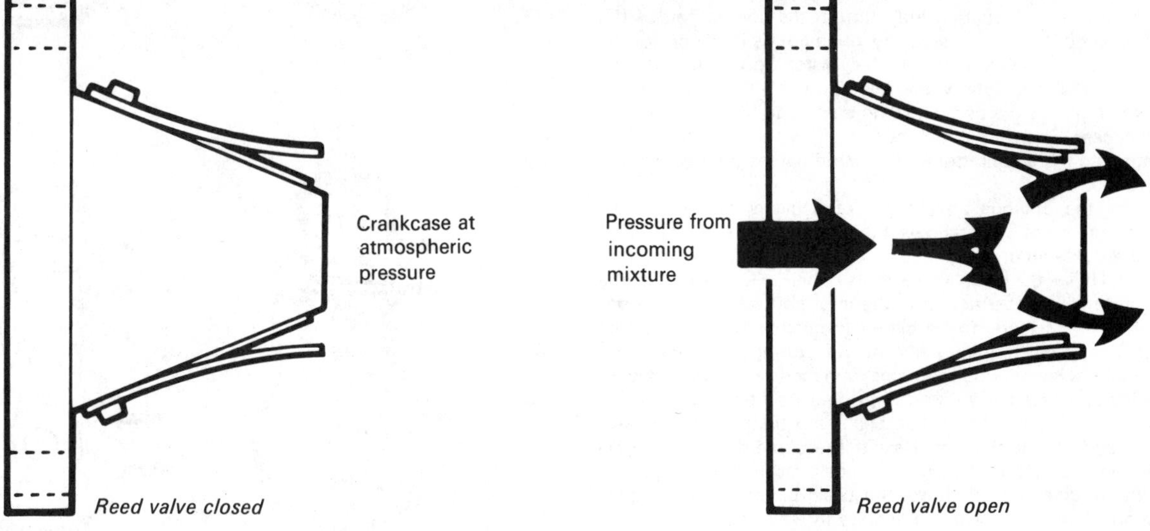

Crankcase at atmospheric pressure

*Reed valve closed*

Pressure from incoming mixture

*Reed valve open*

**Fig. 1.9 Sectioned view of reed valve in operation**

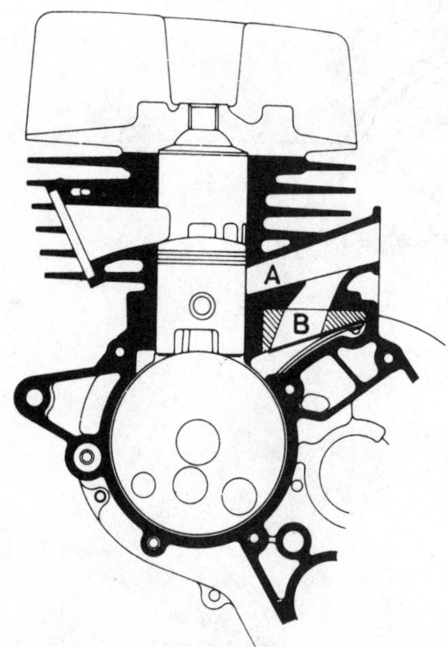


**Fig. 1.10 Suzuki's "Power Reed" system**

*A sectioned view of the TS125ER engine unit, showing how conventional piston porting (A) has been combined with reed valve induction directly into the crankcase (B).*

## 7 Improved two-stroke engine designs: disc valves

In the preceding sections we have seen how the basic piston-ported two-stroke engine relies on the inlet port being uncovered by the rising piston to admit a fresh charge of mixture, and how this tends to reduce the efficiency of the engine. The reed valve is one way of side-stepping the limitations of piston porting, but it is by no means the only one. The disc (or rotary) valve provides an alternative to piston porting, and in some respects it is a better arrangement than the reed valve.

A disc valve consists of a thin steel disc attached to one end of the crankshaft. It is contained between two fibre sealing faces which are attached to the crankcase and to the inside of a disc valve cover. The inlet port passes through the disc valve assembly, and thus is normally closed off by the disc. To permit induction at the correct part of the engine cycle, part of the disc is cut away, opening the inlet port for the required duration, independent of the piston position. As the crankshaft and the disc rotate, the inlet port is uncovered as the cutaway section passes the port, allowing mixture to be drawn directly into the crankcase. The port is then sealed off by the disc, preventing back-leakage into the carburettor as the piston passes top dead centre and starts to fall.

Apart from the obvious advantages of a closer control of the induction timing, a disc valve allows a large inlet port diameter to be chosen, and ensures an unobstructed passage for the mixture entering the crankcase. Unlike the reed valve with its rather bulky valve case, the disc valve presents no obstruction in the inlet port, and thus the gas flow into the engine tends to be better. Its main disadvantages are mechanical complexity requiring fine manufacturing tolerances, and the valve's inability to respond to engine demands like a reed valve. In addition, all disc valves are vulnerable to damage from debris drawn into the engine, the particles of dust becoming trapped in the valve sealing faces and scoring the disc. Despite these, the disc valve works very well in practice and will usually produce a respectable amount of power at low engine speeds, unlike the basic piston-ported engine. The operation of the disc valve is described in Fig. 1.12.

An interesting variation of the disc valve has been used for some years on Vespa scooter engines. Instead of fitting an entirely separate valve assembly, the manufacturers have adapted the standard crankshaft to perform a similar function. The edge of the right-hand flywheel is machined to a very fine tolerance so that it runs a few thousandths of an inch from the crankcase. The inlet port is directly above the flywheel (the cylinder is arranged horizontally on these engines) and thus is blocked off by the flywheel edge. By machining a recess in part of the flywheel it is possible to uncover the port at the required point in the engine cycle in exactly the same way as a conventional disc valve. Although the resulting inlet passage has to be less straight than would otherwise be the case, the system works very well in practice. As a result the engine produces useful power over a wide range of engine speeds, and yet remains mechanically uncomplicated.

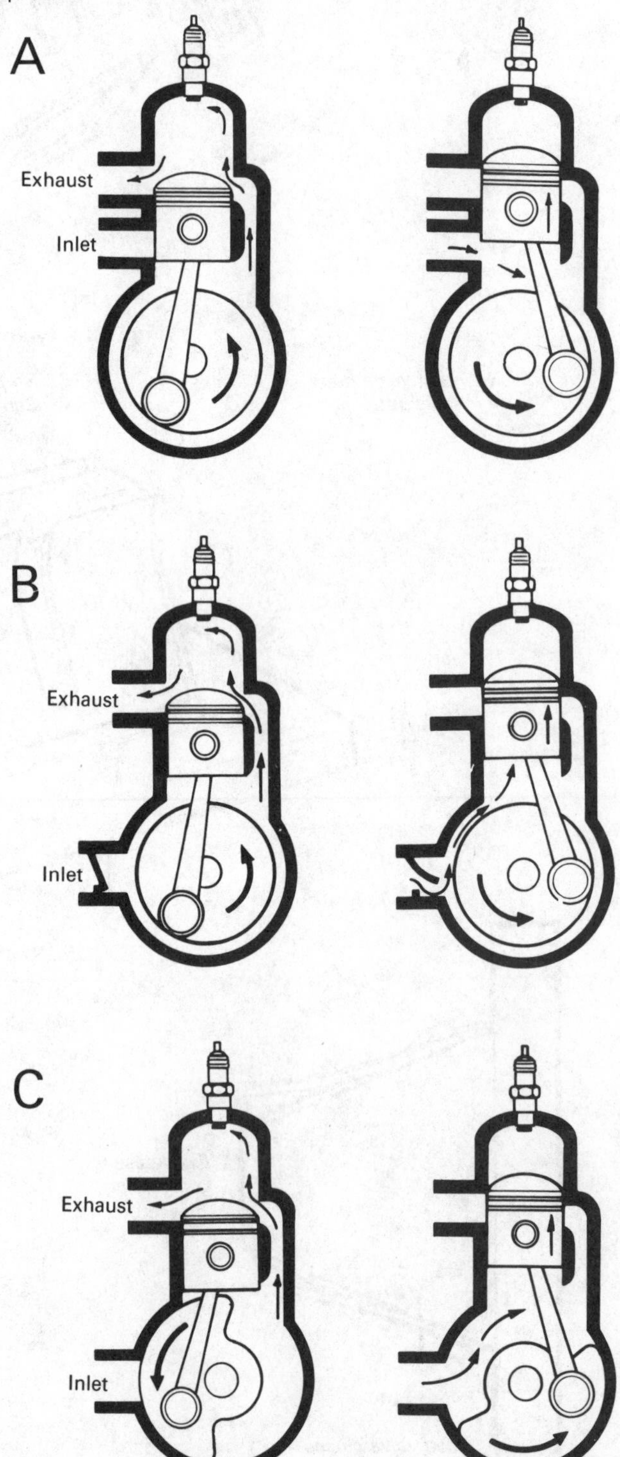


**Fig. 1.11 Two-stroke induction systems compared**

*A Piston porting*
*B Reed valve*
*C Disc valve, or rotary valve*

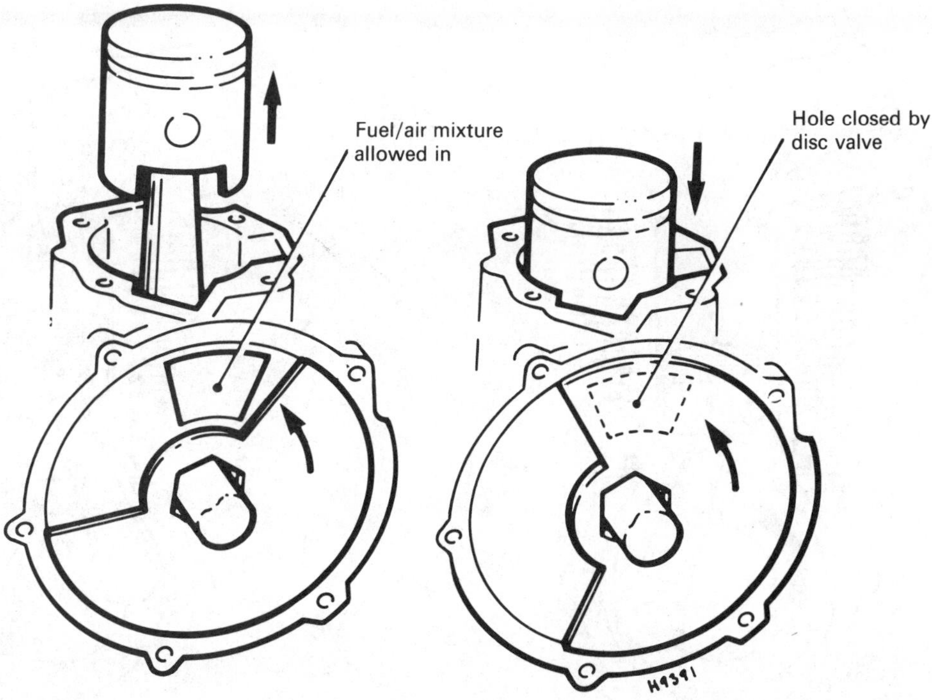


Fig. 1.12 Disc valve operation

## 8 Improved two-stroke engine designs: exhaust systems

Although exhaust systems are covered in detail in Chapter 2, it is only fair to mention them here, if only to underline the importance of exhaust design to the efficient running of a two-stroke engine. Indeed, in many respects the induction and exhaust systems on a two-stroke are very closely linked. In the previous Sections we have discussed ways of getting mixture into the cylinder and exhaust gases out. The exhaust system has a profound effect on both of these areas, and it is recommended that the relevant parts of Chapter 2 are read in conjunction with the above.

## 9 The four-stroke engine

In the preceding Sections describing the operation of the two-stroke engine it will have become obvious that whilst the mechanical principles of the engine are simple enough, the need to burn carefully calculated amounts of fuel at the right time, and disposing of the burnt gases that resulted pose more of a problem. This has led to the continual development of the two-stroke engine to try to improve its efficiency, with the use of reed or disc valves to control induction timing more precisely. Another approach is to allow four strokes for the piston to complete its cycle. This gives the four-stroke engine its name and is the subject of the next few Sections. The accompanying illustration shows the operation of a typical four-stroke engine. It will be noted that the combustion chamber looks a lot more complicated than that of its two-stroke counterpart, but that the ports in the cylinder barrel have gone. With the incoming mixture arriving directly in the combustion chamber, the crankcase no longer plays a part in the combustion cycle. Despite the increased mechanical complexity and the halving of the number of power strokes, the induction and exhaust stages can now be more carefully controlled and thus the engine is relatively efficient.

Mechanically, the four-stroke engine is fairly similar to the two-stroke, and shares the basic components; piston, cylinder, connecting rod and crankshaft. It does, however, have a number of extra components, known collectively as the valve train, and these are all concerned with the control and timing of induction and exhaust. In a way they are the four-stroke's equivalent of the reed or disc valve. There are a number of different arrangements to examine, but they are all different approaches to the same end. Let us start by looking at the basic elements of the valve train.

### Valves

All four-stroke engines feature valves, more correctly known as poppet valves, through which mixture is admitted to the combustion chamber and exhaust gases are expelled. Unlike the two-stroke, the incoming mixture is drawn directly into the combustion chamber, and so that is where the valves are located. On all modern engine designs the valves project down from the cylinder head, and thus these are termed overhead valve, or ohv for short. Until the 1950s there were a few utility machines which employed cheaper but less efficient side-valve engines in which the valves projected up from the top of the cylinder. Given that side-valve engines are now confined to lawnmowers and similar, we will not devote too much time to them.

The poppet valve consists of a circular head attached to a long stem – rather like a large-headed nail. The valve head has a tapered seating face ground on the stem side which is designed to seal against a corresponding face on the valve seat. A seat is incorporated at the hollow dome or combustion chamber end of the inlet and exhaust ports, and is normally kept closed by the valve, which is pulled shut by a strong spring. The valve stem passes through a guide in the cylinder head and emerges through its upper surface, where the valve spring is attached.

### Camshafts

The camshaft is found on all conventional poppet-valved four-stroke engines and is used to open and close each valve at the correct point in the four-stroke cycle. Bearing in mind that the cycle lasts for four strokes of the piston (which equates to two complete revolutions of the crankshaft) and that each valve is required to open once in that cycle, the camshaft is arranged to run at half crankshaft speed. This means that the camshaft completes one revolution for the crankshaft's two, and this is accomplished by the simple arrangement of a gear or chain drive between the two shafts in which the crankshaft gear or sprocket has exactly half the number of teeth of its counterpart on the camshaft. Along the shaft are projections known as lobes whose purpose is to push open the appropriate valve at the required moment. Exactly how this is done depends on the type of engine, and the various systems are described below.

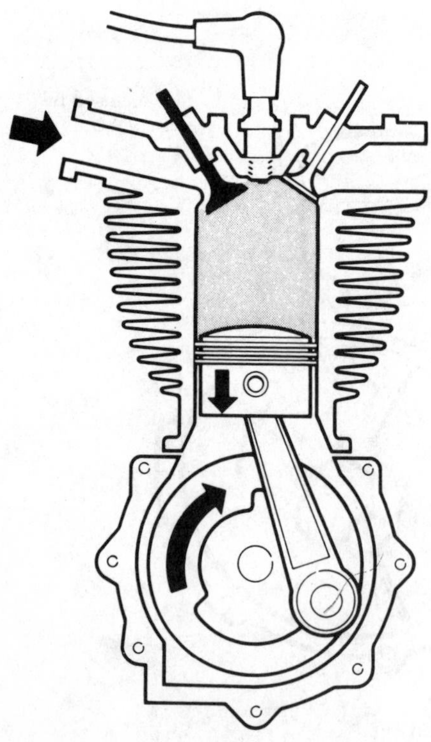

*Induction: As the piston descends the inlet valve opens, allowing the fuel/air mixture to be drawn directly into the combustion chamber.*

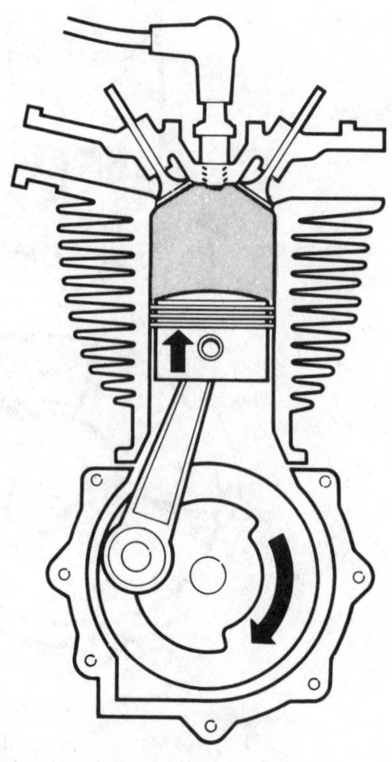

*Compression: The piston starts to ascend with both valves closed. The mixture is compressed.*

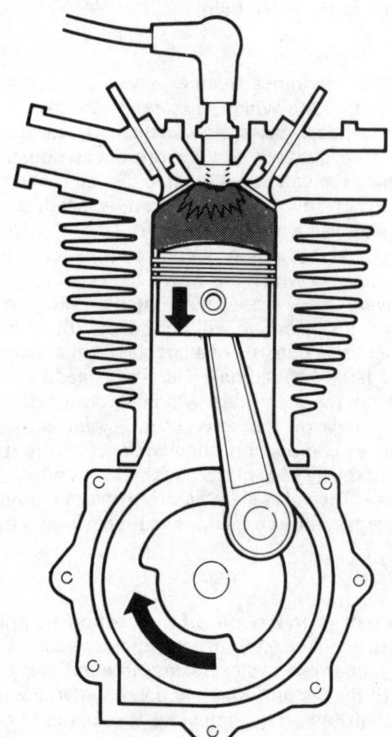

*Ignition: The spark plug ignites the compressed mixture, forcing the piston down the bore.*

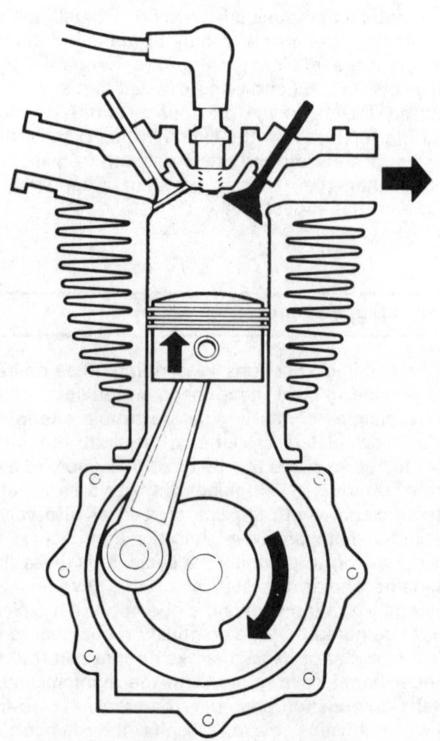

*Exhaust: The exhaust valve opens to allow the burnt gases to be expelled through the exhaust port.*

**Fig. 1.13 The four-stroke cycle**

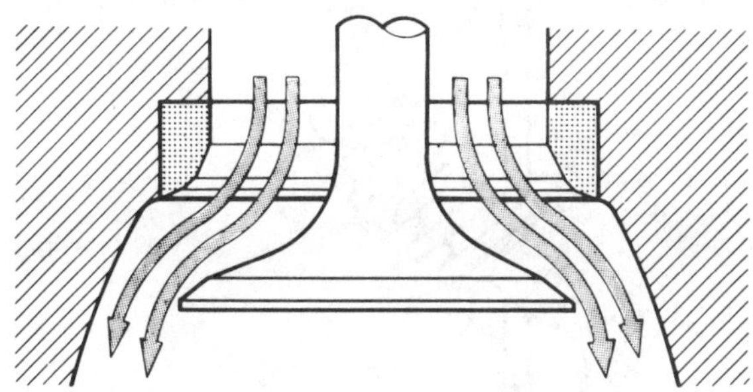

**Fig. 1.14 Section through port and valve showing the flow of mixture into the combustion chamber**

## 10 Four-stroke engine designs

All four-stroke engines are similar in principle, differing only in the way the inlet and exhaust valves are arranged and operated. As with most things on a motorcycle, sophistication tends to lead to complexity, and in achieving higher power outputs the four-stroke engine has been improved a great deal over the years. The various principles are discussed below, starting with the side-valve, which though largely obsolete serves to show the modern overhead cam designs in their true perspective.

### Side-valve (SV)

The side-valve engine is a relatively simple application of the four-stroke principle, using a minimum of mechanical parts to convey movement from the cam lobe to the valve. The camshaft, driven either by gear or chain, is located close to the crankshaft. The cam lobes bear upon short rods, known as 'tappets', running vertically up towards the cylinder. These incorporate screw and locknut adjusters and bear upon the end of the valve stems. The vertical position of the valves means that they are contained in an extension of the cylinder barrel, rather than in the cylinder head as in other four-stroke designs.

The side-valve is probably the easiest and cheapest four-stroke engine to manufacture, and most of the British and US companies made extensive use of it at one time, often powering the utility or economy models of their range. The awkward shape of the combustion chamber, dictated by the position of the valves which were set to one side of the cylinder bore, limited the efficiency of the engine, which produced less power and used more fuel than a comparable overhead valve unit. The inefficiency became more pronounced at higher engine speeds, so the traditional side-valve evolved as a large capacity single of relatively low power ouput. Fitted with large flywheels, it produced a good deal of torque or 'pulling power' at low engine speeds, and thus was a popular choice with devotees of sidecars. These softly-tuned and simple engines were outstandingly reliable, and were very easy to work on if problems did arise. Their demise came about after the second World War, with the advent of improved materials and manufacturing techniques. Faced with far more competition from ohv designs, the side-valve faded away in the motorcycle world, but can still be found on some motor mowers and in similar applications where simplicity and cheapness outweigh any performance considerations.

### Overhead valve (ohv)

Strictly speaking, the overhead valve engine describes all non side-valve four-stroke engines, but is usually used to indicate the pushrod-operated overhead valve unit, rather than overhead camshaft (ohc) types. The layout is very similar to that of the side-valve, but instead of the short tappets of the latter, the cam lobes operate long pushrods running up through a tunnel in the cylinder barrel and head. The pushrods emerge above the cylinder head casting, along with the valve stems. The valves are now incorporated in the upper part of the head casting, hence the 'ohv' designation, and must be pushed downwards to open them. To this end, the pushrod and the end of the valve stem are linked by a short rocker arm, and this usually includes a screw and locknut adjuster to allow the assembly to be adjusted.

The ohv design has a number of major advantages over the side-valve, the main one being the freedom to design an efficient combustion chamber shape. In most respects a hemispherical (a half sphere) combustion chamber is ideal, and the overhead valve design with the valves angled at 45° from vertical produces a combustion chamber shape which works very well indeed. This positioning of the valves allows an efficient gas flow through the engine and more even combustion of the fuel/air mixture. This basic layout of the ohv engine proved perfectly adequate for several decades, and pushrod-type engines are still in production today.

Inevitably, the search for more usable power has brought to light the limitations of the design, at first in racing engines and later in roadgoing versions. Given an efficient combustion chamber design, the way to extract more power from the engine is to raise the operating speed of the engine, and thus the number of power impulses per minute. As the engine speed rises a number of mechanical limitations start to cause problems, notably in the valve train components. With the engine running at high speed the pushrods, valve rockers and the cam followers have to be strong to withstand the loadings imposed on them. Unfortunately, increased strength invariably leads to increased weight, and this brings problems of its own.

As the cam lobe begins to lift the follower and pushrod, and to open the valve via the rocker, these components gradually accelerate. Up to a certain speed there is no problem, but beyond this the weight of the valve train components is such that they are unable to respond quickly enough as the cam lobe passes and begins to fall away again. At this point the valves begin to 'float' despite pressure from the return spring. Not only is the engine speed restricted by this, but the onset of valve float brings with it the risk of the pushrods bending or dislocating, and in severe cases of the inlet and exhaust valves getting tangled inside the combustion chamber. If this occurs, the next time the piston reaches the top of its stroke it smashes into the valves, causing extensive damage. Fitting stronger valve springs is one solution, but this causes more drag, and thus less power, and leads to accelerated wear. The valve train components can be lightened, but this also weakens them.

From the above you will appreciate that the pushrod ohv engine is an efficient design for most purposes, but where very high power outputs and engine speeds are dictated it has a definite limitation requiring a very close look at the way in which the valve train operates. In practice, ohv units are uncommon in modern four-stroke motorcycles for this very reason. Where they are used, such as in Honda's robust and long-running CG 125 single, the resulting machine is a simple and reliable workhorse if an undistinguished performer. In many ways the ohv engine is the current equivalent of the now abandoned side-valve.

### Single overhead camshaft (sohc)

To overcome the problems caused by increasing the weight of the valve train components it is desirable to eliminate as many of the non-rotating parts as possible These are all of the non-rotary parts; the cam follower, the pushrod, the rocker and the valve itself. In the case of the valve little can be done, other than to reduce its weight as far as possible by careful design and the choice of a strong, durable but lightweight material. In racing engines, where manufacturing costs are not important, exotic materials such as titanium can be employed, but this is not really practical for mass production. What can be done is to move the camshaft to the cylinder head, thus eliminating the cam follower and the pushrod. The idea is by no means a new one, and there are many examples of pre-war four-stroke engines with overhead camshafts. Only in the last two decades have manufacturing techniques allowed the principles to be applied to the ordinary road-going motorcycle.

In a typical single overhead camshaft (sohc) engine the camshaft is housed at the centre of the cylinder head, between the valves. On early racing engines the camshaft was driven by bevel gears and a drive shaft running up the side of the cylinder barrel, whilst most standard production designs have opted for a relatively cheap and simple chain drive from the crankshaft. The cam lobes bear on short rocker arms which in turn operate the valves, in a similar fashion to the pushrod ohv engine. The only remaining parts that move backwards and forwards (reciprocating components) are the rockers and valves; not perfect, but a good deal better than coping with the extra weight of pushrods and cam followers as well. A good proportion of modern four-stroke engines are based on sohc operation, and this explains why most modern engines are able to operate comfortably at speeds that would have blown a pushrod engine apart.

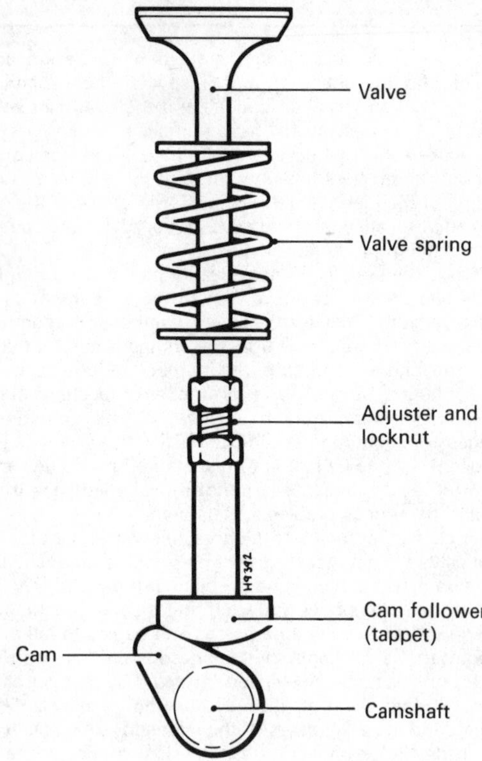


Fig. 1.15 Side valve operation

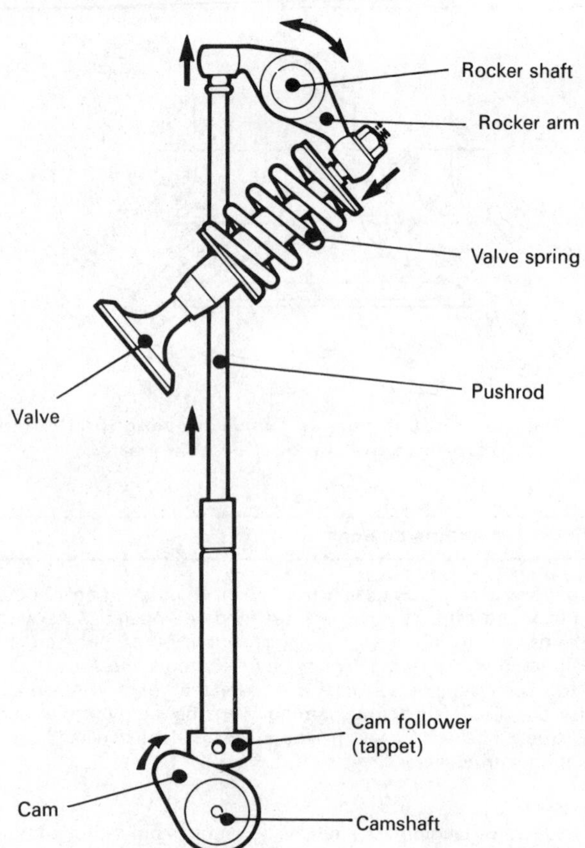


Fig. 1.16 Overhead valve (ohv) operation

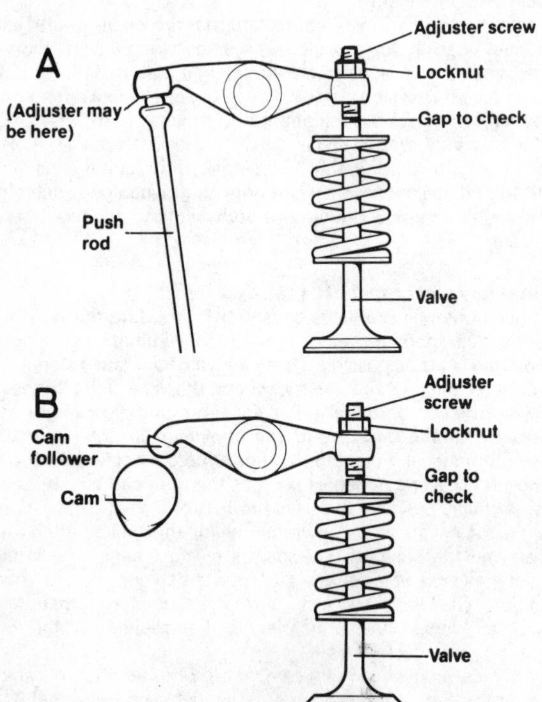


**Fig. 1.17 Comparison of overhead valve and overhead camshaft operation**

**A** *The valve is opened by a pushrod and rocker arrangement, the latter incorporating an adjuster so that the correct clearance between the rocker and valve can be maintained.*

**B** *In this version, the camshaft has been relocated in the cylinder head (hence overhead camshaft, or ohc). The pushrod has thus been eliminated.*

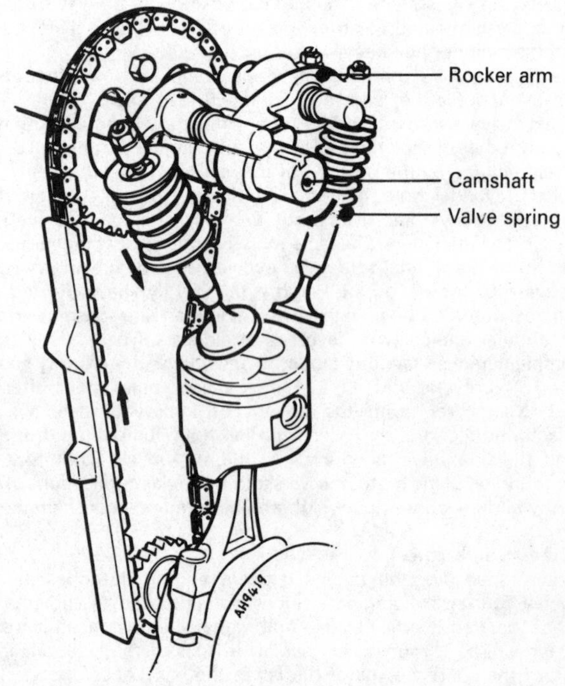


**Fig. 1.18 Single overhead camshaft (sohc) valve operation**

*The camshaft is located between the valves and is driven by a chain from the crankshaft. The valves are opened via short rocker arms*

### Double overhead camshaft (dohc)

The dohc four-stroke engine represents the refinement of the sohc design to eliminate the only remaining avoidable reciprocating weight; the rockers. Instead of the single central camshaft, two are used, positioned directly above the valve stems. Since there is no easy way a conventional adjuster can be fitted, the clearance between the cam lobe and the valve stem must now be set using shims (thin discs of metal made in various thicknesses) and these are normally held in cam followers or 'buckets' running in bores above the valve stems. Most modern large capacity engines use this arrangement, allowing still higher operating speeds.

To sum up, the overhead camshaft engine represents the most common design in four-stroke motorcycles today. That is not to say that development has ceased, though it is unlikely that this basic principle will be supplanted in the foreseeable future. Further development is more likely to be confined to refining existing layouts using improved techniques and new materials, and these are described in the next Section.

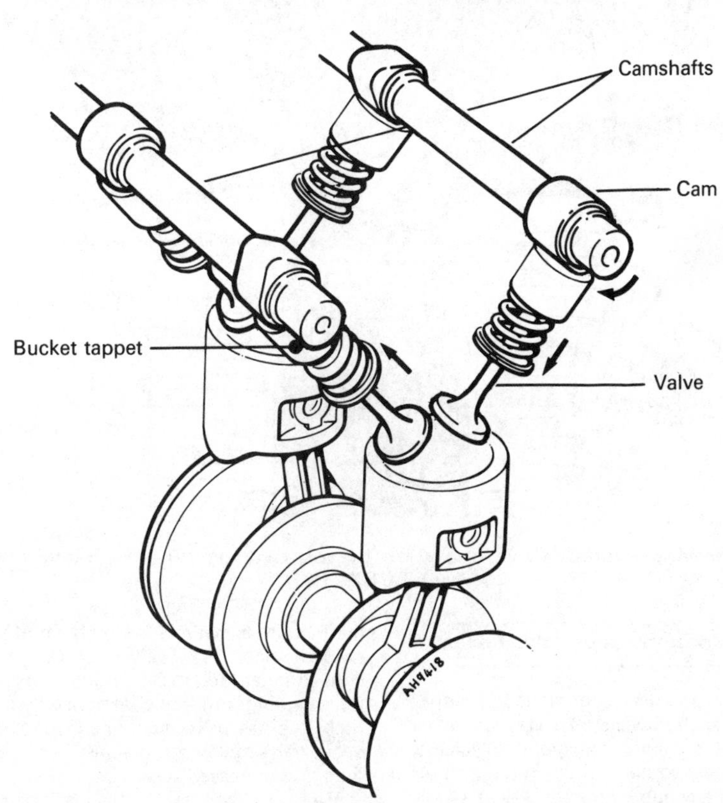


**Fig. 1.19 Double overhead camshaft (dohc) valve operations**

*In this arrangement two camshafts are used, one above each valve or bank of valves. The valves are opened via bucket cam followers or tappets, allowing adjustment by shims and eliminating all but the essential elements of the valve train.*

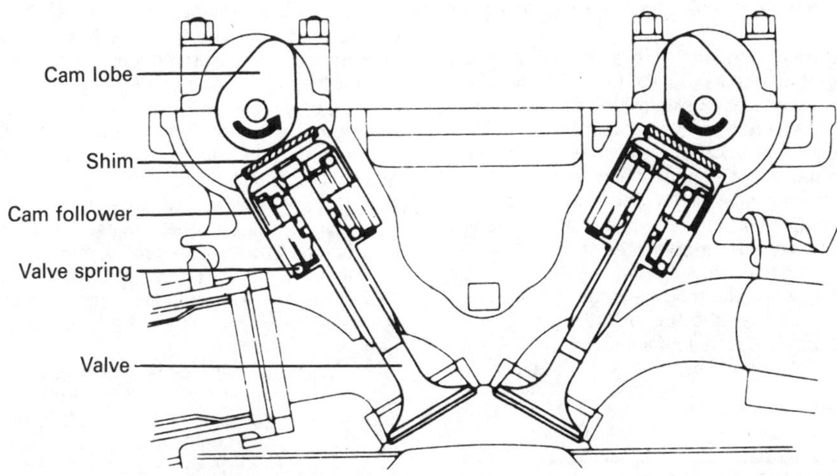


**Fig. 1.20 Section through typical dohc valve train showing cam followers and shims**

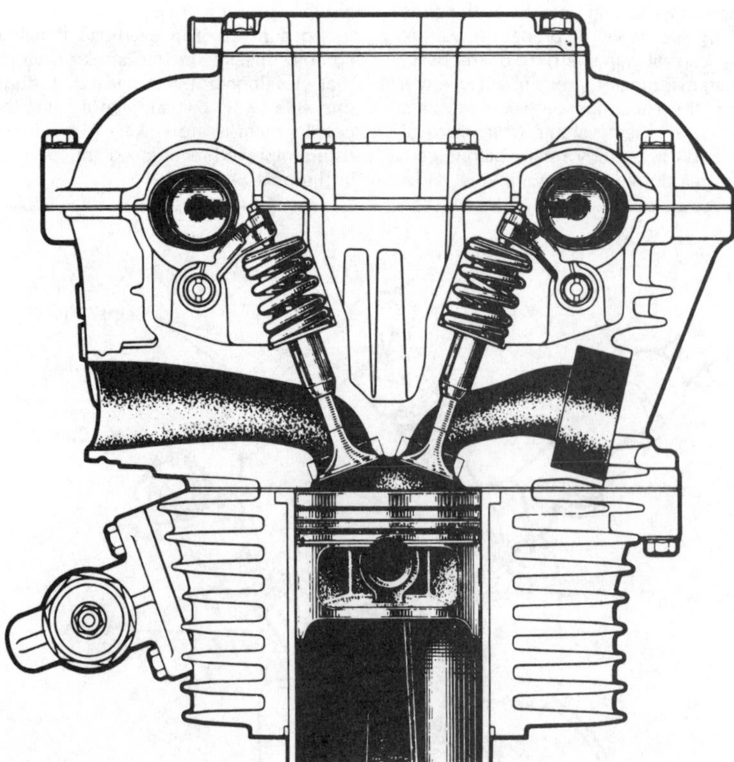

**Fig. 1.21 Dohc valve train showing indirect valve operation by short rocker arms to allow simplified valve adjustment (Suzuki GSX 1100)**

## 11 Improved four-stroke engine designs: four-valve heads

How do you make a well-designed and developed dohc four-stroke go faster? Make it burn more fuel on each power stroke. One way to do this is to fit a bigger carburettor along with correspondingly larger valves. The problem is that there is only so much room in the cylinder head, and sooner or later a point is reached where the valves would touch if enlarged further. To get round the problem, the designers decided to use two smaller valves in place of one big one. Although this may seem complicated at first, it is not significantly more so than a single valve, though interestingly enough it has occasioned the reintroduction of the rocker – a forked one this time to open the two valves simultaneously. The two valves have a combined area greater than that of the large single valve they replace, and because they are smaller and lighter this more that offsets the extra reciprocating weight of the rocker.

In addition to the immediate advantage of a bigger valve area and the preferable central placing of the spark plug, the four-valve head has allowed further development of the gas flow inside the combustion chamber. A good example of this is Suzuki's patented TSCC (Twin Swirl Combustion Chamber). The classical hemispherical cylinder head design is replaced by a more subtle shape where each valve seat area has its own miniature hemispherical recess. The incoming mixture is induced into a swirling motion inside the cylinder, speeding and aiding the rapid filling of the combustion space. As the piston rises, squeezing the mixture into restricted 'squish' areas in the head, the swirling is accelerated so that when the mixture is ignited the flame spreads rapidly, releasing energy from the fuel at the best point for obtaining maximum power from it. Most manufacturers have their own version of four valve heads, and three and even five valve designs have been tried.

## 12 Improved four-stroke engine designs: desmodromic valves

The imposingly-named desmodromic valve arrangement is perhaps the definite answer to the problem of valve float or bounce, the latter caused when the valves strike their seats too rapidly. In all conventional four-stroke arrangements the valve is pulled closed by a return spring, or more commonly, by a pair of springs, one within the other. As has been mentioned, the springs can be made stronger to avoid valve bounce problems, but at the expense of power-sapping drag and increased wear.

Desmo valves avoid this by having the valves closed positively, using a special camshaft lobe profile and a forked closing rocker. The normal or opening cam lobe is of conventional design, whilst the closing cam lobe is a mirror image; the lobe forms a continuous circle except for a dip which corresponds with the opening lobe. The valve opens normally, with the opening rocker pressing down on the stem. As the lobe passes the highest point and the rocker begins to release the valve, the closing rocker pulls the valve shut.

The desmo arrangement offers another advantage in addition to having peace of mind from the positive closing of the valves and the consequent safety of the engine. A factor controlling the efficiency of the engine is valve overlap, where the inlet valve begins to open just before the exhaust valve closes, so that both valves are open at the same time. This helps to scavenge the burnt gases from the cylinder and aids cylinder filling. Overlap is limited in production engines by practical considerations; a margin of safety must be allowed to avoid any risk of the valves touching if the engine is momentarily over-revved. Also, in the interests of mechanical quiet, the cam lobe cannot have too drastic a profile; most designs have 'quietening' ramps to minimise the clatter which would otherwise result. With desmo valves, neither of these considerations need restrict the designer, who is free to employ what would normally be considered unusable cam profiles.

In practice, the desmo valve system is rather exotic and too expensive for normal mass production motorcycles. It is used only by Ducati, but to good effect, particularly in the case of racing engines. Whether it is essential on road-going machines is open to question, particularly in the case of the larger models whose maximum engine speed is limited by other considerations. In the case of the smaller Ducati Pantah unit, desmo valves look more justifiable, and in all cases the arrangement works well. What is beyond dispute is the elegance with which it eliminates the problem of valve bounce.

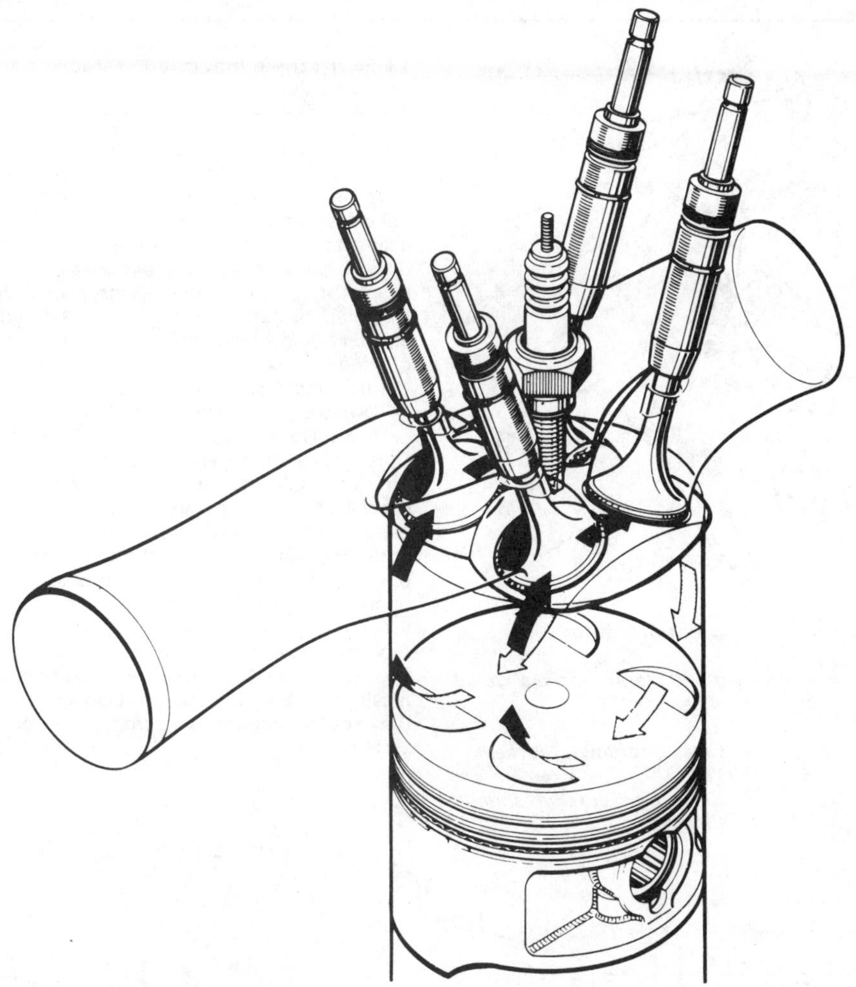

Fig. 1.22 Suzuki's "Twin Swirl Combustion Chamber" (TSCC) head showing the four valves

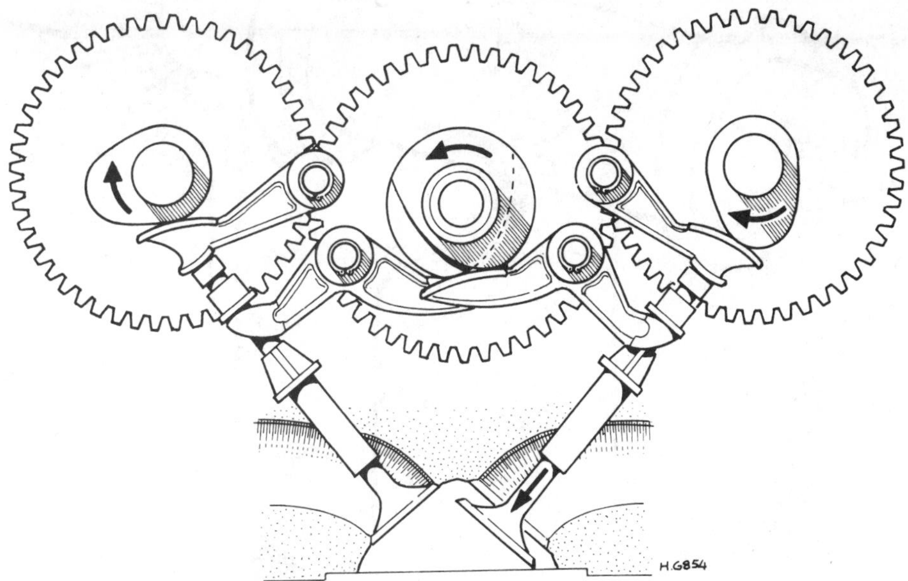


Fig. 1.23 Desmodromic valve operation – early type

*This three-cam arrangement was employed on the early Ducati works racers. The outer cams opened the valves, whilst the single central cam was used to pull them closed.*

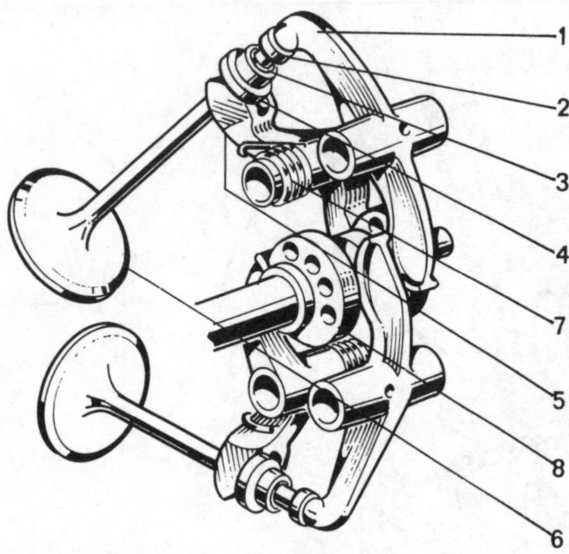


**Fig. 1.24 Desmodromic valve operation – later type**

*In this later design the valve opening and closing rockers are all controlled by the lobes on a single central camshaft*

*1 Opening (or upper) rocker*
*2 Upper rocker adjuster*
*3 Half-rings*
*4 Closing rocker adjuster*
*5 Closing (or lower) rocker*
*6 Valve*
*7 Closing rocker return spring*
*8 Camshaft*

## 13 Four-stroke induction systems: alternatives to the poppet valve

From the preceding Sections it will be seen that the trend in the development of the four-stroke induction system has been to eliminate as far as possible the reciprocating parts in the valve train. Whilst the dohc design comes very close to this, the poppet valve itself remains as a limiting factor. That the poppet valve works cannot be denied, but it does have obvious limitations. Apart from the problem of its reciprocating weight it presents a considerable obstruction to the incoming mixture, causing unwanted turbulence and drag which impede cylinder filling quite significantly. In most current designs a lot of effort has been directed towards compensating for these drawbacks, but the fundamental problem remains.

Over the years there have been innumerable attempts to replace the poppet valve with an alternative valve system, and amongst these the Cross rotary valve design looked the most promising. This took the form of a hollow tube set transversely across the cylinder head in a special chamber. The sleeve was driven at half engine speed and featured a slot in its wall which aligned with the inlet and exhaust ports at the appropriate point in the engine cycle. The valve assembly thus operated in a similar way to the two-stroke's disc valve and offered an unobstructed gas flow into the combustion chamber. Norton tried the valve on its racing engines during the early 1950s, but beset by sealing problems, reverted to poppet valves soon afterwards. Along with sleeve and the Aspin valve, the Cross rotary valve was abandoned mostly because the poppet valve was sufficiently well established to dissuade the manufacturers from further development of an alternative system.

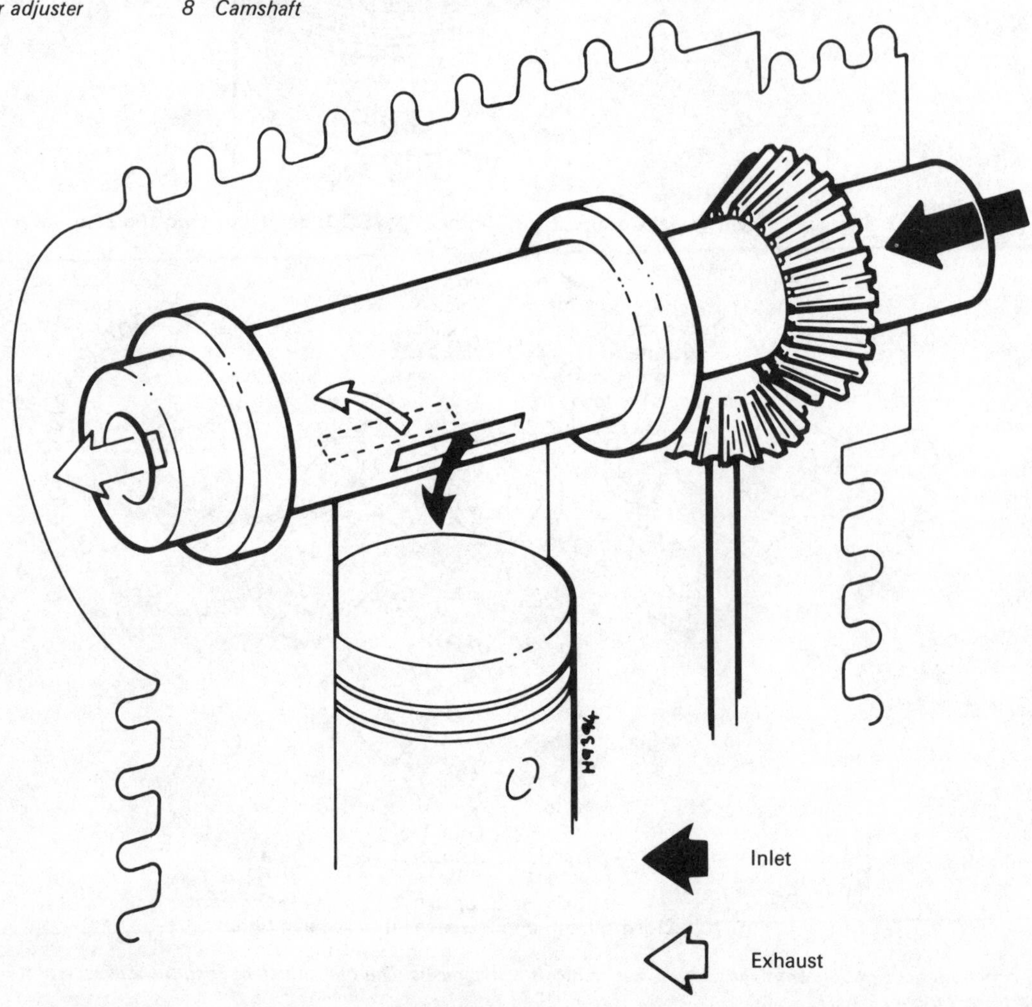


**Fig. 1.25 The Cross rotary vave**

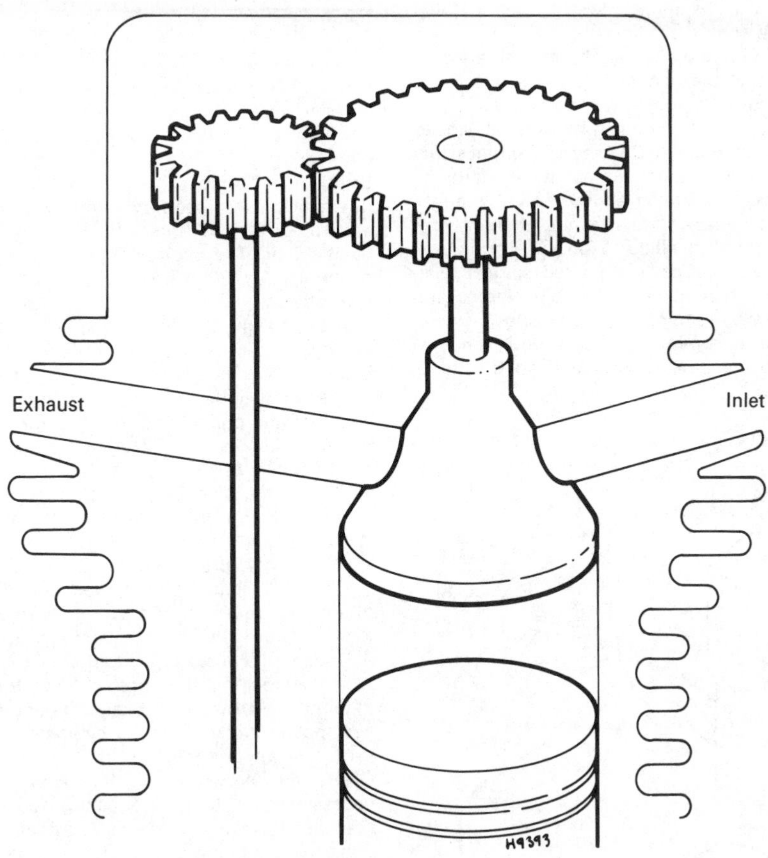


Fig. 1.26 The Aspin valve

## 14 Engine arrangements: the single-cylinder engine

So far we have looked at the two basic engine types used on motorcycles, examining their similarities and differences. In many respects the distinctions between two-stroke and four-stroke engines have become blurred in recent years and there are many areas in which the two overlap. This is also the case with engines of varying numbers of cylinders, and of the way the cylinders are arranged. In the following Sections we will try to establish why engines are produced in such a bewildering number of arrangements.

The simplest arrangement of all is the single-cylinder engine and for many applications it remains the most suitable. Its main virtues are mechanical simplicity and its small size. This means that it is easy and cheap to build and generally less demanding to maintain and service. As such it is ideal for mopeds and commuter bikes, and indeed there are few machines in this category which do not use a single cylinder engine. In off-road sporting applications too, the single combines simplicity with the essential lack of weight and bulk, and thus is universally popular.

If the single cylinder engine is so good, why bother with more cylinders on other machines? Well, the main problem is the vibration which is present in any reciprocating engine. The problem is caused by the crankshaft assembly. If you start with the bare flywheels, these can be spun quite easily in their bearings and cause no vibration problems. As soon as you start to add reciprocating components to the flywheel, namely the crankpin, big-end bearing, connecting rod and piston, you introduce a vibration problem. The crankpin is dealt with quite easily; either remove some of the flywheel material next to the crankin or add a similar amount of weight directly opposite to it, and the assembly is back in balance.

In the case of the remaining components things are less straightforward. The explanation is no less involved, but without an understanding of the problems of the single-cylinder engine, the reasons for multi-cylinder units become rather obscure. The trouble is that the piston and connecting rod do not remain in the same position in relation to the flywheels, and so the out of balance forces are constantly changing as the crankshaft turns. Even though the overall weight of the crankshaft remains constant, part of that weight is constantly changing position, and so there are varying centrifugal forces to deal with. In practice, the biggest cause of imbalance is what is known as the primary inertia force. In simple terms this means that the weight of the piston (and part of the connecting rod, to be more precise) is inclined to try to keep it going at the top and bottom of its stroke. Because of the abrupt change of direction imposed by the connecting rod, the energy is transferred to the rest of the engine unit. This means that for every engine revolution there is one upward and one downward 'pulse' of vibration.

To compensate for this, we could add a further amount of weight to the flywheels opposite the crankpin, so that the total weight of the reciprocating components was balanced out. This is termed a 100% balance factor. By creating a second set of out of balance forces we have effectively cancelled out completely the primary imbalance at the top and bottom of the piston's stroke, and thus have removed the vibration problem entirely – or have we?

Unfortunately not. The trouble is that this arrangement does not work between Top Dead Centre (TDC) and Bottom Dead Centre (BDC) because the added (balance) weight on the flywheels exceeds that of the reciprocating parts in that position. Remember that at mid-stroke of the piston, the weight of the crankpin and part of the connecting rod will be pushing in one direction, but set against this is the full might of our balance weights – far in excess of what is required. The result is severe horizontal vibration caused by secondary imbalance.

There is no real solution to this problem; the only course of action open to the engine designer is compromise. What has to be done is to reduce the primary balance factor so that the secondary imbalance is also reduced without the primary imbalance becoming intolerable. The final balance factor is decided by the maximum designed speed of the finished engine, the type of frame and numerous other considerations, and so it varies between one engine and another, but a balance factor of around 60% is common.

If we look at a few real examples it is immediately obvious that the problem becomes greater as the engine size increases. On a moped engine the piston and connecting rod are so small that the vibration is evident only as a slight buzz felt at the handlebars; hardly a serious problem and barely noticeable in use. On some small machines such as Suzuki's commuter scooter range, the vibration can be isolated almost completely by rubber-mounting the engine. On bigger machines the vibration becomes more noticeable to the point where it starts to impose limitations on the practical maximum engine size. Although there are other considerations, this in part explains why there are no 1000 cc singles. The vibration problem allied to possible structural aspects of the engine internals have effectively limited singles to a maximum of 500 cc or so, and also explain why big singles are traditionally slow-revving engines; by keeping the engine speed down, both wear and vibration are kept to a minimum. More power means more displacement and/or higher engine speeds, and so the need arises for more cylinders.

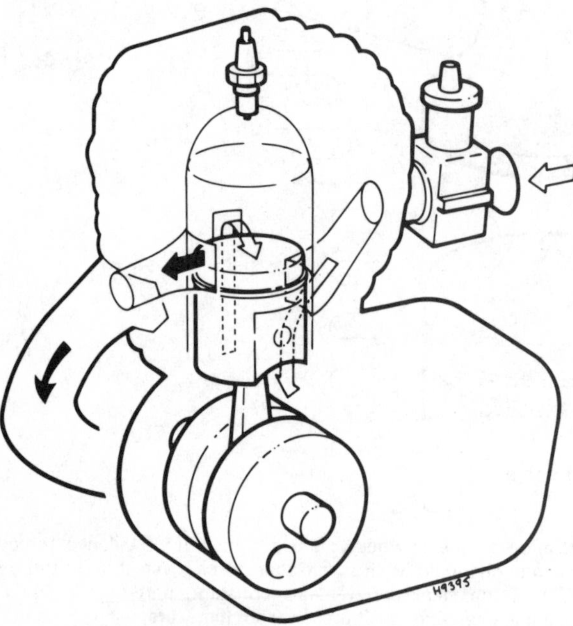


**Fig. 1.27 Typical single cylinder two-stroke**

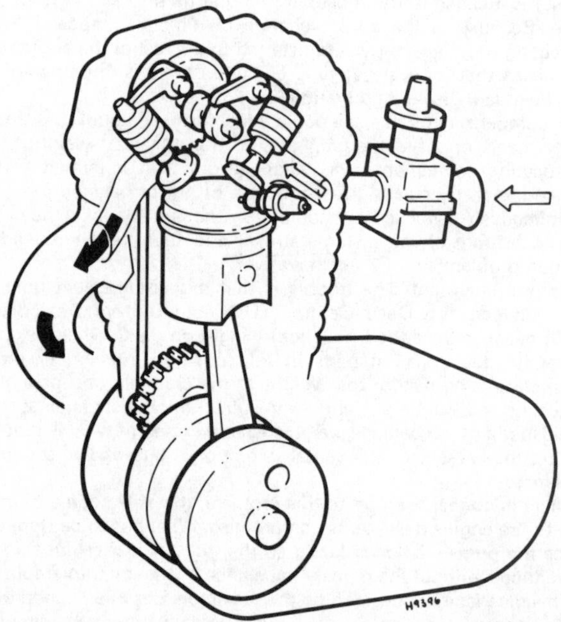


**Fig. 1.28 Typical single cylinder four-stroke**

## 15 Engine arrangements: the parallel twin

### The 360° four-stroke

Historically, the parallel twin was surprisingly like a single-cylinder engine that had been modified to accept two cylinders, pistons and connecting rods. To be a little less obscure about it, the traditional British four-stroke parallel twin had pistons which moved up and down in unison, each cylinder firing on alternate revolutions of the engine, or at 360° intervals, and thus it became known as a 360° parallel twin. The traditional four-stroke single, on the other hand, can be termed a 720° single in view of its one power stroke per two revolutions.

At first sight, the choice of a 360° crankshaft may seem a little hard to explain, because it retains the balance problems of the single, but it is an improvement in some respects. The crankshaft assembly has an increased weight because it is wider to accommodate the extra crankpin and connecting rod, though this is offset to some extent by reducing its diameter. The out of balance forces can be reduced somewhat by employing relatively large diameter pistons with a shorter stroke, so the balance problem, though still there, is reduced. More significantly, the traditional 'thump' caused by the power stroke of a large single is smoothed out by having the two smaller power pulses spread evenly across two revolutions of the engine.

The 360° parallel twin was not without its disadvantages, but offered a number of improvements over the single in the search for more power. The main advantage does not relate directly to the balance problem but rather to the physical limitations of the single. You will remember that the single-cylinder four-stroke fires once every 720° of crankshaft rotation. To keep the engine turning until it reached the next power stroke, massive flywheels were needed, and to avoid an excessive amount of weight these had to be thin and of large diameter. Given the need to keep the piston as light as possible, and the necessity of a long connecting rod, the resulting engine was a so-called long-stroke design. The characteristics of such an engine are good up to a point; it is economical, has a very wide spread of power and can pull with relative ease from low engine speeds. The gear ratios can be widely spread to make use of this generous power band and the machine has a relaxed feel to it. Indeed, the effects of engine vibration are to some extent subjective, and as a rule, quite high levels of low frequency 'thumping' are preferable to a less intense but more irritating 'buzz'.

As soon as you try to make it go faster, however, the drawbacks become apparent. The massive flywheels mean a lot of stored up energy, or inertia, and thus acceleration is confined to a gentle gathering of speed by today's standards. The small bore and long stroke mean high piston speeds and a high rate of wear in these components. As soon as you try to reduce the stroke significantly, the smoothing effect of the large flywheels is lost and the out of balance forces are increased, so the easy-going single becomes more like a mobile road drill.

### The 180° four-stroke

An alternative to the 360° crankshaft parallel twin is to arrange the crankpins so that they are spaced 180° apart. With this arrangement the primary out of balance forces are minimised. At first sight this is a much better choice than the 360° type, and most recent designs have opted for it. The main disadvantage of the 180° crankshaft is that it has uneven power strokes, and it introduces a new problem; the rocking couple.

This curious-sounding effect is evident in all engine designs using more than one cylinder, with the exception of the V-twin, of which more later. Imagine the effect on the crankshaft as one cylinder fires; as the piston is pushed downward the pressure on that end of the crankshaft is increased and there is a tendency for it to try to 'rock' to one side. When the next cylinder fires the effect is repeated with the crankshaft rocking the other way. The only way to eliminate this is to have both crankpins on the same plane, but this is physically impossible with a parallel twin. If you compare the two arrangements you will find that both the 360° and 180° designs have their own particular advantages and drawbacks, making it impossible to say that one is better than the other. To reduce the balance problem further you need (you've guessed it!) more cylinders.

### Two-stroke parallel twins

These are almost invariably built using a 180° crankshaft, and being a two-stroke they show fewer disadvantages when compared to a four-stroke of similar layout. This is because each cylinder fires after every complete revolution of the crankshaft, and thus the firing irregularly found in the four-stroke is no longer a source of vibration. The dreaded rocking couple is still at large, however, and given the higher engine speeds normally found on two-stroke engines, the out of balance forces can result in fairly obtrusive vibration levels. This problem is made worse by the need for the two cylinders to have separate crankcases; this means having a central main bearing and oil seals with the result that the crankshaft has to be wider than on a similar four-stroke. With the added leverage thus obtained at the crankpins, the effect of the rocking couple is magnified.

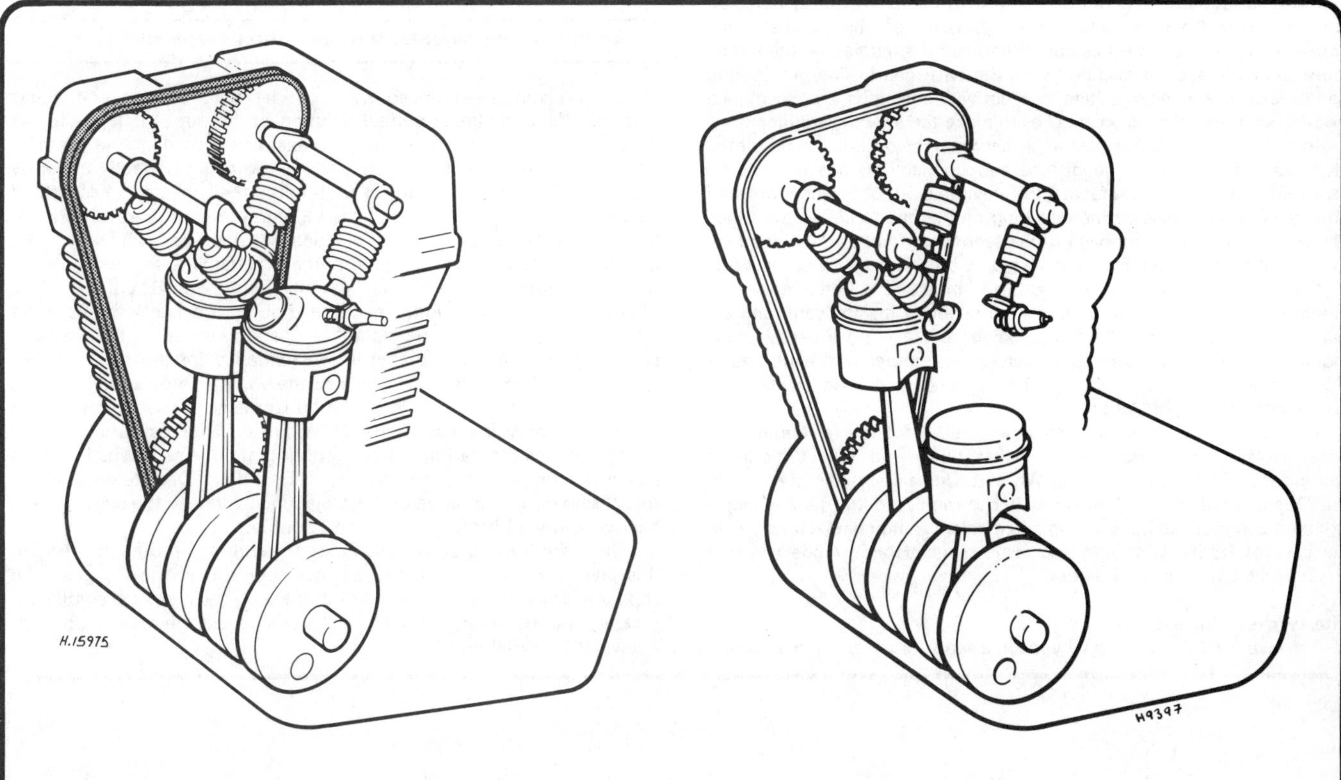


Fig. 1.29 360° parallel twin four-stroke

Fig. 1.30 180° parallel twin four-stroke

Fig. 1.31 180° parallel twin two-stroke

## 16 Engine arrangements: the V-twin

### The four-stroke V-twin

The V-twin engine is almost as old in concept as the motorcycle itself, and the fact that it is still used today is indicative of its basic soundness. The original arrangement of two splayed cylinders sharing a common crankpin avoids the rocking couple problem of the parallel twin, particularly where one normal connecting rod is straddled by the forked rod end of the second cylinder. With the two rods in line, no rocking couple exists, and even where two conventional rods are positioned side-by-side the offset is so small as to make the effect insignificant.

In terms of balance, the best angle between the cylinders is 90°. If the reciprocating weight of the pistons and connecting rods is perfectly balanced (a 100% balance factor) the inevitable out of balance forces of one cylinder are offset by the opposing mid-stroke forces of the other. There is still a residual problem of the secondary forces which combine to shake the engine in a fore-and-aft plane, but these are mild compared to the vibration levels so far discussed. In practice if the engine is mounted in-line, the vibration levels are relatively insignificant, and are mostly due to the 'thump' on each power stroke. With a transversely-mounted engine the secondary forces are more noticeable as a side-to-side shuddering at low engine speeds, but again, far less obtrusive than the parallel twin.

Whilst the 90° V-twin seems an ideal motorcycle engine, its widely-splayed cylinders make it rather bulky and thus difficult to incorporate in a motorcycle frame. Whilst it can be done, as in the case of the Ducati models, it is relatively uncommon. Most V-twin designs exhibit a compromise between optimum balance and compactness, as in the case of Harley Davidson and some recent Honda models with a lesser angle between the cylinders.

### The two-stroke V-twin

The two-stroke V-twin is very much a rarity, but there is one current example in Honda's home-market NS 250. Because it is a two-stroke it is impossible to employ the normal shared crankpin of the four-stroke V-twin, and so inevitably it suffers from the rocking-couple problem common to all two-stroke twins. Even so, the normal out of balance forces of the parallel twin are largely cancelled out.

## 17 Engine arrangements: the horizontally-opposed twin

The horizontally-opposed twin, or 'flat twin' as it is sometimes known, offers an almost perfect solution to the out of balance forces which have affected the designs examined so far, the primary imbalance of one piston and connecting rod being perfectly offset by the other. The only mechanical problem is the rocking couple effect between the two cylinders, but the vibration levels that result are not normally very obtrusive. A more practical consideration is how to fit the unavoidably awkward unit into a motorcycle frame. A few examples of fore-and-aft mounting exist, as illustrated by pre-war Douglas models. This does make for a long machine though and leads to problems when trying to find a suitable location for the transmission components. Another problem is the tendency for the rear cylinder, which is masked by the main bulk of the engine, to overheat.

The best-known example of the horizontally-opposed engine in a modern motorcycle must be the BMW. These, like most other designs of the type, employ a transverse mounting arrangement which in turn makes it a simple matter to adopt shaft final drive. Despite criticism by those who do not approve of the projecting cylinders, the arrangement has worked well for many years and continues to be successful.

There are no two-stroke examples currently in production, though this layout works just as well as in a four-stroke guise. Again, the separate crankcases of the two-stroke engine mean a significant rocking couple, though in practice there is far less vibration than in an equivalent parallel twin.

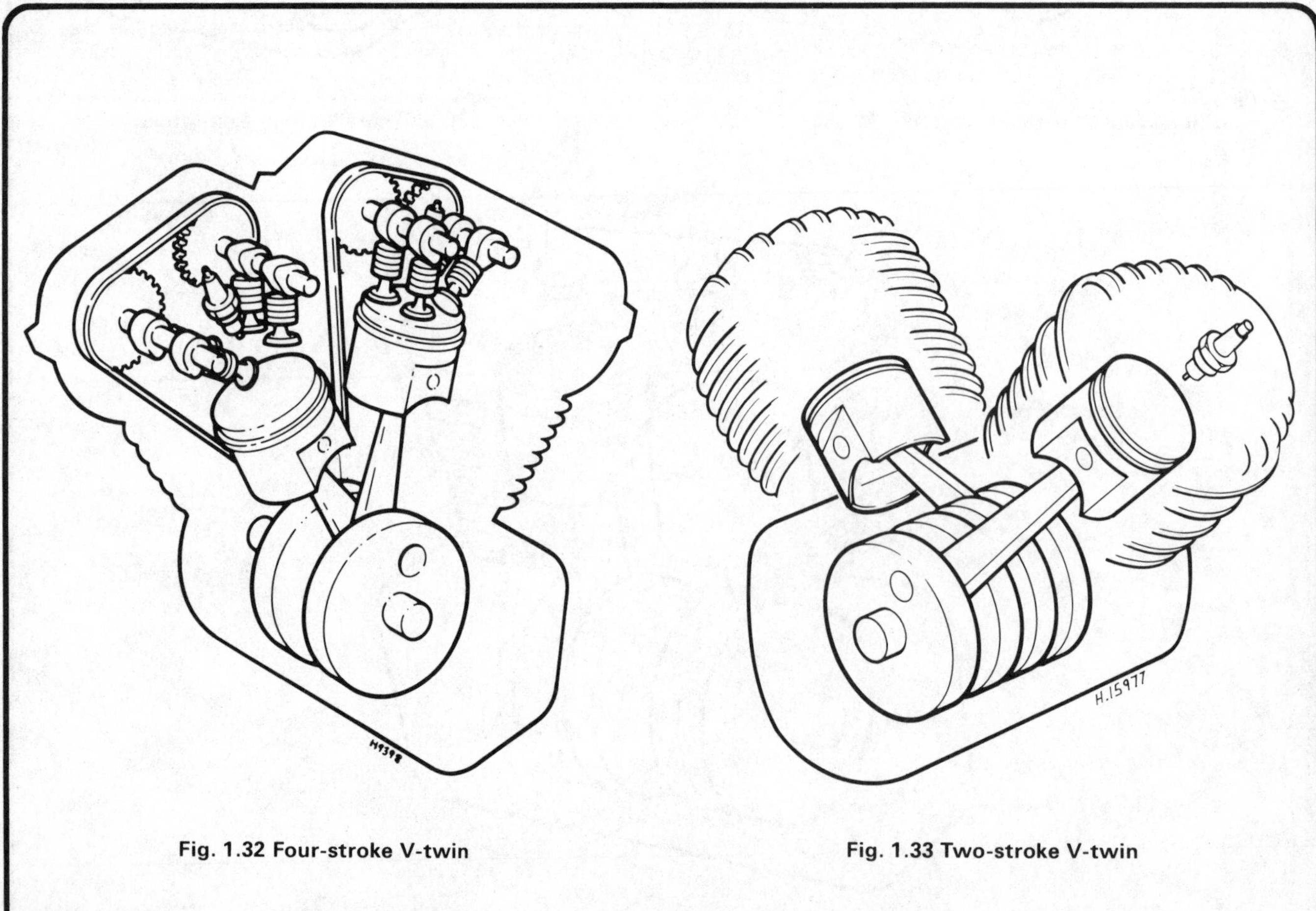


Fig. 1.32 Four-stroke V-twin

Fig. 1.33 Two-stroke V-twin

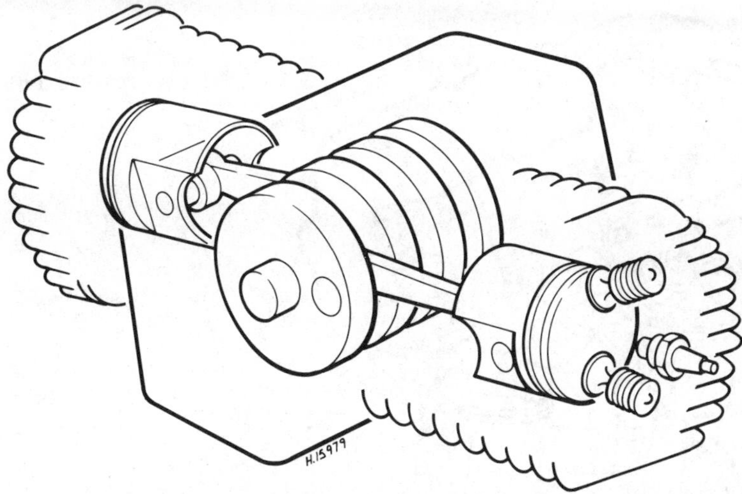


Fig. 1.34 Horizontally-opposed four-stroke twin

## 18 Engine arrangements: the in-line triple

The in-line three cylinder engine is really an extension of the parallel twin in an attempt to strike a compromise between the vibration problems of the latter and the width of a four. This is particularly true of two-strokes whose crankcases begin to grow uncomfortably wide as a triple, and would be positively unwieldy as a four. The two-stroke triple has been a firm favourite in the recent past, with various examples from Suzuki and Kawasaki. Suzuki even went as far as producing a very large two-stroke; the water-cooled GT 750. This remained in production for some years and found a small but loyal following of 'kettle' owners. With their 120° crankshafts the primary forces were quite well balanced, but the complicated rocking couple (rocking triple?) effect gave them a reputation for a fairly high level of high-frequency vibration, especially where the unit was not well insulated from the frame with rubber mountings.

The four-strokes are well represented too, from the BSA Rocket Three and Triumph Trident of the late 1960s, through Yamaha's XS 750 shaft-drive tourer to the only surviving examples; the Laverda triples. In the case of the latter, for many years a 180/360 degree crankshaft was used. That is, when one piston reached TDC, the remaining pair were at BDC and vice versa. In recent years Laverda have adopted a 120° crankshaft and the resulting engine has become far smoother than its sometimes harsh predecessors. In the opinion of most manufacturers, however, the triple has little advantage over the in-line four, and this has become the main-stream large-capacity design during the last decade or so.

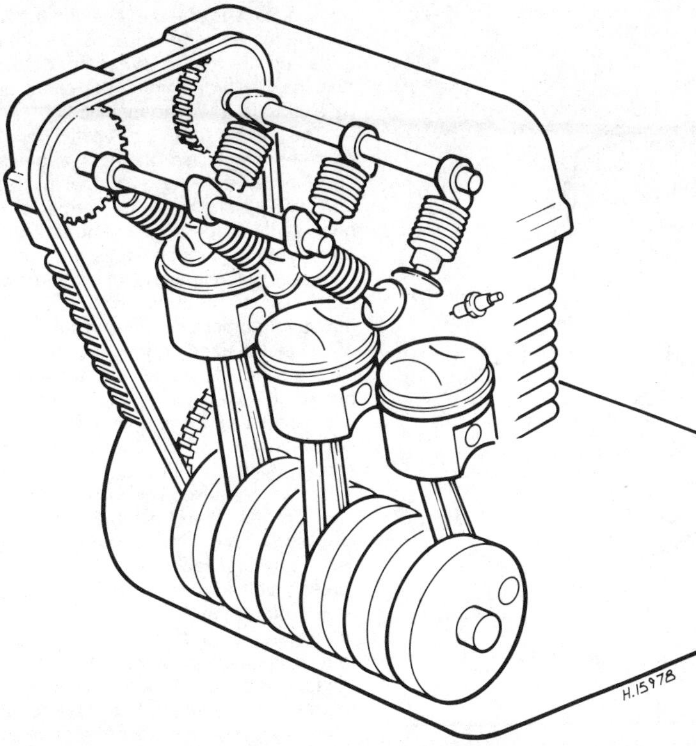

Fig. 1.35 120° in-line four-stroke triple

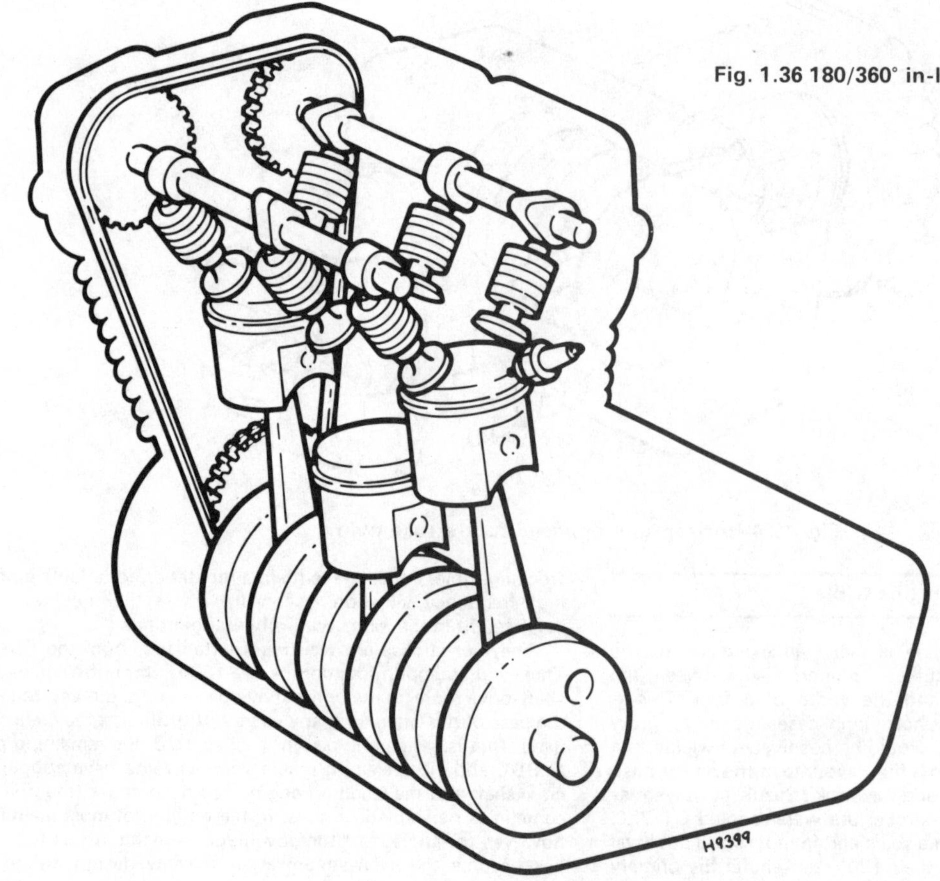


Fig. 1.36 180/360° in-line four-stroke triple

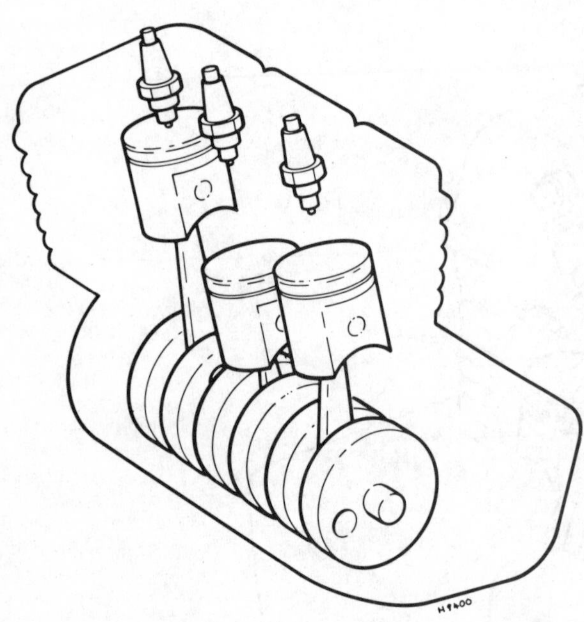


Fig. 1.37 120° in-line two-stroke triple

## 19 Engine arrangements: the in-line four

When Honda introduced its CB 750 Four in 1969 it gave the motorcycling public hitherto undreamed of sophistication, and in so doing laid down the basic arrangement for medium to large capacity motorcycle engines for well over a decade. Of course there was nothing new about the in-line four – car manufacturers had settled on it decades ago as the best compromise between smoothness and compactness for their purposes – but a four cylinder car engine was a large and heavy unit. What Honda did was to bring the four down to manageable proportions, the result being a unit little wider than the parallel twin it was to displace.

The in-line four is basically two 180° twins joined together in a common crankcase. In most engines of this type the crankshaft is arranged so that the two inner pistons move up and down together, and 180° apart from the outer pistons. The crankshaft, although necessarily long to accommodate the four connecting rods and the main bearing journals, does not need to be of large diameter. This is because the relatively frequent power strokes, one at every half-revolution of the crankshaft, obviate the need for large flywheels to maintain momentum. Also of importance is the small size and weight of the pistons and connecting rods, resulting in low primary forces on each individual cylinder, and these spread more evenly than is possible on single, twin or three cylinder units. With a good degree of crankshaft balance and its relatively small diameter flywheels, the four is responsive and can be designed to run at relatively high engine speeds. As such it has found considerable favour from the public and manufacturer alike. The only real problems, apart from the consideration of its sheer mechanical complexitity, is the width of the crankshaft and the inevitable buzzing vibration caused by the secondary and rocking couple forces. Although this is inevitable, the forces involved are not great and the problem is really little more than an irritation in most applications.

To reduce the crankcase width, some manufacturers have resorted to moving ancillary components, like the alternator, to an idler shaft to the rear of the crankshaft, thus allowing the crankcases to be made as narrow as is physically possible. As for the vibration problem, there are only two possible routes; yet more cylinders or the introduction of a mechanical balancer system to cancel out the remaining out of balance forces. We will examine these in subsequent Sections. As for the two-stroke, four separate crankcase compartments are really too unwieldy to be a practical proposition, so the two-stroke in-line four has always been considered a non-starter.

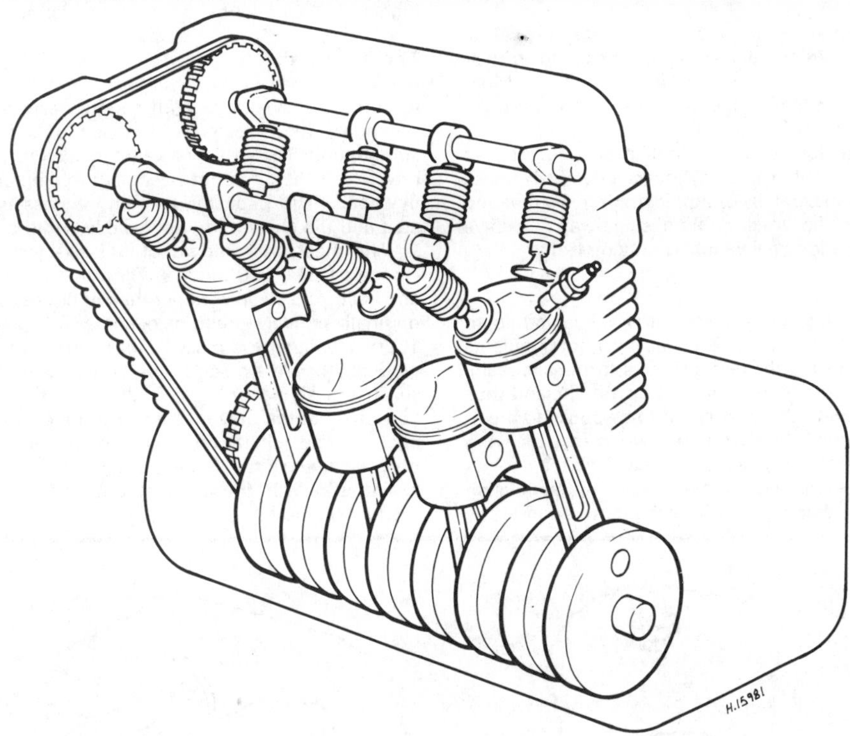


Fig. 1.38 In-line four-stroke four

## 20 Engine arrangements: further variations

In the preceding Sections we have seen the various ways in which engine designers have attempted to improve on the basic single cylinder unit in terms of power output and vibration levels. The process is somewhat contradictory; improve one aspect and the other invariably suffers. This is an essential limitation of the reciprocating engine and demands careful choices and compromises to be made at the design stage if the desired characteristics are to be obtained. If you stop to think about it, the sheer variety of engine arrangements is itself indicative of the designers' dilemma; there is no ideal engine. If there were, it is safe to assume that all manufacturers would use it exclusively, but in reality the best that can be achieved is to select the one which comes closest to fulfilling the requirements of a particular application, and then to incorporate those modifications or improvements that offset the more significant drawbacks. This approach has led to the major motorcycle engine designs discussed above, and has also generated some less common alternatives. In the main, these have had too few advantages over existing arrangements to gain wide acceptance, or have suffered the motorcyclist's traditional distrust of change. In the examples below, some, like the V-three two-stroke may disappear without trace in the coming years, while others, like the V-four four-stroke should offer the first real challenge to the in-line four.

### The V-Three two-stroke

By any standards, the V-three two-stroke is an oddity and seems unlikely to become a popular engine configuration. Initially, the engine appeared as a 500cc GP power unit, the strange layout of the cylinders being chosen to avoid the width problem associated with a two-stroke in-line triple; having reduced the crankshaft width to the minimum possible with separate crankcase compartments, the engine would still have been bulky by virtue of the wide barrels and their transfer ports. By displacing the centre cylinder they would be allowed to overlap somewhat, and the engine width was thus reduced. After Honda racing successes, a road-going derivative, the NS 400R was produced.

### The horizontally-opposed four

Just as the parallel twin was enhanced by the simple expedient of joining two engines to form the in-line four, so too was the horizontally-opposed twin. The resulting engine is exemplified by the Honda Gold Wing models, just about the only example of this arrangement in the motorcycle world. The unit is superbly smooth and gives the Gold Wing the stability that the low centre of gravity dictates. The main drawback is the sheer width of the engine, making it unsuitable for anything other than a large tourer, a role in which it has few rivals. Engine width is a constant problem confronting the motorcycle designer, and although the 'flat four' is almost ideal in every other respect, this one factor is sufficiently important to prevent its extensive use.

### The horizontal in-line four

The trouble with fours, as we have seen, is their width. All engines of this type are far wider than the thickness of the cylinder block, so why not fit them into the frame so that the crankshaft lies in line with the frame, much like a conventional rear wheel drive car. This does work, and the arrangement found a certain amount of popularity in the past, especially in the US. Good examples of this arrangement were the Henderson and Indian fours, and the UK-built Brough and Wilkinson machines. If you look at any of the above the immediate impression is that it is a long machine by virtue of the need to accommodate the long (and rather tall) engine unit in the confines of the frame.

BMW have come up with an interesting variation of the above by laying the unit on its side in the frame. Though a little odd at first sight with its cylinder head running down one side and its crankcase on the other, it does overcome most of the earlier drawbacks. By normal 'four' standards it is quite a narrow unit, and its height is less of a problem. It has the advantages of the conventional transverse four allied to the low centre of gravity of an opposed engine. The BMW K100 series has so far proved successful, though it seems unlikely that other major manufacturers will be inclined to adopt this rather unorthodox approach.

### The Square Four

The Square Four represents another way of doubling the parallel twin to make a four-cylinder unit, this time with two separate crankshafts arranged one behind the other and connected by gears or chain. This arrangement allows the engine width to be kept to that of a twin cylinder unit, with only a small increase in its length, and so provides the advantages of an in-line four without the problem of width.

The most common application of this arrangement was in the Ariel Square Four models. These were all four-stroke engines, and in their final form offered the then remarkable capacity of 1000cc. More recently, the Square Four arrangement has been used in two-stroke racing engines to permit rotary valve induction.

The main problem of the Square Four is that of cooling the rear cylinders. If air-cooled, the front pair of cylinders effectively mask those at the rear, and even with carefully designed finning, overheating tends to become evident in traffic. Water-cooling is one way to resolve the problem, but this means additional weight and complexity.

### The V-Four

Yet another way of arranging four cylinders, the V-Four offers an alternative to the Square Four in terms of compactness but avoids its overheating problems by exposing the rear cylinders to the airstream. In general, the V-Four is no more than a doubled-up V-twin, and thus most of the remarks applicable to the latter can also be applied here. It is possible to arrange the crankshaft with the two crankpins lying parallel (forming a 360° crankshaft), as in the case of the Honda models, and this is the best arrangement in terms of minimising vibration. Another approach, employed by Yamaha, is to arrange the crankpins at 180° to each other. Whilst the resulting vibration is slightly higher, this is offset by the more regular firing of the four cylinders.

### The in-line six

One way of reducing still further the vibration of the in-line four is to add more cylinders. With careful design most of the primary and secondary forces can be balanced out, making the six a notably smooth unit. The six's relatively tiny pistons produce a smooth flow of power and thus it is not necessary to employ large and unresponsive flywheels. The price for this smoothness is mechanical complexity, cost and the sheer and unavoidable width of the engine unit.

The most well known of the six-cylinder motorcycles must be Honda's CBX 1000 models. These have been around for a long time and have sold steadily rather than in dramatic numbers. Though it was originally conceived and marketed as a flagship sports model the CBX 1000 was rather too massive for this role, and over the years the CBX gradually became a sports tourer. Kawasaki have also tried an in-line six in the shape of their Z 1300. Another large machine, this was conceived at the outset as a fast touring machine, and featured water cooling and shaft drive in its specification. Of the European manufacturers, only Benelli saw fit to explore the potential of the in-line six with their Sei model and were the first to market a production model.

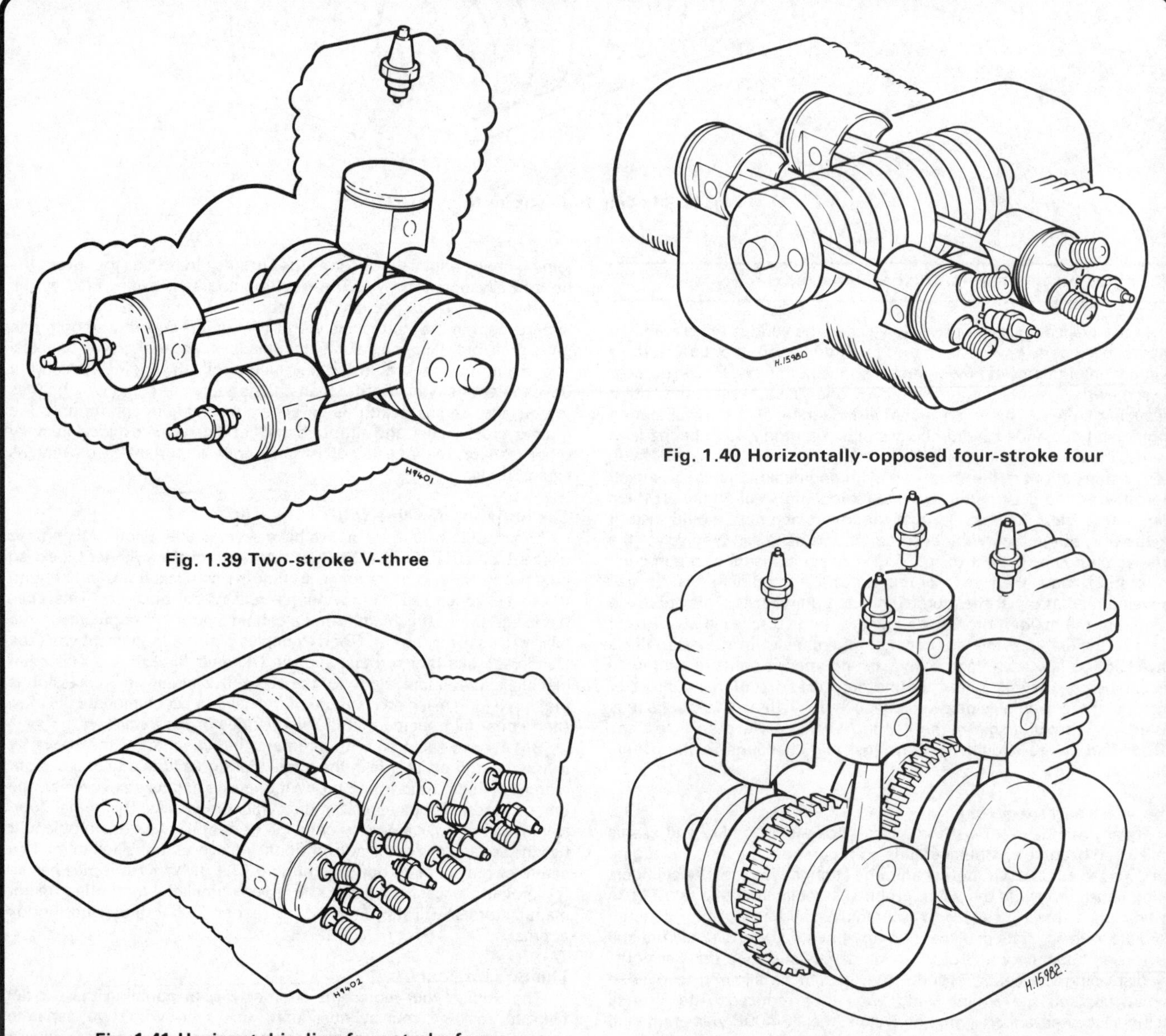


Fig. 1.39 Two-stroke V-three

Fig. 1.40 Horizontally-opposed four-stroke four

Fig. 1.41 Horizontal in-line four-stroke four

Fig. 1.42 The square four

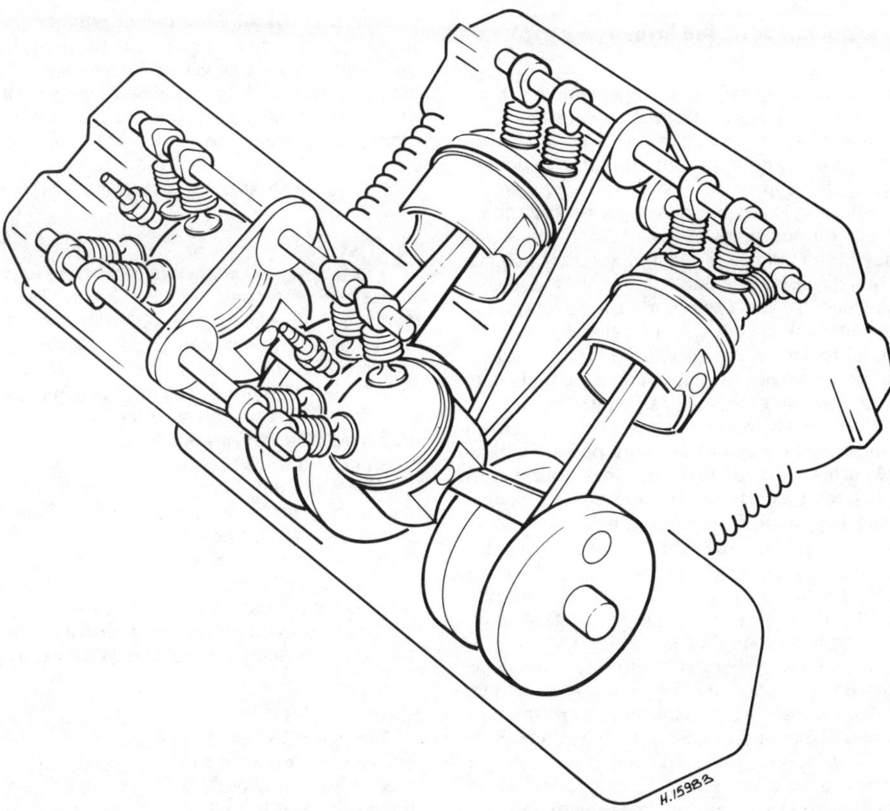


Fig. 1.43 Four-stroke V-four

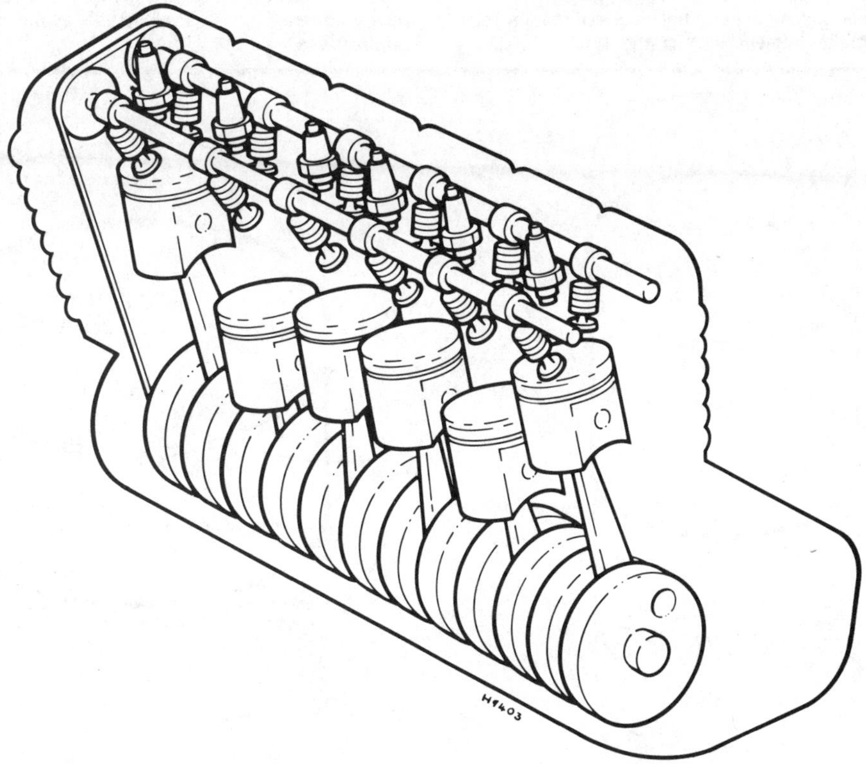


Fig. 1.44 In-line four-stroke six

## 21 The search for more power: bore and stroke

In looking at the various common engine arrangements we have seen how there has always been a dilemma facing the engine designer. Essentially, the engine should be as simple as possible, and thus cheap to manufacture and reliable in use. This approach was most evident in the post-war years where cost effectiveness was a major requirement of any successful motorcycle, and is a major reason for the popularity of the single cylinder engine for many years. Whilst the same requirements remain today in the moped and commuter bike markets, the purpose of the motorcycle in a general sense has evolved. Although it is still used by many as basic transport, it is no longer the case that the main requirement is cheapness and reliability; performance is the main criteria of today's average motorcyclist.

The most obvious way to obtain more power from any engine is to increase its capacity, bearing in mind the considerations discussed in the preceding Sections. Traditionally, however, there have also been very good reasons to concentrate on extracting more power from an engine of a given size. The main one of these in many countries is legislation which often dictates a capacity limit for riders of a certain age or ability. Even where legislation is less restrictive, the cost of insurance increases with a machine's capacity, providing a self-imposed capacity limit for many people. Equally important is the manufacturer's problem of convincing you that his 750cc four is better than all the others, and the best way to do this is to make it go faster/accelerate quicker/look better than its rivals.

We have already seen some of the modifications to the basic two-stroke and four-stroke designs which attempt to make them more efficient in use. Additionally, there are factors which influence the way in which the engine's power is delivered, notably the choice of bore size and the length of the piston's stroke. For any given cylinder capacity there are a number of bore and stroke combinations which may be chosen. In our theoretical engine we could arrange to have the bore diameter equal to the length of the piston stroke, an arrangement known as 'square'. If we increase the stroke and reduce the bore size the engine becomes under-square, or long-stroke, whilst at the other extreme a large bore size could be used in combination with a short stroke to produce an 'over-square' or short-stroke engine.

Before we go any further, two more essential pieces of terminology; bhp and torque. Bhp (brake horsepower) is the unit of measure employed to measure the power produced by an engine at any given speed. Torque can be interpreted most easily as the 'pulling power' of the engine. These two values are established by testing the engine on a device known as a dynamometer over a wide range of engine speeds; from the readings thus obtained the bhp and torque outputs can be plotted as a graph (see example). Without going into the complex mathematics involved, the advantages and disadvantages of the various arrangements can be summarised as follows.

### Long-stroke

The long-stroke engine is characterised by its flat spread of torque across a wide range of engine speeds. The torque is the result of the relatively high leverage exerted on the long connecting rod and is what allows a long-stroke engine to pull strongly from low speeds. The torque curve, if plotted, would show a gentle increase as the engine speed rises, reaching a peak after which it begins to reduce. Given that the engine is at its most efficient when maximum torque is being produced it is obviously desirable to have as flat a torque curve as possible, and in this respect the long-stroke engine excels.

Where the long-stroke loses out is in the overall power available, measured in brake horsepower (bhp). This is very low at low engine speeds, rising in a steep curve and tailing off only at very high speeds. In this respect we need the engine to turn as fast as possible to obtain the maximum amount of power from it, and it is here that the long-stroke is less than convenient; the high piston speed imposes a limitation above which rapid engine wear or damage would result, so this in turn restricts the amount of power available.

### Short-stroke

The short stroke engine can run at higher speeds than can a long-stroke design of similar capacity, and so it is possible to extract more power strokes (and thus more power) in a given time. The drawback is that the shorter stroke means less leverage on the crankshaft, and this in turn dictates a steeper torque curve. In this way the short-stroke is more powerful, but over a narrower band of engine speeds. As you will no doubt have guessed, the answer is a compromise between the two extremes, namely the 'square' engine described above. In practice, most modern motorcycle engines are nearly square in arrangement with slight variations to suit particular applications.

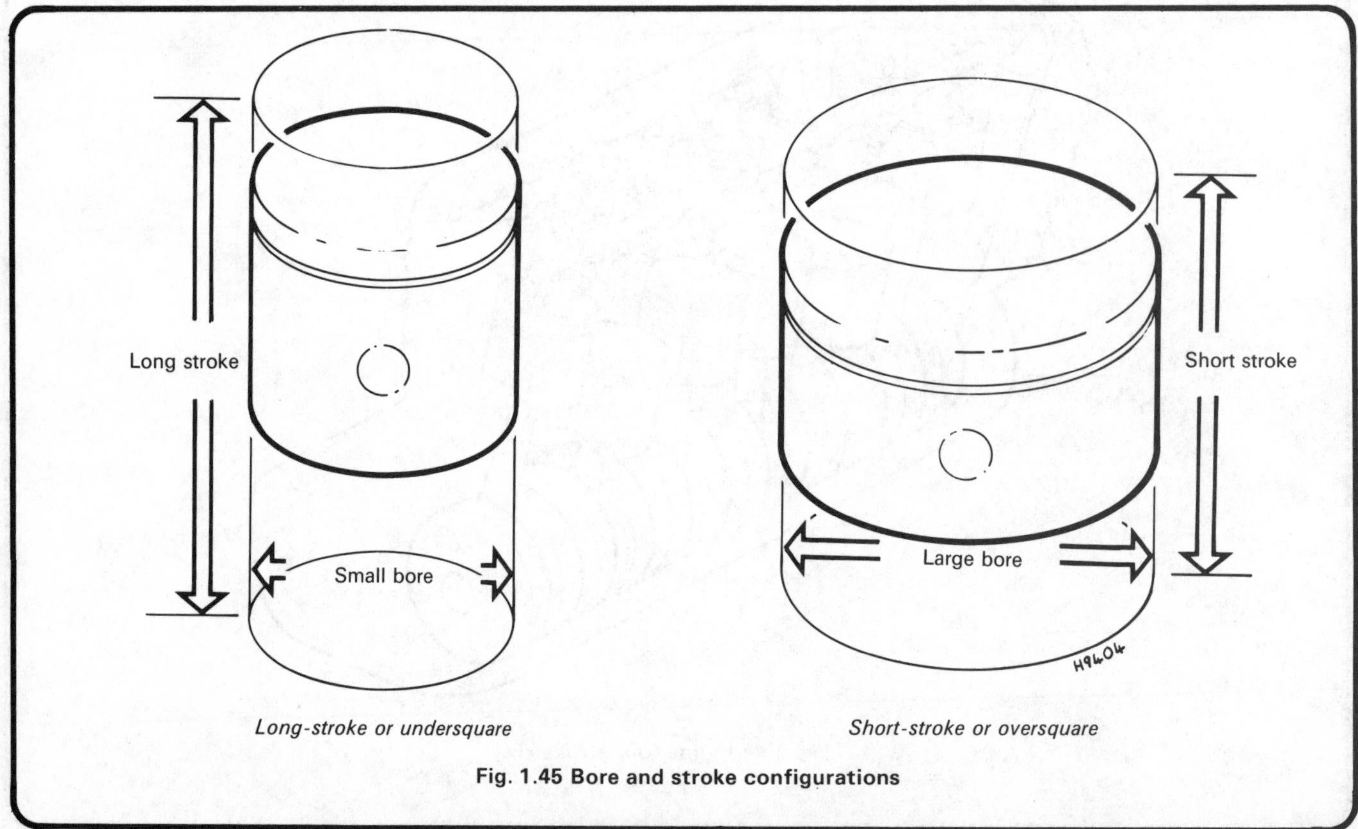


Fig. 1.45 Bore and stroke configurations

## 22 Methods of coping with engine vibration

Having seen how all types of reciprocating engine produce some degree of vibration there remains the problem of what to do about it. In many cases the simple answer is nothing; if the level of vibration is small then it will not be obtrusive in use. On a moped engine for example, the out of balance forces may be quite high, but because the reciprocating components are small, the effect is barely noticeable. Given the same degree of vibration on a much bigger machine – a 250cc or 500cc single for example, and the problem will warrant some attention.

The design of the frame and accessories is important, because these can either damp or encourage vibration. A good example of this is in the handlebars fitted to some machines where sympathetic vibration at the bar ends was found to reach finger-numbing proportions in use. The answer was simply to weight the ends of the handlebars. This altered the resonant frequency of the bar and thus damped out the vibration. Similar techniques are employed to stop handlebar mirrors blurring with vibration and even to prevent recurrent fractures in mounting brackets.

Another approach is to isolate the engine unit from the frame by fitting bonded rubber engine mountings and this can absorb much of the vibration, making the machine feel more comfortable to ride. There are attendant problems due to the need for the engine to be mounted securely in the frame to ensure that the final drive is kept in alignment, and this leads to difficulties on all but the smallest engines.

The methods described so far have been aimed at hiding the effects of vibration rather than eliminating the vibration itself. To do the latter it is necessary to produce further out of balance forces to cancel out those of the crankshaft assembly. The most common method is to use one or more balancer shafts driven from the crankshaft. As the accompanying illustration shows, the forces produced by the weights on the balancer shaft can be arranged to offset the normal vibration in a parallel twin unit, but the arrangement is equally effective in the case of single cylinder machines, to the extent that it has become an almost standard feature on all but the smallest Honda singles.

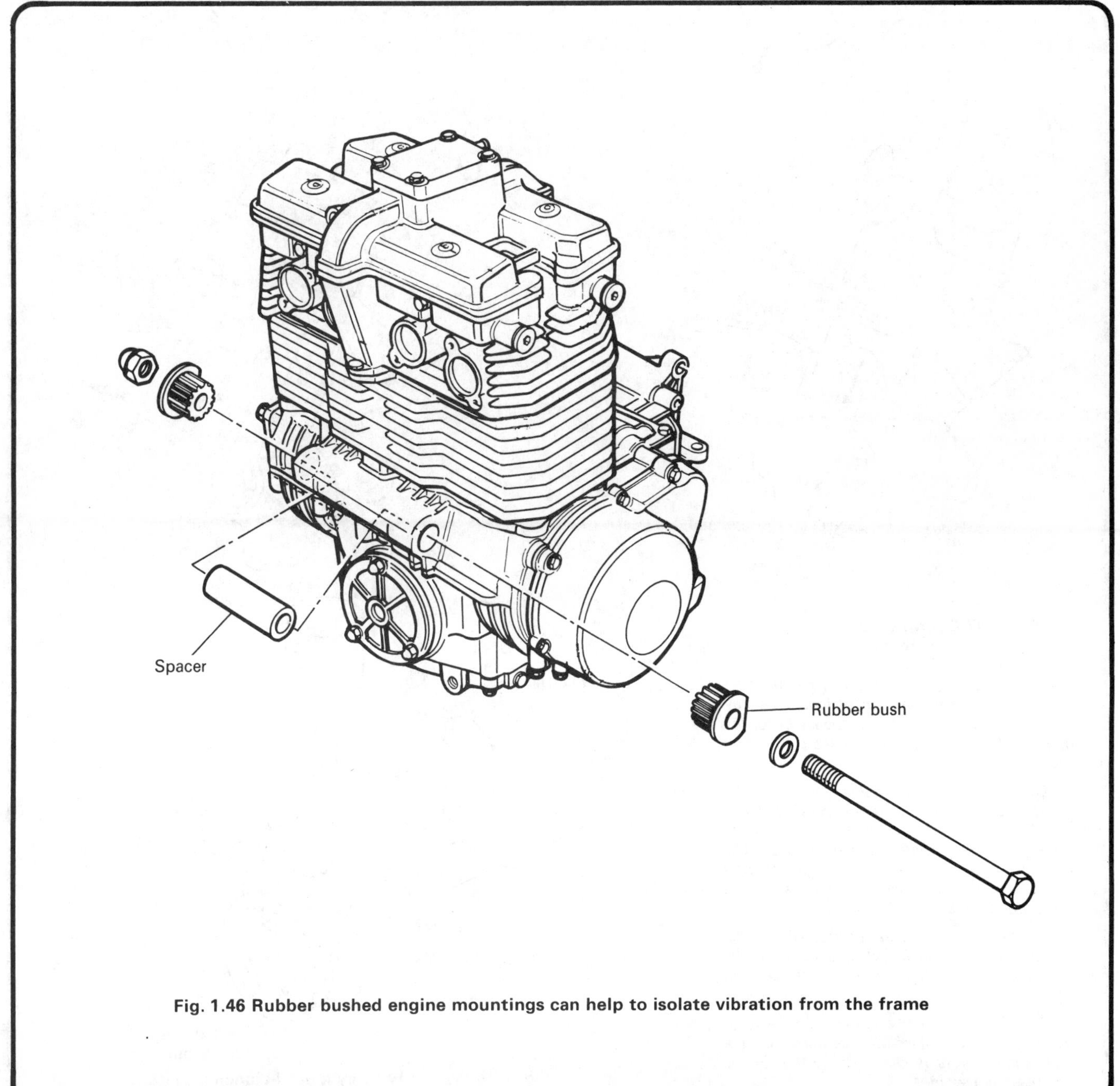


**Fig. 1.46 Rubber bushed engine mountings can help to isolate vibration from the frame**

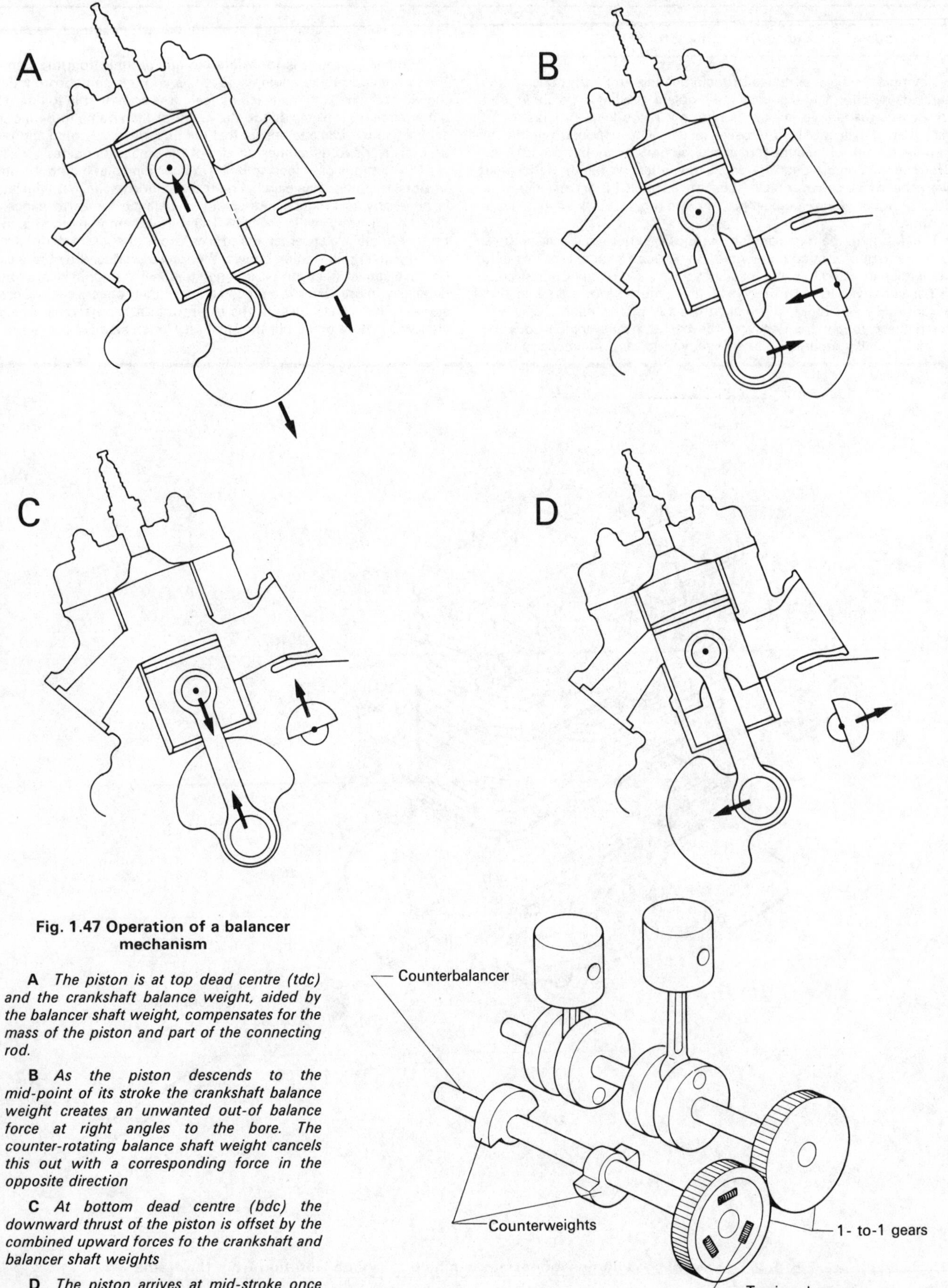


**Fig. 1.47 Operation of a balancer mechanism**

**A** *The piston is at top dead centre (tdc) and the crankshaft balance weight, aided by the balancer shaft weight, compensates for the mass of the piston and part of the connecting rod.*

**B** *As the piston descends to the mid-point of its stroke the crankshaft balance weight creates an unwanted out-of balance force at right angles to the bore. The counter-rotating balance shaft weight cancels this out with a corresponding force in the opposite direction*

**C** *At bottom dead centre (bdc) the downward thrust of the piston is offset by the combined upward forces fo the crankshaft and balancer shaft weights*

**D** *The piston arrives at mid-stroke once more, and the out-of-balance force of the crankshaft weight is cancelled by that of the balance shaft weight*

**Fig. 1.48 Typical twin-cylinder balancing system**

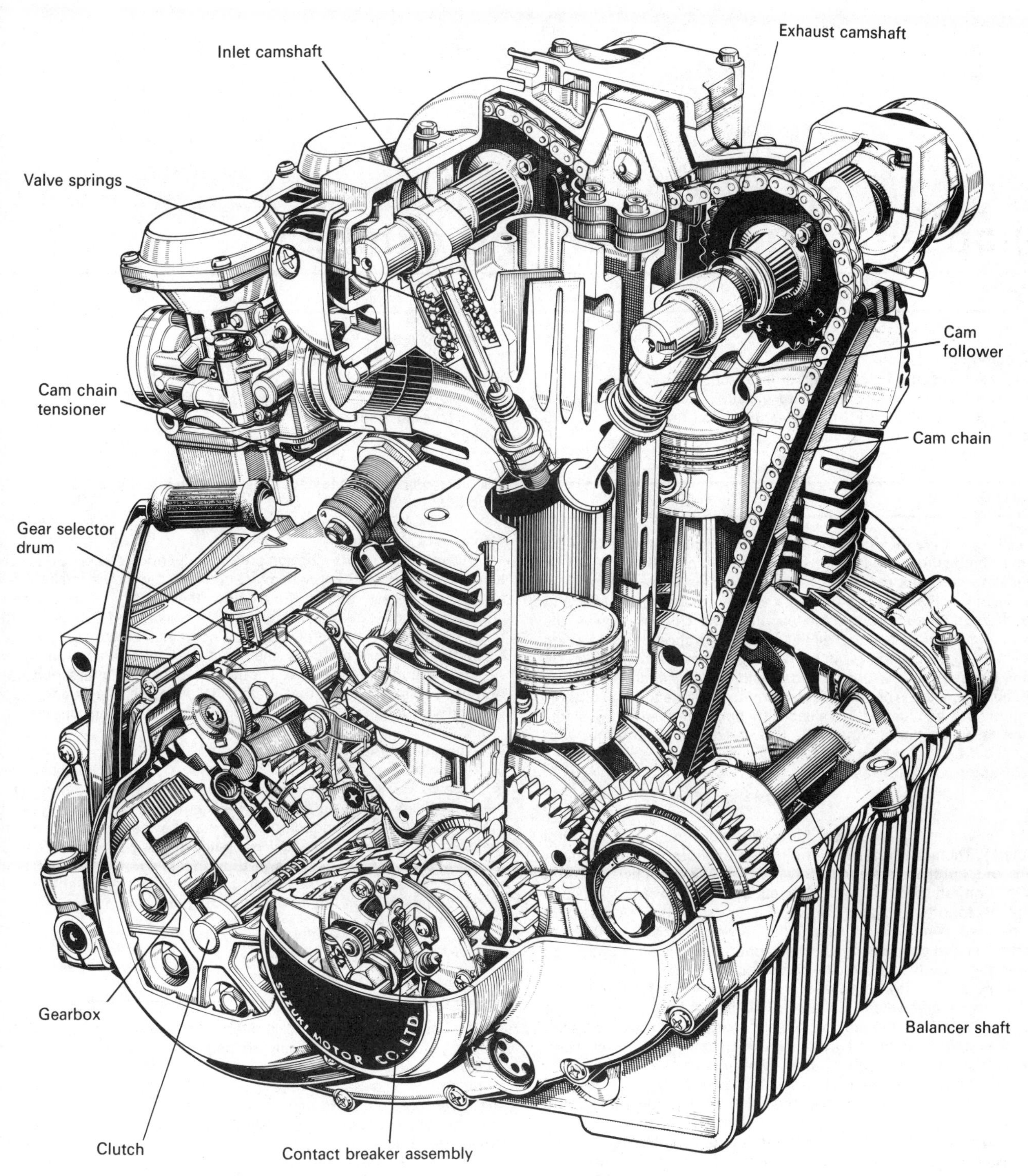


**Fig. 1.49 Sectioned view of the Suzuki GS 400 engine**

*The GS 400 engine unit is a 180° four-stroke parallel twin featuring chain driven double overhead camshafts. The illustration shows the major features of the engine, and also the relative position of the transmission components. Note in particular the crankshaft-driven balancer shaft located at the front of the unit.*

# Chapter 2 Fuel system and exhaust

**Contents**



## 1 Introduction

In Chapter 1 we looked at the basic mechanical components of the internal combustion engine and the ways in which these could be arranged to suit various motorcycle applications. Common to all of these designs is the need to control precisely and accurately the flow of the fuel/air mixture through the engine. This Chapter covers the process of mixing the fuel and air in the correct proportions, delivering this mixture to the cylinder(s) in the required volume to obtain a variety of engine speeds, and disposing of the residual gases after combustion has been completed. Though it is common to separate the functions of induction and exhaust, it is valuable to consider them as a single process in which the energy in the fuel is extracted and turned into useful work and its byproduct, heat. The important elements in this process are described below.

### Fuel

The universal choice of fuel for roadgoing motorcycles is petrol (gasoline). There are a number of other possibilities which we might use instead, but these are either more expensive or less efficient. Petrol is a fraction of crude oil, that internationally important and finite commodity found in deposits below the earth's surface. The crude oil is broken down in refineries by distillation, a process involving heating the crude oil and condensing various fractions as they rise up through a tower divided into temperature-controlled galleries.

The choice of petrol as a fuel is governed by a compromise of two qualities, its calorific value (cv) and its volatility. A high cv is desirable because it represents the amount of heat energy, and thus the useful work, that can be obtained from a given quantity. As the cv rises, however, so the volatility falls, and we require a reasonably volatile fuel. The volatility of a fuel is a measure of how easily it will evaporate at low temperatures, and the lower the volatility, the more difficult the fuel is to burn, hence the need for a compromise.

Having chosen a fuel it is necessary to find out in what ratio it must be mixed with air to ensure complete and efficient combustion; too much air and valuable energy (in the form of fuel) will be excluded from the cylinder, whilst too little air will mean unburnt fuel being expelled with the exhaust gases. The correct ratio of air to fuel is 15:1, whilst the practical limits for successful combustion are between 12:1 and 18:1. Now all we need is a reliable method of delivering this mixture to the engine.

### The carburettor

The carburettor is by far the commonest method of controlling the fuel/air mixture. In the Sections which follow we will look at how it mixes the fuel in the correct proportions, how it is used to control the speed of the engine and how it can adjust to the varying loads imposed on the engine, and how these and other demands have lead to its development. The carburettor is not quite universal, however; some machines employ an alternative method called fuel injection, of which more later.

### The intake system

This rather broad description covers the various components, other than the carburettor itself, which are concerned with the intake side of the process. These include the air filter, the function of which needs little explanation, and the casing in which it is housed. The latter often takes the form of a carefully shaped container known as a Plenum Chamber, and this performs the additional job of controlling and silencing the incoming air. We should not forget the intake port itself. Although this is part of the engine, its diameter, shape and length interact with the carburettor in controlling the incoming mixture.

### The exhaust system

The exhaust system, as its name implies, conducts the spent gases from the combustion chamber to the outside world. In addition to this, the explosive exhaust pulses must be subdued to a tolerable level by the silencer. Another function of the exhaust system is to improve the scavenging efficiency, and this is obviously of great significance in two-stroke engines. Since this in turn affects carburation we should view the above components as part of an entire system, starting at the air filter inlet, through the carburettor and combustion chamber to the exhaust tailpipe.

## 2 Basic carburettor design

The basic operating principle of any carburettor is the venturi. This is little more than a specially-shaped tube, and it works in the following way. If air is drawn through a normal tube with parallel walls it will remain at a constant pressure and velocity along its length, as might be expected. If we now make a reduction in size somewhere in the tube, the air-flow characteristics will be modified; at the point of maximum reduction in size the air-flow will increase in speed, and at the same time its pressure will fall. Thus at the smallest point in the tube there exists a slight vacuum. A venturi is precisely this; a tube with a restriction. In the interests of good gas flow, the restriction becomes progressively greater to its maximum point and then gradually opens out again.

In the accompanying line drawing we can see our simple venturi in cross-section. You will note that at the point of maximum restriction we have added a small drilling, beneath which is a reservoir of fuel. The low pressure area allows fuel to be pushed through the hole by atmospheric pressure, and the stream of fuel breaks up into tiny droplets which disperse into the airstream. If the drilling is of such a size that one part of fuel enters for every fifteen of air we have a very crude but effective carburettor. Fit this device to an engine, which will draw the air through the venturi, and the mixture necessary for combustion will be provided. Easy isn't it?

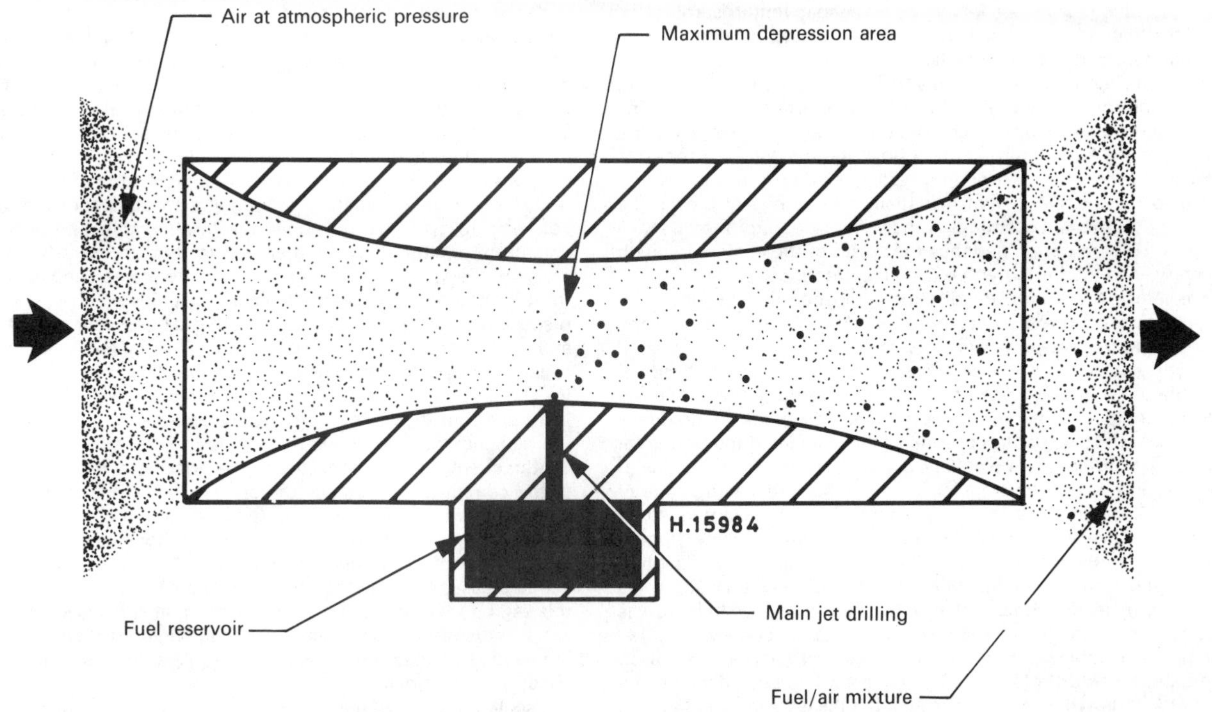


**Fig. 2.1 How a venturi works**

*As air flows through the venturi, the restriction causes it to speed up and lower its pressure. This low pressure area is used to draw fuel through the drilling at the centre of the venturi, and the emerging fuel is atomised as it mixes in the airstream.*

By now you may be wondering why all motorcycles are not fitted with this pleasantly simple and foolproof device. The answer is that it cannot do all that we require of a carburettor. This is not to say that it would not work; it would be quite sufficient for a simple engine running at constant speed and loading. If you have ever dismantled a motor mower's carburettor you may have noticed some similarity – a simple venturi carburettor with the addition of a throttle plate to set the engine speed. Some moped instruments are little more than this, but for most applications we need a more sophisticated device. To find out why, let us examine a few examples and see what needs to be added.

## 3 Carburettor types: the fixed venturi or fixed jet

In Section 2 we created our simple carburettor, and an instrument of this type is known as a fixed venturi type, simply because the profile of the venturi remains constant at all times. To be able to control the speed of the engine we need some sort of movable obstruction to vary the amount of fuel/air mixture entering the engine. This can be achieved by fitting a circular plate, supported on a movable spindle, in the venturi. If the plate is turned so that it blocks the venturi, the air-flow is stopped (and with it the engine). Turn the spindle and the plate will allow air to pass until, when it is at right-angles, it offers little restriction. This arrangement is known as a butterfly throttle. To ensure that the fuel is supplied in the correct proportion it is drawn through a carefully sized drilling. To allow for adjustment to be made, should the need arise, the drilling can be incorporated in a small threaded brass plug, known as a jet.

Meanwhile, we need to make sure of a constant supply of fuel and this needs to be kept at a constant level to ensure consistent operation. This job is done by the float assembly, housed in a float bowl below the main jet drilling. If you want to see an example of how the float system works, go into the bathroom and take the top off the WC cistern. Inside you will see the float, an arm connecting it to a valve and a cistern full of water. Flush the WC and the water level falls and with it the float. This opens the valve and the cistern fills with water until the rising float closes the valve again. The carburettor float valve assembly does exactly the same job, keeping the fuel level constant.

The above instrument would work reasonably well on an engine at normal operating temperature, but if it was cold it could prove impossible to get started. This is because the fuel in the incoming mixture will condense on the cold metal in the engine, and thus would not remain in the finely vaporised form needed for successful combustion. To compensate for this we have to make the incoming mixture very much richer in fuel than normal. This is achieved either by restricting the venturi so that the low pressure in it is greatly increased, thus increasing the proportion of fuel in the mixture, or by providing an alternative supply of fuel through a separate cold-start circuit. Both systems tend to be called 'chokes' but strictly speaking it is only the former system that works by 'choking' the venturi. Once the engine has started it will begin to warm up, and eventually it will be necessary to turn off the cold start device to prevent the engine being flooded by the excess fuel.

If we wish the fixed venturi to operate over a wide range of engine speeds the single jet may not be adequate at all speeds. At very low speeds, for example, the depression (the partial vacuum) in the venturi may not be enough to lift the correct amount of fuel through the main jet, so the engine will falter and die. To compensate for this we could position a second (pilot) jet outlet near to the butterfly throttle plate. With the throttle plate just open there will be a localised venturi effect near it, and this can be used to draw in the extra fuel. As the throttle opens this effect is lost and the main jet takes over.

A similar problem at higher engine speeds can be offset by additional (secondary) jets positioned and sized so that they come into action only when very high depression exists in the venturi. In practice, it is usually necessary to have quite a few jets to provide a constant mixture at all speeds, and the fixed venturi is not commonly used on motorcycles. Until quite recently Harley-Davidson used fixed jet carburettors, but in general they are more often found on car engines.

## 4 Carburettor types: the slide carburettor

The slide carburettor tackles the problem of the changing demands of the engine by altering the size of the venturi, and thus its effect on the main jet, rather than adding further secondary jets as in the above example. For this reason it is known as a variable venturi carburettor. Many of the features described in Section 3 are still applicable, notably the float system and cold start system.

Where the slide carburettor differs from the fixed venturi type is in the way it controls the rate of fuel delivery through the main jet. The main jet is screwed into the carburettor at the most restricted part of the venturi, as in the fixed venturi type. Above it, however, is a movable cylindrical throttle valve housed in a vertical extension of the venturi, and able to rise or fall so that it partially or completely blocks the airflow through the carburettor. It is thus able to control the effective opening of the carburettor, and thus the speed of the engine, in much the same way as the butterfly throttle valve described earlier.

There remains the problem of supplying enough fuel when the depression at small throttle openings is insufficient to lift it from the float bowl, and this is resolved in the same way as has been described for the fixed venturi type. A pilot jet can be fitted on the engine side of the throttle valve, making use of the localised venturi effect at small throttle openings. As the throttle is opened, the pilot jet gradually becomes less effective, control passing to the main jet. If the bottom of the valve were left flat there would be a 'gap' between the influence of the pilot jet and that of the main jet. To avoid this, the leading edge of the valve is machined at an angle, emphasising the venturi effect between the valve and the carburettor bore at intermediate throttle openings. On moped carburettors, the above arrangement is often sufficient, and from the point where the throttle valve is about 1/3 open the main jet in combination with the varying venturi size is enough to control the mixture and engine speed adequately.

On bigger machines, however, the larger carburettor sizes used mean that the venturi effect will not have the correct effect on the amount of fuel drawn through the main jet; if the jet is large enough to supply adequate fuel at high speeds, it will tend to flood the engine at low speeds. Fit a smaller jet and fuel starvation will occur at large throttle openings. To correct this problem an ingenious solution was found; the needle jet.

The needle jet is positioned so that it is flush with or projects slightly into the carburettor bore. The main jet, which is chosen so that it is of the correct size at full throttle, screws into the bottom of the needle jet. Hanging from the underside of the throttle valve is a tapered needle which passes down into the needle jet. At intermediate throttle openings the gap between the needle and the wall of the needle jet is considerably less than the main jet size, and so the fuel flow is controlled by the needle jet assembly. As the throttle is opened, the needle jet allows more fuel to pass through it, and is thus able to adjust to the increased demand. Finally, from about 3/4 to full throttle, the needle valve opening exceeds that of the main jet, and so control is passed to the latter. If the above seems a little complicated, study the accompanying line drawing which should help to show how the needle valve functions.

From the foregoing it should be obvious that the variable venturi of the slide carburettor can eliminate the need for the complicated array of jets and passages which typifies the fixed venturi instrument. This in turn means that the slide carburettor can be made smaller and lighter, both of which are important considerations when building motorcycles. A less obvious advantage is the subtle way in which the various stages of operation overlap and influence each other. We have seen that the stages of operation of the slide carburettor are pilot jet, throttle valve cutaway, needle jet and main jet, but these are really only arbitary divisions; in practice the transition between each stage is quite gradual, and so the careful choice of settings can be used to produce a very smooth response at widely varying speeds and throttle openings. In fact, the slide carburettor has proven to be so well suited to motorcycle use that it has been the usual choice for around half a century. In this time it has evolved quite considerably, and in recent years has developed into a much more sophisticated device to comply with increasingly stringent demands of performance, economy and pollution control.

## 5 Carburettor types: the CV (constant vacuum) carburettor

The constant velocity or CV carburettor is another example of a variable venturi instrument, having much in common with the slide carburettor described above. It differs in that the throttle valve is replaced by a similarly shaped piston, the position of which is controlled not by the throttle twistgrip, but automatically by degree of vacuum in the inlet passage. The overall airflow through the carburettor, and thus the engine speed is regulated by a twistgrip-controlled butterfly valve, much like that of a fixed venturi carburettor. This arrangement allows the instrument to respond to the requirements of the engine, and this effect is best illustrated by looking at what happens in a conventional slide instrument in normal use.

Imagine that you are riding along at a constant speed in top gear.If you wish to go faster, you open the throttle valve and the increased volume of mixture allows the engine to pick up speed until a higher cruising speed is reached. To maintain the correct mixture ratio the throttle should be opened gradually as the engine gathers speed, but in practice most of us simply open the throttle and wait until the engine and carburettor sort themselves out. This means that during the acceleration phase it is common for the throttle valve to be too far open for the particular engine speed. The effective area of the venturi is increased, but the airflow through the instrument, being governed by the demands of the engine, remains low. This in turn means that the venturi effect is temporarily lost, fuel is not drawn through the main jet at the correct rate, and thus the engine is starved. Similarly, if when cruising at a constant throttle setting we come to a hill, the machine may begin to slow down. Assuming we do not change to a lower gear and the throttle position is maintained, the same problem exists. In extreme cases this may cause the engine to misfire or even stall, and this can be seen with the machine running at idle speed. If the throttle is opened suddenly and completely, the engine will splutter for a few moments and may stop completely if it cannot recover the venturi effect quickly enough.

Whilst under normal circumstances few riders will misuse the throttle to the extent that stalling is a problem, the real drawback is more subtle. Just as a gross mismatch between throttle setting and engine speed will cause stalling, so a lesser mismatch will cause a less severe but equally significant variation of the correct mixture strength. In other words, unless you are very conscientious, your motorcycle will be running inefficiently for much of the time, and both performance and fuel economy will suffer. In the case of the CV carburettor, it controls the mixture strength in response to the demands of the engine, the rider merely signalling the required change of engine speed via the butterfly valve. In circumstances similar to those described above, the CV carburettor responds differently. When accelerating, we open the butterfly valve which controls the airflow into the engine. The depression in the carburettor and inlet port remain low at this stage, so the vacuum-controlled piston opens only as far as the present rate of airflow into the engine demands. As this increases, so the piston rises until it balances against the throttle valve opening. This means that the mixture strength is kept at the correct proportions at all times, and the engine is kept running efficiently, irrespective of the rider's ham-fistedness in operating the throttle twistgrip.

As mentioned above, the piston is operated by engine vacuum, or depression, maintaining the velocity of the mixture at a constant level. In consequence, this type of instrument is known variously as constant vacuum or constant velocity (CV) and also constant depression (CD). The significant part of the instrument is obviously the piston, so let us see how it works. There are two basic approaches, using either a close fitting piston in a chamber above the venturi (SU type) or by fitting a flexible diaphragm to the top of the piston to separate it from a vacuum chamber, again above the venturi (Stromberg type). The diaphragm or piston chamber is thus separated into two parts, the upper part connected by a port to the venturi, and the lower part being vented and at atmospheric pressure. If the vacuum level in the venturi is high, the piston is lifted upwards, whilst if it is low the weight of the piston plus a light spring closes the piston. This can best be understood by studying the sectioned examples which accompany the text.

It will be seen that the CV carburettor offers a number of clear advantages over the slide instrument, and that both variable venturi types are better suited to motorcycle use than the fixed venturi or fixed jet types. The difference between the slide and CV carburettor is not so great as might be thought however, and in practice the two types are used according to the type of engine and the overall cost of the machine. In many cases the extra cost of a CV carburettor is felt to outweigh its advantages, and on some more sporting machines, the simplicity and responsiveness of the slide type are felt to be more important than improved efficiency. In consequence, both types may be encountered in a wide range of applications.

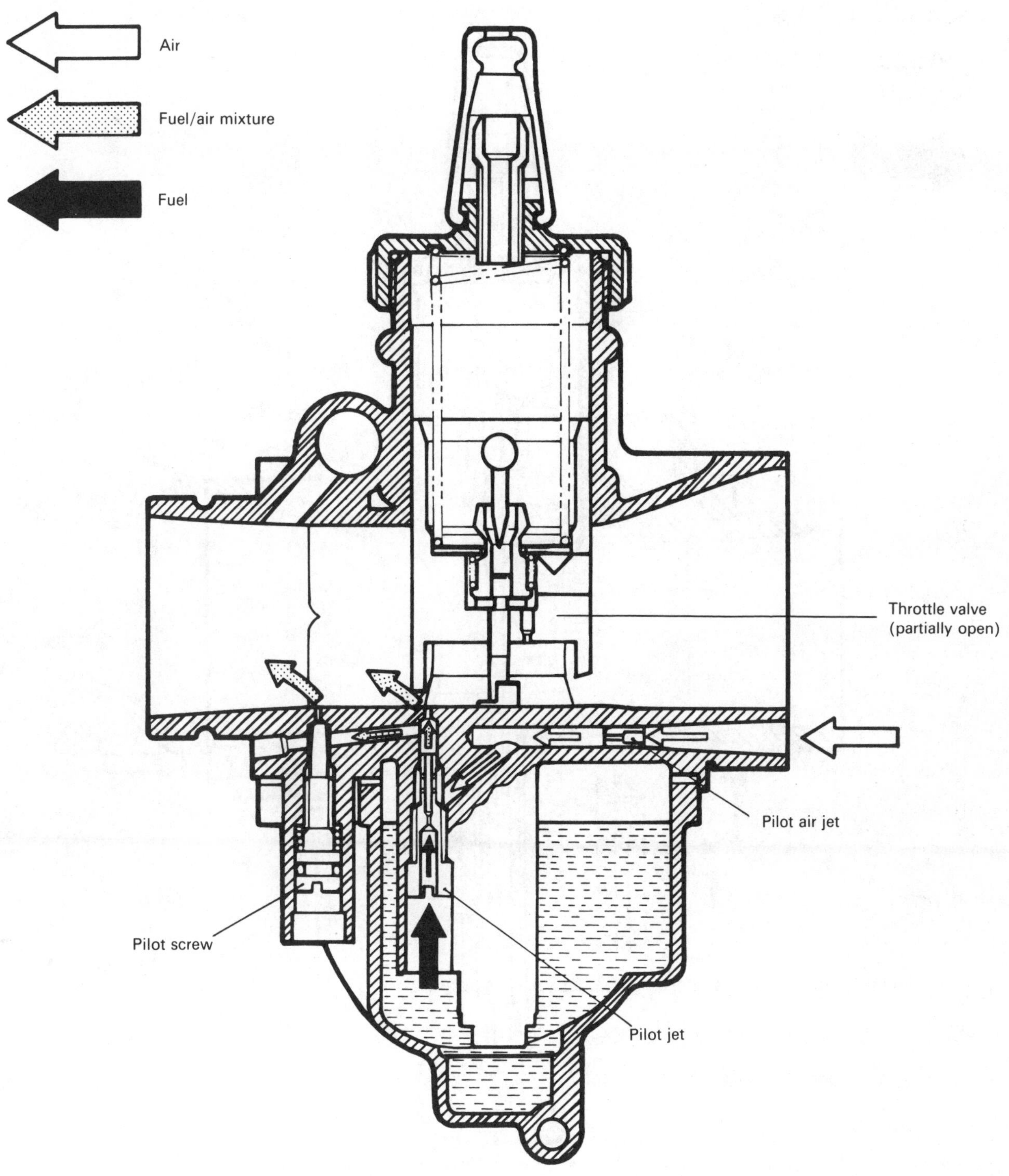


**Fig. 2.2 The pilot, or slow running circuit – slide carburettor**

*In this example, air is drawn through an inlet passage and is regulated by the pilot air jet. Fuel is drawn up through the pilot jet and mixes with the air, the resulting mixture entering the main bore at the pilot outlet, just below the edge of the throttle valve. The strength of the pilot mixture can be varied via the pilot screw and its outlet.*

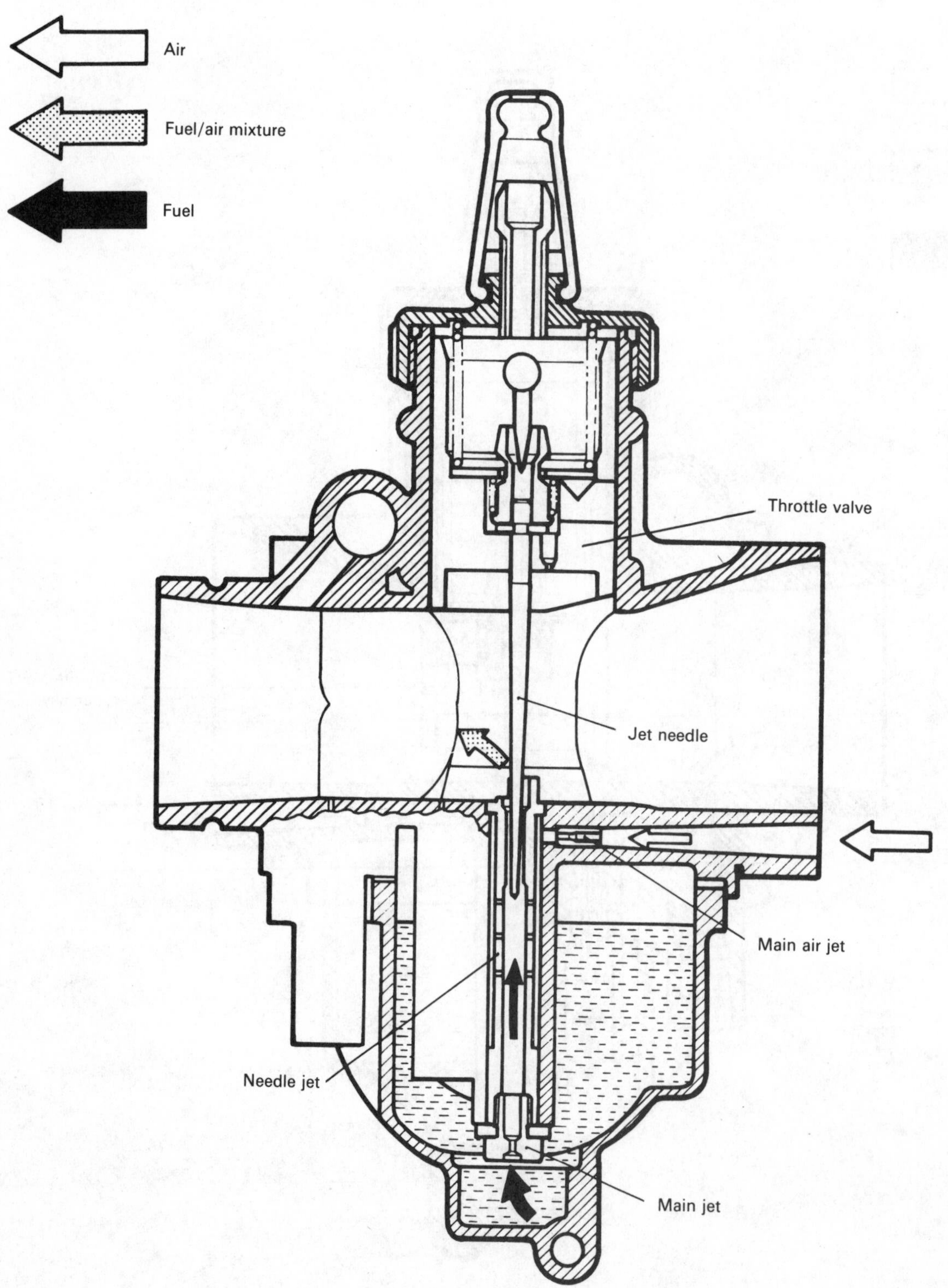


**Fig. 2.3 The main jet circuit – slide carburettor**

*As the throttle valve is opened, the mixture strength is controlled by the main air jet and main jet. Through intermediate throttle openings, the volume of mixture entering the main bore is controlled by the needle and needle jet. Note the air bleed holes in the latter – these help to atomise the fuel using air drawn from the main air jet.*

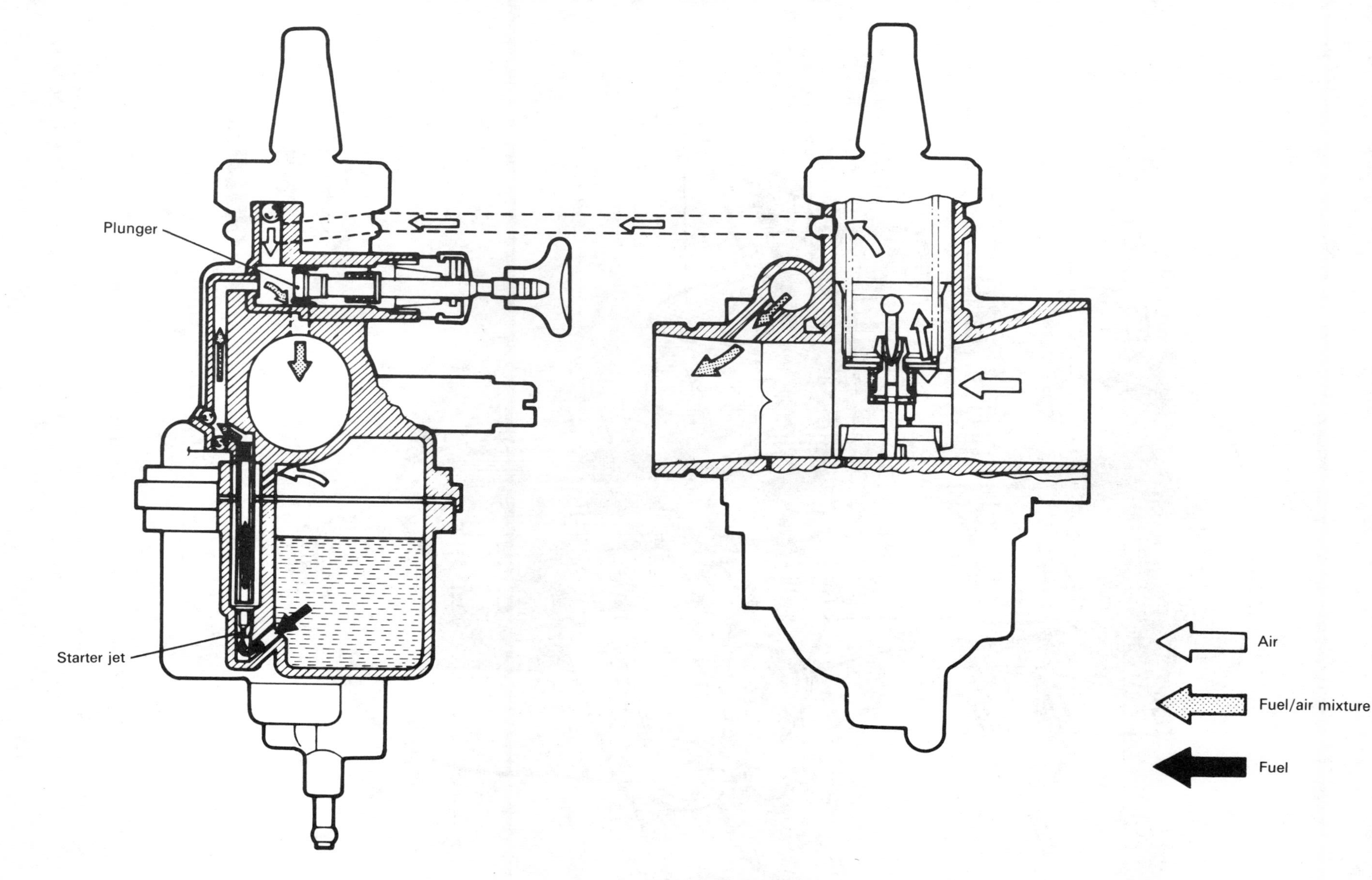


**Fig. 2.4 The cold start system**

*The majority of carburettors are equipped with a plunger-type cold start system in which fuel is drawn up through the starter jet, mixed with air, and fed into the carburettor bore. The system provides an extremely rich mixture for cold starting, and on most arrangements has only an on or off setting. The plunger can be controlled from a knob on the carburettor, or remotely by a cable and lever.*

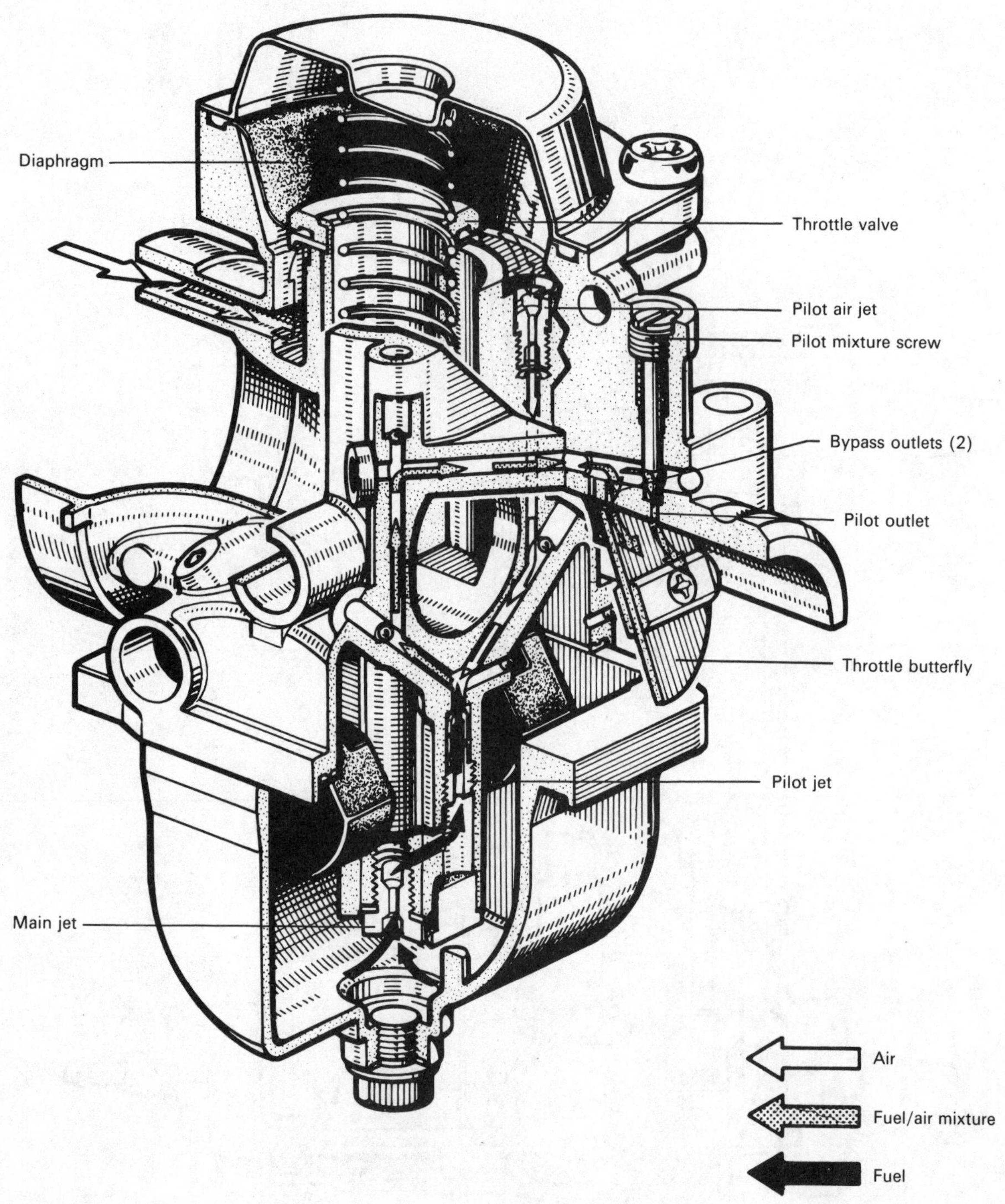


**Fig. 2.5 The pilot, or slow running, circuit – CV carburettors**

*At idle speed the throttle butterfly is almost closed, as is the throttle valve. Air is drawn through the pilot air jet and mixed with fuel from the pilot jet. A proportion is discharged through the pilot outlet(s) whilst the remainder is controlled by the pilot mixture screw to regulate the mixture strength.*

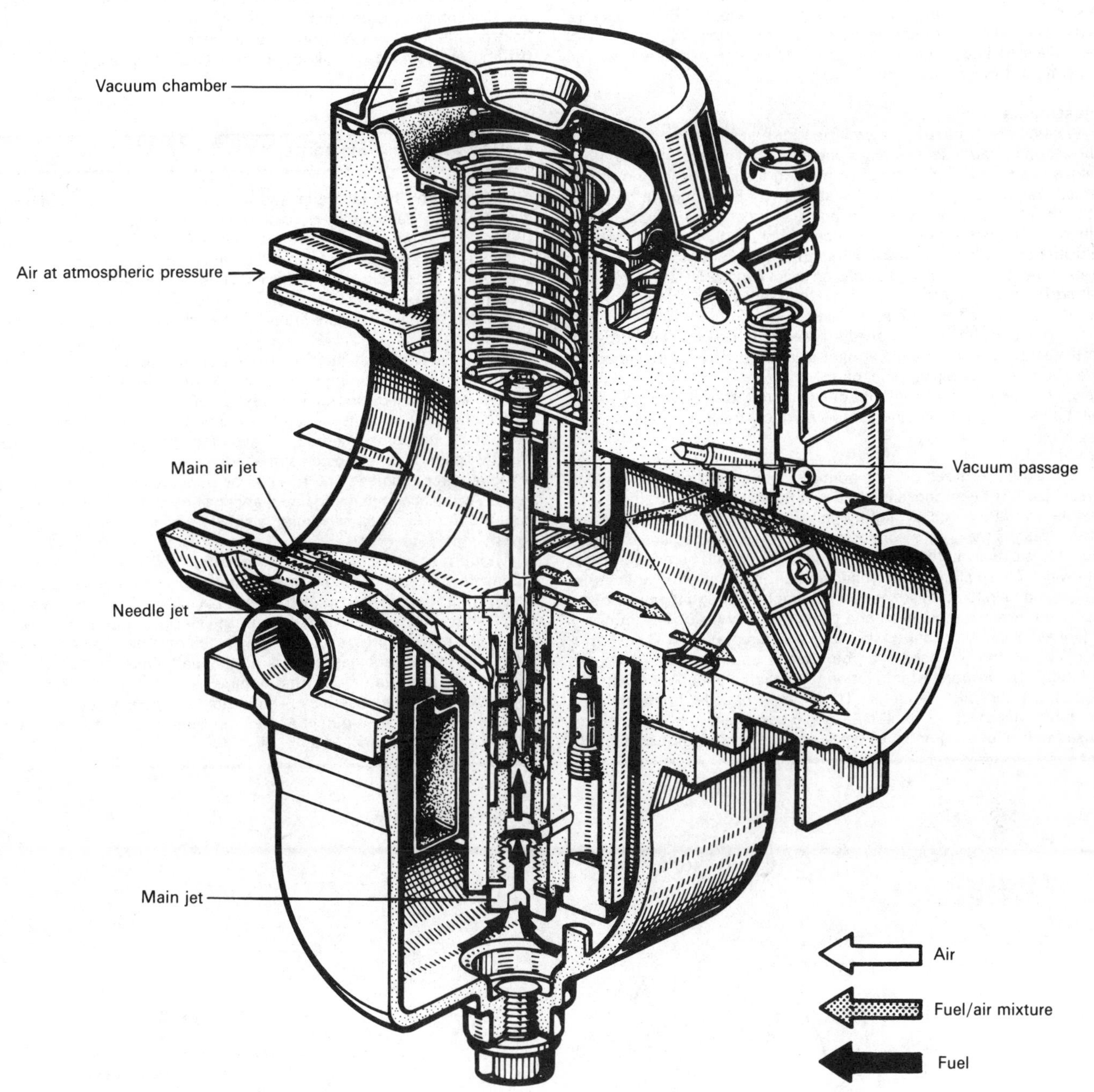


**Fig. 2.6 The main jet circuit – CV carburettors**

*As the throttle butterfly is opened, a low pressure area is created below the throttle valve. This is transmitted to the vacuum chamber via the vacuum passage in the throttle valve. The underside of the diaphragm is open to atmospheric pressure, so the valve rises against spring pressure in response to the vacuum. As the piston rises, the vacuum decreases until the throttle valve is balanced in the correct position for a given engine speed and loading.*

*Air is drawn in through the main air jet where it is mixed with fuel drawn up through the main jet and needle jet assembly. In this respect the CV carburettor works in the same way as a slide type instrument.*

## 6 Slide and CV carburettors in detail

We have seen how the two varieties of variable venturi carburettor work in principle, but in practice there are a number of developments on the basic design which bear closer examination. In some cases these relate to improving the performance of the instrument, whilst others make it more practical to use.

### Adjustments

All carburettors have some provision for adjustment to allow them to be set up to particular machines and operating conditions. The most obvious need is some method of controlling the idle speed, and this is normally provided by an adjustable stop to set the minimum opening of the throttle valve at the desired point. In most cases this takes the form of a knurled screw on the side of the carburettor, though in multi-instrument installations a single throttle stop knob may control all instruments via a linkage. Only on a few mopeds is this control omitted on the grounds of economy; they rely on adjustment of the throttle cable to achieve the same result.

To fine-tune the mixture at idle speed it is necessary to provide some method of controlling the pilot jet. This can be done either by controlling the overall volume of the mixture with a pilot mixture screw, or by adjusting the amount of air entering the pilot circuit using a pilot air screw; both arrangements are widely used.

### Jet selection

The various jet sizes do not normally require alteration once the correct size has been chosen, but if conditions dictate a change it is possible to fit jets of a slightly larger or smaller size. In many carburettors the main jet is connected to the needle jet by an emulsion tube. This is usually in the form of a long cylinder with numerous holes in its walls. These allow a controlled amount of air to enter above the main jet and help to atomise the fuel flowing up through the needle jet. This in turn ensures more even and complete combustion. In addition, the jet needle can be changed to one of a different profile. This allows the effect of the jet needle to be altered quite subtly. On many machines, one or more air correction jets may be encountered in the carburettor's air inlet drillings. These are normally fitted by the carburettor manufacturer to allow a single basic carburettor casting to be used to produce a number of types, and they should not be altered.

### Float adjustment

The level of the fuel in relation to the jets in the carburettor must be set accurately or the mixture strength will be affected at all engine speeds. Most manufacturers specify a fuel level or float height setting, and this can be adjusted by bending the small tang which bears on the float needle. It is worth noting that an incorrect fuel level can create baffling problems, especially on multi-cylinder engines.

## 7 Carburettor refinements

It is perhaps inevitable that the basic carburettor types outlined in the preceding Sections have undergone numerous detail changes to suit various engines, and there are even a few hybrid types, where a slide or CV instrument has been fitted with extra fuel circuits, along the lines of the fixed venturi carburettors. These are normally controlled by primary and secondary main jets in place of the single jet of the standard instrument, and are intended to ensure a more precise mixture control.

When we looked at the CV carburettor, we saw how the standard slide instrument was prone to a temporary weak mixture problem if the throttle was opened too quickly. Despite this single disadvantage, the slide carburettor remains a useful instrument, so inevitably there have been developed other methods of avoiding the weak spot. The most effective method is to provide some means of enrichening the mixture at the required moment, and this can be done by fitting an accelerator pump. As the accompanying line drawing shows, the pump is operated from the throttle valve, producing a small jet of fuel when the valve is raised.

Though not essential to the operation of the carburettor, an automatic cold start or 'choke' is an increasingly common feature. In its simplest form, some moped instruments have a small cam arrangement which shuts off the choke flap if the throttle is opened beyond a certain point. On more sophisticated models a temperature-sensitive unit is fitted. On these machines there is no manual choke control; the unit senses the temperature of the engine, and opens or closes the cold-start circuit as necessary. The system is operated by a bi-metal strip which bends as it gets hot, and can thus be used to operate the choke or cold start mechanism.

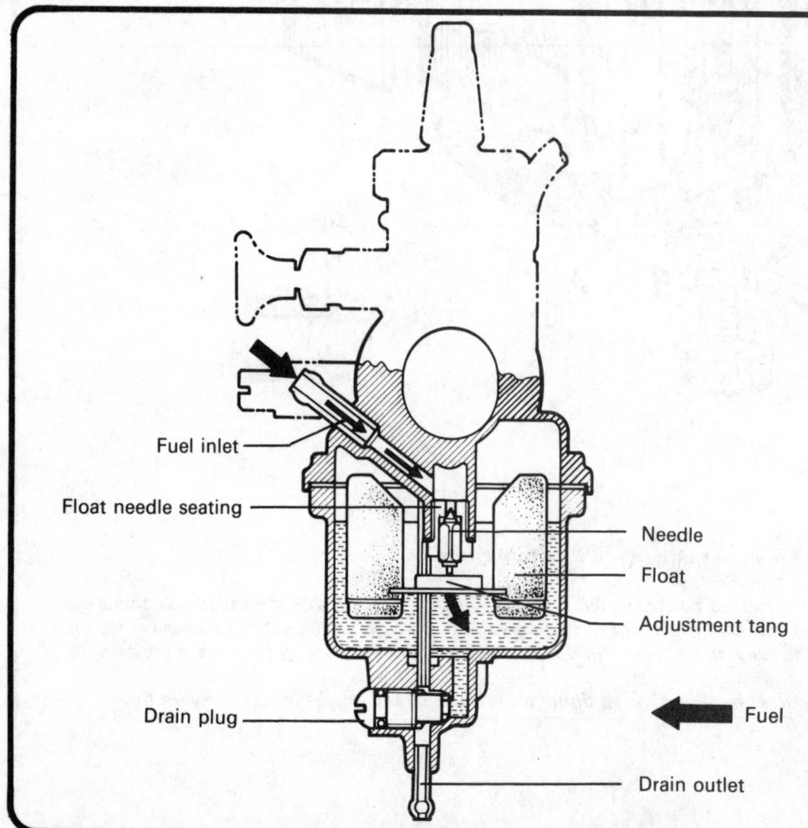


**Fig. 2.7 The float system**

*When the fuel tap is turned on, fuel flows into the float chamber. As the fuel level rises, so does the float assembly. When it reaches a predetermined height the float needle is pushed against its seat, shutting off the supply. An adjustment tang is provided to allow the fuel level to be set to the specified height in relation to the main jet.*

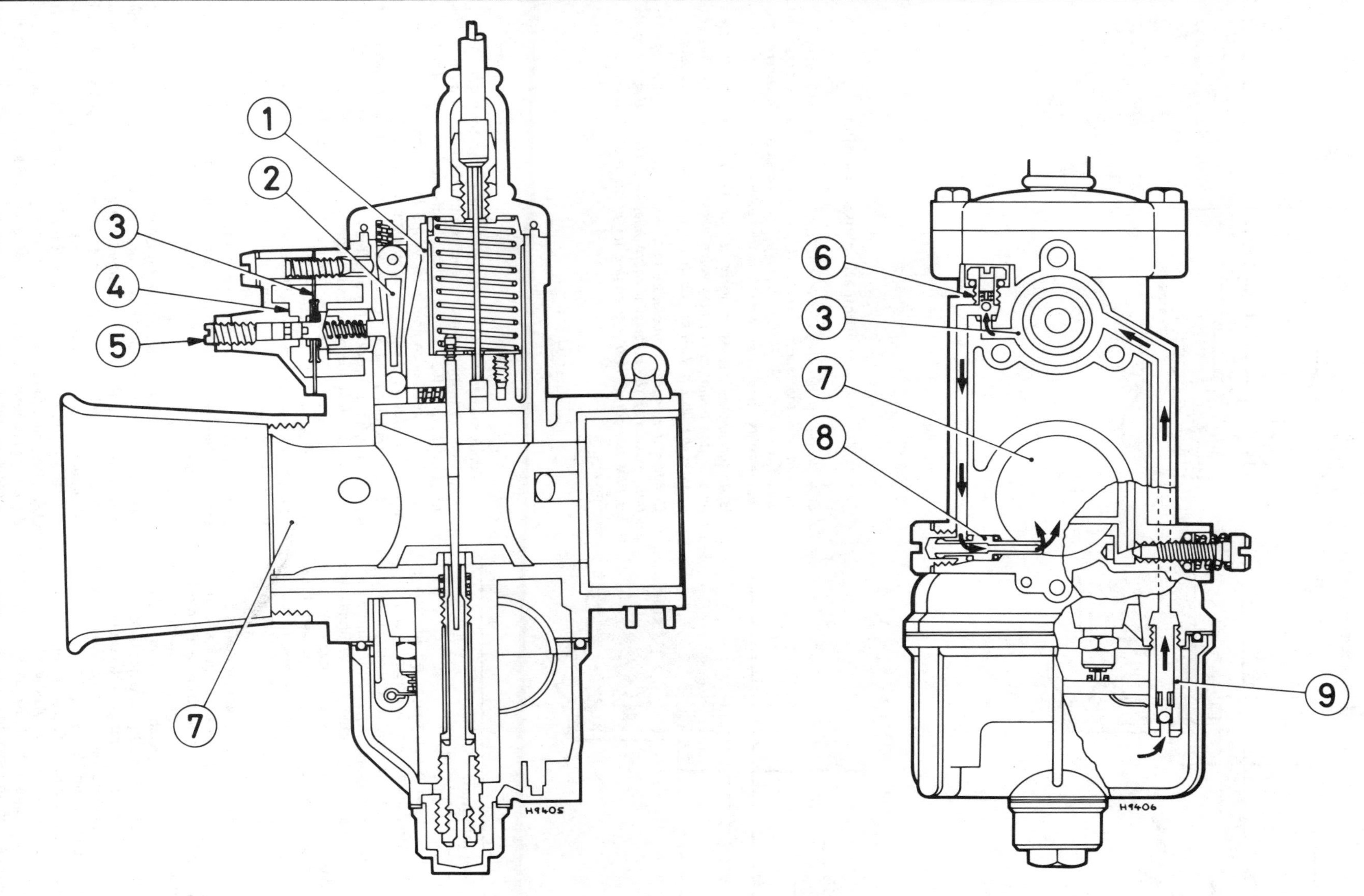


**Fig. 2.8 Accelerator pump operation**

*On this example of an accelerator pump (Dell'Orto PHF) the diaphragm-type pump is controlled by a ramp on the side of the throttle valve (1). As the valve rises, it pushes a lever (2) which in turn depresses the diaphragm (3). Movement of the diaphragm, and hence the amount of fuel injected is set by an adjuster screw (5) and spring (4). The fuel in the pump chamber exits past a non-return valve (6) and is expelled through a jet nozzle (8) into the main bore of the carburettor (7). When the throttle is closed, the diaphragm returns, drawing a fresh charge of fuel up through the inlet non-return valve (9).*

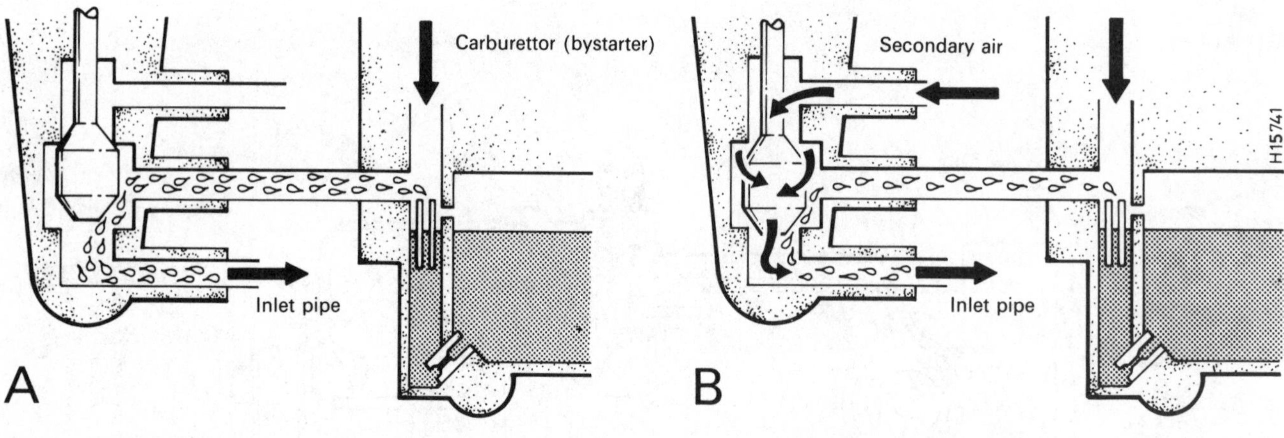


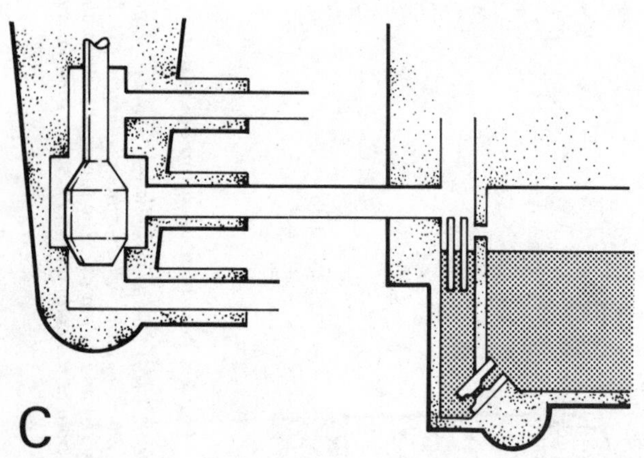


**Fig. 2.9 Automatic choke operation**

**A** *When the temperature is below 10°C, the secondary air passage is blocked by the starter valve. As the engine is cranked an enriched-mixture is drawn through the bystarter chamber and supplements the mixture from the carburettor.*

**B** *As the engine begins to warm up (between 10° and 46°C), the bimetal strip begins to open the valve, allowing extra or secondary air to enter the system. This means that the enriched mixture is diluted.*

**C** *When the engine temperature rises above 46°C, the valve opens fully, closing off the outlet pipe to the inlet tract. The cold start circuit is thus turned off until the engine temperature again drops below 46°C.*

## 8 Turbocharging and fuel injection

In recent years there has been an upsurge of interest in turbocharging as a method of extracting more power from an engine of a given capacity. Previously, turbochargers were used mainly in racing applications by virtue of their cost and complexity, and the unfortunate tendency for the 'blown' engine to be rather fragile under the additional pressures placed on it. Technological advances have allowed car and motorcycle engineers alike to develop satisfactory systems for road-going vehicles, and most of the Japanese producers have taken the opportunity to release a few models to test public reaction.

The turbocharger consists of a compact turbine unit driven by the exhaust gases and turning at very high speed. At the other end of the turbine shaft is an impeller unit, and this is used to force air into the engine at above atmospheric pressure. With a greater volume of air entering the combustion chamber during each induction stroke, a correspondingly greater amount of fuel can be admitted and burnt, thus producing more power. The turbo unit also incorporates a pressure-sensitive valve arrangement to prevent manifold pressure rising above a certain limit; usually about 15 psi.

Most turbo designs employ an electronic fuel injection system to control the quantity of fuel delivered to the cylinder at any given engine speed and pressure. This arrangement avoids the technical problems of using carburettors at high pressures, and can ensure a degree of accuracy that would otherwise not be possible. The basic principle of fuel injection is to maintain at a constant pressure a circuit of fuel between the tank and a pump unit, any unused fuel being vented back into the tank. A solenoid-operated injector nozzle is fitted in each inlet port, and at the required point in the induction stroke, the correct quantity of fuel is injected as a high-pressure spray. The fuel is thus forced into the engine quickly and in a finely-atomised form, ideally suited for rapid and even combustion. An electronic control box monitors engine speed, temperature and boost pressure to allow the fuel quantity to be constantly corrected.

Although most turbocharged engines employ some sort of fuel injection as a matter of course, injection can also be used on standard production engines. Though relatively uncommon due to the increased cost and complexity, fuel injection offers significant advantages in terms of accuracy over long periods; an important point on multi-cylinder engines where the gradual deterioration of carburettor tune is often not noticed until the engine is running quite badly. Whilst there is little that can be done to test or repair an injection system at home, the need should not arise unless a part of the system has failed, rather like electronic ignition.

The advantages of turbocharging are less clear, even though at first sight it seems to be an easy route to more power. Despite the undeniable fact that a turbocharged 650cc motorcycle will rival a conventional 900cc model in terms of performance, it shows few real advantages when the two are compared more closely. The turbo will cost about the same or more than the 900cc non-turbo, it will cost about the same to run and insure, will weigh little less and may prove difficult to sell when it has seen a few years' use. Many people take the conservative option and buy the 'old fashioned' 900 as a known quantity, and if this attitude continues to prevail it seems likely that the Turbo will turn out to be little more than Hi-Tech marketing at its most extreme.

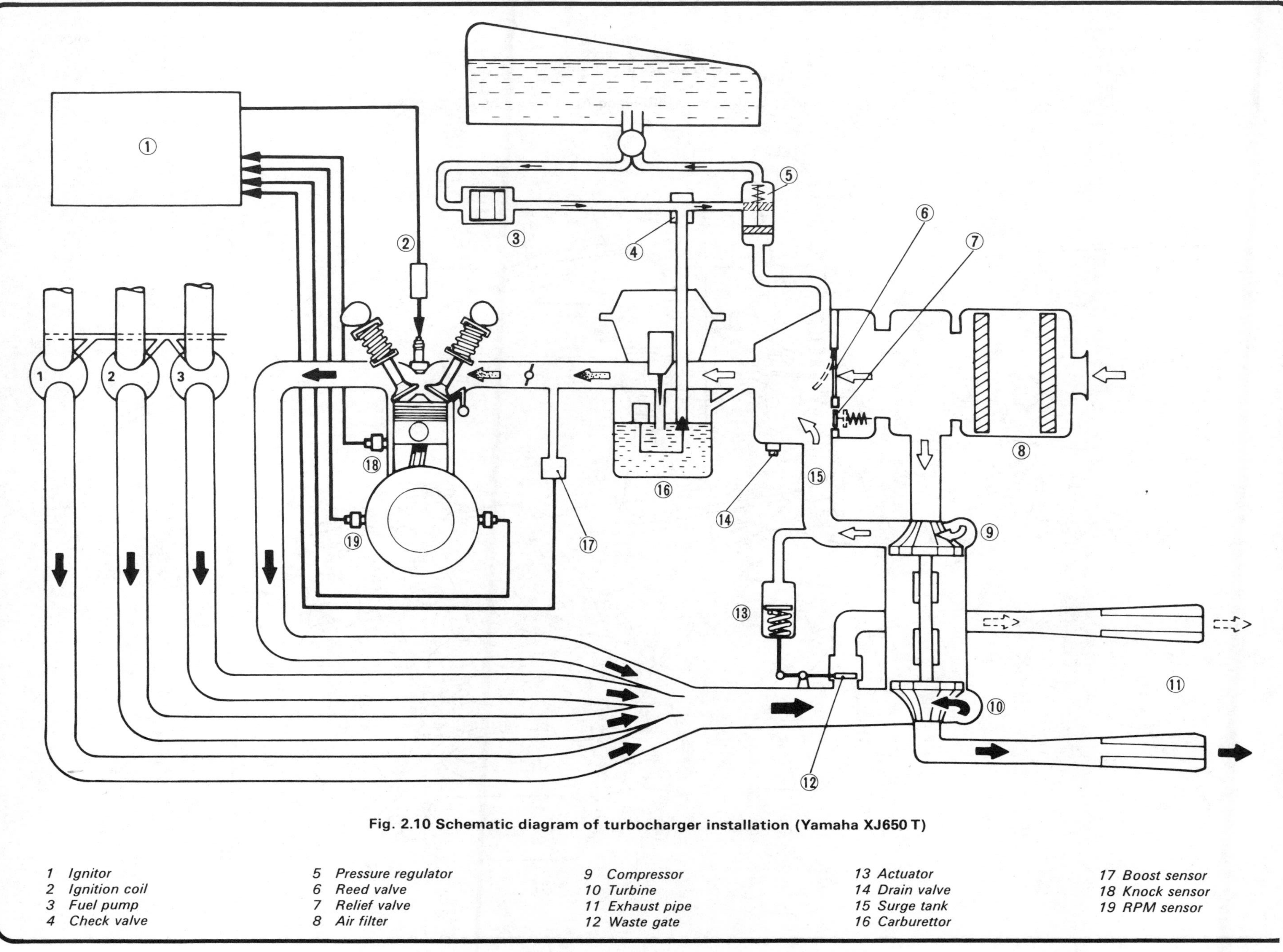


**Fig. 2.10 Schematic diagram of turbocharger installation (Yamaha XJ650 T)**

*1 Ignitor*
*2 Ignition coil*
*3 Fuel pump*
*4 Check valve*
*5 Pressure regulator*
*6 Reed valve*
*7 Relief valve*
*8 Air filter*
*9 Compressor*
*10 Turbine*
*11 Exhaust pipe*
*12 Waste gate*
*13 Actuator*
*14 Drain valve*
*15 Surge tank*
*16 Carburettor*
*17 Boost sensor*
*18 Knock sensor*
*19 RPM sensor*

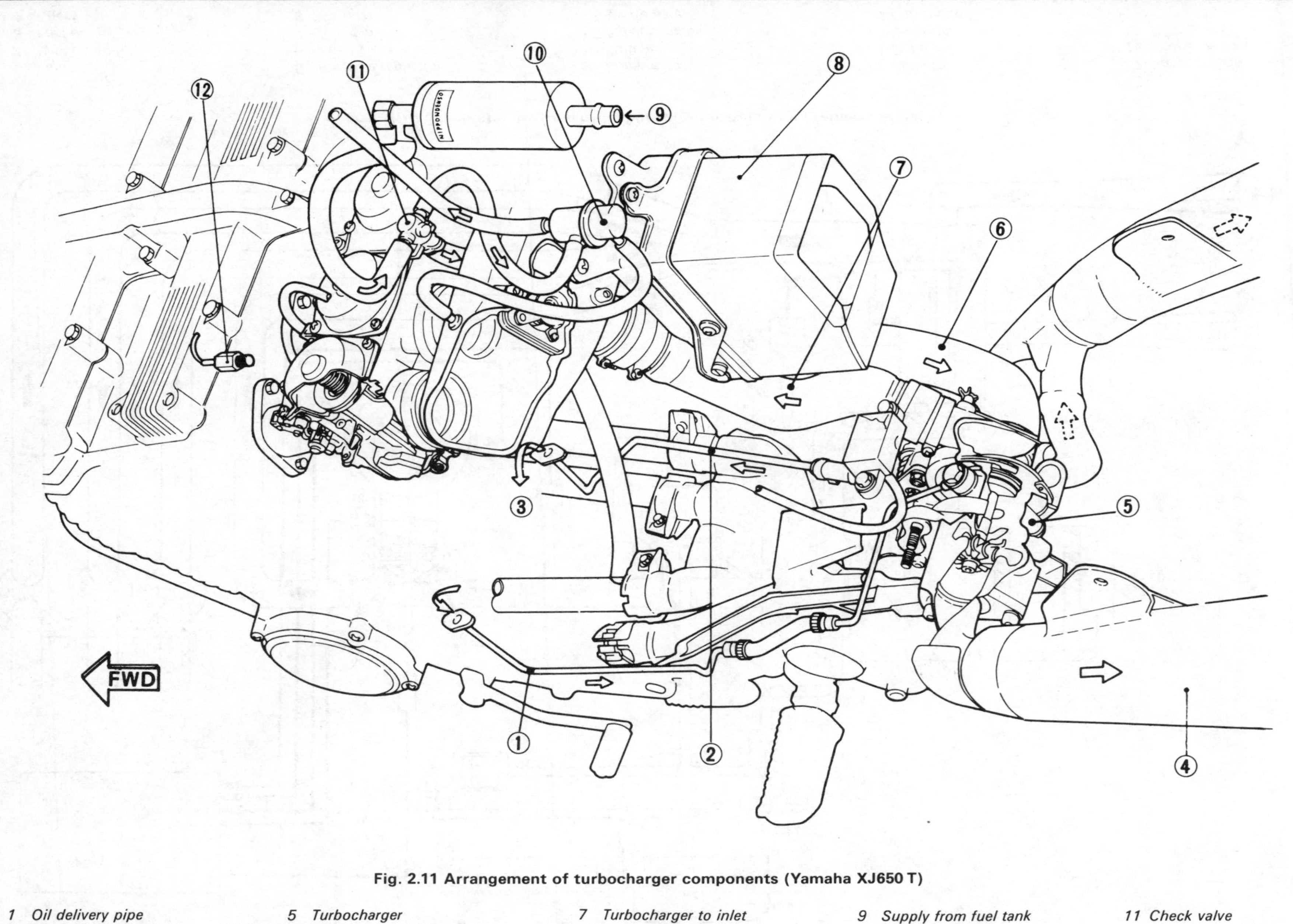


**Fig. 2.11 Arrangement of turbocharger components (Yamaha XJ650 T)**

*1 Oil delivery pipe*
*2 Oil return pipe*
*3 Oil pump pipe*
*4 Exhaust*
*5 Turbocharger*
*6 Air filter to turbocharger duct*
*7 Turbocharger to inlet manifold duct*
*8 Air filter*
*9 Supply from fuel tank*
*10 Pressure regulator*
*11 Check valve*
*12 Knock sensor*

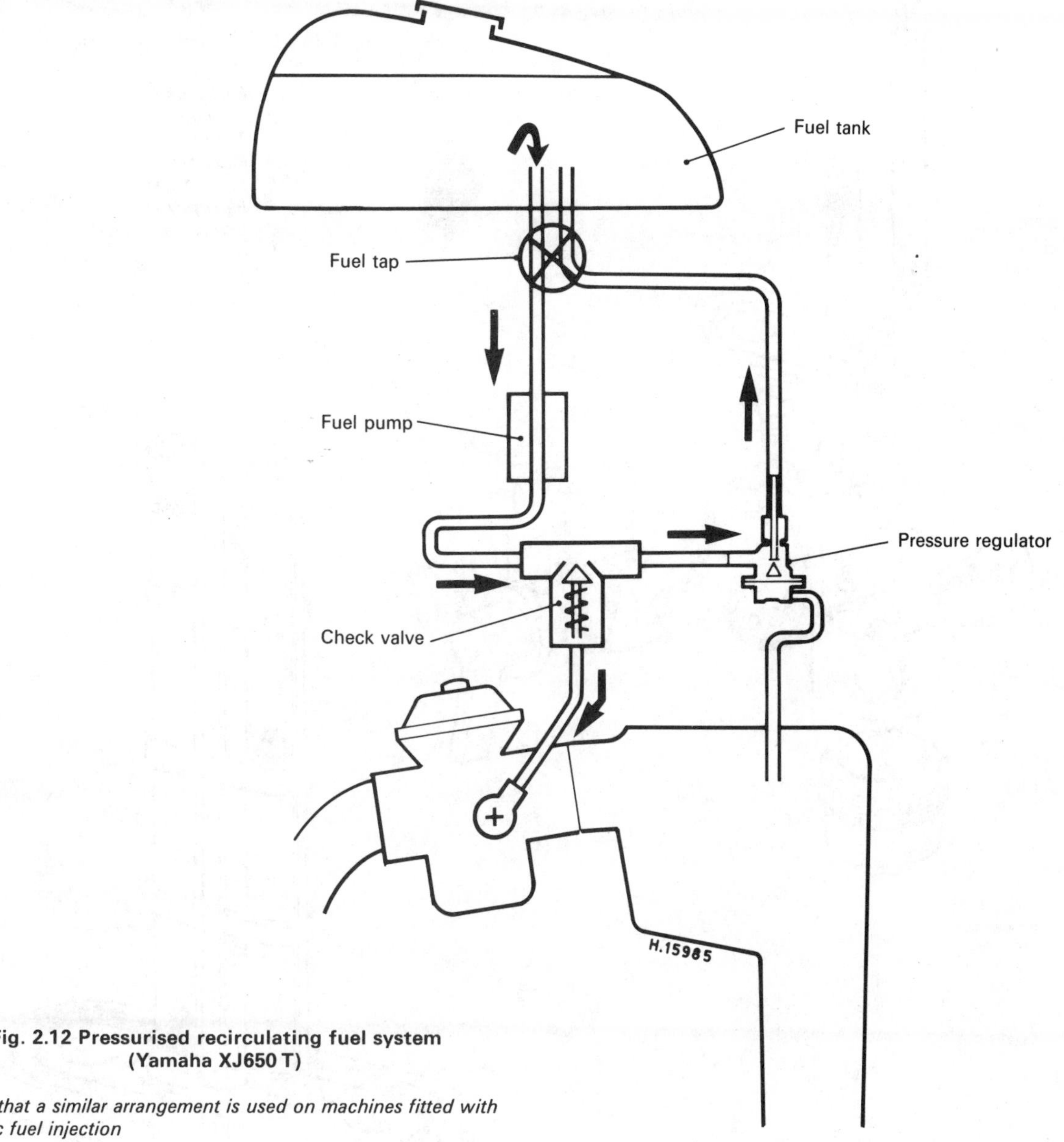


**Fig. 2.12 Pressurised recirculating fuel system (Yamaha XJ650 T)**

*Note that a similar arrangement is used on machines fitted with electronic fuel injection*

## 9 The fuel tank and tap

On almost all motorcycles, the fuel is contained in a tank above the carburettor(s) and is fed by gravity to the float bowl(s). Whilst this is not the best arrangement in terms of weight distribution, it does mean that the need for a mechanical or electrical pump is avoided. It has the incidental advantage that there are few alternative positions on most machines that would allow sufficient room to fit a fuel tank. There are exceptions to this; the Vespa scooters, for example, have the fuel tank below the dualseat and housed inside the monocoque frame section. Given the compact and low position of the engine unit, the gravity feed to the float bowl could be retained.

To control the fuel flow, some sort of tap is normally fitted. At first sight this may seem superfluous, given that the float assembly is performing much the same job. In practice, the fuel tap provides additional security against fuel leakage, allows the provision of a 'reserve' setting and allows the fuel pipe to be disconnected without having to drain the tank. On many machines the tap is manually operated. A small lever on the side of the tap selects the OFF, ON or RES positions as required, the internal rotor allowing fuel to flow through the selected port to the fuel pipe. Projecting up into the tank from the tap body is the fuel filter. This is designed to trap the inevitable debris which would otherwise block the carburettor jets. It also incorporates a short stand pipe, providing the main feed in the ON position. When the fuel falls below the level of this pipe, the tap can be switched to the RES setting, giving an additional supply of fuel and warning that refuelling is required.

On most larger machines an automatic vacuum-operated fuel tap is a common alternative to the manual type. The tap is operated by a flexible diaphragm inside the main body. This is connected by a synthetic rubber hose to the inlet port of the engine. The depression which exists in the inlet port when the engine is running opens the fuel tap, supplying fuel to the carburettor. As soon as the engine stops and the inlet port returns to atmospheric pressure, the tap closes. In most vacuum-operated taps there are additional manual reserve settings, and also a priming position. The latter allows the carburettor float bowls to be filled after they have run dry or have been drained; without this facility it would be necessary to crank the engine for a long time until sufficient fuel had flowed through to allow it to start. The PRI position also allows the diaphragm arrangement to be bypassed in the event of it becoming damaged. On some recent scooter-type commuter machines, the usual tap lever has been dispensed with entirely. The tap can be set to the normal ON or PRI positions using a screwdriver, but the reserve setting has been omitted in favour of a fuel level gauge.

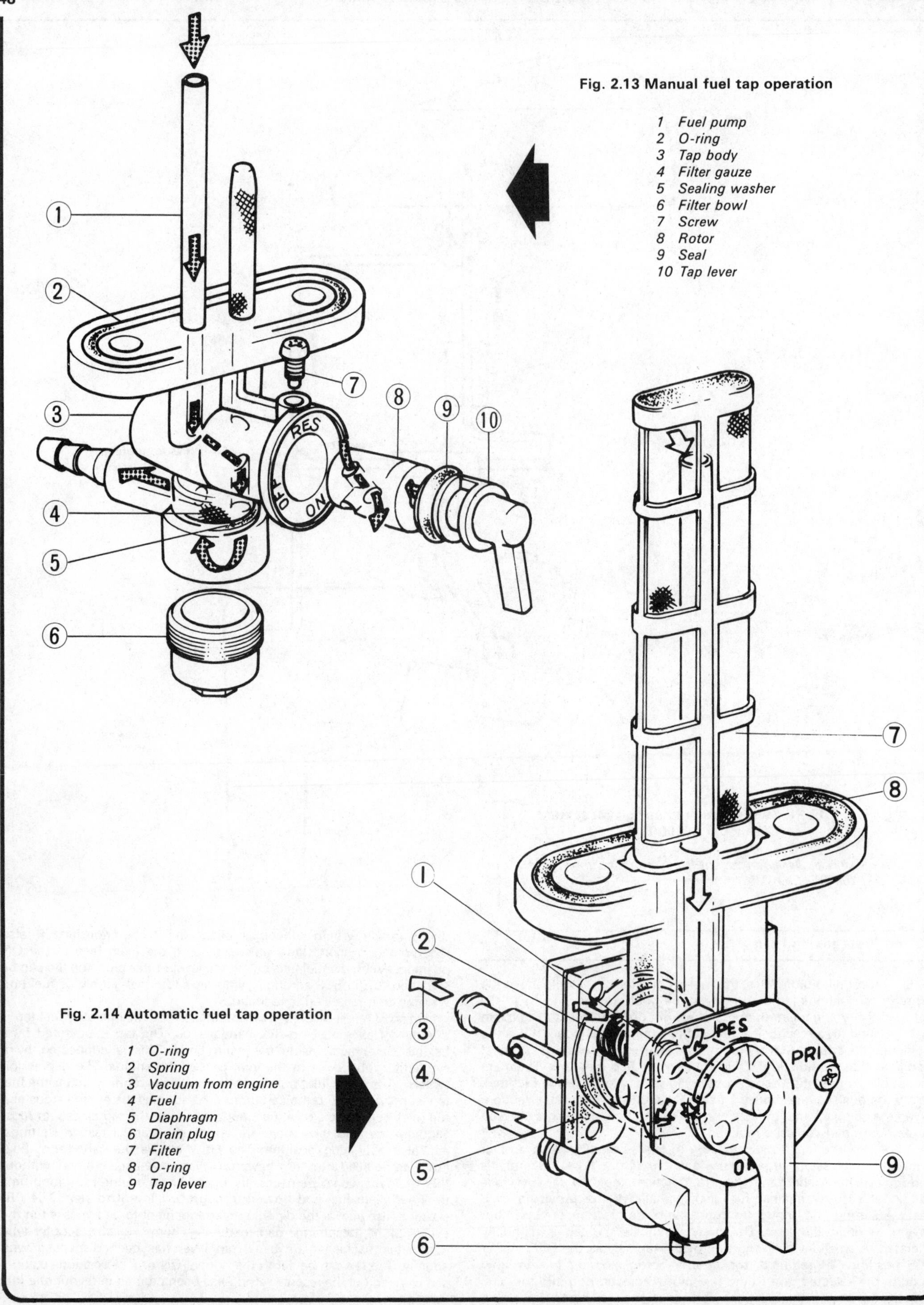


Fig. 2.13 Manual fuel tap operation

1 Fuel pump
2 O-ring
3 Tap body
4 Filter gauze
5 Sealing washer
6 Filter bowl
7 Screw
8 Rotor
9 Seal
10 Tap lever

Fig. 2.14 Automatic fuel tap operation

1 O-ring
2 Spring
3 Vacuum from engine
4 Fuel
5 Diaphragm
6 Drain plug
7 Filter
8 O-ring
9 Tap lever

## 10 Air filters

Though the reasons for fitting an air filter to an engine need little explanation, it is worth considering the ways in which a supply of clean air can be achieved. Like most other components on motorcycles, the air filter has become increasingly sophisticated over the years; the early wire mesh arrangements having been replaced by the far more effective pleated paper or oil-impregnated foam filters used today. Both types are effective methods of trapping the airborne dust which would otherwise enter the engine to wear away the various moving parts, and it follows that to run the engine with the filter missing or damaged is to effectively reduce its life quite drastically.

Most four-strokes and many two-strokes use a filter element of pleated resin-impregnated paper. The resin impregnation prevents the paper from becoming saturated by moisture and thus disintegrating. The pleated arrangement presents the maximum filter area within the limits imposed by the filter housing. This allows the pores in the paper to be kept as fine as possible to trap almost all of the incoming dust, and at the same time avoids restricting the air-flow to the engine. The oil-impregnated foam elements found on many smaller two-strokes are rather coarser in texture, and at first sight might seem less effective as filters. In practice, the oily surface presented to the incoming air catches a good deal of the dust.

All types of filter element require regular maintenance, but rarely receive it; it is too easy to ignore the filter on the assumption that it should be good for a few more miles. In reality, the performance of the filter falls off gradually until it begins to affect the mixture strength or to allow dust to pass through it. In the case of the paper elements, the pores in the paper will become more and more clogged, air will pass through it less freely and the mixture will become excessively rich. With foam types, once the oily coating is covered by dust particles it will be unable to trap further dust until the filter element has been cleaned and re-oiled.

The casing in which the filter is housed fulfils a secondary role as a plenum chamber; that is, it holds a volume of relatively still air from which the engine can draw its next charge. On two-strokes in particular this is important, because the constantly varying air pressure and velocity around the engine would otherwise make it difficult to ensure constant mixture strength. It is not uncommon for racing two-strokes based on road machines to retain the original filter housing/plenum chamber to prevent any fall-off in performance. This effect is less significant on four-strokes where the air is drawn more positively into the combustion chamber.

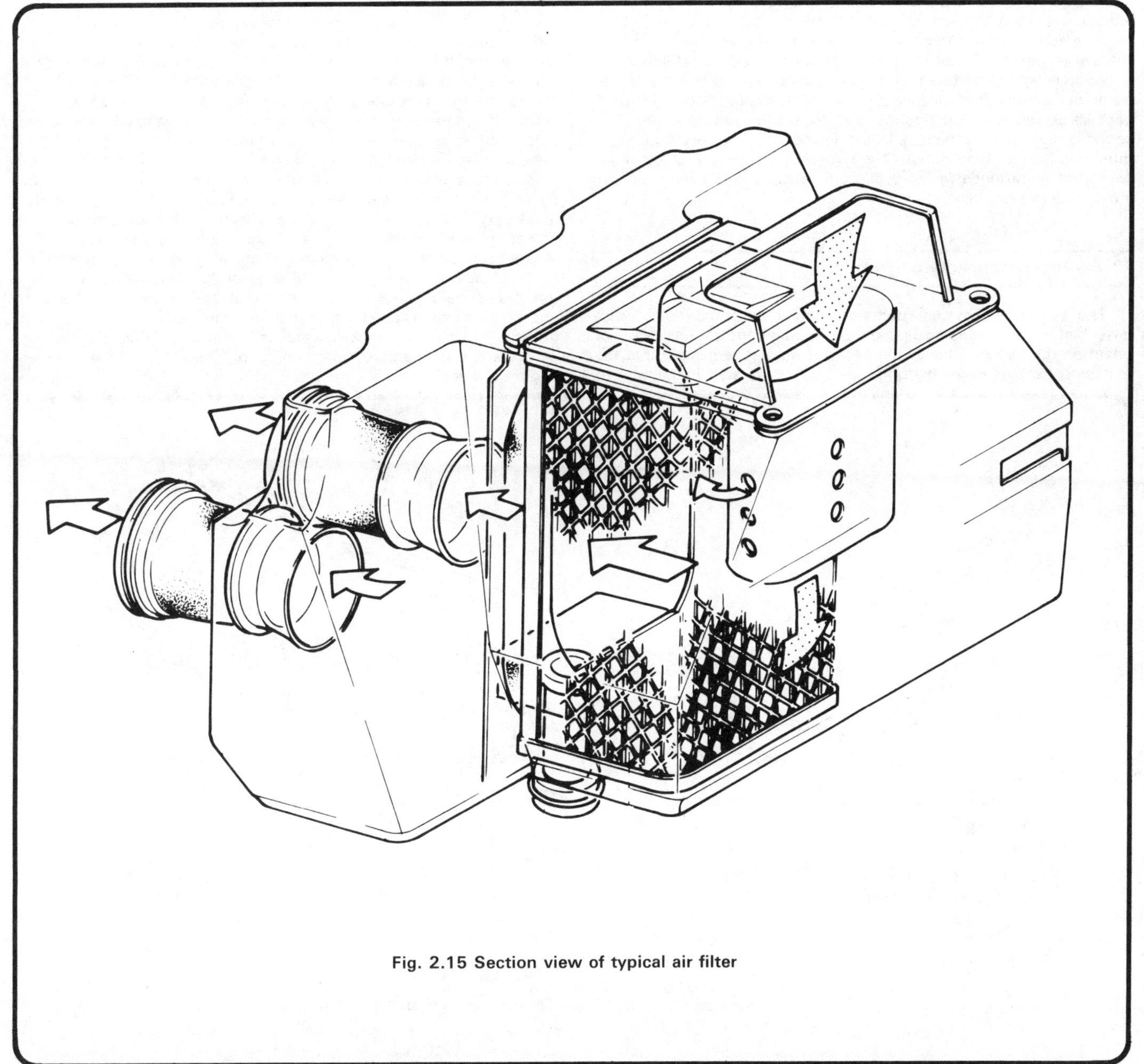

Fig. 2.15 Section view of typical air filter

## 11 Exhaust systems: four-stroke

The main purpose of the exhaust system is, of course, to direct the expelled exhaust gases clear of the machine and rider in a controlled manner. If the hot gases were to be expelled directly from the exhaust port, not only would the noise be unbearable, but any residual fuel would burn off explosively on contact with the oxygen in the surrounding air, so a pipe is used to re-direct the gases down and towards the back of the machine. This allows the gases to cool somewhat, and thus lessens the tendency towards unwanted external combustion. Given the explosive nature of the proceedings inside the combustion chamber, the emerging exhaust gases tend to be rather noisy in rejoining the outside world, and thus require toning down somewhat.

The term 'silencer' may be a little optimistic, but it is a remarkable device for all that. The object is to allow the gases to pass as freely as possible, whilst absorbing the surplus energy that manifests itself as noise. This is often accomplished by absorption; the fast-moving gases are slowed by allowing them to expand into the body of the silencer. The pulses of noise are further fragmented by allowing them to pass through perforated baffles, or through an expanded metal mesh and into a pad of mineral wool or similar. In other words, the harsh initial vibration is broken down into smaller sound waves, many of which cancel each other out. By the time the exhaust gases exit from the silencer tailpipe the noise has been subdued to an acceptable level.

Another approach to silencer construction is to split the silencer body into a number of smaller compartments, the gases being routed backwards and forwards through them in a rather tortuous path. The sound waves are repeatedly reflected, losing a little energy each time, until they exit at the tailpipe. The two above approaches are often combined to produce the very efficient systems in common use on most modern machines.

## 12 Exhaust systems: two-stroke

The two-stroke system performs much the same job as that described in the preceding Section, but in addition has a more direct effect on the performance of the engine. You may remember that the emerging exhaust gases perform a secondary function by helping to draw the fresh mixture up into the combustion chamber through the transfer ports, and that in the same way the fresh charge helps to scavenge, or push out, the exhaust gases. On simple moped or commuter bike systems the design is chosen to work as effectively as possible. Where power is an overriding consideration, however, there is the intriguing possibility of free power, based on the natural tendency for the exhaust pulses to resonate within the system.

This effect can be improved by careful design of the exhaust pipe and silencer as an integrated unit. The system is so constructed that the exhaust pipe gradually flares into a tapering silencer body, with a smaller reversed cone at the end, terminating in a small tailpipe. This arrangement is known as an expansion chamber, and is found on most high-performance road models and all racing machines. It works by controlling pressure waves within the expansion chamber to obtain better cylinder filling than would otherwise be possible.

As the exhaust port is uncovered, the gases rush out and into the exhaust system, assisted by the incoming charge emerging from the transfer ports. The exhaust gases move down the expansion chamber as a wave, gradually expanding and losing velocity. When the wave hits the reverse cone it is compressed and a proportion is reflected back up the system as a reverse pulse. By this time the combustion chamber is more than full, and the excess mixture is now beginning to fill the upper end of the exhaust pipe. As the piston covers and closes the transfer ports, the reverse wave reaches the port, ramming the extra mixture back into the combustion chamber where it is trapped by the rising piston. In this way there is a slight 'supercharging' effect, and the engine will produce more power than it could normally.

The snag is, though, that the reverse wave can only be synchronised to create this effect at a specific engine speed; above and below that speed, the engine runs as normal. To utilise the effect, the system must be carefully tuned to make maximum use of the extra power, and the kick as the engine reaches the narrow band of extra power can usually be felt quite clearly. Though of limited duration, this represents a little extra 'free' power, if at the expense of consistent power delivery. For the latter reason, expansion chambers are normally avoided on commuter machines, where an unexpected or sudden surge of power could prove unwieldly or even dangerous in heavy traffic. It should also be clear from the above that a badly designed after-market expansion chamber may not have the desired effect, and in some cases may make overall performance noticeably worse, particularly if the carburettor jetting is not altered to suit the changed engine characteristics.

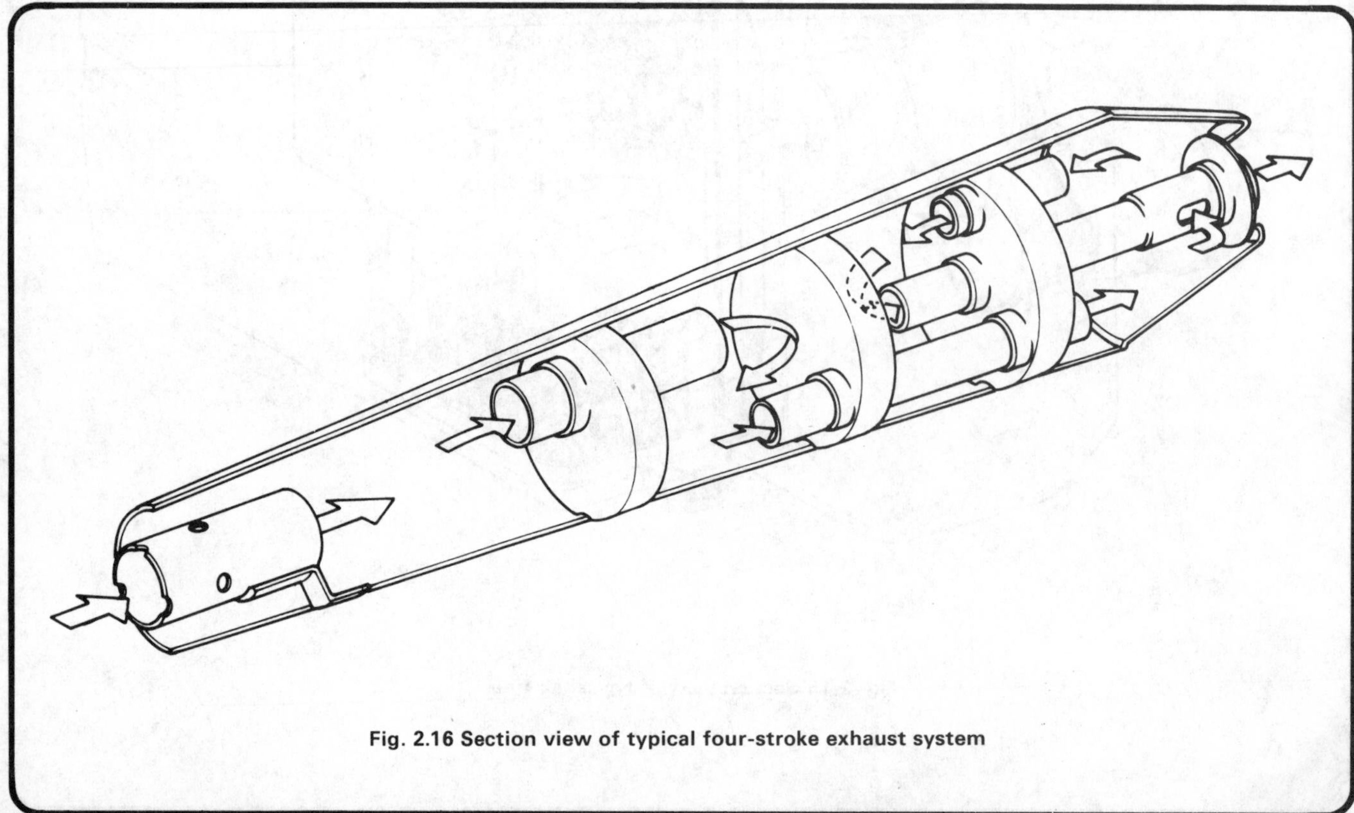

Fig. 2.16 Section view of typical four-stroke exhaust system

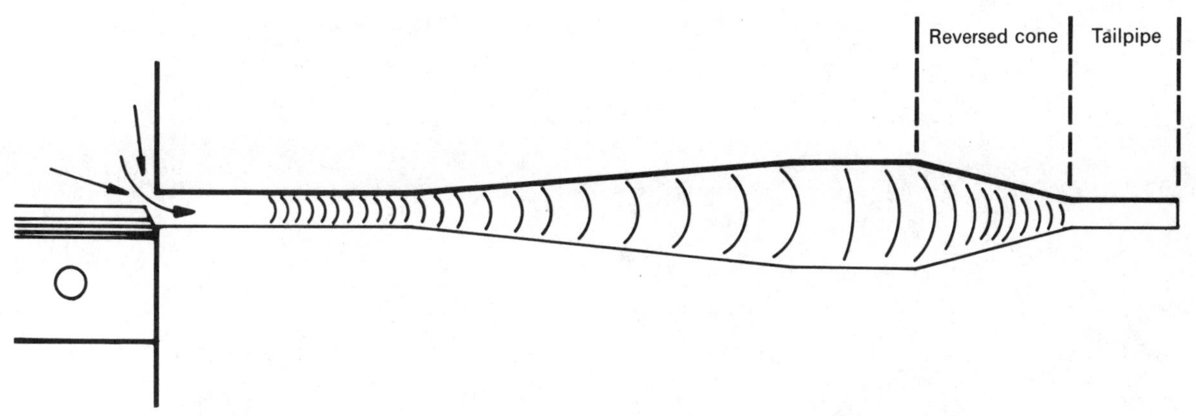


*As the exhaust port opens spent gases rush out into the exhaust system. The gas travels down the system as a high pressure wave gradually expanding and losing velocity until it reaches the reversed cone.*

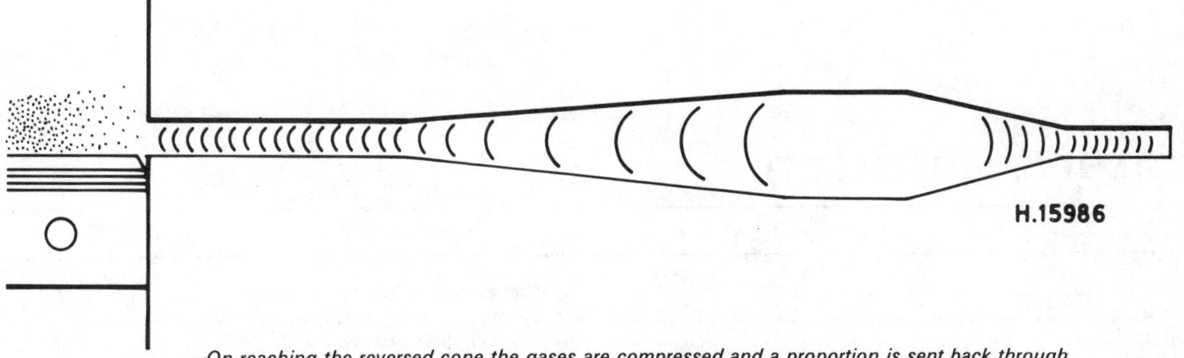


*On reaching the reversed cone the gases are compressed and a proportion is sent back through the exhaust system in the form of a reverse pulse. This has the effect of stopping fresh mixture escaping down the exhaust system before the piston closes the exhaust port.*

**Fig. 2.17 Section view of two-stroke expansion chamber exhaust system**

# Chapter 3 Ignition

## Contents



## 1 Introduction

Having looked at the mechanical aspects of two-stroke and four-stroke engines, and also at the ways in which the fuel/air mixture is fed into the cylinder for combustion, we can now discuss the process of ignition. For the engine to work it is necessary to devise some method of initiating combustion at precisely the right moment in each engine cycle, and the universally popular method is to employ a brief high-tension spark. The high tension spark is applied to an insulated electrode at the centre of a spark plug, where it is coaxed into jumping to earth (ground) across a small air gap.

The essential elements of any ignition system are as follows. Firstly, there must be some method of generating an electrical current to power the system. Even though the power is derived from a battery in many cases, it is essential that the battery is kept charged or the system would soon fail as the battery became depleted. The charge from the battery or from a separate source coil is then applied to an ignition coil. This device converts the current from a low voltage/high current, or 'low tension' feed to the high voltage/low current, 'high tension' form necessary if the plug electrodes are to be jumped. To control the timing of the ignition spark, we require some sort of switch, either in the mechanical form of a contact breaker, or its electronic equivalent, the pickup assembly. In the Sections which follow we will examine each aspect of the system in more detail.

## 2 The power supply

The subject of generating electrical power is covered in detail later in this book, and so we will avoid duplicating it in this Chapter. Suffice it to say that we require a constant low voltage supply from which the ignition spark may be derived. In its simplest modern form this can be an ignition source coil incorporated in the main generator assembly, and this arrangement can be found in most simple moped ignition systems and in many electronic ignition systems. Its main advantage is that it offers a simple source of power which is unaffected by loads on the machine's electrical system. The only real drawback is that at very low engine speeds, such as those prevailing when trying to start the machine, the power output of the source coil may be insufficient to produce a strong spark. In practice, the designers will have ensured that this problem does not normally occur, though the added demands imposed by a fouled or badly adjusted spark plug may lead to starting difficulties.

The alternative to the above approach is to draw power from the main electrical system, and this system is common where the machine has a full electrical system with a battery to supply power with the engine stopped or at cranking speeds. This avoids the possible starting problems which may sometimes be encountered with direct systems, but has its own problems in the event of a flat battery; we must recharge the battery before the engine can be started. On larger machines with electric starters the problem can be compounded. If the battery is partly discharged and the drain imposed by the starter motor is sufficiently high, there may not be enough energy to start the engine. This is why on cold winter mornings it may be necessary to resort to kick starting or pushing the machine to get it running.

## 3 The ignition coil

The need for an ignition coil arises because of the requirement for a very high voltage capable of jumping across the gap between the spark plug electrodes; air being a poor conductor of electricity, the voltage or pressure in this part of the ignition circuit must be high to overcome the resistance offered by this gap. The coil makes this possible by allowing the low voltage supply from the battery or source coil to be transformed into a high voltage (or high tension) supply. The resulting high tension circuit is of correspondingly low amperage, but is nevertheless ideal for ignition purposes. Without resorting to electrical theory this is best illustrated in the following manner. If you take a hose with water flowing from its open end, it will not travel far before falling to the ground, but this can be changed by restricting the end of the hose. The flow of water remains the same, but because it must pass through a restricted opening it emerges at a much higher speed, producing a jet which will travel a considerable distance.

The ignition coil achieves a similar effect by a process called electromagnetic induction. Put simply, this effect occurs when an electrical current flows through a wire; a weak electromagnetic field is created around the wire, and this field can be induced in a second wire as a small current if it is passed through the electromagnetic field of the first. If the current in the first wire is switched on and off, the same effect is achieved in the second wire as the field builds up and collapses; in other words the second wire can be moved through the field, or the field can be moved past the wire to obtain the same result. With a single wire this effect is very weak, but it can be greatly increased by winding two separate coils of wire, one on top of the other.

In a working ignition coil the primary (low tension) and secondary (high tension) windings are built up one over the other around an iron core, the latter being used to concentrate the effect of the field, or 'flux density'. The primary windings consist of a few hundred turns of copper wire, whilst the secondary windings, which terminate in the thick high tension lead, have many thousands of turns. When power is applied to the primary windings the magnetic field is created. If the low tension circuit is now broken, the field collapses and as it passes through the secondary windings, the desired high tension pulse is induced.

There are two basic types of coil in common use on motorcycles. The canister type has a central iron core around which is the secondary winding. The primary winding is outside this, and the whole assembly is housed in a metal canister. Sometimes the canister is filled with oil to aid the dispersal of heat generated in the coil. More common on recent models is the moulded coil, in which the position of the primary and secondary windings are reversed on the central laminated iron core. The whole assembly is then encapsulated in resin to resist the effects of vibration commonly found on motorcycles. Though both types do the same job, the moulded coil is the more popular choice because of its robust construction.

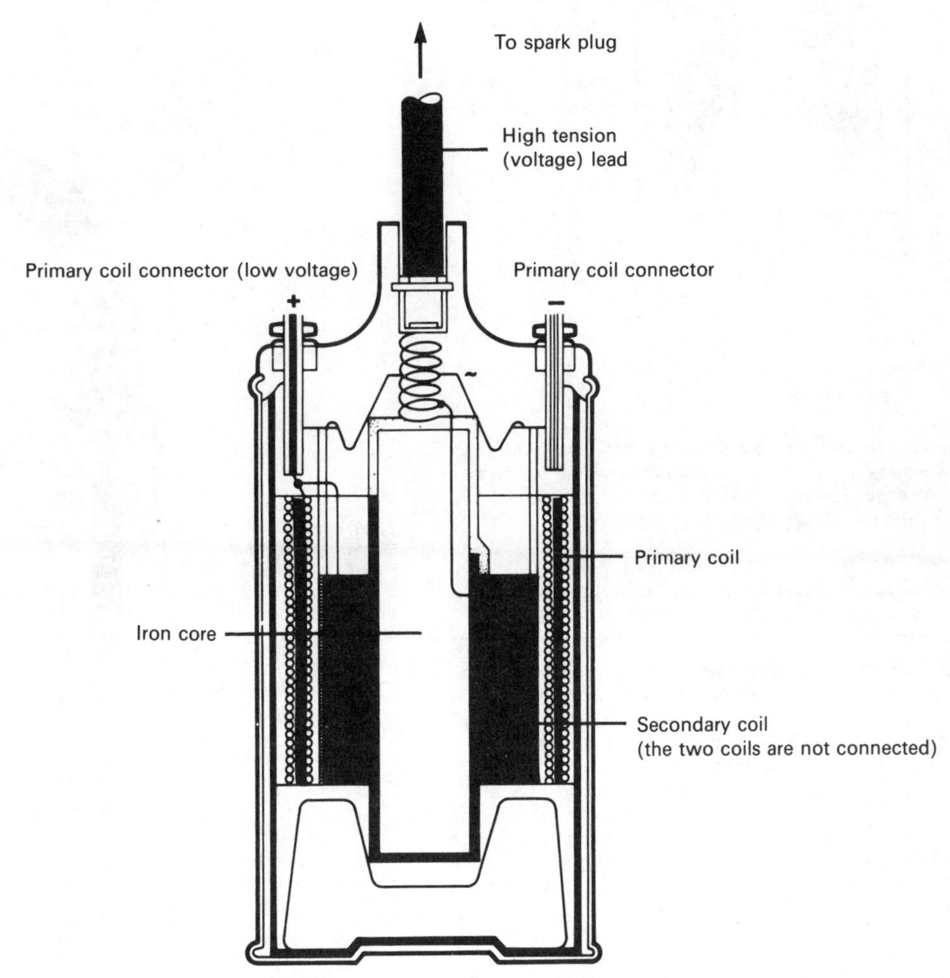


**Fig. 3.1 The canister coil**

*At the centre of the canister is an iron core, around which is wound the secondary windings. It is connected to the central high tension terminal. Outside of this is the primary coil which is connected to the (+) and (–) low tension terminals.*

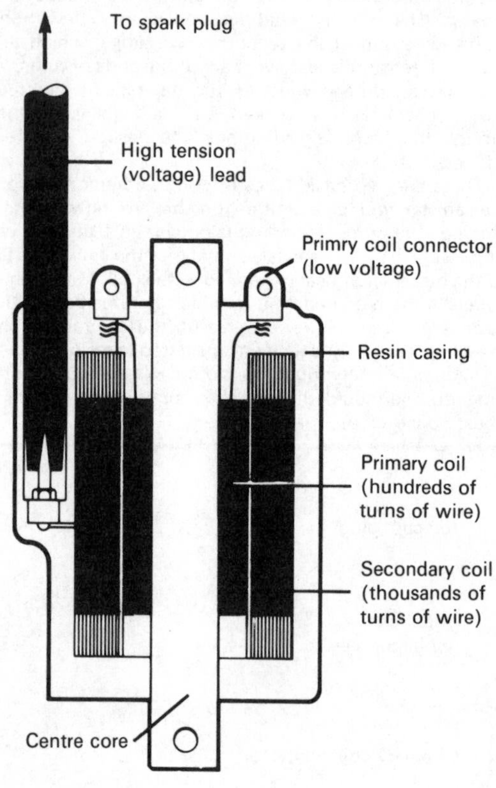


**Fig. 3.2 The moulded coil**

*The primary coil is wound around a laminated iron core, whilst the secondary coil is wound on top of this and is connected to the high tension lead at one edge. The whole assembly is then encapsulated in resin to protect it from the effects of moisture and vibration.*

## 4 The spark plug

The spark plug is an expendable part of the ignition system, designed to perform its job for a limited period and then to be renewed when it becomes worn and eroded. Its purpose is to conduct the HT pulse into the engine, where the spark jumps across its electrodes to earth. At the top of the plug is a round terminal to which the HT lead is connected. This is in contact with the central electrode which is normally made of a nickel alloy to resist the effects of heat and the corrosive elements in the fuel. On some plugs, the electrode is made from more exotic alloys of silver, platinum, palladium or gold. These are designed to offer even greater resistance to erosion, and to perform well under particularly adverse conditions.

The central electrode passes through an insulator, projecting through it at the lower end. The insulator serves to protect the central electrode from electrical leakage, and to shield it from much of the engine's heat. By varying the amount by which the 'nose' of the insulator projects, it is possible to control the plug electrode operating temperature to suit specific engines, and this is why plugs are produced in standard and projected nose versions.

The insulator is retained in the metal body of the plug by a spun-over lip at its upper edge. To prevent gas leakage there are seals fitted between the central electrode and the insulator, and between the insulator and body. The plug body is formed from steel, and is usually cadmium plated to prevent rusting. The upper part of the body incorporates the hexagon with which the plug is tightened and removed. At its lower end it is threaded to allow it to be screwed into the cylinder head, and a collapsible metal sealing ring is fitted. At the extreme lower edge is fitted the earth electrode. This is welded to the plug body and provides the path to earth for the ignition spark.

The spark plug is remarkable for both its low cost and for the demanding role which it fulfils so reliably. In fact, the low cost of the plug is deceptive; this is largely due to the vast numbers in which plugs are manufactured and is no reflection on its precision. The demands placed on spark plugs by modern engines are such that they are produced in a bewildering array of sizes, reaches and grades.

Apart from obvious considerations such as thread size, and choosing the correct reach to ensure that the electrodes are positioned in the right place in the combustion chamber, the plug electrodes must be kept at the correct operating temperature. The correct temperature range in most applications is between 400°C and 800°C, and this is adjusted to a particular engine by selecting the appropriate grade of plug. If the engine runs hot, it is necessary to fit a grade of plug which will dissipate heat from the electrodes rapidly. In such a case a plug with a short insulator nose is chosen, and these are termed cold or 'hard' plugs. Conversely, if the engine runs cool heat must be retained longer at the plug electrodes, and this demands a long insulator nose. This type of plug is more common on older or less highly tuned engines and is termed a hot or 'soft' type. You may care to note that there is absolutely no relationship between 'hot' plugs and 'hot' engines; a popular misunderstanding which seems to persist.

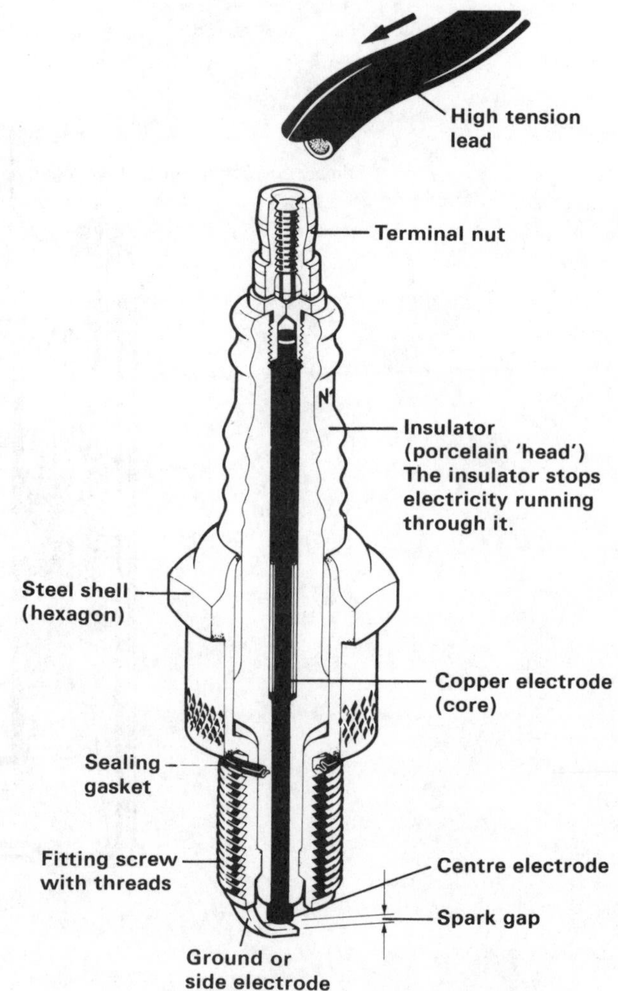


**Fig. 3.3 The spark plug**

*A section through a typical spark plug. Note that in some applications the copper centre electrode is replaced by a platinum or gold-palladium type.*

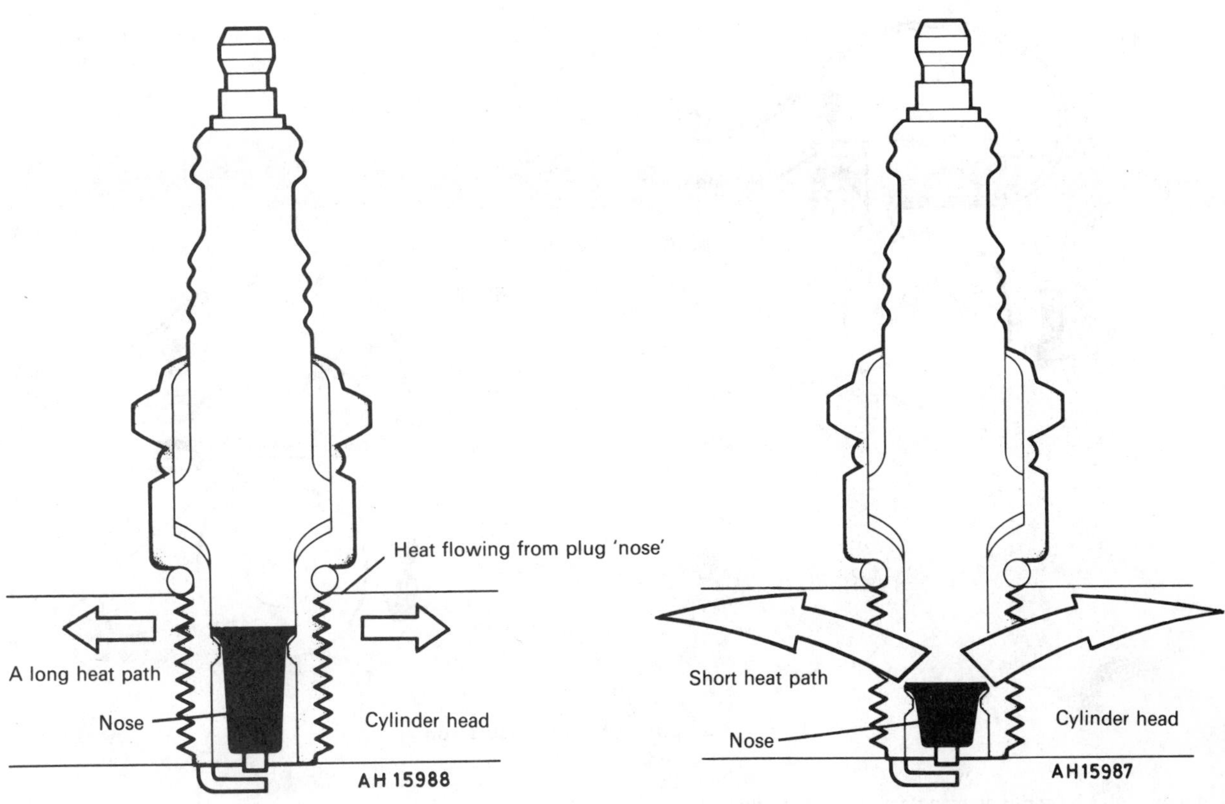


Fig. 3.4 A hot (or soft) spark plug

*This type of plug has a long insulator nose to limit the rate of heat loss from the electrodes. It is used where plug fouling is likely to occur.*

Fig. 3.5 A cold (or hard) spark plug

*This type of plug has a short insulator nose to encourage heat loss from the electrodes. It is used where the plug is likely to suffer from overheating.*

## 5 Flywheel generator ignition systems

The flywheel generator (or flywheel magneto) ignition system is about the simplest way of obtaining an ignition spark, and as such has been popular for many years on small engines. It has the advantage of deriving its power directly from its own source coil and thus does not demand a battery for starting purposes. The flywheel generator unit is in fact a small alternator of the rotating magnet type. It consists of a cast alloy rotor containing cast-in permanent magnets. This is attached to one end of the crankshaft and spins with it, acting as an additional flywheel. Inside the rotor, and mounted separately on a fixed circular plate called a stator, are the ignition source and lighting coils. As the rotor spins, the fields of the magnets pass repeatedly through the coil windings, and thus induce a current in exactly the same manner as that described above for the ignition coil.

As its name suggests, an alternator produces alternating current (ac). This is because the polarity of the magnets in relation to the coils is constantly changing from north to south, and this in turn means that the current induced in the coils flows one way, then reverses and flows the other way. As may be expected, there is a dead point between the two extremes at which no power is produced, but since this fluctuation takes place very rapidly it is of little importance as far as the lighting system is concerned. Those of you who own or have owned a machine with a flywheel generator will no doubt be aware of the way in which this fluctuation can be seen; flickering lights at tickover.

The principle of operation of the ignition circuit relies on energy transfer, and works as follows. The ignition source coil forms a circuit with the primary windings of the ignition coil. Between the two is the contact breaker assembly, and this is connected in parallel with the coils. If the contacts are closed (which they are for much of the time) the current flows through them and thus back to the source coil. The ignition coil is thus short-circuited and receives no power. The contacts are opened by a cam at the correct point for ignition to occur, and the position of the rotor is arranged so that the output from the source coil is at its maximum as the contacts separate. The current from the source coil must now flow through the ignition coil primary windings, where the HT spark is induced, firing the spark plug. It is this transfer of energy to the ignition coil which gives the system its name.

There are a couple of points to note about the above. Firstly, that it is important to time the contact separation to make full use of the available current; if they opened at a 'dead' point in the cycle there would be no current flow, and no spark. Secondly, that there is a final component in the system which we have so far ignored. This is called a capacitor (it is also frequently referred to as a condenser, which is rather misleading). The capacitor can be thought of as a sort of short-term battery; it can store a small charge and then discharge it again when required. In this application its purpose is to stop the contact breaker points from acting like the spark plug. This is necessary because the contact faces move apart quite slowly by electrical standards, and when they are just moving apart they provide a more tempting path to earth than the ignition coil primary windings. To prevent the charge from jumping across the contacts a capacitor is connected across them, this will store any residual current, and thus prevents contact burning.

The flywheel generator ignition system, then, is a simple and inexpensive method of providing an ignition spark. In practice it works quite well, providing that full use is made of energy transfer at the correct point in the generation cycle. It is due to the limitations imposed by this that most stators cannot be adjusted to vary the

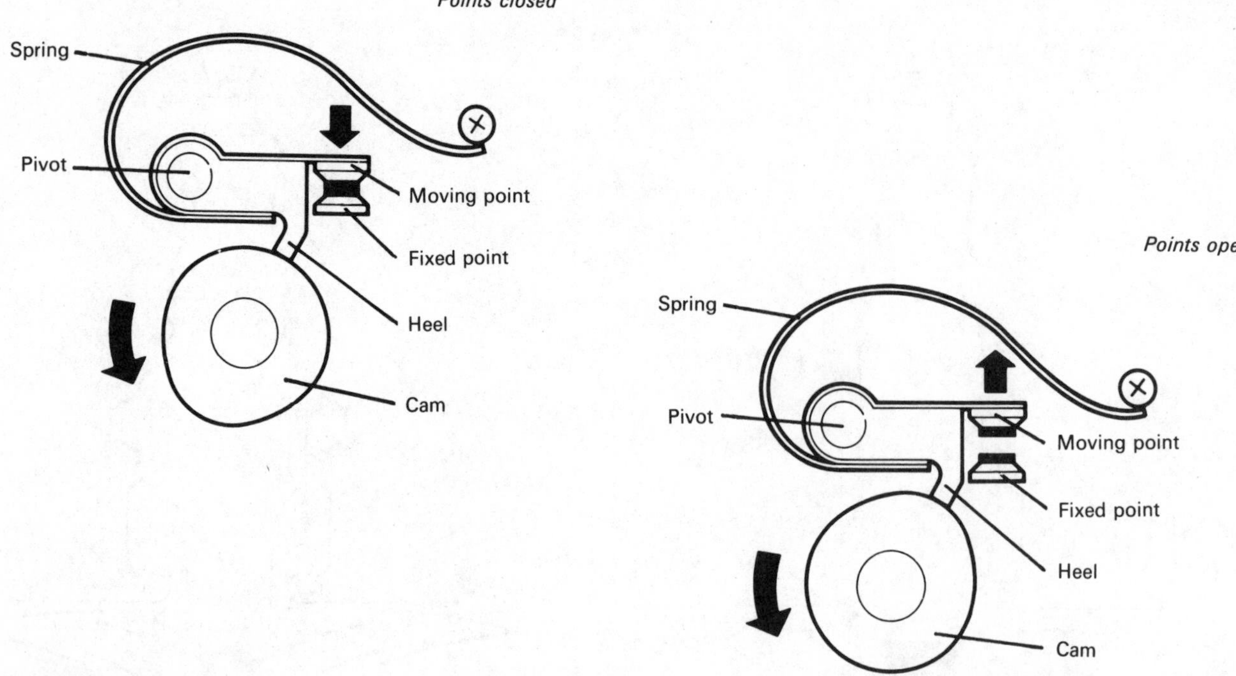


**Fig. 3.6 Contact breaker operation**

ignition timing; this is set during manufacture and can subsequently be altered by only a small amount by varying the contact breaker gap. Whilst this is sufficient on small engines, on larger machines the need to be able to advance the ignition point as speed increases becomes greater, and so energy transfer systems are no longer adequate. The reasons for this, and the solution to the problem are discussed below.

## 6 Battery and coil ignition systems

On small capacity engines, with small combustion chambers, it is acceptable to have a fixed ignition advance. This means that an allowance is made for the length of time taken for the spark to ignite the mixture and for combustion to take place. This is by no means instantaneous, and so it is necessary to arrange for the spark to occur in advance of the piston reaching the top of its stroke (TDC). In any given bore size, the time taken for combustion to be completed will remain constant, but the speed of the engine varies widely. In an engine with a large bore, the spread of the combustion flame takes an appreciable amount of time, so the lag in the power stroke is more pronounced. To compensate for this it is necessary to arrange for the plug to fire earlier in the cycle as the engine speed rises, and thus the ignition advance cannot remain fixed, but must adjust automatically. You will remember that with the simple energy transfer system this is not possible, because the contacts would then be opening when the source coil was not at full strength, so an alternative (and constant) supply of power is now required.

Our new power source is derived not from a source coil, but from the main electrical system of the machine. Given the more advanced nature of the larger machines, a more substantial and stable supply is required for both ignition and lighting purposes, so we must resort to a battery system. The flywheel generator is replaced by a more substantial alternator, the output of which is rectified (converted to direct current, or dc) and regulated so that it can meet the changing demands placed on it. The battery acts as a reservoir of power to keep the supply constant at low speeds and when the engine has stopped, and it is the inclusion of the battery which demands a dc recharging system.

The battery and coil ignition system works in a similar way to the flywheel generator type, but there are some important differences. The battery supplies power to the primary windings of the ignition coil, and the circuit is completed by the closed contact breaker points. These are connected in series (in line) with the coil rather than in parallel (across) it, as in the case of the flywheel generator version. The magnetic field generated in the primary windings is maintained until the cam opens the contact breaker points. As this occurs, power to the primary windings is interrupted, the field collapses, and a high tension pulse is induced in the secondary windings, creating the ignition spark. A capacitor is included in the circuit and fulfils the same role as it did in the flywheel generator arrangement.

With a constant, regulated supply to the ignition coil, we can now obtain an ignition spark at any point in the engine cycle, providing the facility for variable spark advance. In earlier magneto-based systems, this was often manually controlled. A handlebar lever was provided to allow the ignition to be retarded during starting and at low speeds, or advanced as required as engine speed increased. This works well enough for a simple four-stroke single (provided you remembered to retard the ignition before starting to avoid being kicked back enthusiastically!) but on more complex high-performance engines it becomes almost essential to have constant and automatic adjustment of the timing. This can be provided by an automatic timing unit (ATU).

Instead of fixing the contact breaker cam directly to the camshaft (four-strokes) or crankshaft (two-strokes) it is included as part of the ATU. The unit comprises a baseplate with a central support pin which carries the cam. The cam can turn on the pin, but its movement is controlled by two spring-loaded bob weights. At rest and at low speeds, the springs hold the cam in its retarded position, but as the engine speed increases the weights are flung outwards, turning the cam and thus advancing the ignition.

From the above it can be seen that the battery and coil ignition system offers a number of advantages over the flywheel generator type, and that it is essential where centrifugal ignition advance is required. The chief drawbacks are that it is dependent on power from the battery to allow the engine to be started, and it has more moving parts. This in turn means that wear occurs in more areas of the system, and that regular maintenance is required to keep the system working efficiently. To improve precision still further it is necessary to eliminate as far as possible all of the mechanical parts of the system, and this is exactly what electronic ignition does.

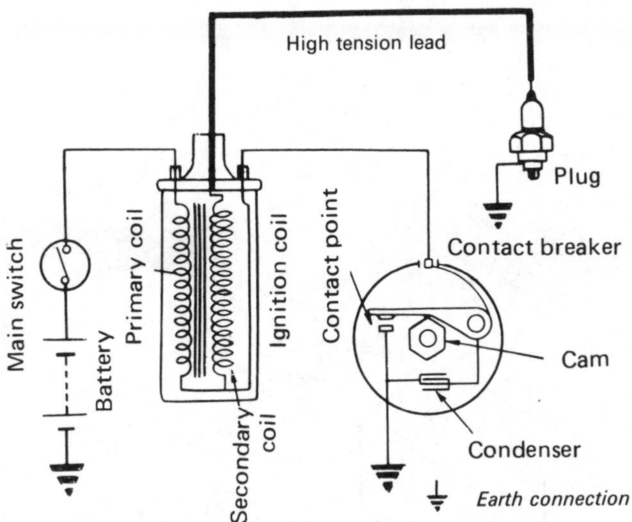


**Fig. 3.7 A battery and coil ignition system**

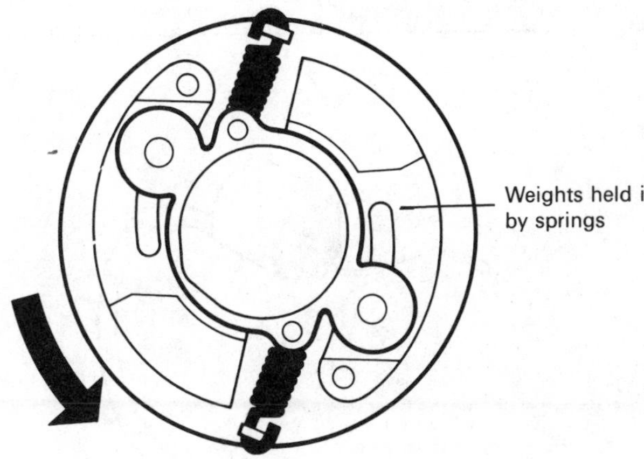


*Unit at low speed (not operating)*

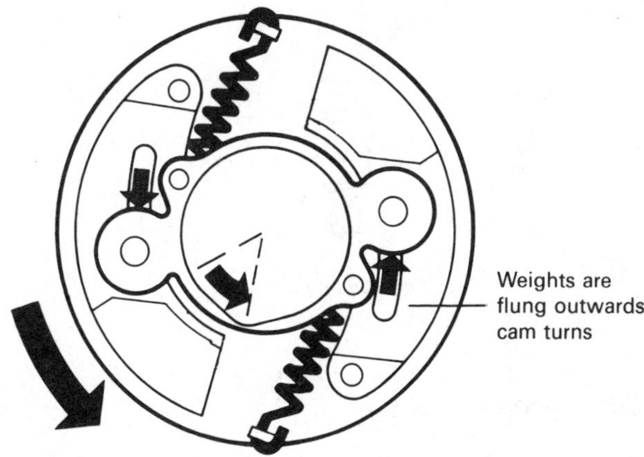


*Unit fully advanced (high speed)*

**Fig. 3.8 Automatic timing unit (ATU) operation**

## 7 Electronic ignition system

The Achilles heel of both of the systems discussed so far is the inclusion of mechanical parts. It is difficult to manufacture components like contact breakers and ATUs with sufficient precision to ensure reliable operation, and even when this is achieved the effects of wear take an inevitable toll during normal use. Starting with the contact breaker itself, the moving contact is subject to wear at its pivot, and to a greater extent at the fibre heel which bears upon the cam face. After a period of use this wears down and the contact gap closes, necessitating periodic adjustment and eventual renewal. The contact faces themselves suffer from erosion caused by the slight arcing which takes place each time they open. This problem is reduced by the fitting of a capacitor, but eventually the removal of material from one contact and the deposition of the same on the other contact mean that the assembly must be renewed. The ATU, so important on larger engines, is also subject to wear over a long period, and it will gradually allow the firing to become more and more erratic.

The above problems can be solved in part by a transistor assisted coil (TAC) ignition system. This arrangement removes much of the electrical load on the contacts, and thus more or less eliminates the erosion problem. Many early systems worked on this basis, but most currently-used circuits have dispensed with the contact breaker entirely and in so doing have made the TAC system obsolete, so we will not dwell too long on this type.

The most popular type of electronic ignition system in use on motorcycles is the capacitor discharge ignition (CDI) type. The mechanical contact breaker assembly is replaced by a small pickup or 'pulser' coil on the alternator stator. A magnet in the rotor sweeps past the coil inducing a tiny signal current which is fed to the CDI unit and thus indicates the firing point. Many of you will recognise the CDI unit as a sinister black box, the contents of which are sealed in resin, and which in the event of failure costs a lot of money to replace. The ethics of parts pricing policy aside, it is interesting to have some idea of what goes on inside the unit.

Most CDI units contain a thyristor, a capacitor and a couple of diodes, though there may also be additional circuitry to control ignition advance. The first of these items, the thyristor, functions as an electronic switch. Its two main connections control the flow of current, much the same as the contact breaker. Instead of a mechanical cam arrangement, the thyristor has a third connection; when a small current is applied to this, the device conducts the main current and will remain conductive until this falls to a low level. At this point the thyristor reverts to an 'off' state until it receives the next trigger signal from the pickup. The thyristor is also known as a silicon-controlled rectifier and often abbreviated to the initials SCR.

The next important element in our black box is the capacitor, which we know from the earlier systems. As before, this device stores a charge, in this case a few hundred volts derived from the source coil or the battery supply. When the trigger current is applied to the thyristor, it conducts, allowing a short pulse of energy to flow through the ignition coil primary windings. This in turn induces a powerful HT spark from the secondary windings to ignite the mixture. All this, and not a moving part to be seen.

The characteristics of CDI ignition are such that the spark at the plug is far more precise and powerful than in a conventional system, and so ignition is both more accurate and less prone to fouling. Since there are no mechanical parts there can be no wear, and thus once the timing has been set it will require no further attention. Where automatic ignition advance is required, this can be achieved by using a secondary pickup circuit to modify the trigger point by the desired amount. The ways of doing this are diverse and introduce unnecessary complication to the discussion – suffice it to say that it can be done, and that it works very efficiently. Those wishing to investigate the matter further can refer to more specialised works on the subject, but the fact remains that it is of little practical value. This brings us to the often-heard cry; "Give me a good old-fashioned contact breaker system any day". There may have been some justification for this in the early days of electronic systems, when reliability was rather dubious. Current systems tend to last rather better however, and it is doubtful if the accusation of expensive replacement parts bears close examination. Whilst the 'black box', if it does fail, can be expensive to renew, it normally lasts for a very long time. What price the numerous sets of contact breakers and the time spent adjusting them?

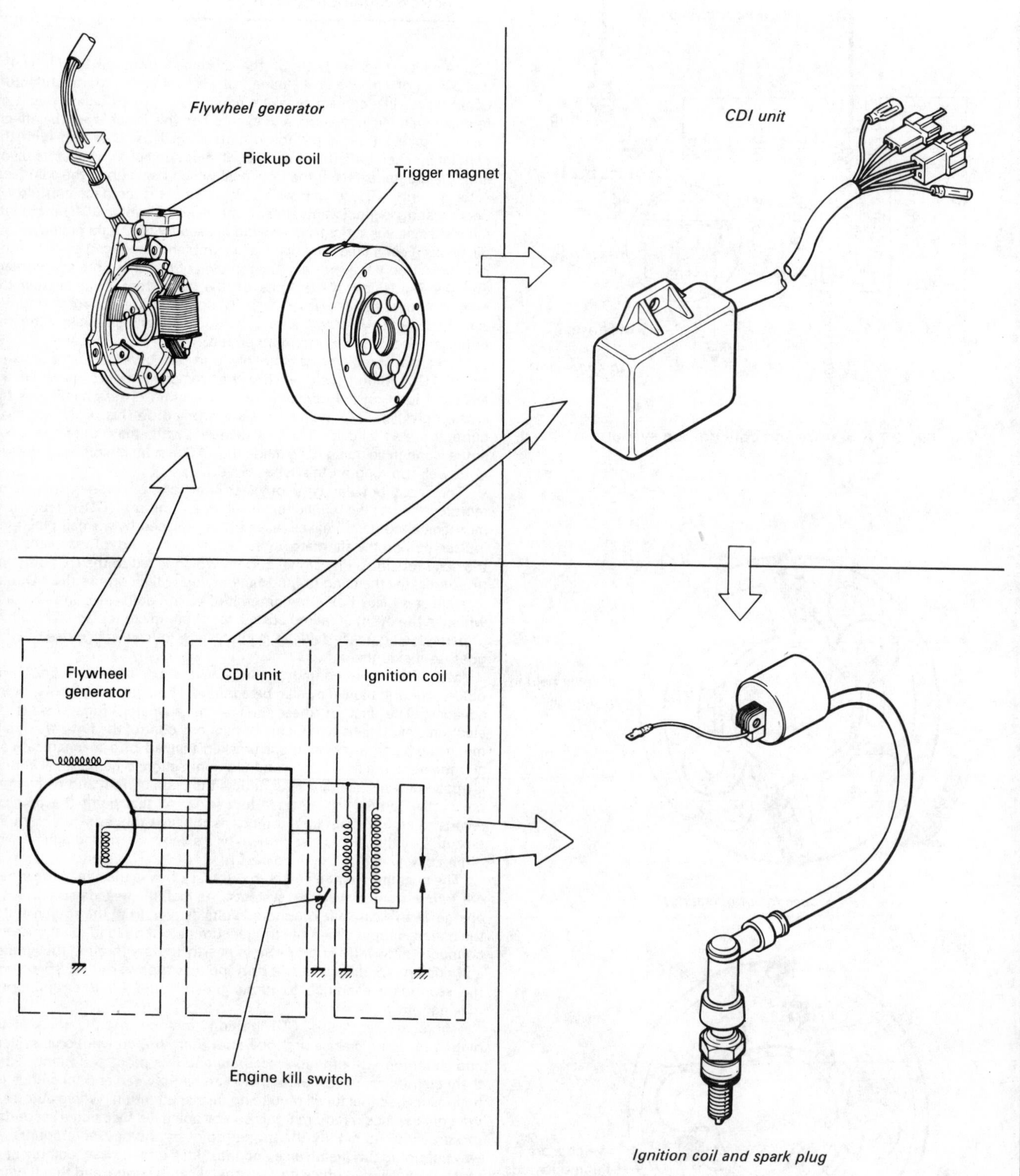


**Fig. 3.9 Capacitor discharge ignition (CDI) components**

*This illustration shows the elements in a typical CDI system (Suzuki DR125 shown) together with the circuit diagram for this particular system.*

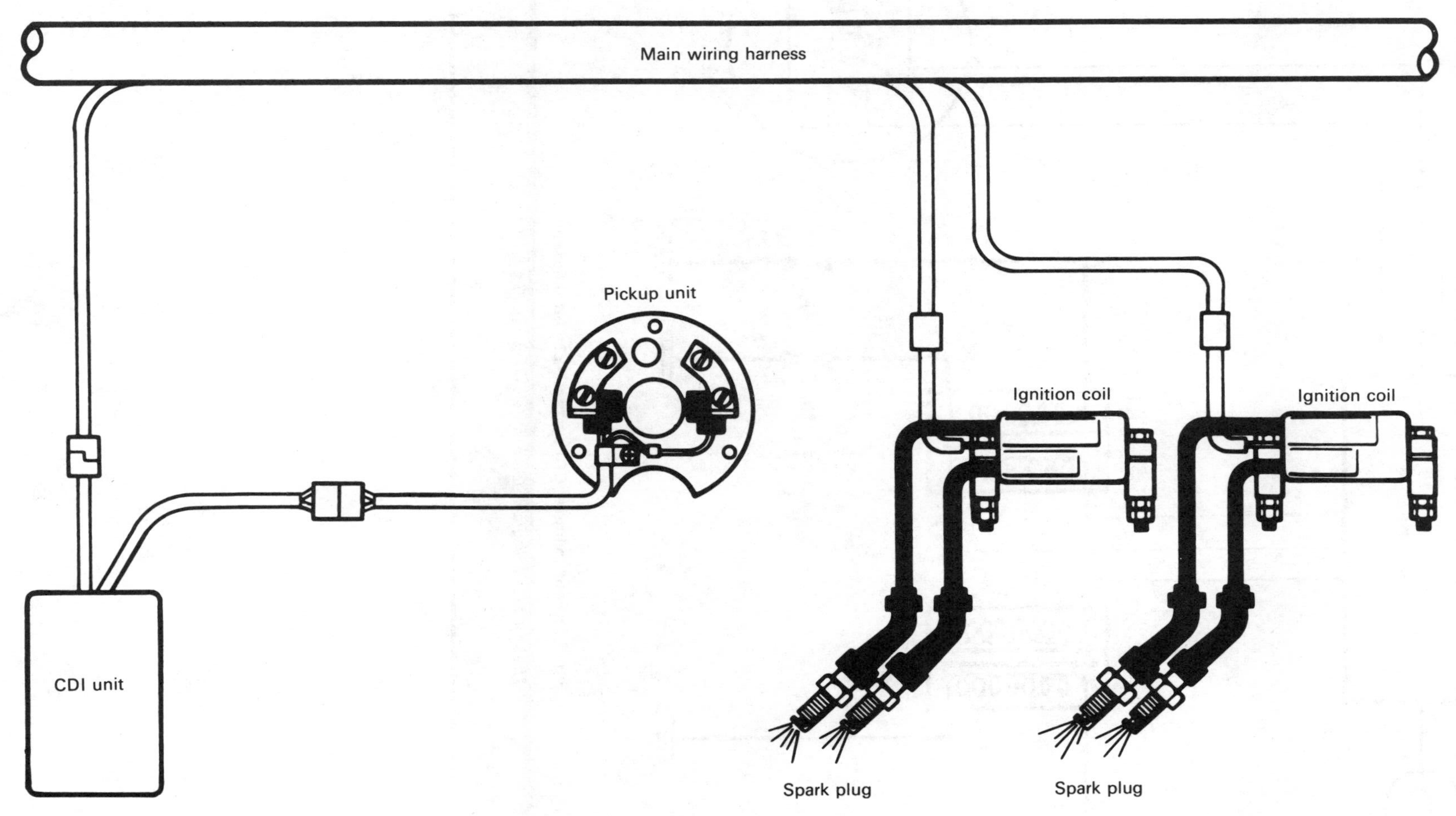


**Fig. 3.10 A typical four-cylinder type CDI system**

*This drawing shows the layout of the various ignition components. Note that two plugs are operated by a single coil and pickup. This means that each plug sparks twice per engine cycle, an arrangement known as a "spare spark" system because one of the two sparks occurs during the exhaust stroke.*

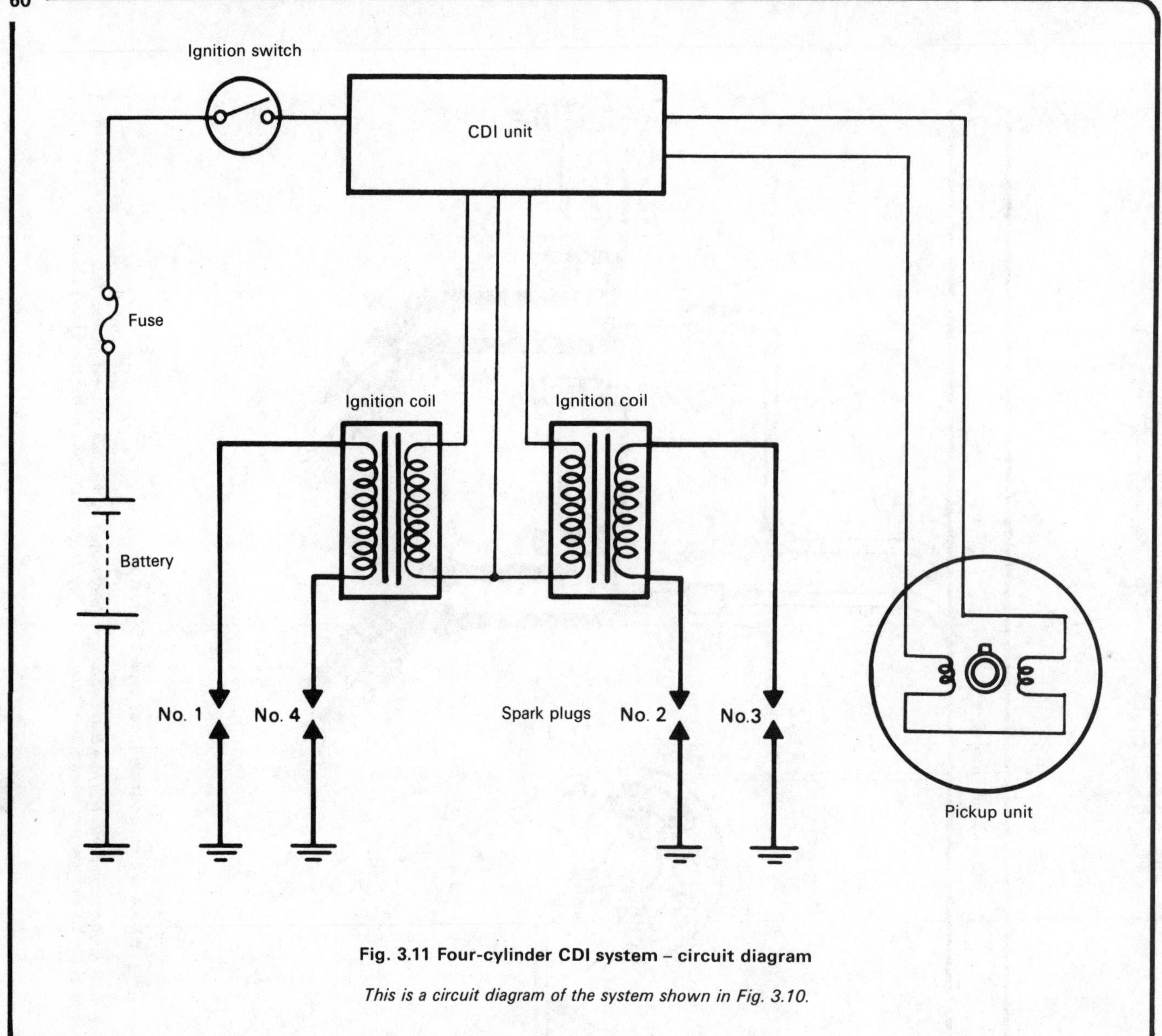


**Fig. 3.11 Four-cylinder CDI system – circuit diagram**

*This is a circuit diagram of the system shown in Fig. 3.10.*

# Chapter 4 Transmission

**Contents**



## 1 Introduction

All powered two-wheelers require some method of transmitting drive from the engine to the rear wheel. In its simplest form, the moped with single-speed automatic transmission performs the job with the minimum of complexity, whilst some of the larger machines employ far more sophisticated and complex systems. Much depends upon the role of the machine in question and the level of performance expected from it; the moped is merely required to propel the rider at moderate speed on short journeys, and so the need for a complex transmission system does not arise. On larger machines, the range of road speeds is far greater, and it is this which dictates the use of a gearbox to provide a number of gear ratios.

Ideally, of course, the engine would be able to provide a continuous supply of power from a standstill to its maximum speed without having to alter the gear ratio at all, but in practice there is a limit to the speed at which the engine can be run without the risk of mechanical failure. This means that the 1000cc motorcycle would be little better than a moped if confined to one gear, even though it produces many times the power of the moped. On the other hand, if we provided the moped with a wide selection of gear ratios it would not produce enough power to attain very high speeds.

## 2 Clutches

An essential feature of all machines produced today is some form of clutch to allow drive to the rear wheel to be disconnected whilst still leaving the engine running. This was not always so, and very early machines employed a form of direct drive using a belt between pulleys on the crankshaft and the rear wheel. This worked up to a point, but it did mean that to stop at a junction it was necessary to stop the engine as well. It follows that the engine could not be started with the machine stationary, so it was necessary to push-start it on each occasion – hardly a convenient arrangement.

The way to avoid the problems described above is to fit a friction clutch somewhere between the engine and rear wheel. This allows the drive to be disconnected, and has the incidental advantage of allowing gearchanges to be made where a gearbox is employed. With the exception of automatic gearboxes, all motorcycle clutches are of the friction type. These are usually manually-operated from a handlebar lever, but some smaller machines use a simple automatic centrifugal clutch. The two arrangements are described below, and should be studied in conjunction with the accompanying line drawings in the interests of clarity.

### The manual clutch

The simplest form of friction clutch would consist of the crankshaft terminating in a circular plate, and fitted close to it, a corresponding plate and shaft. If there was a small gap between the two plates, the engine could run with the second shaft remaining stationary. If we now move the second shaft until its plate is in contact with that of the crankshaft, the friction between the two would turn the second shaft. In this way power from the engine could be applied to the second shaft or disconnected from it at will.

On a more practical level, let us look at how this principle is applied on most motorcycles. Power from the engine is available at the crankshaft, and this is used to drive the clutch via gears or a chain. This stage is known as the primary transmission, and reduces the speed of the rapidly revolving crankshaft to a more moderate level. The clutch assembly is mounted on the end of the gearbox input shaft, its outer drum supported on a bearing and thus free to turn even if the machine, and thus the input shaft, is stationary. Inside the drum, the clutch centre is bolted to the shaft end and thus turns with it.

The centre and the drum are both slotted (splined) to engage their respective plates. The friction (drive) plates engage in the outer splines of the drum, whilst the plain (driven) plates engage on the inner clutch centre splines. A varying number of plain and friction plates are fitted alternately, and this controls the amount of friction area available. On a small machine fewer plates are necessary than on a larger, more powerful model. Outside of the plates is a pressure plate which clamps the clutch plates together under spring pressure. This means that the alternate plates are held tightly together as a group and thus turn together, transmitting drive to the input shaft. To disconnect drive the clutch pressure plate is pushed away from the clutch plates, against spring pressure. This allows the individual plates to separate and slip in relation to each other, so the clutch centre and the plain plates can stop while the clutch drum and the friction plates continue to turn.

### Centrifugal clutch

This type of clutch is commonly used on mopeds, where its automatic operation frees the rider of unnecessary controls. This means that, with the exception of the throttle twistgrip, the machine can be as easy to operate as a bicycle. The clutch unit consists of a clutch centre which is attached to the end of the crankshaft. Around the edge of the clutch centre are two or more friction shoes, very similar to drum brake shoes. These are pivoted at one end, and are held against the centre by springs. Outside the centre and running close to the friction surface of the shoe is a drum. This is carried on a bearing on the crankshaft end, and thus can remain stationary even when the crankshaft is turning. The drum incorporates the driving sprocket or pulley which eventually transmits drive to the rear wheel.

At low engine speeds the clutch centre spins with the crankshaft and the drum remains stationary. As engine speed rises, centrifugal force acting on the pivoting shoes throws them outwards and into contact with the drum surface. In this way the drum begins to revolve with the crankshaft and the machine moves off. When the throttle is closed the shoes are drawn away from the drum by the return springs and drive is disconnected. It will be appreciated that this simple arrangement is ideal in moped designs where simplicity of operation is an important requirement, but it does have the disadvantage that it is not easy to incorporate a gearchange. This is because it is necessary to de-clutch during the change, and so a manual control is normally required. One way of getting round the problem is to arrange a method whereby the clutch is disconnected as the gearchange control is operated, and this system does work, though not with such control or smoothness as is found in manual systems. Another possibility is to employ a fully automatic transmission using two or three ratios. These are used widely on mopeds and on the small scooter-type commuter bikes which have become popular in recent years, and the system is discussed later in this Chapter.

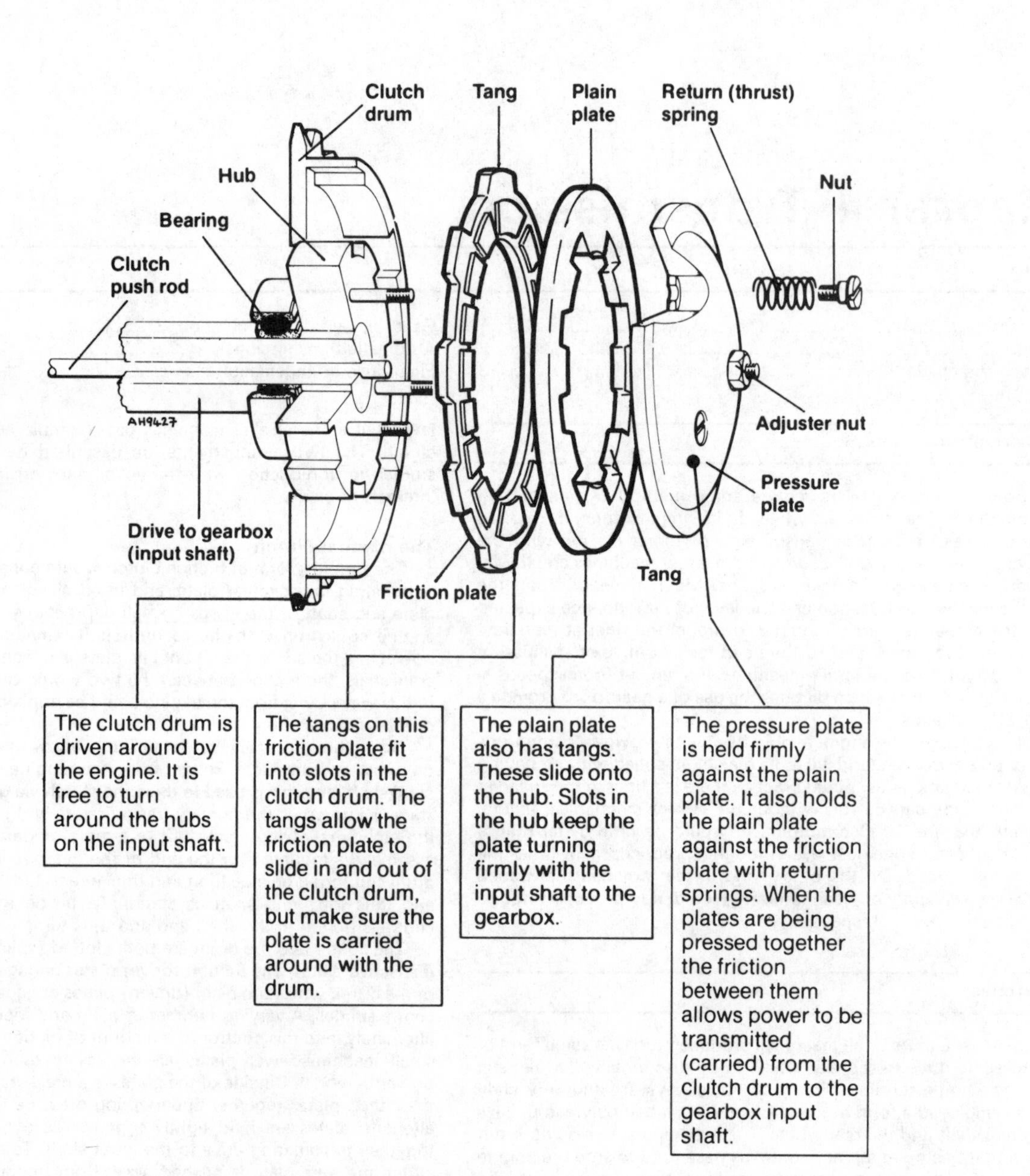


**Fig. 4.1 A simplified manual friction clutch**

*In this example a simplified clutch having only one plain and one friction plate is shown; real clutches have several pairs of plates.*

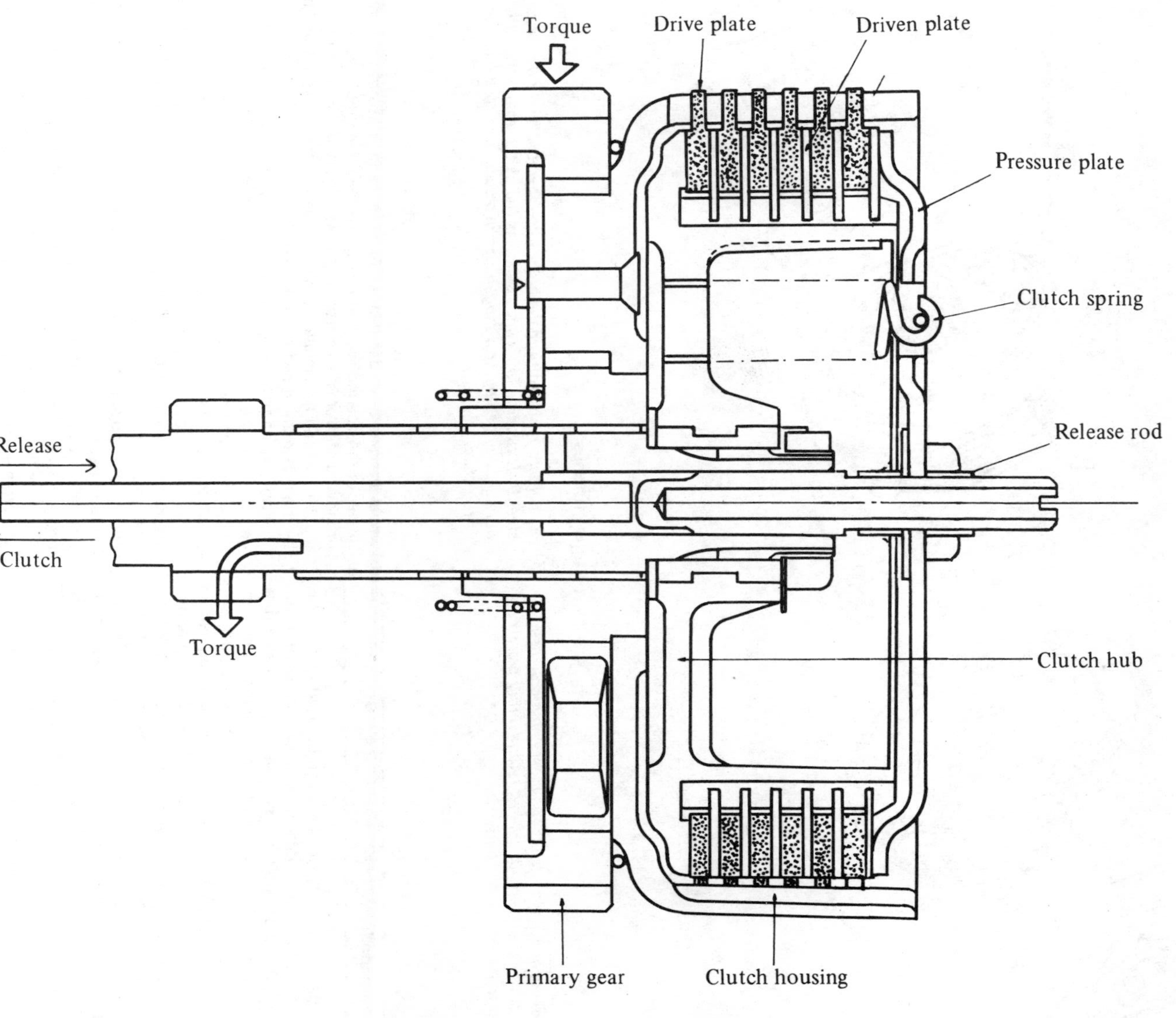


**Fig. 4.2 Sectioned view of a friction clutch**

*This is a more realistic example of a multi-plate friction clutch, shown in section. Note that in this example extension springs are used.*

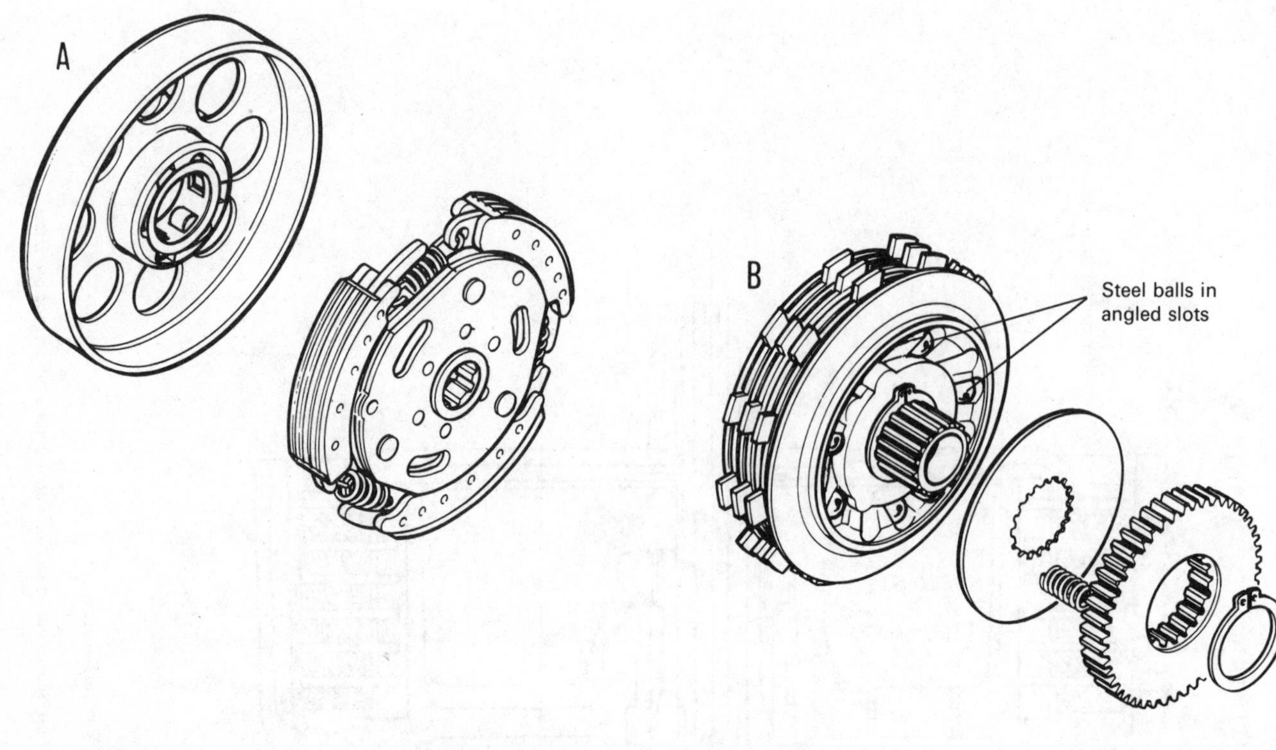


**Fig. 4.3 Centrifugal clutches**

**A** *The shoe-type centrifugal clutch is the most commonly used arrangement. The shoes are flung out against return spring pressure until they begin to turn the clutch drum.*

**B** *Plate-type centrifugal clutches are operated by a number of steel balls running in inclined slots. As the clutch spins, the balls fly outwards, engaging or disengaging drive according to the application of the clutch.*

## 3 Why are gears needed?

The principle of gearing is fairly simple; it can be used to alter the speed of a rotating shaft to a useful rate for a specific purpose. If for example the shaft is turning at 2000 rpm and we wish to halve that rate, then we must fit to the shaft a drive gear having half the number of teeth of the driven gear. For every two rotations of the drive gear, the driven gear will thus turn once. When we look at gearing as applied to motorcycle transmissions, there is another factor to be considered; not only does the gearing change the engine speed to a rate which translates to the desired road speed, it also determines the number of power strokes applied during each revolution of the rear wheel. Thus in bottom gear, there will be numerous power strokes, and thus more power, during each revolution than in successively higher gears. This is necessary to allow the machine to overcome inertia when moving off from rest, and this can be demonstrated by trying to pull away in top gear. Even on the most powerful machine the engine will be unable to get it moving and will stall; it is necessary to build up to the final ratio in stages.

As we have seen, the requirement for gearing comes about as a direct result of the characteristics of the internal combustion engine. Taking an imaginary engine, useful power may only be produced in a relatively narrow band between about 2000 rpm and 8000 rpm. First of all it is necessary to reduce this rate of revolution to something that, at the rear wheel, represents a reasonable road speed. This is dependent on the outside diameter of the wheel, itself an element in the gearing, and the power output of the engine. In the case of a single-speed moped, for example, we may find an overall reduction of around 15.00:1. This means that for every 15 revolutions of the engine, the rear wheel will revolve once. This ratio will have been chosen after the wheel size has been decided, and will make best use of the available power. If the gearing were too high, the machine would be incapable of moving off from a standstill. If it were excessively low, however, the machine would accelerate rapidly, but its top speed would be limited by the maximum speed of the engine.

With an engine of greater capacity and power, a much higher gearing could be used to attain a higher top speed, but there remains the problem of moving away from rest. Even though the engine is more powerful, it is still limited by its power band, and so it becomes necessary to add intermediate gears to build up to the final gear ratio. These must be spaced so that as maximum revs are reached in one gear, selection of the next gear will drop the engine speed to the lower end of the power band. Ideally, the ratio would be continuously variable between the lower and upper requirements, but systems of this type have yet to prove generally usable on motorcycles. Instead we find a selection of fixed ratios which change the gearing in steps. On the majority of machines five gears are used, this being about the best compromise between the ideal spacing of the ratios and the problems that using more would introduce; imagine how tedious changing up through ten gears would become. More importantly, the time taken at each change, where the machine is not accelerating, would probably make it slower overall than a similar model with fewer gears.

## 4 Gearbox layout and operation

For many years, motorcycles employed gearboxes of the mainshaft/layshaft type in which power was fed in at the clutch, mounted on one end of the mainshaft. From here, it was fed through the appropriate set of gears to emerge at the correct ratio at a sleeve gear surrounding the clutch end of the input shaft. In this way, movement through the gearbox started and finished at more or less the same point, and this was ideally suited to the machines of that era, with their separate engine, primary drive and gearbox assemblies. There were, inevitably, variations on the above layout. In some applications, the sleeve gear was fitted at the opposite end of the mainshaft, and thus the drive crossed over from one side of the machine to the other. Alternatively, the power could be fed in at the sleeve gear to emerge at the input shaft. The second shaft in this type of gearbox, the layshaft, was blind at both ends, and thus served only to provide the means of changing the gear ratios using pairs of gears of various sizes.

More common on recent machines is the all-indirect gearbox. This differs from the mainshaft/layshaft type in that the power is fed in on one shaft and out on the other. In the interests of clarity it is convenient (and logical) to refer to these as the input and output shafts respectively, though some tend to cling to the older terminology of mainshaft and layshaft. In most designs the gearbox is of the crossover type; power being fed in via the clutch at the right-hand end of the input shaft and emerging at the final drive sprocket on the left-hand end of the output shaft.

The accompanying illustration shows a theoretical two-speed all-indirect gearbox to indicate the principles of operation. As shown, the gearbox is in neutral. The input shaft pinions are splined onto the shaft and thus are turning with it. The output shaft gears are free to turn on plain portions of the shaft, and are thus rotating whilst the output shaft itself remains stationary. To engage 1st gear, the gearchange lever is operated, and this in turn moves the selector drum. A cam profile in the drum face throws the sliding collar towards the output shaft 1st gear pinion (A). The sliding collar is splined onto the output shaft, so when its dogs engage with those of the gear, power is transmitted to the shaft and the final drive sprocket. Second gear is selected in the same way using the other pair of gear pinions. In both cases, to avoid the damage that would result if the dogs were thrown into sudden engagement, the clutch is used to disengage drive to the input shaft. The shaft will slow down and stop allowing the gears to mesh smoothly. The clutch can then be let out to apply drive through the gears to the rear wheel.

In real life things are less clear and straightforward than in our example, but the same principle applies. In the average motorcycle gearbox, the sliding collar is omitted to save space. Instead, some of the gears themselves are used, and are slid a slight distance along the shaft whilst remaining in constant mesh with their opposite number. In the plan view of a five-speed gearbox, it will be seen that the gears are not arranged sequentially along the shafts, but are fitted in as and where convenient to make the assembly compact and efficient. In a five-speed box, three selector forks are needed to move the gears to the correct positions, and the three selector grooves are indicated by arrows. Though a little hard to follow at first, the power flow shown in each of the five ratios gives a good indication of how most motorcycle gearboxes function, so it is worth spending a little time studying it.

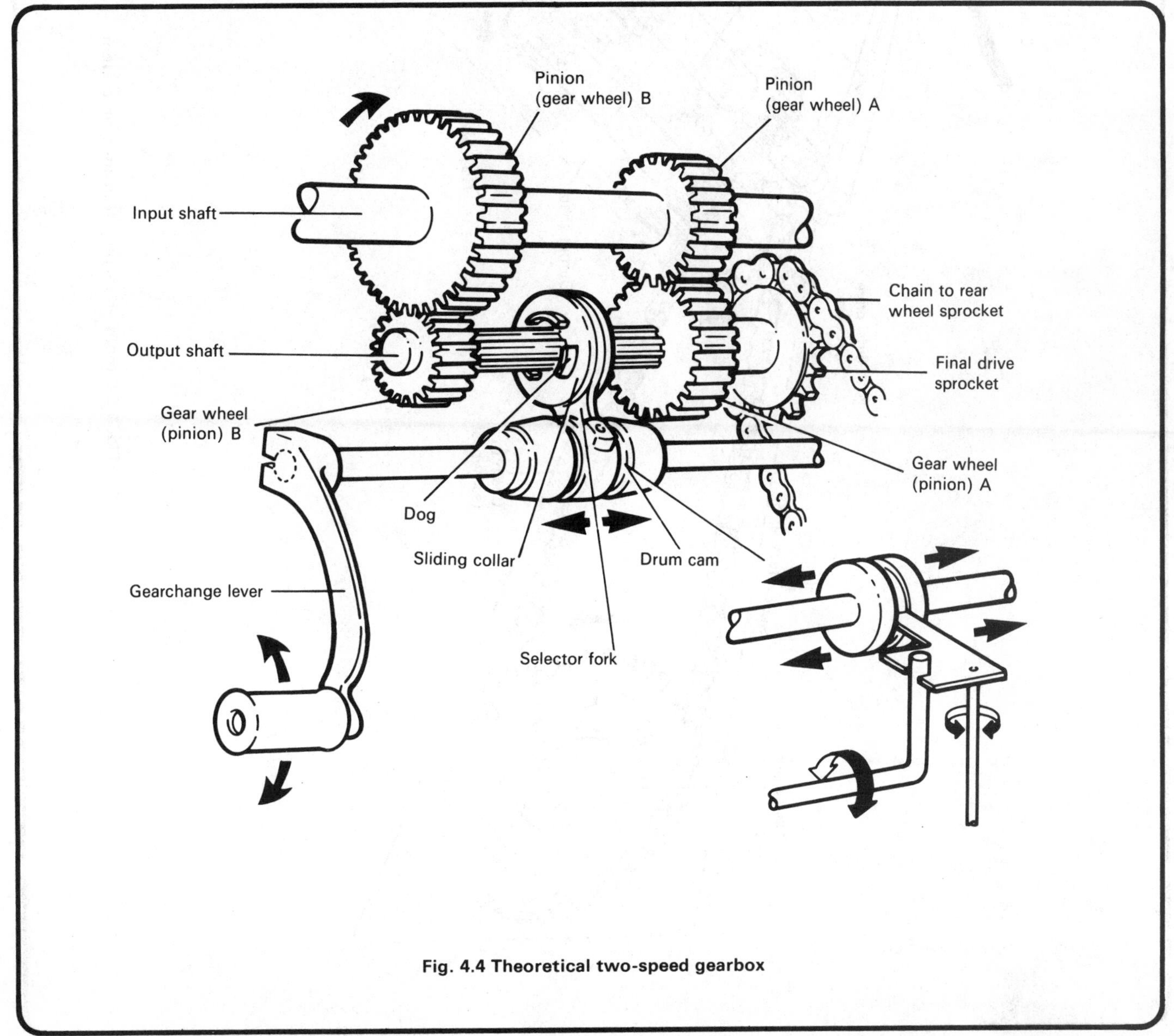


Fig. 4.4 Theoretical two-speed gearbox

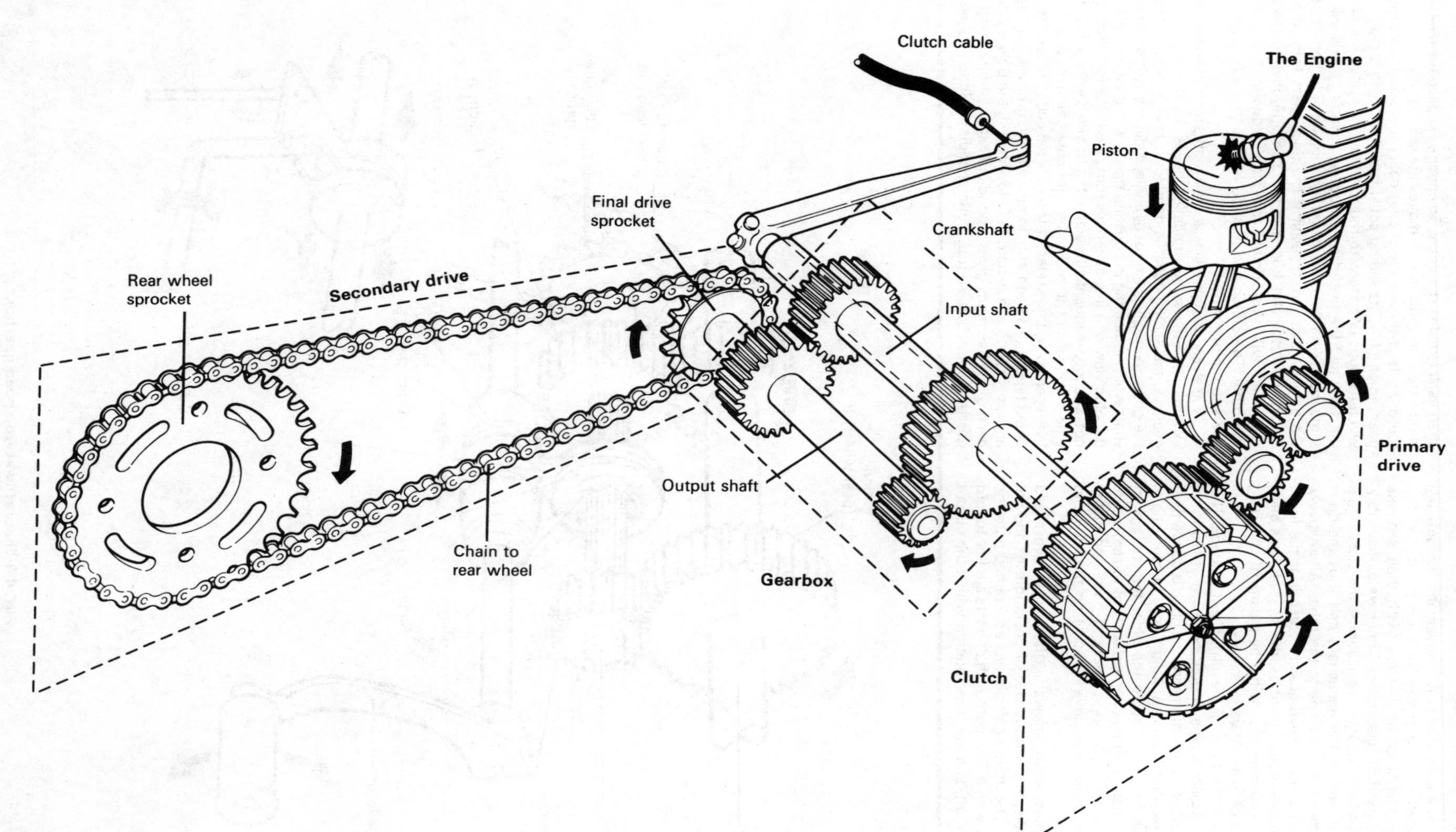


Fig. 4.5 Simplified manual transmission system

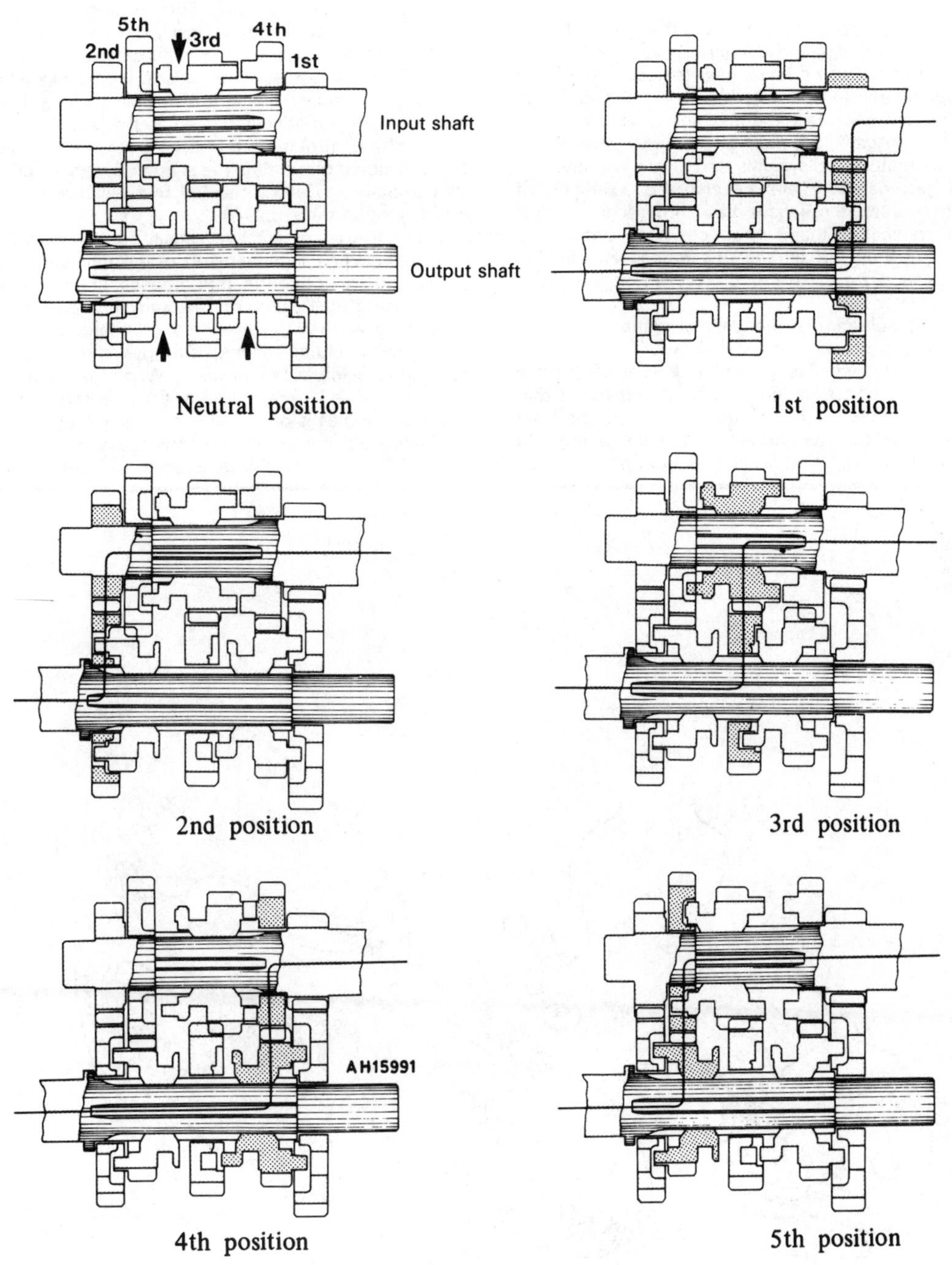


**Fig. 4.6 Typical 5-speed constant mesh gearbox**

*In the six drawings the gearbox is shown in section, the power flow through the various pairs of gears being indicated by shading.*

## 5 Automatic transmissions

Whilst it is quite possible to produce a single-speed moped that works well enough for most purposes, it can be advantageous to have some choice of gearing. One approach is to fit a full manual gearbox similar to those used on full-sized motorcycles. This, allied to a 50cc two-stroke engine developed to produce the maximum amount of power, can result in a completely different type of machine; a sort of miniature motorcycle. These were very popular in the UK for some years, providing the sixteen year old rider with a way of getting around the legislation which limited him or her to a machine of this capacity. The machines provided an example of how a particular size of engine capacity could be developed to its maximum potential, and many of the models were capable of 45 or 50 mph. Eventually, the 'sports moped' was legislated out of existence in the UK, largely as the result of hysterical press reports of 'killer mopeds' wiping out the nation's youth. What was a blow to the sixteen year old did, however, bring about a return to the original concept of the moped, now without pedals. The new 'no-peds' were limited to a maximum designed speed of around 30 mph, and since there was no possibility of competing on performance, the various manufacturers have sought to out-sell each other on other features.

The sports moped may be a thing of the past, but there are still good reasons for adopting some kind of gearing. A popular approach is to fit a normal top gear, supplemented by a lower gear (or gears) to permit more rapid acceleration when starting from rest. The extra ratio(s) can be invaluable in traffic, and will allow the machine to start on (and negotiate) steep inclines. Again, this can be a purely mechanical arrangement, similar to motorcycle systems and using a manually-operated clutch and gearchange. There are plenty of examples of mopeds with extra gears, and these have been around for several decades. The only real drawback is that it introduces more controls and thus complication for the rider. Given that the moped is intended primarily as simple transport for the non-motorcyclist, an automatic arrangement has its attractions.

One more promising solution is the variable ratio belt drive transmission used by Vespa on some of its mopeds. This utilises a conventional centrifugal clutch which engages the drive as the throttle twistgrip is opened. More important is the centrifugally-operated split pulley which transmits drive via a V-belt to the rear wheel. The front and rear pulleys are both formed in two halves, the rear unit being held together by spring pressure. The front pulley is controlled by the wedging action of rollers, and the assembly functions as follows: At rest, the two halves of the front pulley are fully apart and the rear pulley is pushed closed by its spring. This gives an effectively low ratio as the machine moves off, and thus brisk acceleration. As the speed rises, the rollers are thrown outwards and this closes the gap in the front pulley. The drive belt must now ride over a bigger diameter, and this forces apart the rear pulley, giving it a smaller working diameter. In this way the gear ratio is gradually altered as the machine gathers speed, with no need for control from the rider. As the machine slows on steep hills or when slowing in traffic, the sequence is reversed. The lower ratio is then available to allow the hill to be climbed or to provide better acceleration in traffic.

Another way of achieve similar results is to fit more than one centrifugal clutch. Arrangements of this type are more widespread and varied, and are not confined to mopeds. In its simplest form, there is a normal centrifugal clutch on the crankshaft end, and this takes up the initial drive. At the rear wheel end, or in the engine casings themselves is a second clutch having stronger springs and thus remaining inoperative below a certain speed. When the second clutch comes into operation, drive is transmitted at a higher ratio, the first clutch being bypassed by means of a ratchet arrangement or similar.

There are many variations of the above system, and much depends on the way in which the transmission is laid out. In the case of the

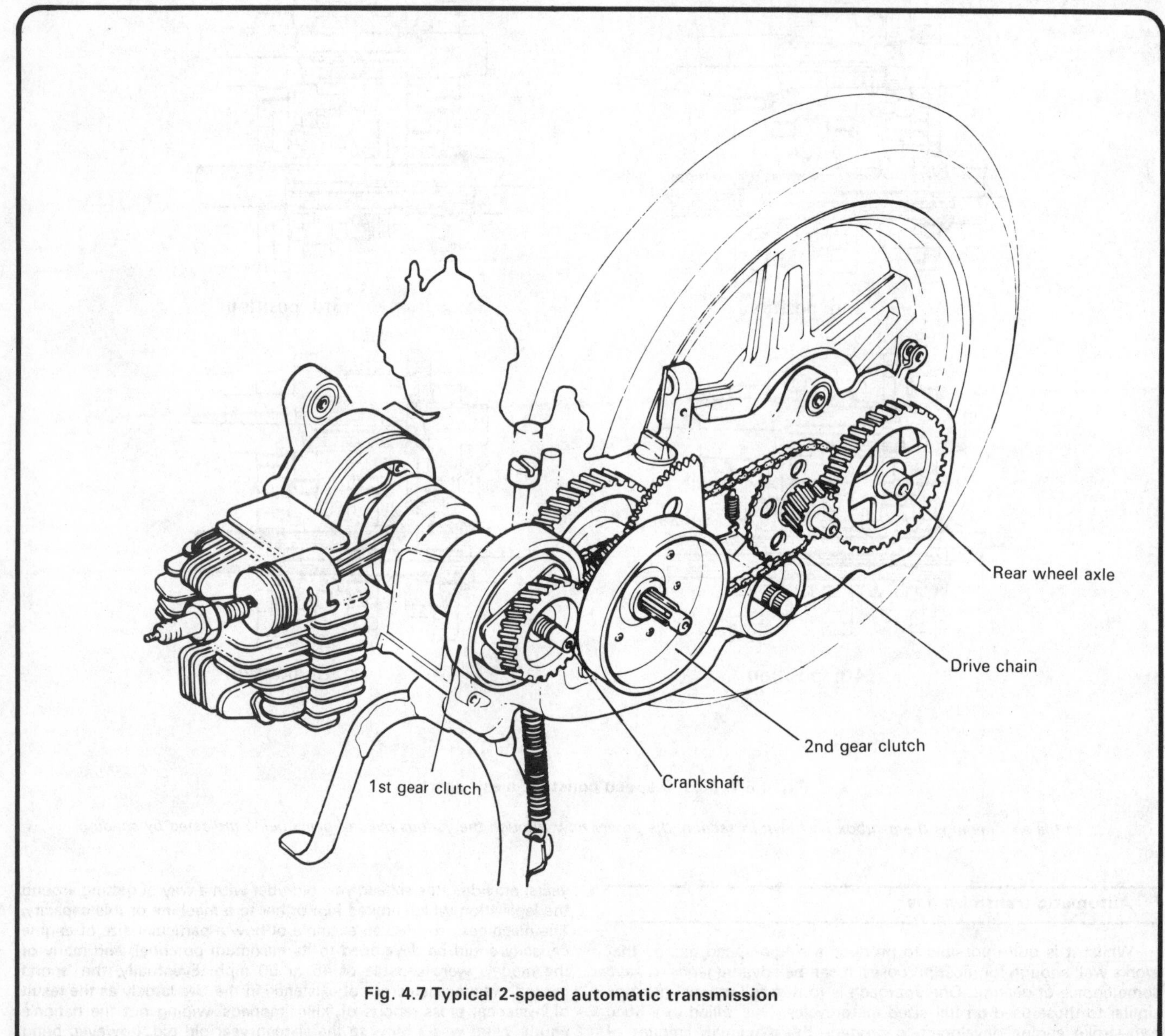


Fig. 4.7 Typical 2-speed automatic transmission

popular scooter-styled commuter mopeds, the second speed clutch is often located at the rear of the transmission casing, near to the stub axle which carries the rear wheel. The principle has been elaborated on machines like Suzuki's CS 125 scooter. In this machine a three-speed transmission is used, operated by shoe-type centrifugal clutches for the 1st and 2nd gears. The 3rd gear is operated by a centrifugal multiplate clutch. This is similar to conventional manual clutches, but it is operated by steel balls being flung outwards as the clutch revolves, rather than by a pushrod arrangement. The crankshaft-mounted 1st gear clutch operates in the normal way, transmitting drive to the stub axle. As engine speed rises, the second gear clutch engages and the drive from the 1st gears is interrupted by a one-way clutch. When the 3rd gear clutch engages, the drive from 2nd gear is disconnected in a similar manner. The transmission is designed so that the change between 2nd and 3rd gears occurs at a point determined by the amount of load on the engine. In this way the transmission will remain in 2nd longer if accelerating or climbing a hill than it would if under a light load.

The other route to automatic transmission is considerably more complicated, and does not use a friction clutch. A device called a torque converter is used instead, in conjunction with high and low gears. The torque converter is a somewhat difficult device to come to terms with, and for that reason its inner workings will be left to more specialised works to explain its finer points to those who wish to know more. For our purposes it is sufficient to know that it employs a hydraulic drive system which allows torque multiplication to replace most of the gears on a conventional machine. In theory, only one gear is really essential, but in practice there are advantages in using more. The system is essentially the same as that employed in cars with automatic transmission, and the same drawbacks apply.

Principally, these concern the power loss through the torque converter and thus the loss of performance and fuel economy when compared with a manually operated equivalent. A secondary problem is that of transmission creep at road junctions – annoying in a car, and potentially dangerous on a motorcycle. For most people, automatic transmission can be regarded as not having characteristics suited to what is required of a motorcycle, and this may be the main reason why automatics of the torque converter variety have never been welcomed. Honda have made two forays into this rather difficult area with the CB750A and CB400A Hondamatic models. To be fair to Honda, and to Moto Guzzi with their Hydro-Convert model, they did work well. It seems that no-one wanted to buy them.

## 6 Final drive arrangements

The method of transmitting power to the rear wheel varies widely according to the layout of a particular machine. In some cases it forms an extension of the main transmission, terminating in a short stub axle to which the wheel is attached. This can be seen in scooters and many mopeds, particularly those using variable speed transmissions. In the conventional motorcycle design, however, there is a separate secondary transmission between the gearbox and the rear wheel, and it is the various arrangements of this type which we will be examining in this Section.

### Chain drive

The earliest motorcycles employed a belt drive to the rear wheel, and this worked satisfactorily where the power output was low. The leather or later rubber drive belts did have a tendency to slip when wet, though, and this and the increasingly powerful engines being developed soon necessitated a stronger and more reliable system. Chain drive was an obvious choice, being compact and relatively easy to arrange on most conventional designs. Despite the fact that the chain itself is mechanically complicated with its numerous links and rollers, its adaptation to motorcycle final drive poses no great problems. As a transmission medium, roller chain is surprisingly efficient, but only when in good condition. In practice, road dirt soon takes its toll on an unprotected chain, and efficiency soon falls off.

Dirt sticks to the side plates of the chain, and will eventually work its way into the rollers where it acts as a grinding paste, literally wearing the chain away. To reduce this problem the chain needs to be kept clean and well lubricated. Where chains were used inside the engine casings it was obvious that they were comparatively long-lived, a timing chain outlasting its exposed final drive equivalent many times. In the 1950s much attention was given to the problem of chain wear, leading to the introduction of automatic oilers and full enclosures. These were very successful in extending the life of the chain, and also in reducing the amount of maintenance required, and it may seem surprising that with very few exceptions, enclosures are no longer fitted today. The reason for this is simply that no-one liked the look of them. The average motorcyclist, it seems, is so conscious of the appearance of the machine that efficiency is gladly sacrificed for it. Of current production models, MZ seem to offer the neatest form of enclosure with a cast alloy cover around the rear wheel sprocket and fairly unobtrusive synthetic rubber tubes covering the upper and lower chain runs. Honda's CG 125 comes with a traditional pressed steel enclosure; efficient but rather clumsy in appearance.

If the public refuse to accept an enclosure, the only other option is to find a way of keeping the dirt out of the rollers. The chain would still require cleaning and external lubrication, but the wear problem could be much reduced. The O-ring chain does just this by fitting tiny O-ring seals to keep the grease in each roller and the dirt out. This type of chain is more expensive, and is often heavier and bulkier as well, but these disadvantages are outweighed by the extended service life offered.

### Toothed belt drive

One alternative to the traditional chain is the toothed belt. This, as its name suggests, is a flat belt with teeth moulded into its inner face and running on correspondingly toothed pulleys. Although the idea is simple enough, it is only in recent years that companies like Uniroyal have been able to develop reinforcing materials capable of carrying the high loadings imposed by motorcycle final drive systems. The toothed belt is slightly less efficient than a new, clean chain, but in use this difference is soon negated. The belt system is lighter and quieter than chain, does not require maintenance or adjustment, and provides a much smoother drive.

To date, there has been little sign of a general swing to toothed belt in place of chains, though Kawasaki and Harley-Davidson have each released models using the system. The only real drawbacks are the increased width when compared with a chain, and the problem of what to do if a belt breaks on the road. This last point has been a frequently heard 'what if' type of criticism, though in reality the owner is no worse off than one with a broken endless chain. A temporary spare belt can be fitted to get you home, and fitting a new belt is not too difficult (and certainly a lot cleaner than fitting a chain). It remains to be seen if toothed belt drive will be widely adopted in place of the chain. The results to date look promising, but this ignores the main unknown factor; the fickle and conservative buying public.

### Shaft drive

Many years ago the motor industry abandoned the drive chain and adopted the drive shaft in its place. Motorcycles, too, have been using shaft drive for many years, though it has never looked like replacing the chain. It is hard to deny that shaft drive is the best final drive medium of the lot. It is robust, clean and needs no maintenance apart from changing the oil in the rear wheel bevel casing. It can be argued that it is expensive, heavy and that it absorbs a lot of power. Shaft drive enthusiasts will counter that one shaft drive unit is cheaper than a lifetime's supply of chains, that it is not that much heavier than a chain and its sprockets, and that it is more efficient than a worn and dirty chain.

To use shaft drive effectively it helps if the engine is transverse, its crankshaft running in line with the drive shaft. If you look at machines like all BMWs and Moto Guzzi V-twins, and at Honda's CX500 and derivatives, you can see the advantages quite clearly. If the engine is mounted in-line it is first necessary to turn the drive through right-angles before it can connect to the shaft. This might seem complicated, but a look at Yamaha's XS750 and XS1100 show that it can be fairly neatly done. The main drawback with shaft drive is its initial cost; it can be argued that it will add enough to the initial price tag to persuade a potential buyer to opt for a similar but cheaper chain drive model from a rival company. There are more subtle side effects of shaft drive that those who really hate the idea are quick to point out. The first of these is harshness in the transmission. What is really meant here is that the 'give' in a chain which helps smooth out hamfisted throttle control is not there with a shaft drive system. The other is the strange inclination of some shaft driven machines to alternately rise or sink at the back end. This is caused by the shaft trying to climb up or down the bevel gear under load or on overrun, but it is more disconcerting than a real cause for concern.

Grease
Pin
O-ring or seal

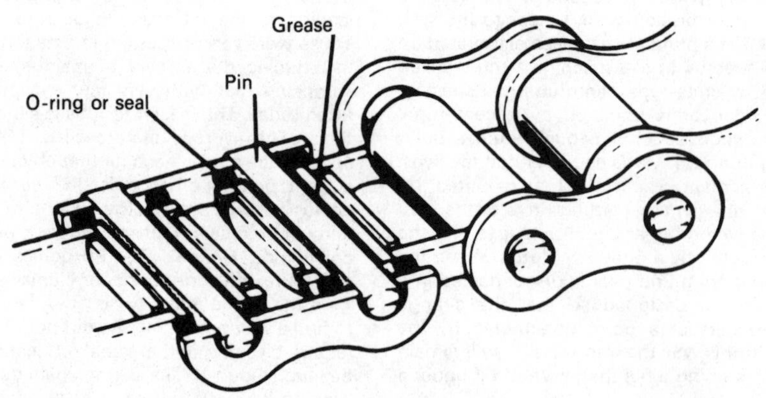

**Fig. 4.8 Section through a typical O-ring chain showing how the chain pins are sealed**

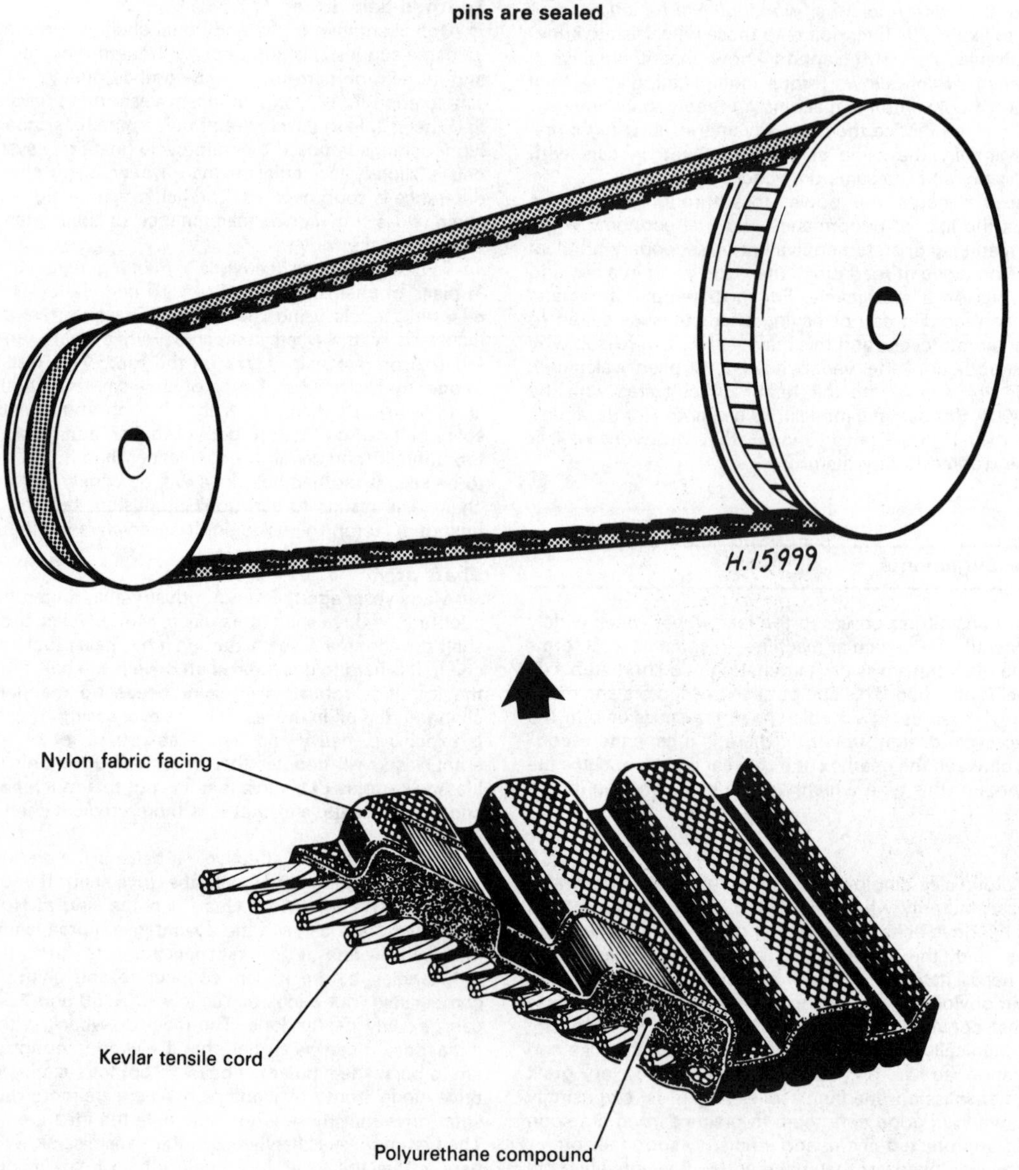

H.15999
Nylon fabric facing
Kevlar tensile cord
Polyurethane compound

**Fig. 4.9 Toothed belt final drive**

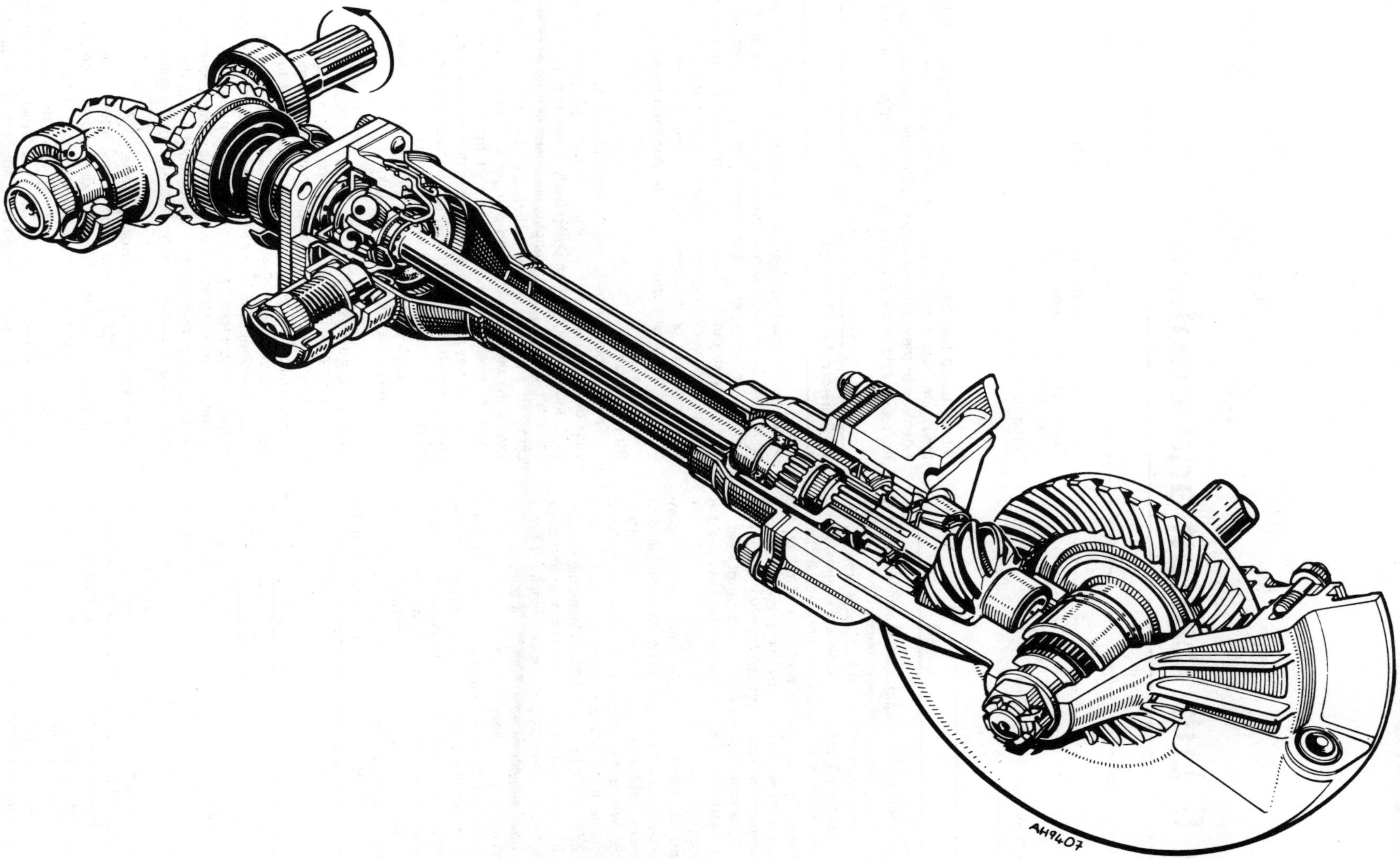

Fig. 4.10 Shaft final drive

# Chapter 5 Lubrication and cooling

**Contents**



## 1 Introduction

The internal moving parts of the engine are machined to fine tolerances and to a smooth finish to minimise wear. When viewed under a microscope, however, apparently smooth surfaces are actually quite rough, and to minimise the friction and heat which would occur if the surfaces were in contact it is necessary to introduce a film of lubricant to separate them. By maintaining a coating of oil on the internal surfaces of the engine, the various parts are effectively cushioned and held apart from each other. If the lubrication should fail at any point, there will be a rapid and localised build-up of heat. In extreme cases this may cause the affected areas to become welded together, and this is known as seizure.

In addition to its main role, the oil performs a number of secondary jobs. The oil film effectively covers the internal parts, excluding air and acidic deposits which would otherwise cause corrosion to take place. On four-stroke engines, where the oil is constantly recirculated through the engine, it carries away any contaminants formed during combustion to be trapped in the oil filter, and thus cleans the engine. The oil is also used to improve sealing between the piston and rings and between the reed and disc valves on two strokes. Finally, it helps to disperse heat from areas subject to very high local temperatures such as the piston, rings and cylinder bore surface.

Despite the high efficiency of modern engines, fuels and oils there remains the problem of heat. Ideally, an engine would convert all of the energy in the fuel into work, and would be mechanically frictionless, and thus would remain cold. In practice there is a considerable amount of unwanted heat generated in all engines, and this must be kept to a reasonable level to prevent damage. This can be done directly, by radiating heat into the surrounding air, or indirectly by conducting the heat away with water which is then cooled in a radiator.

## 2 Four-stroke lubrication

On all modern four-strokes a circulating oil system is used. An engine-driven pump forces the oil through passages in the engine castings, or though external pipes, to the main areas of stress in the engine. The main feed directs a high pressure supply to the big-end and main bearings. A second feed, often at a lower pressure, takes oil to the top of the engine where it lubricates the rockers, cams and valve gear before draining back down to the crankcase. On some engines, a drilling in the connecting rod takes oil up to the small-end bearing, the emerging oil splashing on the piston and cylinder walls to lubricate and cool them. Others rely on the oil vapour present in the crankcase and on splash lubrication to protect these areas.

There are two basic systems employed on four-stroke engines, and these differ in the way the oil is stored on the machine. In the case of a 'dry-sump' system, the oil drains down into the bottom of the crankcase where it is picked up through a strainer by the return side of the oil pump and transferred to an external oil tank. More common today are 'wet sump' systems in which the oil is contained in an extension of the crankcase known as a sump or oil pan. This eliminates the return side of the system and is thus simpler in operation.

## 3 Four-stroke oil pumps

In the circulating lubrication system of the four-stroke it is necessary to provide some means of forcing the oil through the drillings or oil pipes in the engine, the obvious choice being an engine-driven pump. There are three basic types of pump commonly used in motorcycle engines; the plunger pump, the gear pump and the eccentric rotor or trochoidal type. Of the three the eccentric rotor design is the most popular choice on current machines.

### Plunger pumps

The plunger pump is most commonly found on older machines with dry sump systems, and thus it has feed (delivery) and return (scavenge) plungers. The pump body is mounted near the end of the camshaft, and the pump plungers are operated from an offset pin in the camshaft end. This drives a sliding block which in turn raises and lowers the plungers. The feed plunger is of smaller diameter than the return plunger, and this ensures that the amount of oil ultimately finding its way to the crankcase is less than the return side of the pump can cope with. This means that the crankcase is kept clear of residual oil which would otherwise touch the flywheels, causing drag. At the bottom of each pump chamber is a one-way valve which controls the flow of oil to the engine and oil tank.

### Gear-type pumps

The gear-type pump consists of a pair of meshed gears running in a closely confined chamber. The pump chamber is machined to fit very closely around the gears, the teeth of the latter running only a few thousanths of an inch from the chamber walls. Oil at the inlet side of the pump is trapped in between the pump body and the space between each pair of gear teeth, and is thus carried around to the outlet side. In a dry sump engine, a second stage of the pump provides the return or scavenge to the tank. As with the plunger pump, the return side must be of greater capacity than the feed to keep the crankcase clear of oil.

### Eccentric rotor, or trochoid pumps

This type employs a pair of concentric rotors inside a circular pump body. The shapes of the inner and outer rotors will be best understood by looking at the accompanying illustration. The four-lobed inner rotor is so designed that as it turns, taking with it the five-lobed outer rotor, the cavity between the lobes becomes larger and then smaller. By positioning inlet and outlet ports on one face of the pump body, oil is drawn in through one and expelled through the other as the cavity volume changes. This may appear a little obscure, but as in the case of the Wankel engine, its operation is best understood by looking at an example.

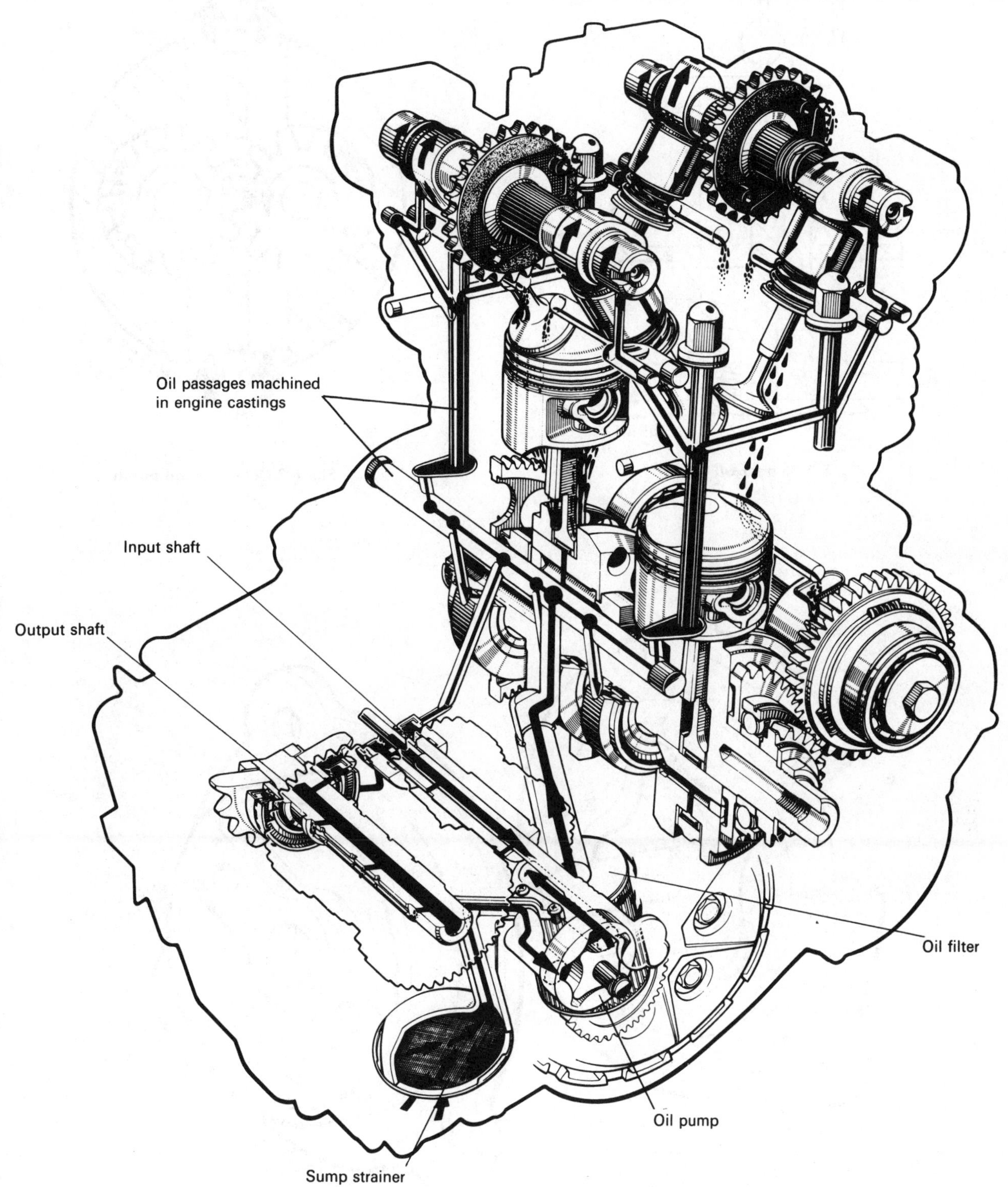


**Fig. 5.1 A typical wet-sump lubrication system**

*This example shows the way in which oil is distributed from the sump to the various engine components requiring lubrication. The oil drains back down to the sump to be filtered and recirculated.*

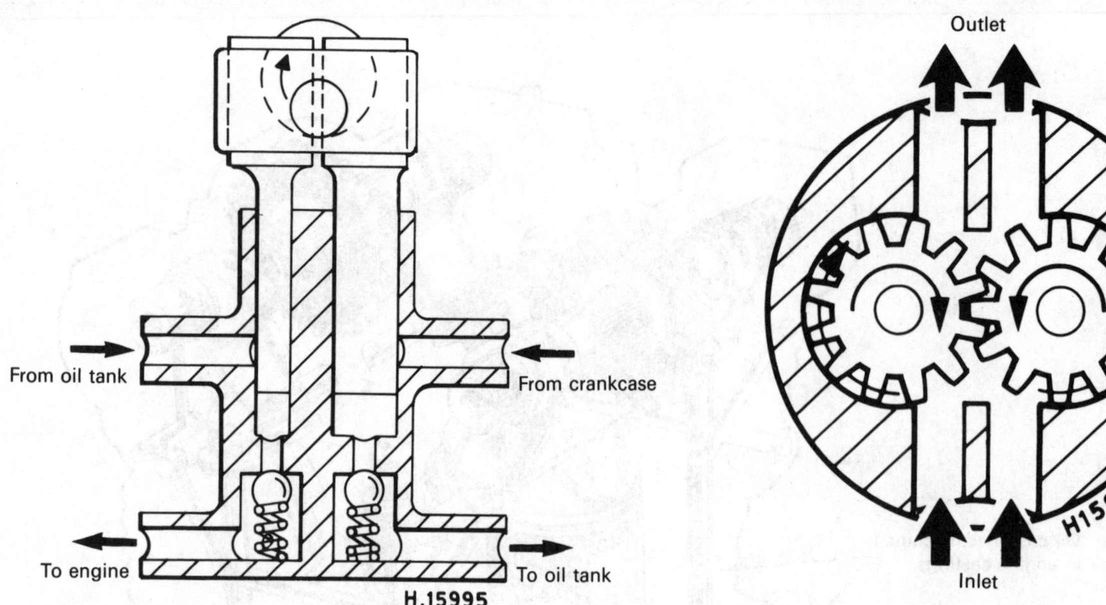


Fig. 5.2 Plunger oil pump

Fig. 5.3 Gear-type oil pump

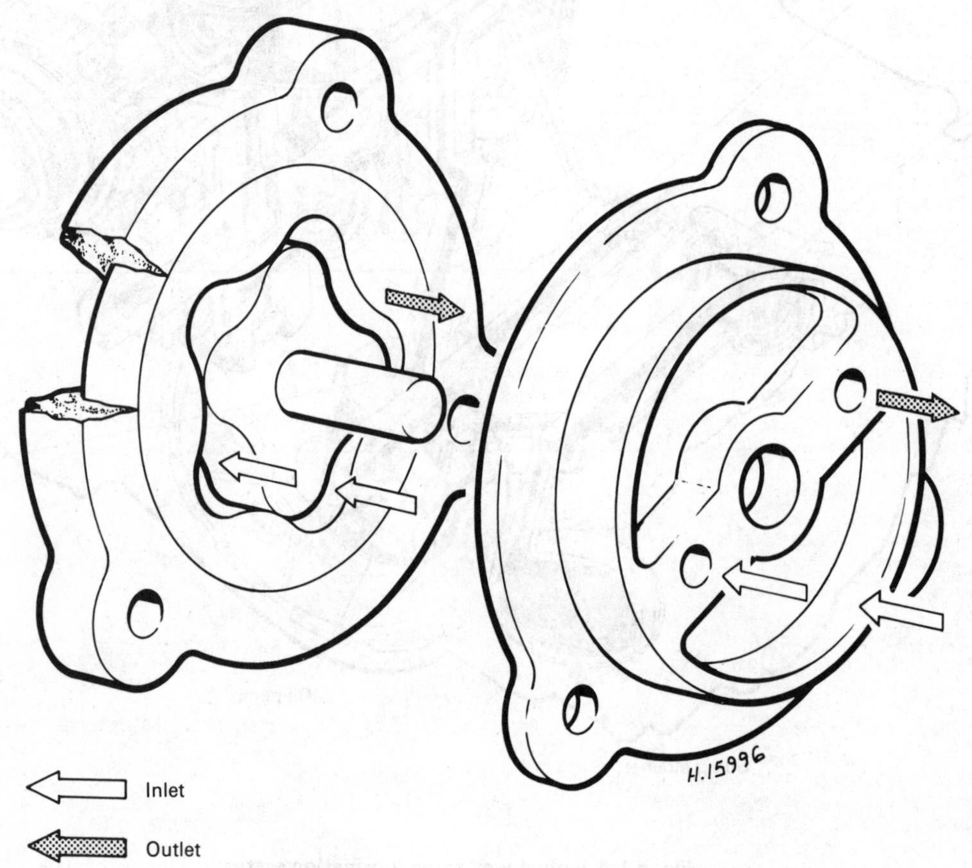


Fig. 5.4 Trochoid oil pump

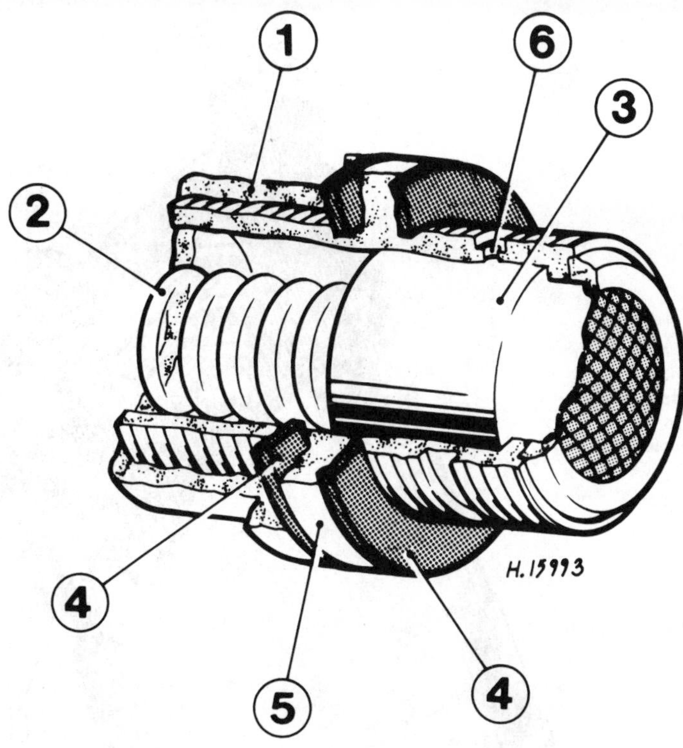


Fig. 5.5 Oil pressure relief valve

*1 End cover*
*2 Spring*
*3 Valve*
*4 Sealing washer*
*5 Valve housing*
*6 Outlet hole*

## 4 Four-stroke lubrication systems: pressure relief and bypass valves

In addition to the check valves or non-return valves which ensure that oil passes in the correct direction round the system, a pressure relief valve is normally fitted to limit the overall pressure in the system. The valve is held closed against oil pressure by a spring. As the oil pressure rises it eventually reaches a point where it forces open the relief valve and allows excess oil to drain back to the crankcase. The relief valve is necessary when the engine is running at high speed to prevent the engine oil seals and gaskets from being burst under excess pressure.

The bypass valve is another type of pressure relief valve, this time designed to open only when internal resistance in the oil filter is such that the flow of oil is likely to be seriously interrupted. In normal circumstances the valve should never open, but if regular oil and filter changes are ignored, the filter element will eventually become badly obstructed. The bypass valve, as its name suggests, bypasses the filter and allows the oil to continue to circulate. The oil is now unfiltered, however, so the contaminants in it are carried round the engine and will cause accelerated wear.

## 5 Four-stroke lubrication systems: oil coolers

As has been mentioned, the circulating oil performs a valuable job in transferring heat from the localised high temperature areas of the engine. The temperature of the oil governs to some extent its thickness, or viscosity; the hotter it gets the thinner it becomes. To prevent the oil from thinning to the point where its lubrication properties might be inadequate, it must be cooled before it is returned to the engine. In a dry sump system the oil tank radiates a good deal of the accumulated heat and this is aided by the cooling effect of the air flowing past it. In the case of wet sump engines, the sump extension of the crankcase is often finned to present the maximum surface area to the air.

In some applications, notably racing engines and some high performance road engines, this natural dispersal of heat may not be sufficient when the machine is ridden hard or in hot climates. To improve the rate of heat loss an oil cooler is fitted. This consists of a small radiator mounted at the front of the machine in the airstream. The oil is passed through the radiator and is thus cooled to a more acceptable level. Oil coolers may be fitted as accessories, though it is uncommon for this to be necessary unless the engine has been modified to produce more power than standard. If, as is often the case, an oil cooler is fitted for cosmetic reasons, there is a danger that the oil will be cooled excessively, and in many respects this is worse than overheating the oil. The extra cooling capacity will delay the engine in reaching its normal operating temperature, and this in itself in undesirable. When fitting an accessory oil cooler it is well worth choosing a type which offers thermostatic control. This allows the cooler to come into operation only when it is really needed.

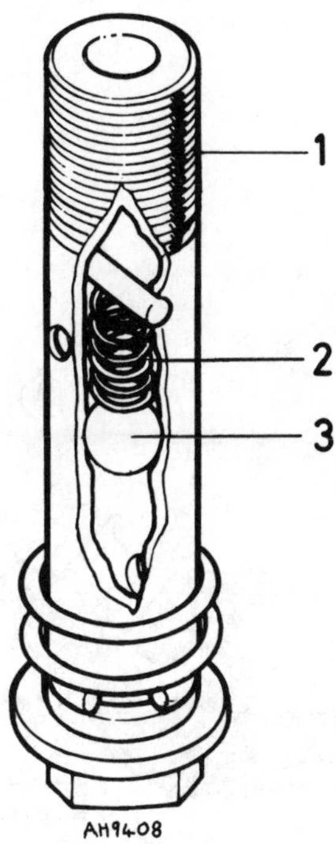


Fig. 5.6 Oil filter bypass valve

*1 Valve housing*
*2 Spring*
*3 Steel ball*

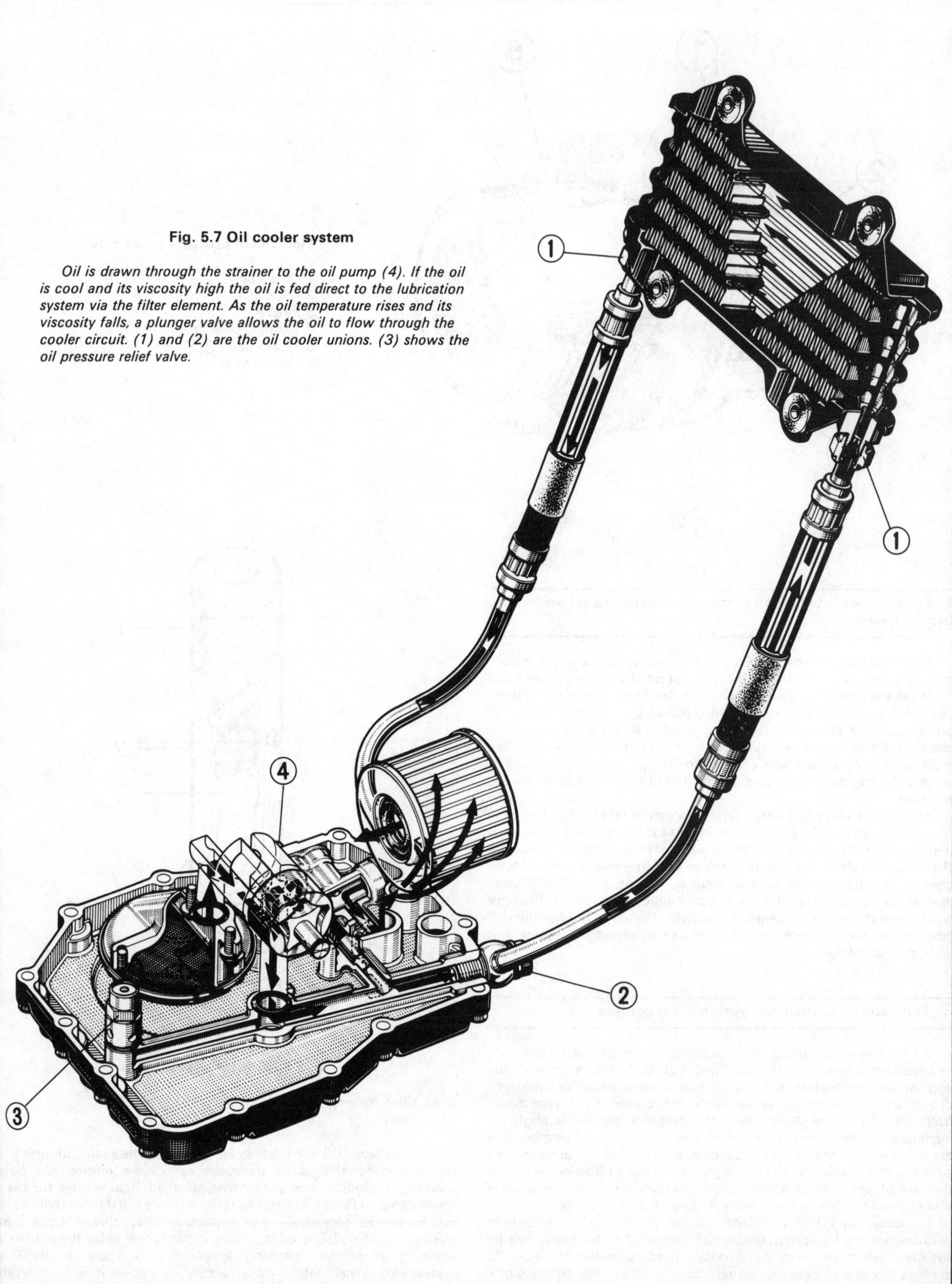


**Fig. 5.7 Oil cooler system**

*Oil is drawn through the strainer to the oil pump (4). If the oil is cool and its viscosity high the oil is fed direct to the lubrication system via the filter element. As the oil temperature rises and its viscosity falls, a plunger valve allows the oil to flow through the cooler circuit. (1) and (2) are the oil cooler unions. (3) shows the oil pressure relief valve.*

## 6 Two-stroke lubrication systems

It is not possible to use a circulating oil system in a two-stroke engine because of the crankcase's secondary function as a pumping chamber; the oil would be drawn with the fuel/air mixture into the combustion chamber through the transfer ports. Instead, two strokes employ a so called total-loss system in which the oil used for lubrication is drawn in in small quantities and is gradually burnt or expelled with the exhaust gases.

In its simplest form, a small percentage of oil is mixed with the fuel in the fuel tank. When the fuel/air mixture is drawn into the crankcase and compressed, some of the oil condenses on the engine parts to lubricate them, whilst the residual oil is burnt and expelled with the exhaust gases. This approach is known as premix, the fuel often being known as 'petroil' due to its oil content. The ratio of oil to petrol is very low; usually about 20:1 or 50:1 in the case of modern engines. Despite the small quantity used it is impossible to do anything other than provide the amount needed by the engine at full load. Inevitably, this means that at lower speeds there is an excess of oil which results in oily exhaust smoke.

Pump-fed arrangements avoid this problem by allowing the rate of oil delivery to suit the throttle opening. By connecting the throttle twistgrip to the pump it can be regulated by altering the effective stroke of the pump as required. The oil is carried in a separate tank and is usually gravity-fed to the pump. The pump lubrication system is now almost universal on all but competition engines, where lightness and simplicity are more important.

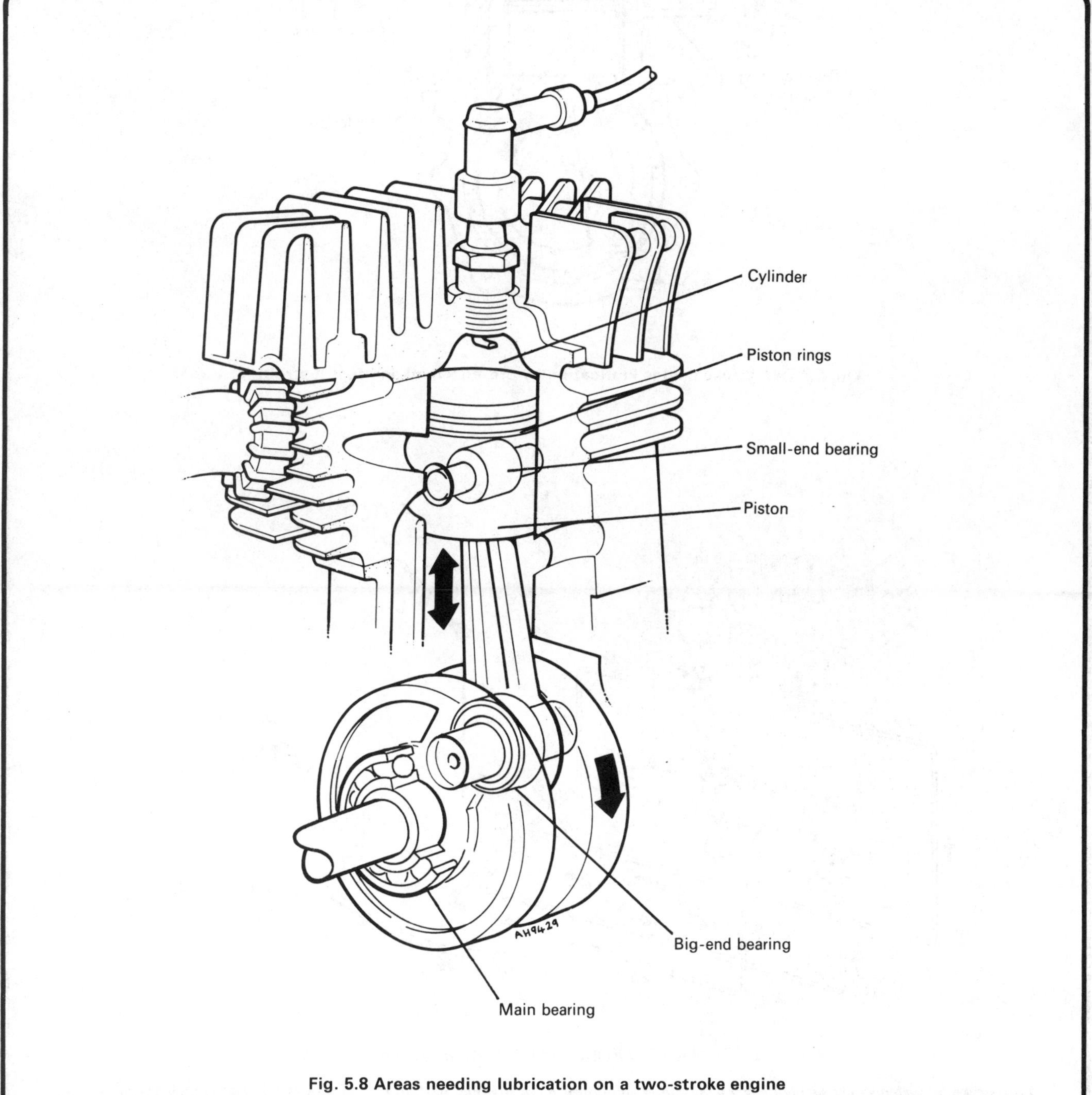


Fig. 5.8 Areas needing lubrication on a two-stroke engine

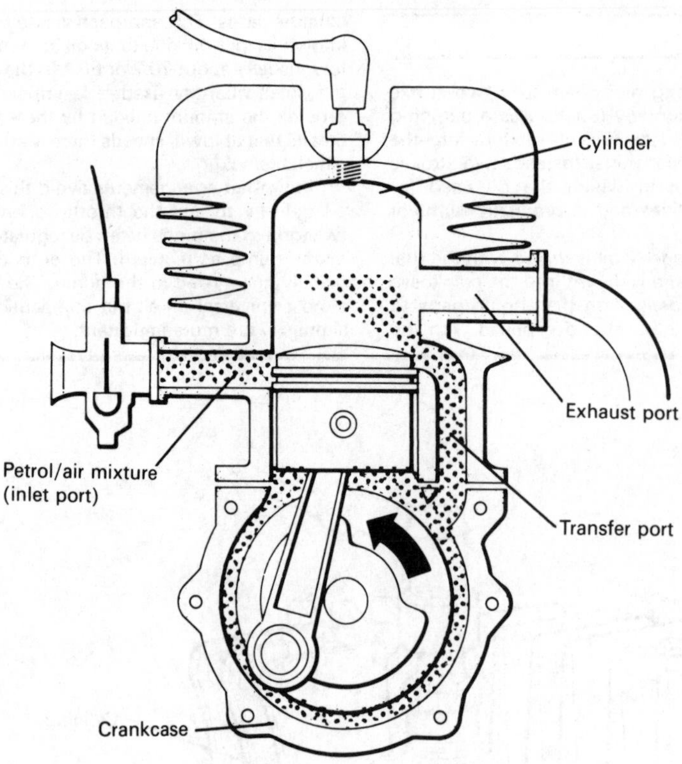


**Fig. 5.9 Two-stroke engine lubrication by pre-mixed oil and fuel (petroil)**

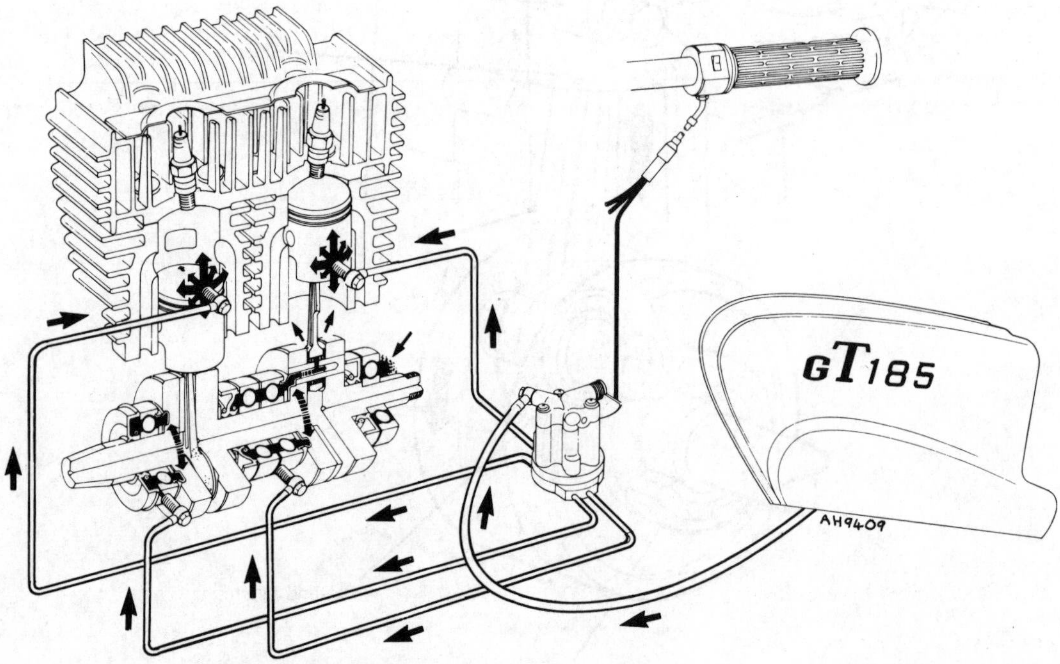


**Fig. 5.10 Pump-fed lubrication system**

*Two-stroke oil systems may simply deliver a measured amount of oil to the inlet port. In this version (Suzuki GT185) the cylinder walls and engine bearings are all lubricated directly.*

## 7 Air cooling

With the build-up of heat in certain areas of the engine comes the need to disperse this heat to prevent distortion and seizure of the components concerned. The simplest method is to increase the surface area of those parts so that the required amount of heat can be lost to the air, and this is done by incorporating cooling fins in particularly hot areas. If you look at any air-cooled engine you will notice immediately that the main area or heavy finning is, not surprisingly, the cylinder head and barrel. The crankcase area is not in immediate contact with the heat from combustion and so needs little or no finning. The exception to this generalisation is in the case of wet sump four-strokes, where finning is used to help cool the oil.

The principles of air cooling were established along with the first motorcycles, and little has changed in the intervening years. The designer must calculate the fin area to suit the rate at which heat must be dispersed, and this is why finning may vary from one engine to another. In the case of a road machine, for example, the cooling effect is aided by the machine's passage through the surrounding air. This is less true of a trials bike, because it is often working hard whilst moving only slowly. This is why many offroad engines have heavy finning. Another way to employ air cooling is to fit ducting over the finned areas and then cool them by blowing air from a fan through the duct, as in the case of a scooter, for example. Although power is lost in turning the fan, this method gears the rate of cooling to the engine speed, rather than the road speed, and thus is more closely geared to the engine's cooling requirements. To exercise even closer control we need to use a better cooling medium; water.

## 8 Water cooling

The main disadvantage of air cooling is the wide range of operating temperatures under which the engine must function. The problem of varying rates of expansion and contraction of the various engine components means that manufacturing tolerances have to be quite low, and the rate of heat production of a large or highly tuned engine can sometimes prove difficult for air cooling to cope with. Forced air cooling using an engine-driven fan goes some way towards improving the situation, but fan cooling a large engine leads to understandable extra bulk.

Water cooling resolves most of the problems associated with air cooling, at the expense of extra weight and complexity. The hot areas of the engine, the cylinder head and barrel, incorporate a water jacket or a system of passages. The water jacket is connected to a radiator by a pipe running from the top of the jacket to the top of the radiator. A second pipe runs from the bottom of the radiator to the bottom of the cooling jacket. The water in the jacket absorbs the heat from the engine and becomes less dense than the cooler water in the radiator. This heavier water runs in through the bottom hose, displacing the heated water upwards and into the radiator. The water loses heat as it passes down through the radiator until it eventually becomes quite cool as it nears the bottom. In this way the water automatically circulates, needing no mechanical assistance to do so. The arrangement is known as a thermosyphon cooling system. Where a greater rate of cooling is required, or where the water passages or radiator offer a great deal of resistance to the thermosyphoning water, it may be necessary to fit a water pump to assist the flow.

One immediate problem with water is that it tends to boil at temperatures regularly exceeded by the engine – an undesirable state of affairs since the resulting steam would not contribute to cooling the engine and might blow the cooling system apart. This can be avoided by running the system under pressure. As the pressure is increased, so is the boiling point of water, and in this way the boiling problem can be shifted past the normal temperature range of the engine. The radiator (or more often the coolant expansion tank) is closed by a pressure cap designed to withstand a pre-set pressure before venting any excess through a small pipe.

Many water cooling systems are controlled by a device called a thermostat. This is a temperature-sensitive valve which closes off circulation until the engine reaches the correct temperature. By doing this it allows the engine to warm up more rapidly, and so minimises the higher wear rates present when an engine is running below its correct temperature.

Other problems which beset a water-based cooling system are corrosion and freezing. If plain tap water were used, the impurities in it would speed up the rate of electrolytic action between the various metals in contact with the water. In other words, the system would act a little like a battery, with metal being eroded and deposited as the current flowed in the system. This can be avoided by using only distilled water, but in practice most manufacturers add inhibiting chemicals to prevent the problem altogether. Along with the inhibitors is usually added ethylene glycol to prevent the water freezing when the machine is parked in cold weather. If this antifreeze solution is omitted the expanding ice will usually destroy the fragile radiator and may warp or crack the cylinder head.

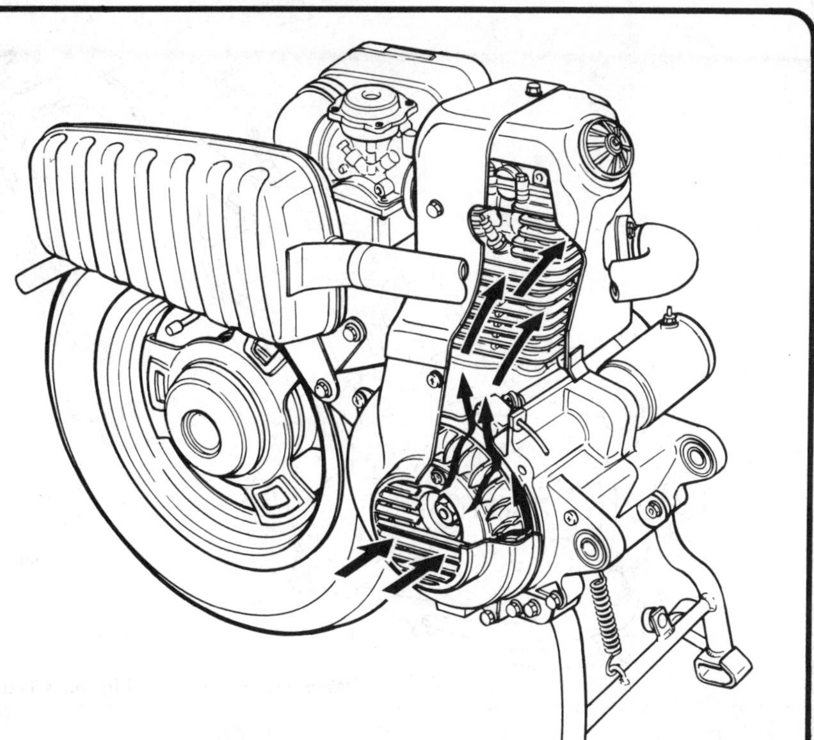

**Fig. 5.11 Forced air-cooling**

*Fan powered air cooling systems of this type are often found on scooter engines. The ducting directs the air past the relevant engine components.*

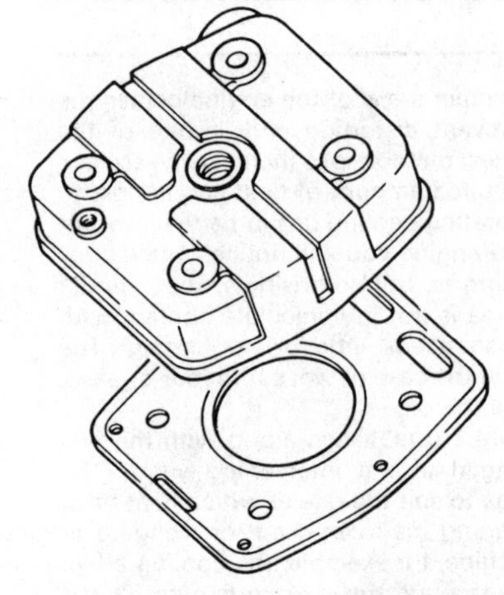

**Fig. 5.12 A water-cooled cylinder and head**

*Note the water passages cast into the cylinder and head. A drain plug is provided to permit the coolant to be drained prior to overhaul*

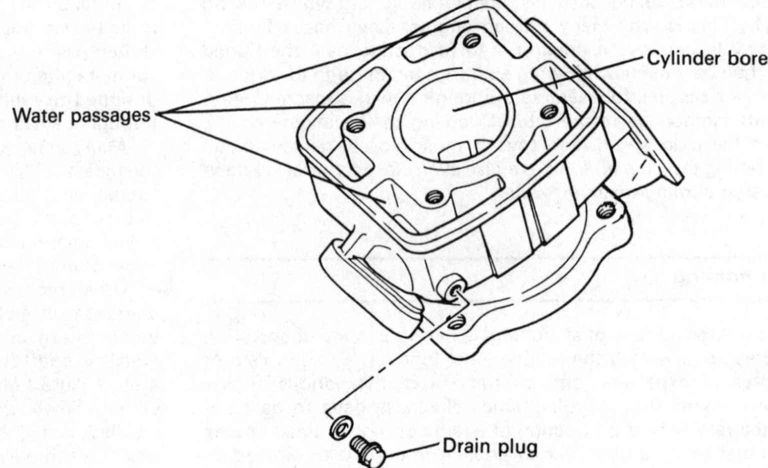


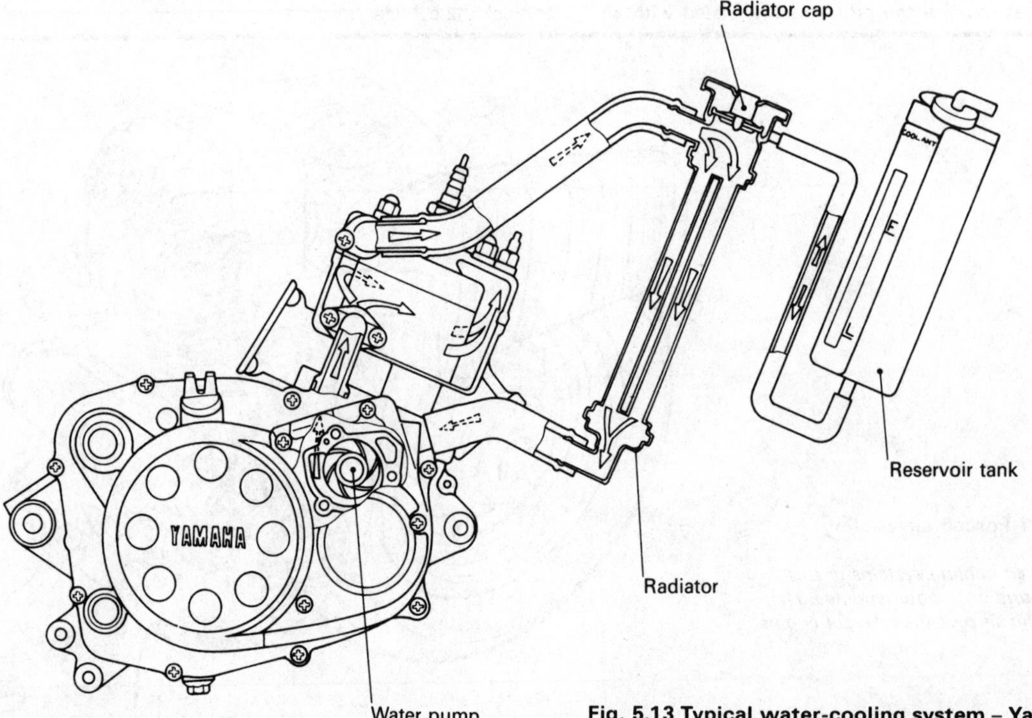


**Fig. 5.13 Typical water-cooling system – Yamaha RD125 LC**

# Chapter 6 Wheels, tyres and brakes

## Contents



## 1 Introduction

Irrespective of its construction, the job of the wheel is to support the tyre accurately and reliably despite the loads imposed on it by braking, acceleration and road surface irregularities. In addition, the wheel must be as light as possible – two contradictory requirements. Though little attention is paid to the wheel it has developed over the years to match the increasing demands placed on it by successively more powerful engines.

Tyres, too, appear commonplace at first glance. In truth they are far more complicated than you might think, and again have developed with the motorcycle into the sophisticated items we now take for granted. The tyre has to provide safe, reliable performance under a wide range of loads, speeds, temperatures and weather conditions. They are fundamental to the rider's safety, but have to be kept down to a reasonable price; for all of its technology, the tyre remains a disposable item.

The brakes must be able to disperse almost instantly the stored-up energy of a large, fast moving motorcycle and its rider. There may be enough energy there to demolish a sturdy wall, but we need to be able to bring it under control in a matter of seconds, and in a less destructive way. The brake has to convert the energy into heat and to radiate that heat very rapidly to achieve this feat – a fact which rarely crosses our mind when riding.

Taken together, the three areas discussed in this Chapter are perhaps the three most important safety-related items. Each is fulfilling a complex job in a most inconspicuous manner.

## 2 Spoked wheel construction

The spoked wheel, with which almost everyone is familiar in one way or another, is really quite a remarkable device. It has three main elements; the rim, the hub, and the spokes which connect the two. Spoked wheels have been used on every imaginable vehicle over their many years of popularity, and even using the most advanced materials it is difficult to find a method of constructing a wheel that is much better. Perhaps it is the very familiarity of the spoked wheel that makes us take it for granted, but if we stop to think about how it works it begins to seem a very strange device indeed.

The hub is simple enough. It is really just a tube through which the wheel spindle passes, carried on a pair of bearings so that it can turn easily. It also has two flanges which provide a method of locating the domed heads of the spokes. The rim, too, is fairly straightforward; just a shaped band of metal which carries the all-important tyre and provides the anchor point for the outer end of the spokes. It is the spokes themselves which are the most remarkable part of this type of wheel. If you look at a spoked wheel on a parked motorcycle it may occur to you to wonder how the spoke nearest the ground can support all that weight. After all, if you took a spoke and pushed the ends together it would bend and collapse quite easily, and this is true of a lot of spokes in a wheel. The point is that the spokes have little compression strength, but a great deal of tensile (pulling) strength. When you look at a motorcycle with spoked wheels it is literally hanging from the spokes uppermost in the wheel; the remaining spokes are only locating the hub in the centre of the rim and preventing the rim from bowing outwards under the weight of the machine.

Another consideration is the loading imposed under braking and acceleration; in each case the rim and hub are under pressure to twist in relation to one another, and so the spokes must be so arranged to cope with these forces. The spokes are fitted in a tangential pattern, rather than in a radial pattern to accomplish this, as shown in the accompanying illustration. If the wheel is viewed edge on, it can be seen that each alternate spoke runs from the rim to opposite sides of the hub. This results in a triangulated structure which will resist any tendency for the rim to move sideways in relation to the hub. On a motorcycle these thrust loadings are not very great because the machine banks through corners, so the forces tend to be felt as downward pressure on the centreline of the wheel. This is not the case where a sidecar is fitted, and many sidecar enthusiasts have their wheels rebuilt to provide greater strength in this direction.

The rim is made from chromium-plated steel or aluminium alloy and can be of a number of different sections. These are chosen to suit a particular application or tyre size. The spokes are secured at the rim by thin sleeve nuts called nipples. These thread onto the spoke end to allow the wheel to be trued initially and to permit subsequent tensioning. The ends of the spokes are ground off flush with the head of the nipple and then covered by a rim tape to prevent chafing of the inner tube. The necessity for a hole in the rim to take the nipple prevents tubeless tyres from being used on spoked wheels. At the root end of the spoke is a round head which is fitted into a countersunk hole in the hub flange. The spoke is often turned through 90° at this point, though on some wheels a straight spoke is chosen for additional strength. The hub itself may take the form of a straightforward spool type, or may be enlarged to incorporate the brake drum.

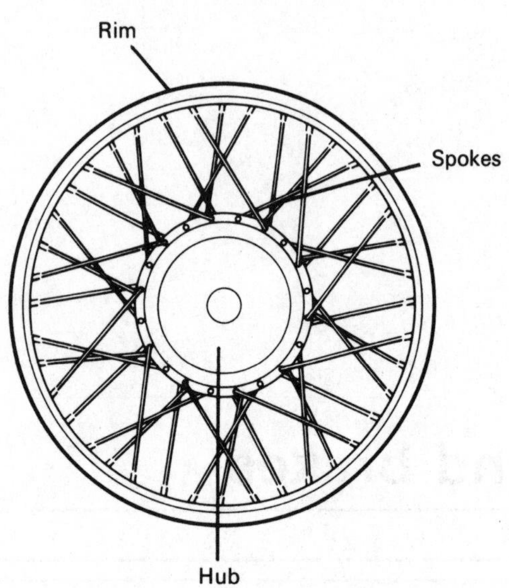


**Fig. 6.1 Wire spoked wheel construction**

*Note that the spokes are not arranged radially from the centre line of the hub; the angled arrangement is used to brace the wheel against the torque of the engine (rear wheel) and that of braking (both wheels).*

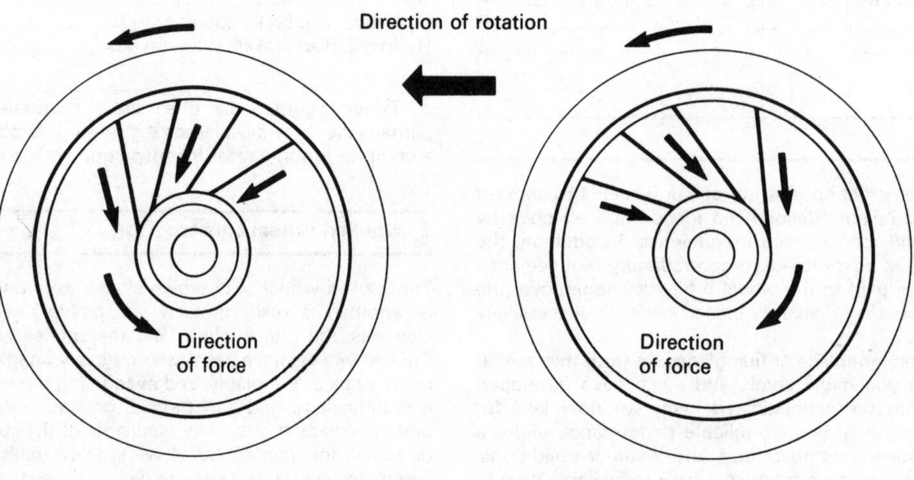


**Fig. 6.2 Spoke loadings in a wire wheel**

*These illustrations show a wheel with only one set of spokes in position. Note how the two sets of spokes are designed to absorb loadings in different directions*

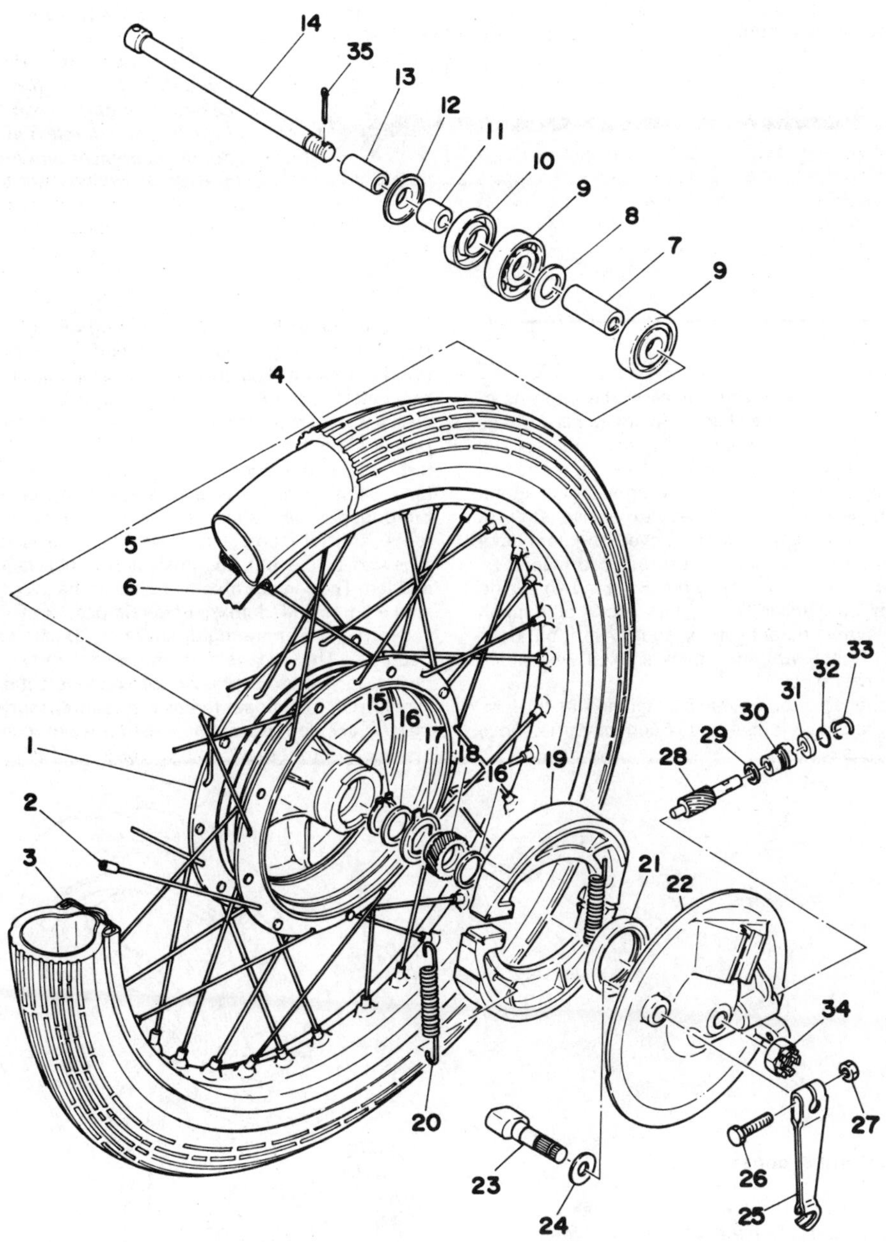


**Fig. 6.3 Construction of a typical spoked wheel**

*This sectioned view through a typical spoked wheel shows its construction, together with the tyre and tube and a drum type front brake. Rear wheels are of similar construction.*

*1 Hub*
*2 Spoke set*
*3 Wheel rim*
*4 Tyre*
*5 Inner tube*
*6 Rim tape*
*7 Bearing spacer*
*8 Washer*
*9 Wheel bearing*
*10 Seal*
*11 Distance piece*
*12 Cover*
*13 Sleeve*
*14 Wheel spindle*
*15 Circlip*
*16 Washer*
*17 Driving dog*
*18 Driving gear*
*19 Brake shoe*
*20 Spring*
*21 Oil seal*
*22 Brake plate*
*23 Fulcrum*
*24 Washer*
*25 Actuating lever*
*26 Pinch bolt*
*27 Nut*
*28 Driven gear*
*29 Washer*
*30 Body*
*31 Oil seal*
*32 O ring*
*33 Clip*
*34 Castellated nut*
*35 Split pin*

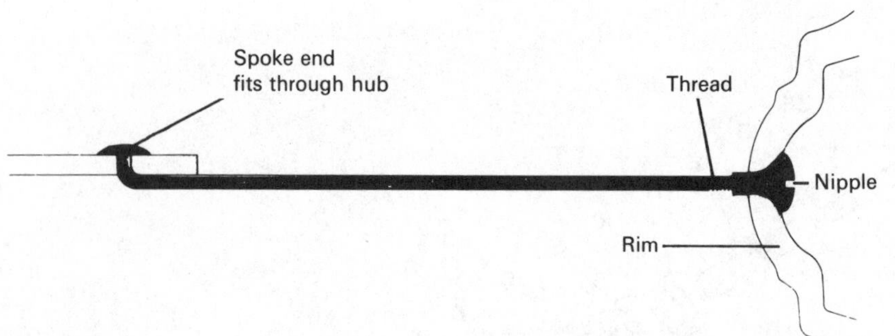


**Fig. 6.4 How spokes are fitted**

*The spoke has a domed head which fits through a hole at the hub end. The spoke passes through holes in the rim and is secured by a threaded nipple. This can be used to set up the rim alignment when the wheel is first built, and allows subsequent adjustment.*

## 3 Cast alloy wheel construction

Cast wheels first appeared on racing machines in the interests of weight saving and greater precision. They had an incidental advantage in that the width at the hub could be much less than a wire spoked type, and this simplified the fitting of disc brakes. The original racing wheels were made from magnesium alloy and were significantly lighter than an equivalent wire wheel. This material is very expensive and is of limited life, being prone to corrosion and cracking over long periods of use. To avoid sudden failure under prolonged use on road machines, the domesticated versions which soon followed the trend in racing developments have usually been made from a less exotic aluminium alloy. The resulting wheel is more durable and is equally stiff, but does not have the advantage of lighter weight – many spoked wheels are lighter than the equivalent cast type.

The wheel is cast in one piece and is then machined at the rim, spoke edges and hub, to produce a wheel that is perfectly true. Once finished, the wheel needs no trueing or adjustment, and maintenance is confined to ensuring that the surface finish of the wheel is kept in good condition. The absence of spoke nipples allows suitable wheels to be fitted with tubeless tyres, though it is important to note that some cast wheels are suited only to tubed types because of porosity or the profile of the tyre well.The use of a cast wheel is now almost universal, but despite the undeniable advantages, there are drawbacks. There have been instances of cracks appearing on the wheel as a result of prolonged impact stresses. This usually causes cracking at the spoke roots, and although a complete fracture is rare, the wheel must be renewed to prevent this possibility, since failure of this type is often sudden. The same problem applies in the event of an accident. Whilst a spoked rim will deform under impact and can be rebuilt, the cast version is far more rigid and may break or suffer invisible stress fractures. This means that the wheel must often be renewed as a precaution unless sophisticated crack detection facilities are available. Worse still, the impact forces may be transmitted to the forks or frame, making accident repairs an expensive proposition.

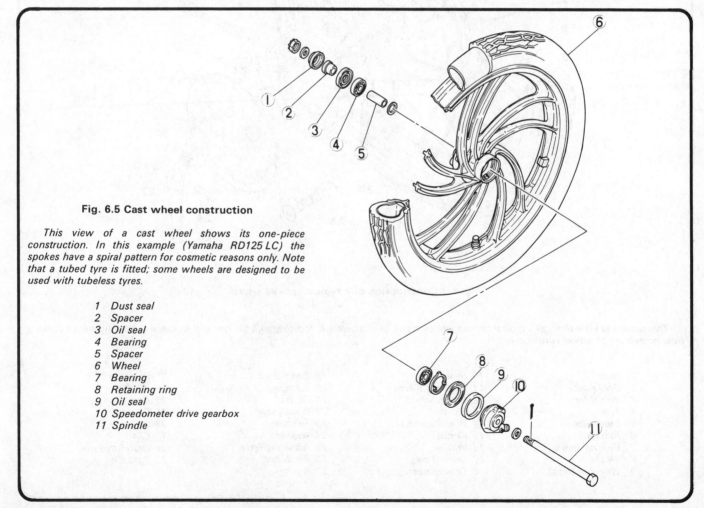

**Fig. 6.5 Cast wheel construction**

*This view of a cast wheel shows its one-piece construction. In this example (Yamaha RD125 LC) the spokes have a spiral pattern for cosmetic reasons only. Note that a tubed tyre is fitted; some wheels are designed to be used with tubeless tyres.*

*1 Dust seal*
*2 Spacer*
*3 Oil seal*
*4 Bearing*
*5 Spacer*
*6 Wheel*
*7 Bearing*
*8 Retaining ring*
*9 Oil seal*
*10 Speedometer drive gearbox*
*11 Spindle*

## 4 Composite wheel construction

The composite wheel is a hybrid between the wire spoked and cast alloy types, intended to combine the advantages of both. From the point of view of manufacturing, various rim profiles can be built onto a basic hub/spoke combination, and this reduces costs appreciably. The rim is an extruded alloy section, similar to the alloy rims used on wire spoked wheels, but without the spoke holes. This allows the use of tubeless tyres. A flange on the inner face of the rim provides an attachment point for the spokes. These are made from pressed steel or alloy, and can be riveted or bolted to the rim and hub. In use, the composite wheel is much the same as a cast wheel, but can be designed to deform in a controlled manner during a crash. This avoids transmitting the impact forces to the frame or suspension. The best known example of composite wheel construction is probably Honda's Comstar wheel. This, like a cast wheel, must be renewed if it becomes bent or buckled, though there are others, like the British-made Astralite, which can be rebuilt in the event of accident damage.

## 5 Split rim wheels

This type of wheel is uncommon in the motorcycle world, but can be found on some scooters and on most All Terrain Vehicles (ATVs). The wheel is formed from steel pressings and is in two halves. The rim halves bolt together at the centreline, and thus can be separated to permit easy tyre changes. This type of construction is ideal where a wheel of small diameter is needed because it avoids the problems of working the bead over the rim which would otherwise make tyre fitting a nightmare. In the case of scooter wheels an inner tube is fitted, but a tubeless tyre is fitted to some ATVs, requiring an O-ring seal to be fitted between the two rim halves.

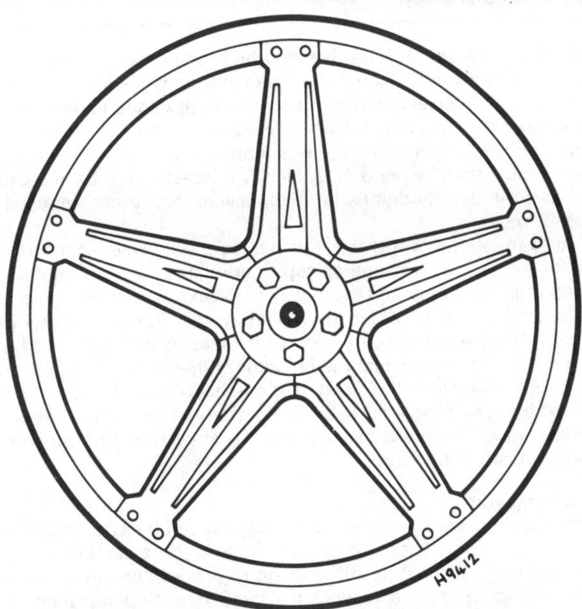


**Fig. 6.6 Composite wheel construction**

*Composite construction allows various rim sizes and profiles to be built onto a common hub unit. The pressed steel or aluminium spokes are attached by bolts or rivets at the hub and rim.*

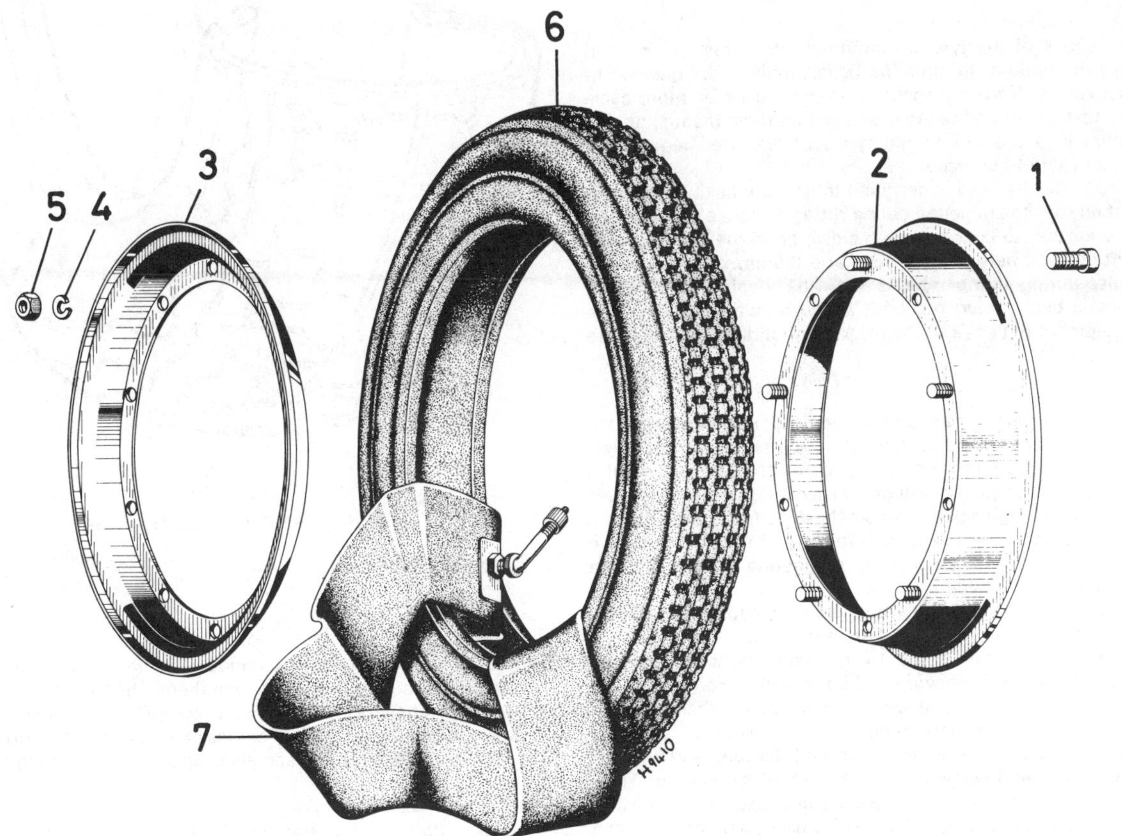


**Fig. 6.7 Split rim wheel construction**

*1 Bolt*
*2 Rim half*
*3 Rim half*
*4 Spring washer*
*5 Nut*
*6 Tyre*
*7 Inner tube*

## 6 Tyre construction

Tyres are one of those subjects which could easily take up the remainder of this book. Though a consumable item like oil and fuel, the tyre is a very complicated device. Every tyre built is labour, material and technology intensive, a factor which is reflected in its price. Amongst all road vehicles the motorcycle asks more of its tyres than any other. Not only must the tyre perform faultlessly if disaster is to be avoided, it must do so under conditions far more severe than those imposed by cars and trucks.

The foundations of a tyre are its casing plies; layers of rubberised synthetic fibre cords laid one on top of another at varying angles and bonded together in the finished tyre. The casing plies are covered by a layer of soft rubber to which the tread layer is bonded. At the inner edges of the tyre is the bead, a carefully shaped and reinforced area which holds the tyre against the rim edge. Where the tyre is designed for tubeless operation the bead is more heavily reinforced and the inside of the tyre is covered with an airtight layer of rubber, known as an airseal liner. To understand the function of each part of the tyre, let us look at each one in turn.

### The casing plies

The casing plies are what controls the shape of the tyre, both at low speeds and at high speed where the centrifugal forces are trying to distort it. The plies must be stiff enough to prevent the adverse effects of this distortion, and to prevent the tread from rippling under hard acceleration and braking. In contrast to the above, the plies must allow the tyre to flex in a controlled manner to absorb surface irregularities and thus keep the tread in constant contact with the road, and this is achieved by the alternate diagonal layers of plies. Many motorcycle tyres have four plies, and this is denoted on the tyre sidewall as 4PR, or four ply rating. Where a stiffer carcase is needed, the tyre may use six plies.

### The beads

The inner edges of the tyre are moulded into a reinforced bead which locates the tyre on the rim. The bead profile is designed to fit correctly on a variety of the rim sections normally used on motorcycle wheels, and most tyres can therefore be used on most manufacturer's rims. Occasionally a specialised rim type will be used requiring a particular type of tyre to be used.

With tubed tyres, the bead is designed to be fairly flexible so that it can be stretched over the rim edge during fitting. Where a tubeless tyre is fitted, its beads are stiffer and a much closer fit on the rim. This is to ensure an airtight seal between the bead and the rim, and may cause some difficulty during fitting. This is why the repair and fitting of tubeless types is best carried out by a specialist who will have the necessary equipment to carry out the work without damage to the tyre or rim.

### The tread

The tread is the visible part of the tyre and is composed of a synthetic rubber compound chosen for its grip and wear properties. The compound must be chosen carefully to suit the application of a particular tyre; a soft compound will give excellent grip, but may wear away very rapidly at high speeds where heat builds up in the tyre carcass. A harder compound will reduce the rate of wear, but the grip will be reduced. It will be seen that the compound used must be a compromise between the two.

Under ideal riding conditions it would be advantageous to have a tyre with a completely smooth tread to ensure that the maximum amount of rubber was in contact with the road surface, and this is why in racing 'slicks' are used whenever conditions permit. For road use, it is essential that the tyre can cope with all types of weather and road surface conditions. If a slick were to be used on a wet road, a film of water would be trapped between the tread and the road surface, and the tyre would slip on this film. The network of grooves or sipes moulded into the tread allows the surface water to escape to the sides of the tyre, and the slight flexing of the tread is used to pump the water film clear. It will be appreciated that the tyre's ability to cope with water will be reduced as the tread wears down, and this is why most manufacturers recommend that a tyre should be renewed when worn down to about 2mm, rather than the UK legal minimum of 1mm.

In the case of off-road machines, a different tread pattern is used to cope with the muddy or dusty surfaces. The heavy block tread of the motocross knobbly is designed to bite into a loose surface which would clog a road tyre in seconds. The tread blocks are shaped to throw off any mud trapped between them. The trials type tyres used on both trials and trail bikes are a compromise between road and motocross treads; the blocks are less heavy (and thus do not destroy the surface so readily) and can also cope with road use to some extent.

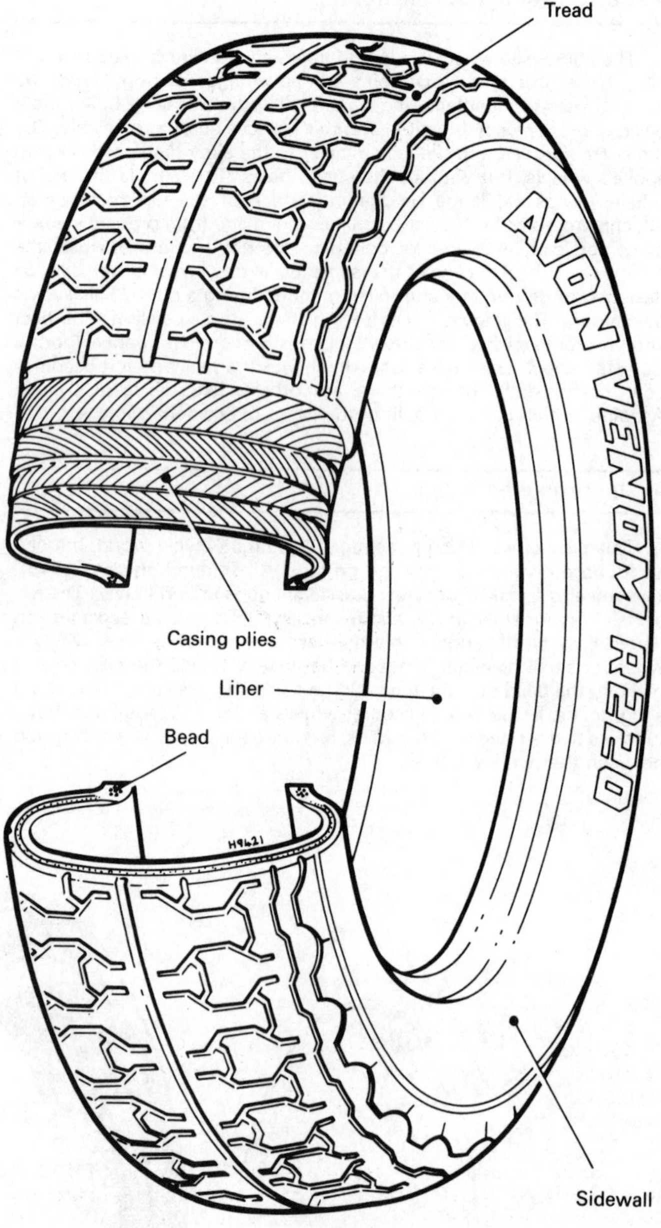


Fig. 6.8 Tyre construction

### Tubed and tubeless tyres

The motorcycle has traditionally used tubed tyres for the simple reason that this is the only type that can be fitted on a wire spoked rim due to the holes for the spoke nipples. The tube is simple a thin rubber bag with a one-way valve which allows the tyre to be inflated with air to the specified pressure. Tubes have a number of disadvantages. If punctured, the tube will tear quite readily, and this can result in a sudden deflation or blowout. It is also possible for some degree of movement between the tyre and rim under acceleration or braking.

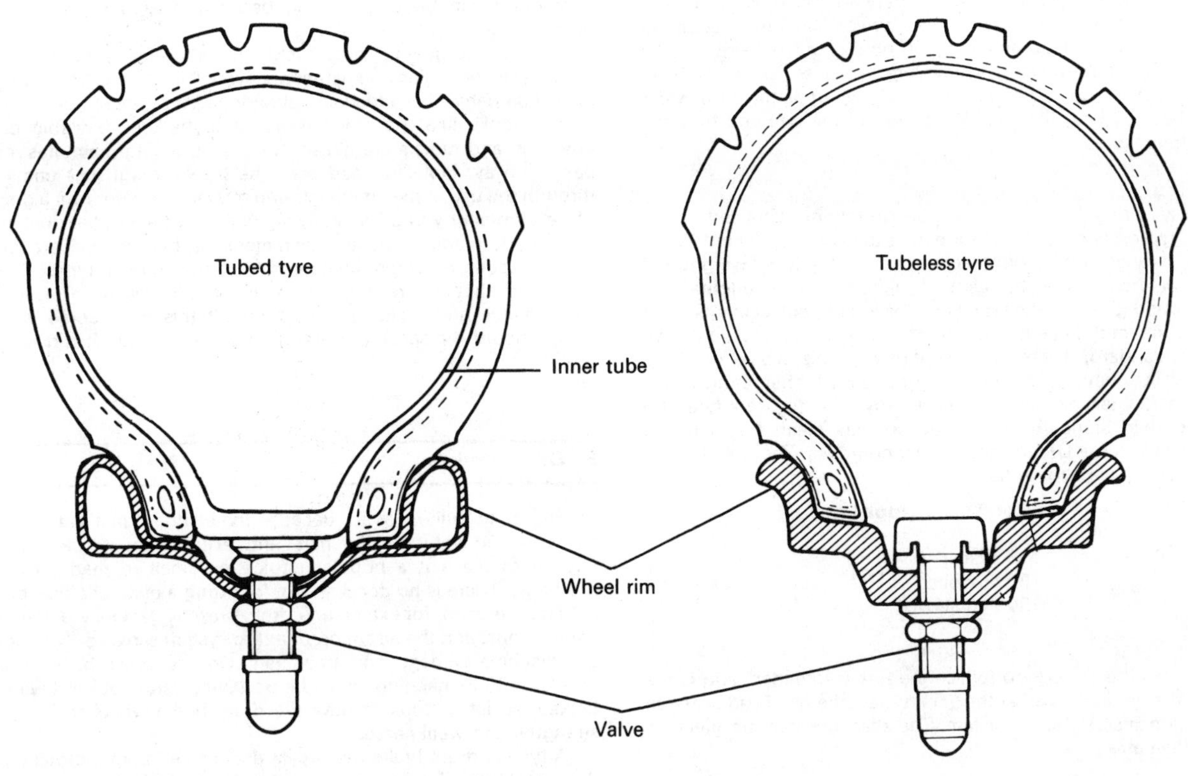


**Fig. 6.9 Tubeless and tubed tyres**

*In the case of a tubeless tyre, the seal is formed between the wheel rim and the tyre bead, the air valve being fitted into the rim. With tubed tyres the valve is attached to the tube; the seal between the tyre and rim is not so important, and the rim need not be airtight.*

This can drag the tube round the rim, tearing out the valve. The other drawback is the tubed tyre's tendency for heat build-up especially when used at constant high speeds. This affects the rate of wear of the tyre and also indirectly requires a slightly harder compound to be used to combat this problem.

With the appearance of the cast and composite wheel, the opportunity was taken to adopt the tubeless tyre. Instead of an inner tube, the inside of the tyre is coated with a thin airseal liner, and a seal is made between the rim and the tyre bead. The air valve is fitted into the rim. The tubeless tyre reduces or avoids most of the problems outlined above, and as a general rule is safer in use. The only real drawback is that it can be hard to fit or remove without the correct equipment, and roadside repairs are almost impossible in the UK. This is because UK laws require a tubeless tyre to be repaired off the wheel using a headed plug, rather than the straight plug which can be fitted from the outside. Given the inability of a motorcycle to carry a spare wheel, this can make punctures a very inconvenient incident.

## 7 Tyre types and markings

The sidewall of most motorcycle tyres contains a wealth of information concerning its construction, dimensions and its intended application. The size marking is of obvious importance, and thus a good place to start. For many years the section (width) and the diameter of the tyre have been given in inch sizes, though this is now gradually being changed to metric sizes. At present the two equivalents are being produced concurrently and this is likely to continue for some years yet. A typical sidewall marking might look like one of the following:

4.10H 18
or 100/90H 18

The two tyre sizes shown above are roughly equivalent, the first being an Imperial (inch) size and the second the metric equivalent. In the case of the Imperial tyre, the markings can be read as follows. The '4.10' denotes the tyre's section, or width in inches. The 'H' gives the speed rating, and this is described in more detail below. The '18' indicates the diameter of the wheel rim in inches. In the case of the metric version, '100' denotes the section in millimetres. The second figure, '90' expresses the aspect ratio of the tyre – the height of the tyre from bead to tread centre as a percentage of its width. In this example, given the 100 mm width, the height is therefore 90 mm. As with the first example, the speed rating is shown by the 'H' and finally we have the rim diameter, oddly enough still given in inches. Let us look in greater detail at some of the above terms.

### Aspect ratio

This marking follows the rim size marking and is separated from it by an oblique stroke; /. Where the tyre height is the same as its width, it has a 100% aspect ratio. This is considered as being a standard figure, and so is not included on the sidewall. Where the tyre has an aspect ratio of less than 100% it is termed a low profile type, and the aspect ratio is usually shown on the tyre wall. There are a few exceptions to this rule however. The low profile tyres which are now becoming popular allow a wider tread area without increasing the height of the tyre sidewall. This in turn means a stiffer tyre, with less risk of instability at higher speeds. In some applications it allows updating to a wider section without altering the overall diameter of the tyre and thus the gearing of the machine.

### Speed rating

The speed rating letter indicates the maximum sustained speed possible on the class of machine for which the tyre is intended. More importantly, it takes into account factors such as the likely weight and handling characteristics of that class of machine, so the original tyre fitment is a good guide to the rating of subsequent replacements. As a general rule, the rating, like the section and aspect ratio, should not be varied from standard. There are exceptions to this where one tyre manufacturer may have found a fitment of slightly higher rating works better on a particular machine. It is never advisable to use a tyre of a lower rating than standard, and to do so may mean that you are breaking the law in the UK and some other countries. The speed rating letters and speeds are shown below:

| Speed rating | Max. speed (mph) |
|---|---|
| R (reinforced) | 95 |
| S | 113 sustained |
| H | 130 sustained |
| V | 130 and above |

### Diameter

This denotes the rim size for which the tyre is intended, and is the diameter of the rim measured at the point where the tyre bead seats on the flat section inside the raised rim. The diameter may be given in inches or millimetres.

### Other markings

The sidewall may carry further sets of letters and numbers, and also direction arrows. The latter are used to indicate the correct direction of rotation for a particular tyre. For example, the plies in a front tyre may be arranged to give it particular strength under braking. If the tyre is reversed on the rim, this extra reinforcement will not be used to advantage and the tyre may wear very quickly. Where a tyre is suited to front or rear fitment, it needs to be braced against acceleration when on a rear wheel and braking if fitted at the front, so two opposing arrows may be found, marked FRONT and REAR.

A maximum pressure figure may be found, and this indicates only the maximum safe pressure that the tyre is capable of withstanding. It is NOT an operating pressure, which will be much lower. Finally, all recent tyres are marked either TUBED TYPE or TUBELESS, for reasons which should be self-evident. It follows that a tubed type tyre is not suitable for use without an inner tube, even on a tubeless rim. Equally, a tubeless tyre can only be used on a non-tubeless rim if an inner tube is fitted.

## 8 Radial ply tyres

Until very recently, all motorcycle tyres have been of crossply construction. This refers to the way alternate layers of plies have been laid in an 'X' pattern to provide stiffness in the sidewall. It goes without saying that to have the sidewall deforming along the machine's centreline would be very unpleasant – the bike would squirm from side to side in much the same way as it does on a deflated tyre. It would be impossible to control properly, and this is why crossply construction has always been necessary on two-wheeled vehicles.

In the case of twin-track vehicles like cars the situation is different; given the in-built stability of the car, and the fact that the wheels do not bank significantly, it is positively advantageous to have a very flexible sidewall. Not only does this allow the tread to conform easily to ripples in the road surface, it means that under heavy cornering forces, the tread is able to remain flat on the road without being pulled up by a stiff and unyielding sidewall. An incidental but very useful advantage is that the thinner and lighter construction does not generate or retain as much heat as an equivalent crossply, and thus its operating temperature range is narrower. This in turn means that a softer compound can be used, giving better grip without suffering from overheating.

Despite the obvious drawbacks the radial has much to offer as a motorcycle tyre. Early experiments were far from encouraging, and many companies have tried and abandoned the concept over the years. It now looks like the radial is about to become a viable product, however, and radials are already in use on racing machines, and are becoming available for road use. The breakthrough has come about through the use of new materials and techniques, and from a great deal of development work. The early signs are that the radial does provide better performance and wear characteristics, but the tyres are currently rather expensive when compared to conventional types. It seems inevitable that future improvements should result in even better performance and/or lower prices, and if this does come about the radial should replace the crossply in the same way it did in the car world.

## 9 Drum brakes

The drum brake was for decades the standard method of bringing any wheeled vehicle to a halt, and even today its simplicity and cheapness make it a popular choice on small to medium capacity machines. There is no good reason for fitting a hydraulic disc brake on a 30 mph moped, for example. A drum brake is generally better in such applications, and the adoption of a disc system serves only to enhance the machine's image and price tag. On the other hand, a typical 1000cc/600 lb machine would be positively dangerous if it were drum braked, so let us look at how the drum brake works to discover its strengths and weaknesses.

A typical drum brake has a cylindrical steel drum, normally part of the wheel hub. The drum is covered by the brake backplate on which is mounted the brake shoes and operating cam(s). At rest, the friction material of the shoes is held slightly clear of the drum. When the brake lever is operated, the cam(s) force the shoes outwards against the drum surface, slowing the wheel and thus the machine. In its simplest form the brake has a single cam, the other end of the shoes being located on pivot pins. This means that the moving end of one shoe 'bites' harder against the drum, aided by the drag from the drum surface creating a self-acting or self-servo effect. In other words, the energy of the rotating drum is used to improve braking effort. This effect applies to what is known as the leading shoe. By contrast, the corresponding end of the remaining shoe tends to be forced away from the drum, and is known as the trailing shoe. The above arrangement, utilising one leading and one trailing shoe, is generally known as a single leading shoe brake, or sls for short.

To obtain extra braking effort without increasing the overall size of the drum, each shoe can have its own cam at the leading end, and its own pivot at the trailing end. The two cams are operated via an adjustable linkage by one cable, and the arrangement is known as a twin leading shoe, or tls, brake. To extract yet more effort from the brake, it can be made double sided, with a tls brake fitted on each side of the wheel. This arrangement is by no means common, but was used primarily in racing applications before the introduction of the disc brake.

The sls and tls drum brakes described above work very well in the right applications, and in some respects are preferable to a disc arrangement. The system is simple, and requires no complicated hydraulic operation to be effective. Drum brakes tend to offer more 'feel', allowing the brake to be controlled easily and accurately. This is particularly desirable on the lightweight machines to which drum brakes are most often fitted. The real problem of the drum brake is heat. The bigger and more powerful the brake, the more heat is generated during braking. If this builds up in the linings it will eventually reduce the braking effort as the friction material becomes glazed over, a condition known as fade. The heat can be dispersed better if the drum is ventilated, and many tls brakes employed air scoops to direct air past the shoes and thus cool them. Unfortunately, the air scoop also worked well as a rain scoop, and the water itself reduced efficiency. The timely introduction of disc brakes led to their rapid adoption on larger capacity models, whilst the smaller and less powerful machines have retained the drum type.

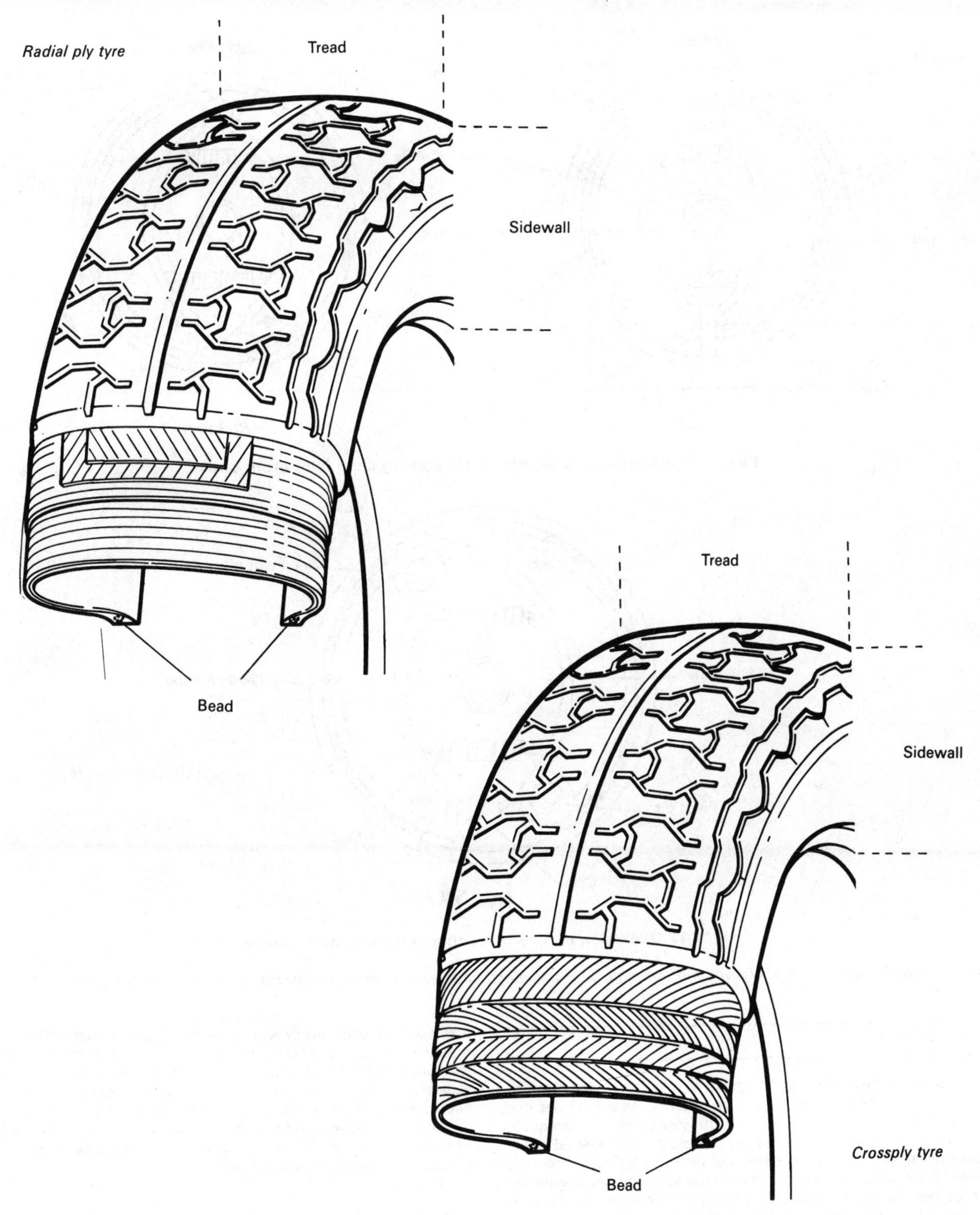


**Fig. 6.10 Comparison of crossply and radial ply tyres**

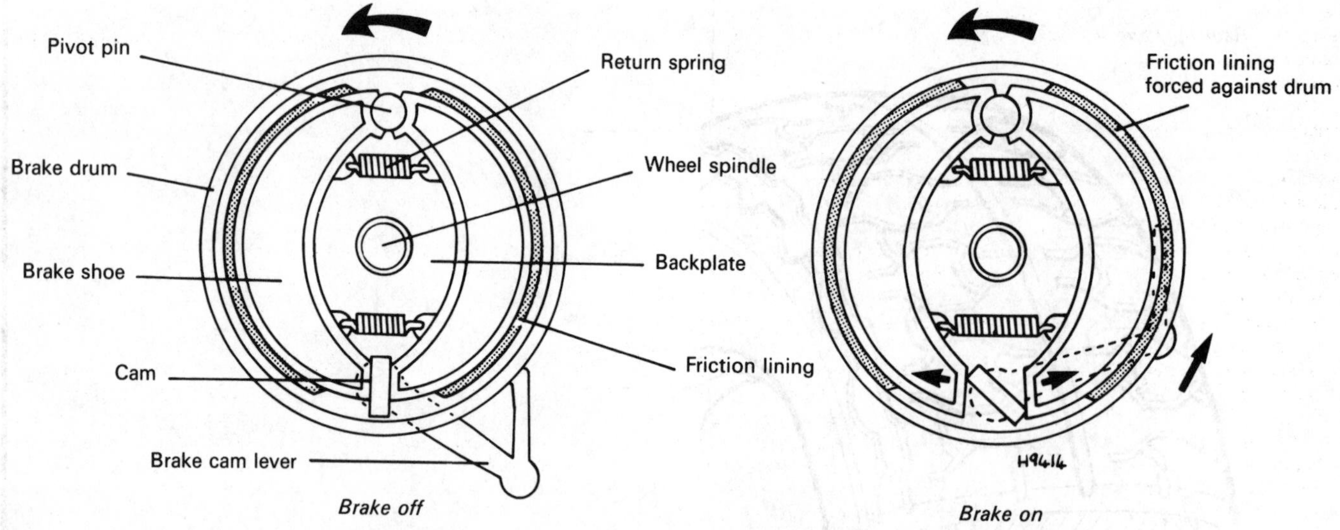


Fig. 6.11 Operation of a simple single leading shoe (sls) drum brake

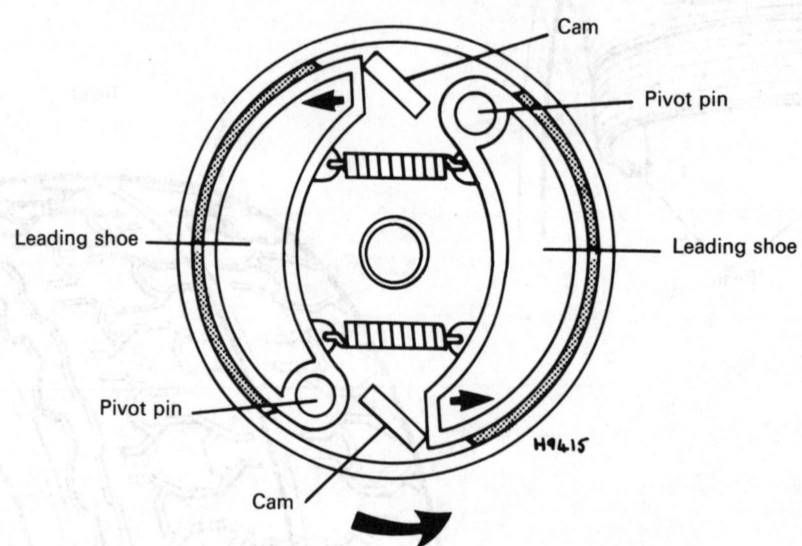


Fig. 6.12 Operation of a twin leading shoe (tls) drum brake

*Note that each shoe has its own pivot and operating cam, allowing much greater braking effect than is possible with a single leading shoe unit.*

## 10 Disc brakes

The disc brake first appeared on aircraft in response to the problem of coping with the heat generated in a drum brake. As aircraft became heavier and faster the drum brake soon proved woefully inadequate when attempting to stop it. The idea was simple enough: Get rid of the enclosed drum, and fit instead a flat cast iron or steel disc. The disc turned with the wheel, whilst attached to the adjacent suspension leg was a caliper. Its action depended upon two hydraulically-operated pistons which in turn moved two friction pads in response to the brake control. When operated, the caliper clamped the pads hard against the sides of the disc. The brake, being open to the air, was able to disperse heat much more readily than a drum, and so the fade problem was much reduced. Using hydraulic operation, great pressure could be exerted, and thus a small, light, fade-free and very powerful brake could be produced.

Before long, the same set of problems beset the racing world, and it was perfectly logical to adopt the same solutions as the aircraft and car world were now using to good effect. It was now a matter of time before the disc brake found its way onto a road machine, and, after the first few accessory disc brakes appeared for use on existing models, the first mass produced production version appeared in 1969 on Honda's revolutionary CB750. Since then the disc system has been used almost exclusively on all medium to large displacement machines, and as has been mentioned, has made cosmetic appearances on mopeds. The systems used have developed somewhat, though the basic principle remains unchanged. In the next Section we will look in detail at the various aspects of the disc system.

## 11 Hydraulic disc brake operation

With few exceptions, disc brakes are operated hydraulically, rather than mechanically. This method is chosen because it is a convenient way to apply relatively low lever pressure over a broad spread of movement to the high pressure/low movement action required at the caliper. All hydraulic systems make use of the fact that, unlike gases, liquids are not compressible. The particular liquid most suited to hydraulic use is a specially formulated mineral oil. This has very carefully designed properties to resist boiling, and should never be replaced with another type of oil. One disadvantage of hydraulic fluid is that it is hygroscopic. This means that it will absorb moisture from the surrounding air, and as it does so its resistance to boiling is decreased. This is the main reason that the fluid must be changed regularly, though it also flushes the system to remove any dirt which might otherwise cause wear.

The master cylinder consists of a cylinder and piston assembly, usually incorporating a fluid reservoir. When the brake lever or pedal is operated, the piston is pushed along the cylinder, displacing fluid from its outlet and along a hydraulic pipe. When the lever is released the fluid and piston can move back to their original positions. The reservoir is connected to the cylinder via a port which is open when the piston is at rest. This allows the system to be constantly topped up. When the piston begins to move, the port is covered, preventing pressure in the system from forcing fluid back into the reservoir.

The master cylinder and caliper(s) are connected by rigid metal pipes and specially reinforced hydraulic hoses which allow unrestricted suspension movement. At the lower end of the hydraulic line is the caliper, consisting of one or two pistons and cylinders, depending on the type used. Unlike the master cylinder, the piston is of large diameter, and it is this difference in size which makes use of the hydraulic effect. When the master cylinder piston moves, say 10 mm along its bore, a certain volume of fluid is forced along the hydraulic pipes to the caliper. Here it must displace the caliper piston, but because this is of much greater diameter it need only move perhaps 1 mm to accommodate the fluid. In this way the pressure exerted over the normal lever movement is concentrated into a small range of movement at very high pressure at the caliper. Inevitably, heat is generated during braking, but the surface of the disc is open to the airstream and can thus lose the heat much more readily than an enclosed drum. The pads prevent the heat from being transferred back to the hydraulic fluid by virtue of the insulating properties of the friction material. This, incidentally, is why pads must always be renewed well before the friction material is worn away; if this is not done, the heat can get to the caliper and may cause the fluid to boil. The resulting air bubbles, being easily compressed, make the brake spongy and ineffective.

Both the master cylinder and caliper pistons are sealed by specially designed synthetic rubber seals which act rather like the piston rings in an engine, preventing pressure and fluid loss from the system and the ingress of air. The caliper seal is specially shaped so that it twists slightly as the piston moves. This is sufficient to pull the piston back into the caliper when the brake is released, returning fluid back up the pipe to the master cylinder. This means that the range of movement at the pads is very small; just sufficient to ensure that the pads are clear of the disc when the lever is at rest. As the friction material of the pads wears away, the caliper piston needs to move further to bring them into contact with the disc surface. The piston distorts the seal as before, but beyond a certain point it moves through the seal and into a new position. In this way the system is self-adjusting, and can compensate automatically for pad wear.

Disc brakes are almost universal on larger capacity models, giving good braking performance without the attendant problems of cooling which beset large drum units. It is common to fit a twin disc arrangement on the front wheel. This allows very powerful braking and also distributes the braking force evenly on both sides of the wheel. Rear disc brakes are also used, though the need is not so great here. This is because of the effects of weight transfer during braking. It is common for 75% of the machine's weight to be concentrated on the front wheel during braking, and this in turn means that most of the available tyre traction is also at the front. In these circumstances it is a disadvantage to have excessive braking power at the rear wheel, so a rear disc unit will be comparatively weak. It can be argued that the superior fine control and 'feel' offered by a drum unit makes it a better choice, and many manufacturers retain a rear drum for this reason.

In the past, disc brakes on some motorcycles were notorious for poor wet weather performance. This is due to the water film which builds up on the disc and must be swept clear before braking can commence. The problem can be worsened by a poor pad material, and by the use of stainless steel or chrome-plated discs. The grainy structure of cast iron makes this an ideal disc material, but it has the disadvantages of poor cosmetic appearance after the surface has rusted a little. Drilled discs help to improve the rate at which water is removed, but by far the most effective innovation has been the introduction of sintered metal pads. These have a limited quantity of metal particles embedded in them, and as a result tend to wear unevenly. The rippled surface allows the high spots to bite through the water film much more quickly than conventional pads.

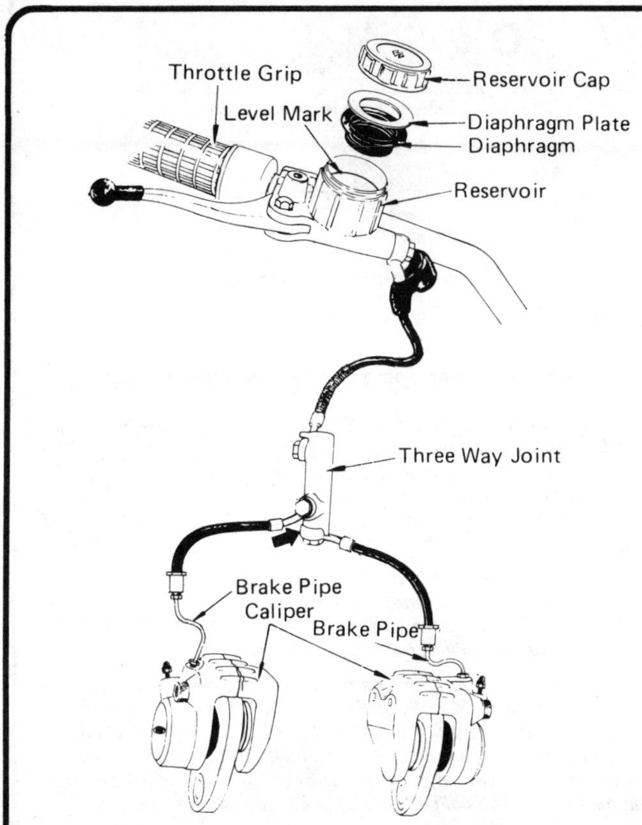


**Fig. 6.13 Typical twin hydraulic disc brake system**

*The master cylinder is connected to the two calipers by flexible hydraulic hoses and steel brake pipes. The flexible hoses allow the necessary movement during steering and suspension movements.*

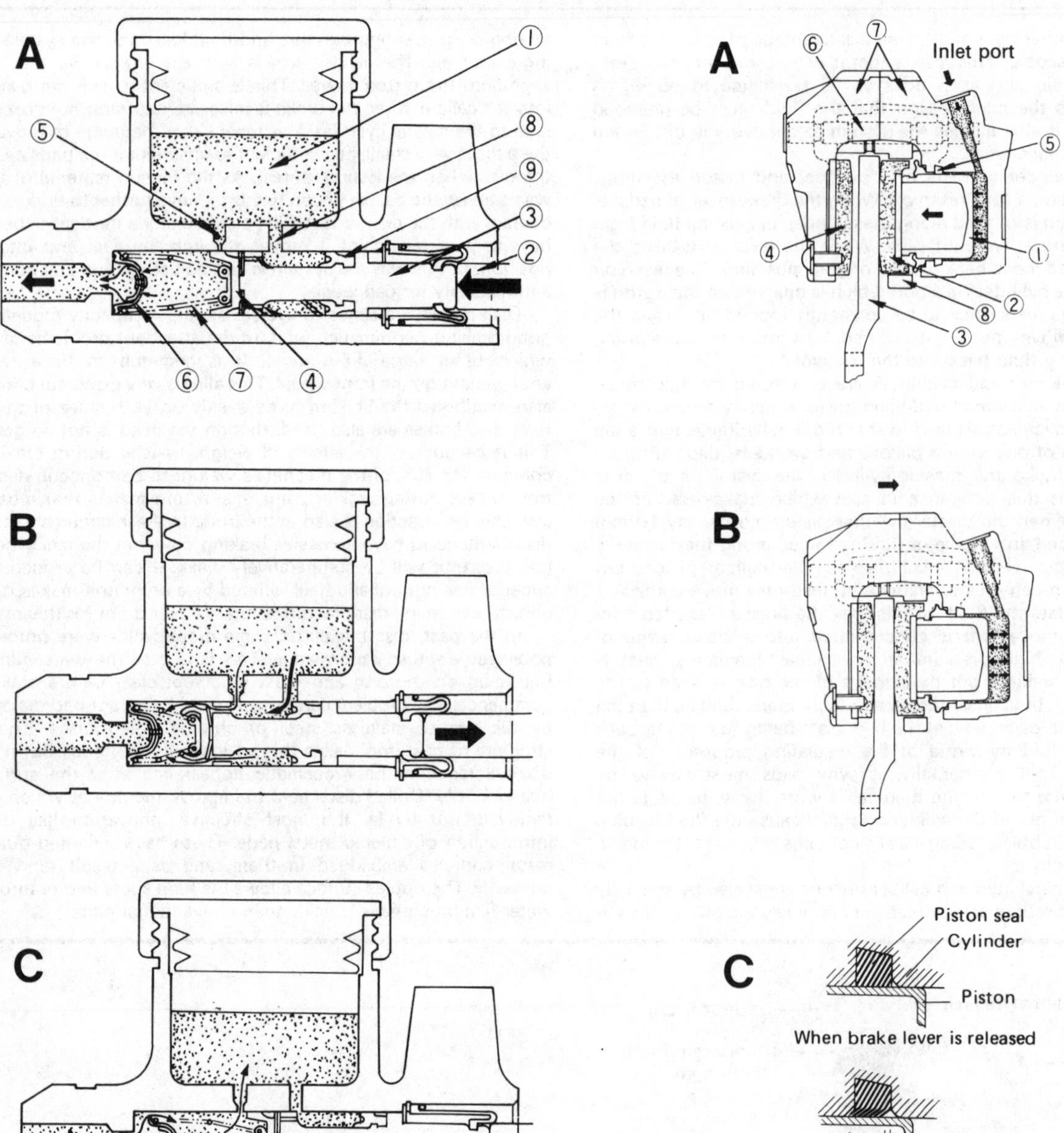


**Fig. 6.14 Master cylinder operation**

**A** *Applying the brake. The end of the brake lever (2) pushes the master cylinder piston (3) along its bore. Once the return port (5) has been passed by the primary cup (4) fluid is forced past the check valve (6) and along the brake hose to the caliper.*

**B** *Releasing the brake. Once lever pressure is released the spring (7) pushes the piston assembly back up the bore. Until the pressure in the brake line is significantly higher than that of the master cylinder body, the check valve remains closed and fluid is drawn past the primary cup via small bleed holes in the piston. Once the check valve opens, fluid flows back from the caliper until pressure is equalised.*

**C** *Completion of return stroke. With the piston at rest, fluid continues to flow past the check valve and back to the reservoir. When the check valve is closed by the pressure of the return spring, the fluid continues to flow via a small notch in the end of the body until the pressure in the system is equalised.*

**Fig. 6.15 Caliper operation (single piston type)**

**A** *Brake applied. Fluid from the master cylinder enters through the inlet port and begins to push the piston (1) along its bore. The piston continues to move until the pad surface (2) contact the disc (3). To obtain equal pressure on both sides of the disc, the caliper body (7) is able to slide along the caliper axle (6) until the fixed pad contacts the far side of the disc.*

**B** *Brake released. When the brake lever is released the piston seal (5) which distorts under braking will return to its original position. The amount of movement is very small, but is enough to move the pads just clear of the disc surface.*

**C** *Piston seal operation. As mentioned above, the piston seal is designed to distort slightly as the brake is applied. This allows the seal to be used to return the piston when the lever is released. As the pads wear, the piston is pushed through the seal to compensate, but will always be returned by a standard amount. This means that the caliper automatically adjusts for pad wear.*

## 12 Hydraulic disc brakes: caliper types

### Opposed piston calipers

In an opposed piston caliper, the caliper body is bolted rigidly to the fork leg (or swinging arm if used as a rear brake). These are two opposing cylinders and pistons, each with its own pad. The two cylinders are connected by an internal passage, so hydraulic pressure is equal in both. This means that when the brake is operated, both pistons move towards the disc, clamping the pads against each side of it. This was the original caliper design and is still widely used by European manufacturers, notably Lockheed and Brembo.

### Single piston, or floating calipers

The single piston caliper is widely used on Japanese machines and approaches the problem of exerting equal pressure on both sides of the disc mechanically, rather than hydraulically. The caliper body is mounted on a bracket via a pivot or sliding pins which allow it limited sideways movement. The body houses only one piston, the remaining pad being fixed on the opposite side. When the brake is operated, the piston pushes the pad against the disc surface. With continued pressure, the caliper body swings or slides until the fixed pad is pressed against the opposite side of the disc.

The single piston design eliminates problems sometimes found with twin-piston units, where corrosion jams one piston. This leads to unequal pressure being exerted on the two pads, and thus handicaps braking efficiency. The drawback with the single piston type is corrosion or wear in the pivot or sliding pins. This too can cause unequal braking effort and can also allow chattering between the bracket and caliper.

### Other caliper arrangements

The two basic types described above cover the majority of applications found in the motorcycle world. There are variations and developments of these, however, and these are concerned with obtaining better braking performance. To increase the area of friction material in contact with the disc surface without increasing the disc size, it is necessary to fit elongated pads to cover a wider arc of disc. This could be done by fitting additional calipers, but in practice it is convenient to merge these into a single, double piston unit. Many manufacturers now use calipers of this type, either as opposed or single piston arrangements.

Another approach, not yet established on production machines, but of increasing popularity in racing circles, is to fit a large diameter disc to the wheel rim, rather than the hub. This means that the disc is passing through the caliper at higher speed, but that less pressure is needed to stop it. The caliper is inverted, operating from the inner edge of the disc, but the system is in most other respects conventional.

Honda have produced a variation of the above in their 'Inboard Ventilated Disc' system. This employs an inverted caliper mounted on a cover plate in a similar fashion to the brake backplate assembly of a drum brake. The double piston caliper is inverted as in the above arrangement, though the disc is still carried on the wheel hub. The disc is a complex casting with ventilation slots between the two surfaces. This and cooling scoops in the cover plate ensure a supply of air to cool the otherwise enclosed assembly. The result is rather like a combination of a disc and drum brake. It tends to make the wheel to which it is fitted much more difficult to remove and replace.

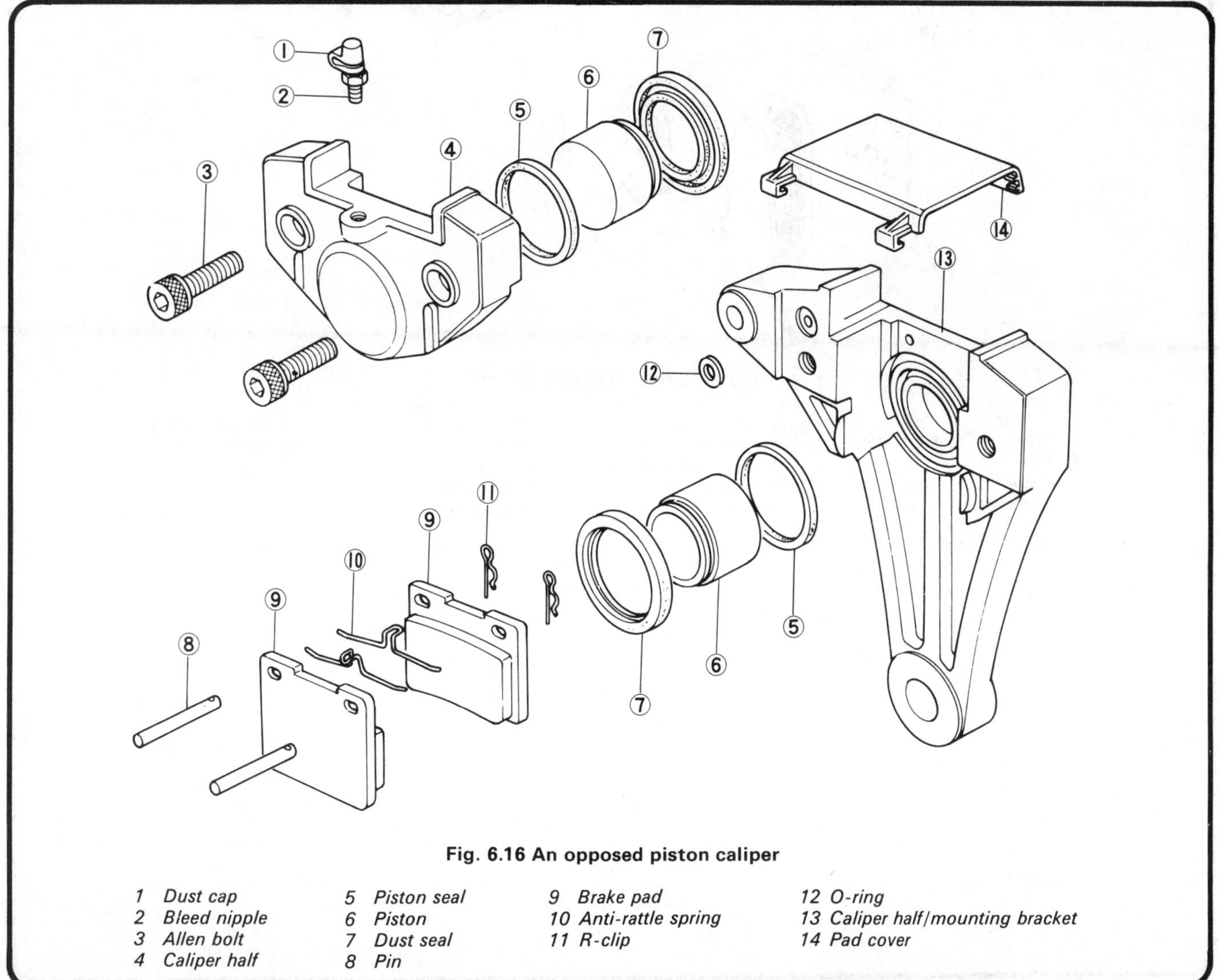


**Fig. 6.16 An opposed piston caliper**

*1 Dust cap*
*2 Bleed nipple*
*3 Allen bolt*
*4 Caliper half*
*5 Piston seal*
*6 Piston*
*7 Dust seal*
*8 Pin*
*9 Brake pad*
*10 Anti-rattle spring*
*11 R-clip*
*12 O-ring*
*13 Caliper half/mounting bracket*
*14 Pad cover*

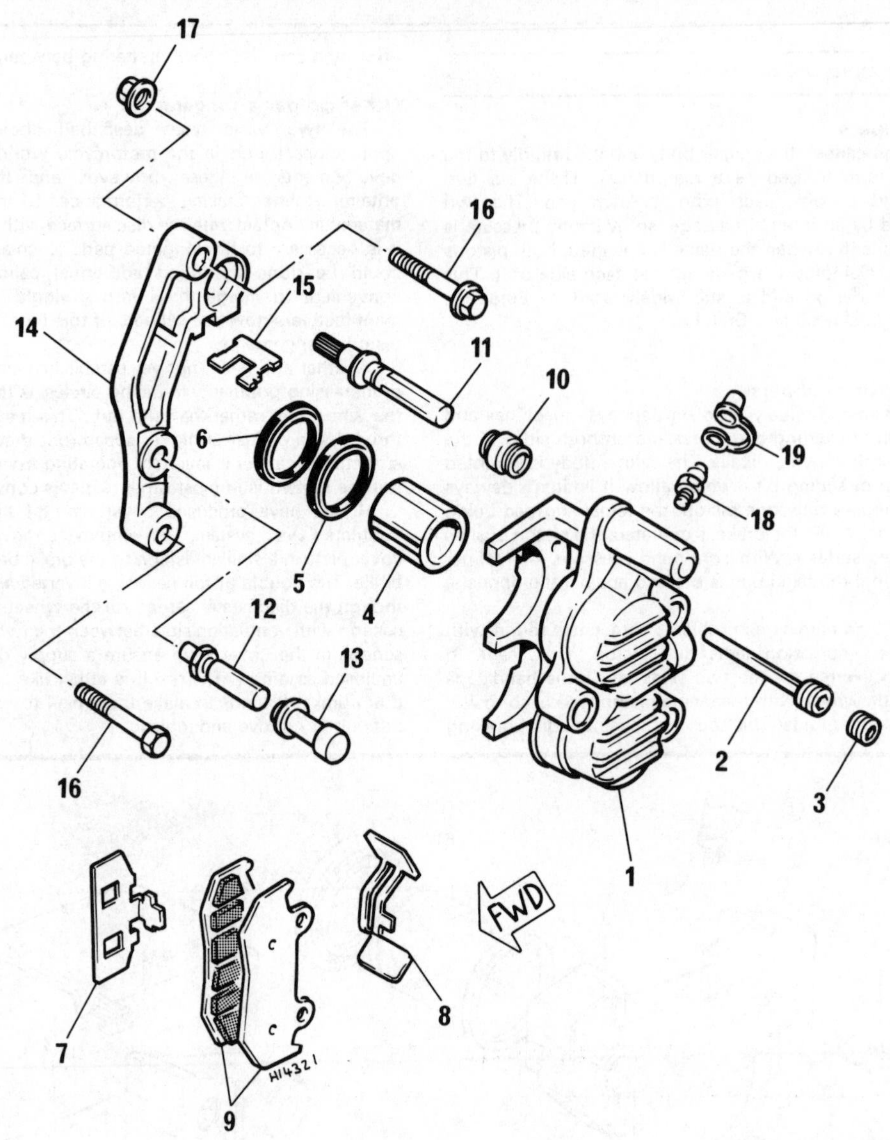


**Fig. 6.17 A twin piston caliper**

1 Caliper
2 Brake pad retaining pin
3 Plug
4 Piston
5 Piston seal
6 Dust seal
7 Anti-squeal shim
8 Anti-rattle spring
9 Brake pads
10 Seal
11 Axle bolt
12 Axle bolt
13 Bush
14 Mounting bracket
15 Retainer
16 Mounting bolt
17 Nut
18 Bleed nipple
19 Cap

# Chapter 7 Front suspension and steering

**Contents**



## 1 Introduction

The steering arrangement commonly used on most powered two-wheelers is derived from that of the bicycle, namely a pair of forks which support the front wheel and which are able to pivot in relation to the frame to permit steering. There have, of course, been numerous refinements of this basic arrangement, most important of which is the introduction of suspension. Suspension systems are many and varied, and for this reason we will concentrate only on those types currently in use, leaving the girder fork and its associated designs to more specialised works. Similarly, we will not dwell on the more exotic developments which have yet to gain widespread acceptance.

## 2 Telescopic fork

This, as its name suggests, works in much the same way as a telescope. Each fork leg consists of an inner tube (stanchion) which is clamped in the fork yokes (of which more later). Fitting closely over the stanchion, is the lower leg, often a light alloy casting, and sometimes fitted with renewable bushes. The two legs are fitted in parallel and attached at their lower ends to the wheel spindle. Inside each leg is a coil spring, so the weight of the machine is supported by the springs, which are able to deflect slightly to allow the wheel to ride over irregularities in the road. To prevent the suspension from bouncing uncontrollably, some form of damping is usually incorporated.

The most usual damping arrangement is to fit a valve or specially sized hole in the base of the stanchion, and then to fill the lower leg with oil. As the lower leg is deflected upwards, the oil is trapped and must flow up through the valve or drilling and into the stanchion. This imposes a resistance on the movement of the suspension, which is repeated on the downstroke. As a result, any tendency towards bouncing is prevented. In practice, there needs to be little damping effect on the upstroke – it is better if the wheel can move easily in response to bumps. On the downstroke, however, the damping effect can be stronger. This is usually achieved by a two-way damping valve which offers less restriction in one direction than the other, or by having a simple by-pass valve to allow a fairly unrestricted flow on the upstroke.

The construction of the telescopic fork varies widely, and each manufacturer seems to have his own ideas about the finer points. The overall principle, however, remains the same. In the line drawings that accompany this Chapter are examples of telescopic forks, and these should be studied to gain some idea of the variations of the basic arrangement. You will soon note that a number of detail refinements appear in the various forks in common use. The more significant of these are discussed below.

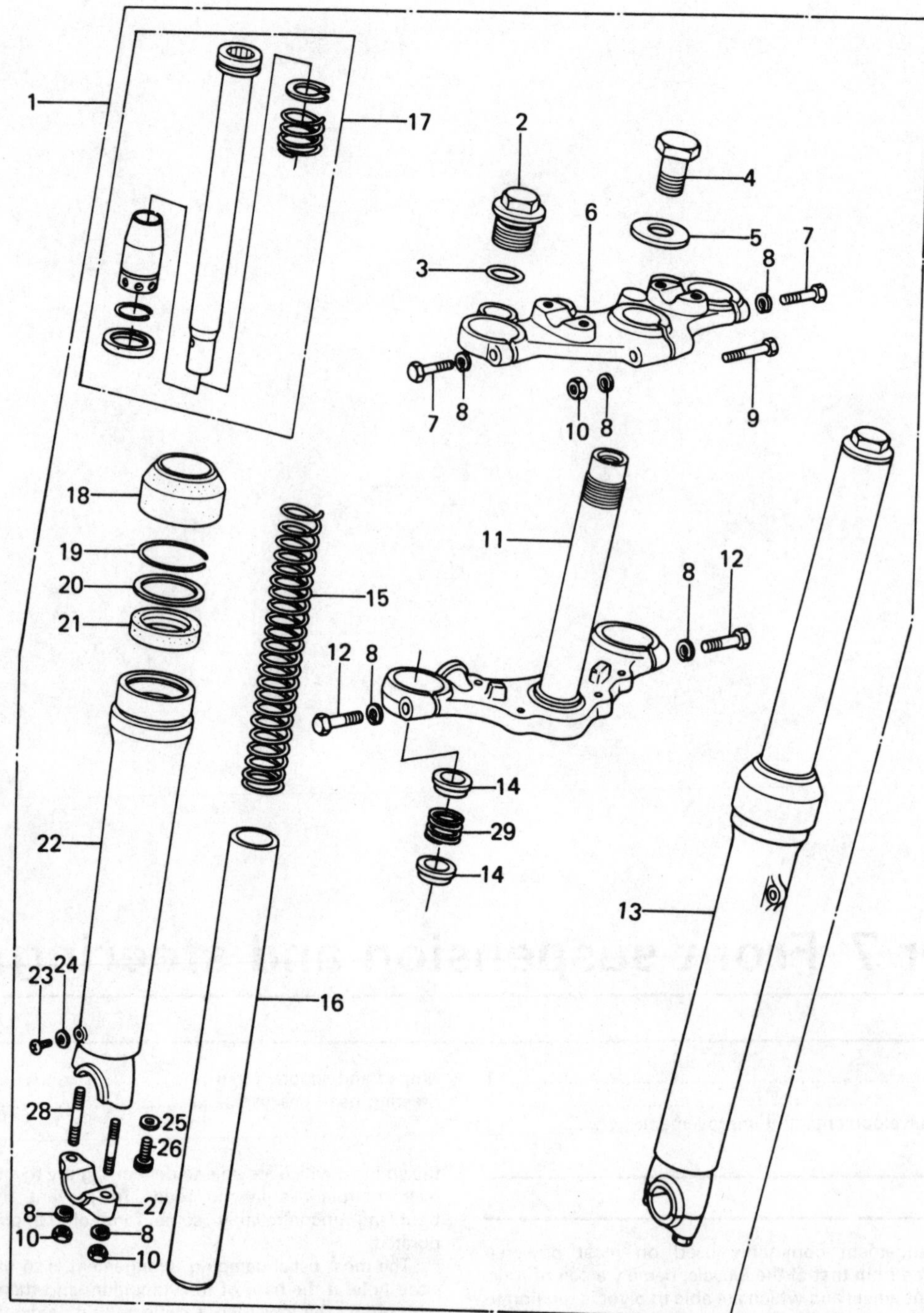


**Fig. 7.1 Component parts of a typical telescopic front fork – Kawasaki KL250**

*1 Front fork assembly complete*
*2 Fork top bolt*
*3 Sealing washer*
*4 Steering stem bolt*
*5 Washer*
*6 Top yoke*
*7 Bolt*
*8 Spring washer*
*9 Bolt*
*10 Locknut*
*11 Steering stem and lower yoke*
*12 Bolt*
*13 RH lower leg*
*14 Spring seat*
*15 Fork spring*
*16 Fork stanchion*
*17 Damper rod assembly*
*18 Dust seal*
*19 Circlip*
*20 Washer*
*21 Oil seal*
*22 LH lower leg*
*23 Drain screw*
*24 Fibre washer*
*25 Fibre washer*
*26 Damper bolt*
*27 Clamp half*
*28 Stud*
*29 Rebound spring*

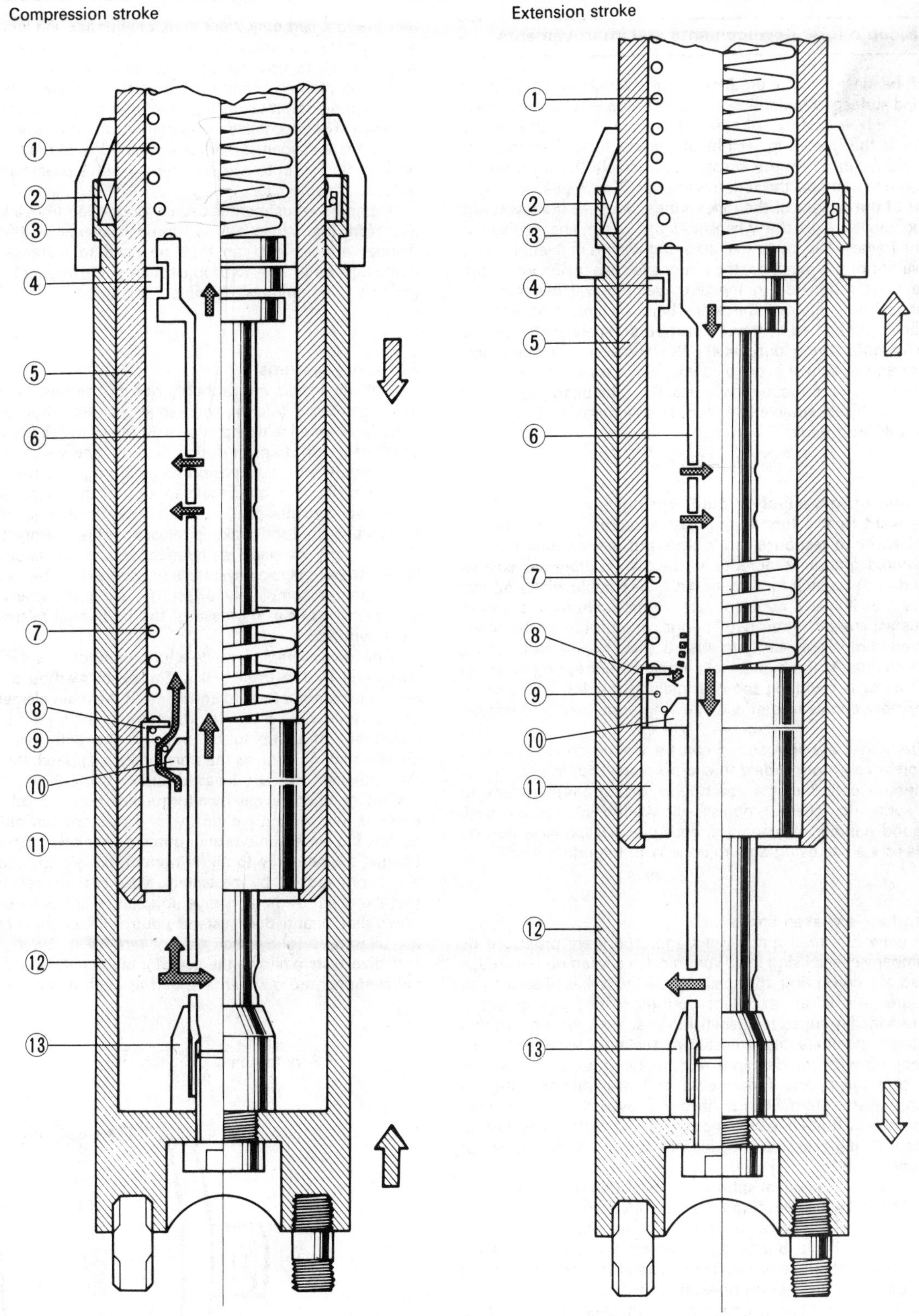

**Fig. 7.2 Fork operation showing flow of damping oil – Kawasaki Z200**

*1 Main fork spring*
*2 Oil seal*
*3 Dust seal*
*4 Piston ring*
*5 Fork stanchion*
*6 Damper piston assembly*
*7 Rebound spring*
*8 Damper valve seat*
*9 Spring*
*10 Valve*
*11 Valve body*
*12 Lower leg (slider)*
*13 Damper rod seat*

## 3 The telescopic fork: developments and improvements

It would be desirable to produce a fork which could respond quickly to road surface irregularities, and it is this quest which has been behind most developments of the telescopic fork. One major consideration is the unsprung weight of the machine. This refers to those items NOT carried by the suspension, namely the front wheel, the brake components and the fork lower legs. (To be precise, it also includes part of the weight of the fork springs, because the lower end of the spring moves with the wheel and the upper end is fixed in relation to the frame). The lower the unsprung weight in relation to the remaining weight of the machine, the better the suspension will work, because the large difference in the two weights will minimise the amount of shock transmitted to the rider. There is a limit to how far the front end can be lightened without disproportionately high costs in materials or manufacturing difficulties. Next time you are out, note how the front end of almost every bike you see looks the same; this is the state of the art on production machines. So if the unsprung weight is at its commercially acceptable limit, further changes must be made in the way the fork itself works.

### Multi-rate and progressively wound springs

What we want from a fork is progressive action; that is, the fork should move easily in response to a bump, but the resistance of the movement should gradually increase as the fork compresses so that large bumps do not cause it to 'bottom out'. The trouble with a normal coil spring is that it has a constant rate. Some manufacturers have looked at this aspect and fitted two springs, one on top of the other. The first spring compresses easily to absorb small ripples and bumps, giving a smooth ride. As the bumps get bigger, the first spring becomes 'coil bound', its coils touching together making it solid. The second, stiffer, spring now comes into effect, allowing continued and heavier springing.

As an alternative, a single spring can be wound so that its coils become progressively more widely spread from one end. In this type of spring, successive coils become coil bound, giving another route to progressive springing. These progressively wound springs are now used on a good number of machines, and give a responsive ride on normal roads as well as being able to cope with the odd pothole.

### Air forks and air-assisted forks

Air forks were first tried many years ago, and were produced by Dowty, a company specialising in air springing in aircraft undercarriage struts. Instead of a coil spring, the space inside the fork is filled with air under pressure. Air is an excellent springing medium, giving a progressive rate ideally suited to suspension use. The problem was that seal technology and materials available at the time were not really capable of coping with the demands and neglect found in their new home. If a seal failed, the fork would collapse, necessitating an expensive specialist rebuild. Things have improved a lot since then, and air forks are now quite reliable. The problem of seal failure, though much reduced, is still present, and this has led to the popularity of air-assisted springing.

In this type of fork the initial springing is provided by conventional coil springs. The forks are also fitted with air valves, often linked by a hose to ensure equal pressure in each leg. The advantages of air springing are thus available, but because the air pressure is much lower than in an air fork, seal failure is less rapid. When the seal does fail, the fork can still operate using spring pressure only.

One final point. There is a commonly-held belief that air forks provide adjustable damping. Though the air pressure in the fork does affect the damping to a small degree, air itself is a very bad damping medium. This is because it is easily compressed and is why it is such a good springing medium. The damping effect is still provided by forcing oil through a restriction, and thus damping can only be adjusted by altering the size of the restriction.

### Adjustable spring preload and damping

Some of the more sophisticated forks bristle with adjusters, giving the facility to set up the fork for almost any conceivable use or condition. The need for adjustment really serves to underline the fact that the fork can only work at its best under fine limits of loading and surface type, but the provision of adjustment does at least go some way towards compensating for its weaknesses.

Spring preload adjustment consists of altering the effective length of the spring and thus raising or lowering its initial rate to suit different loadings. The mechanism is usually a cam arrangement similar to that used on rear suspension units, but built inside the top of each leg. The preload can be set to hard for touring with a passenger or luggage, and reduced for solo use.

Damping adjustment is usually controlled from a knob at the top of each fork leg. When this is turned it alters the effective size of the damper orifice, and can thus be used to increase or decrease the damping effect. The two adjustments are frequently found together, giving a wide range of possible combinations.

### Anti-dive systems

Anti-dive forks are probably one of the best developments yet in fork technology, offering some measure of control for one of the most basic faults of all telescopic forks. In the previous Chapter we noted the effect of weight transfer during braking, and visible evidence of this is the way the front suspension dives during braking. This is more than discomforting though: because much of the suspension movement is taken up by the diving effect, the front suspension is virtually inoperative until the brake is released. This is a great pity, because at the very time we need really effective and subtle control of the front wheel, the suspension system is only partially effective. The problem of dive can be completely offset by using an alternative suspension arrangement but in the case of the traditional telescopic fork we are stuck with it.

Anti-dive systems provide a form of automatic damping adjustment controlled by the front brake. The exact method of operation varies from one manufacturer to another, but the main elements of all systems are as follows. When the machine is being ridden normally, the movement of damping oil through the anti-dive unit is relatively unrestricted. As soon as the front brake is applied, the restriction inside the anti-dive unit is increased, either hydraulically from the braking system, or mechanically by a torque link from the caliper. The damping effect is increased dramatically, and the fork can only compress very slowly. If a large bump is encountered, a small diaphragm valve will be opened momentarily to allow normal movement, and so the suspension is not 'locked' by the system. Most systems provide an adjuster so that the effect of the anti-dive unit can be set as required. It should be noted that all anti-dive systems control the effects of this drawback of the telescopic fork – they do not remove it. Even so, the use of an anti-dive system allows the use of a much lighter and more responsive initial spring and damper rate, and as such it is a major improvement.

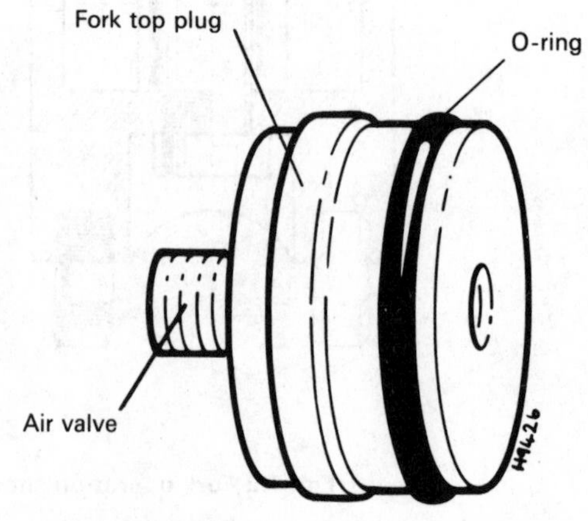


**Fig. 7.3 The simplest form of air assistance – fork top plug with air valve fitted**

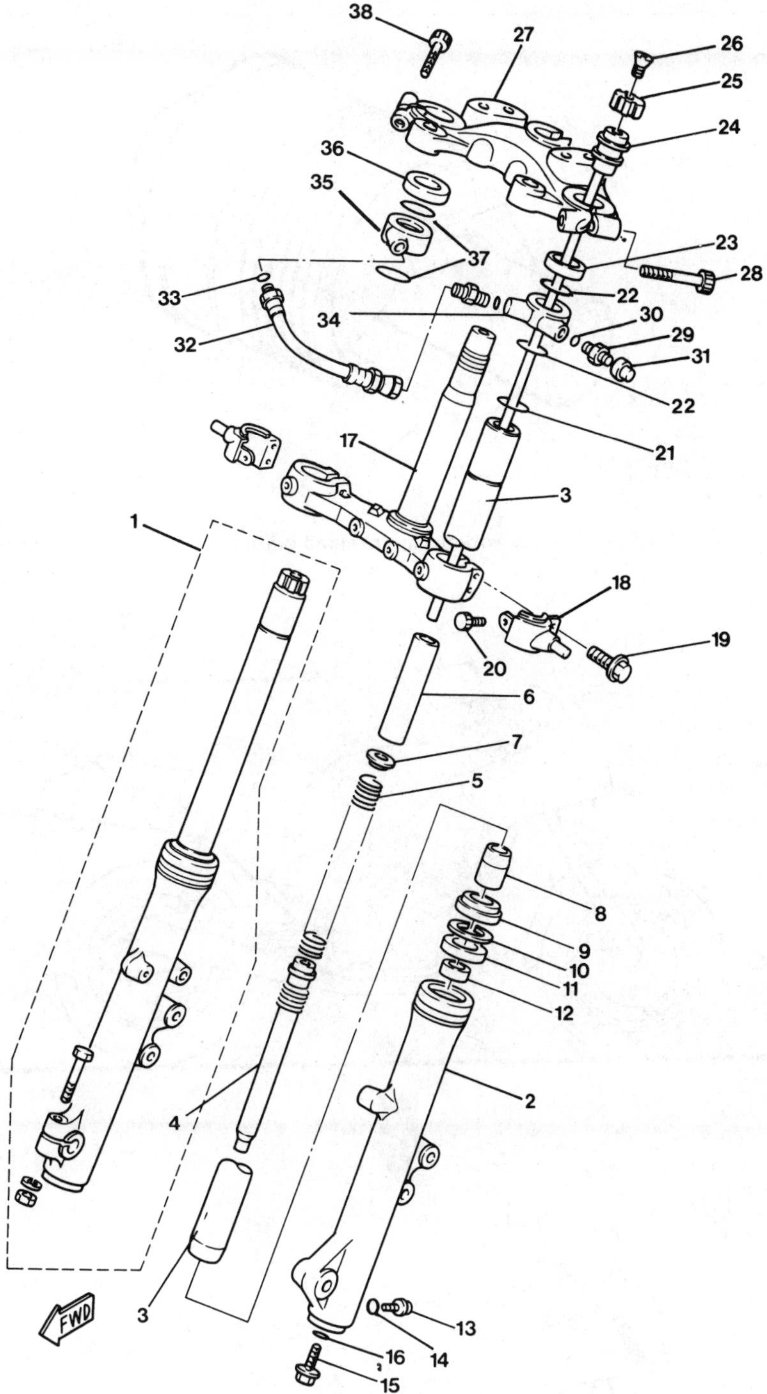


**Fig. 7.4 Air-assisted forks with adjustable damping – Yamaha XJ750 J**

*Note in particular the air connecting hose (32) which links the fork legs to ensure equal pressure. Damping rate is controlled by knurled knobs (25) at the top of each leg.*

*1 RH fork leg*
*2 LH lower leg*
*3 Stanchion*
*4 Damper rod*
*5 Fork spring*
*6 Spacer*
*7 Spring seat*
*8 Damper rod seat*
*9 Dust seal*
*10 Circlip*
*11 Oil seal*
*12 Bush*
*13 Drain screw*
*14 Sealing washer*
*15 Bolt*
*16 Sealing washer*
*17 Lower yoke/steering stem*
*18 Shroud*
*19 Pinch bolt*
*20 Bolt*
*21 O-ring*
*22 O-ring*
*23 Seal*
*24 Plug*
*25 Adjuster knob*
*26 Countersunk screw*
*27 Upper yoke*
*28 Pinch bolt*
*29 Air valve*
*30 O-ring*
*31 Valve cap*
*32 Air hose*
*33 O-ring*
*34 LH air union*
*35 RH air union*
*36 Seal*
*37 O-ring*
*38 Pinch bolt*

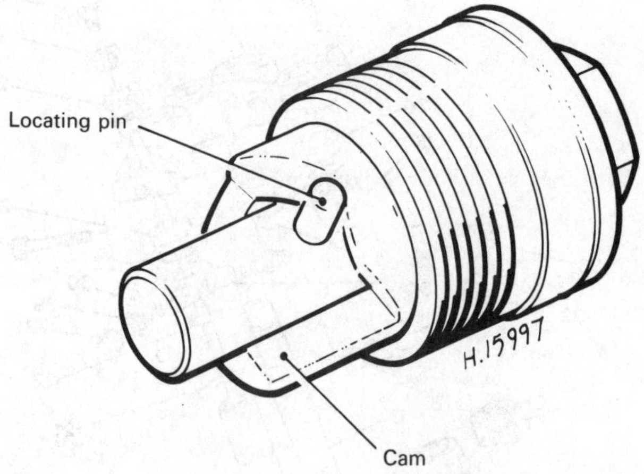


Fig. 7.5 Fork spring preload adjuster

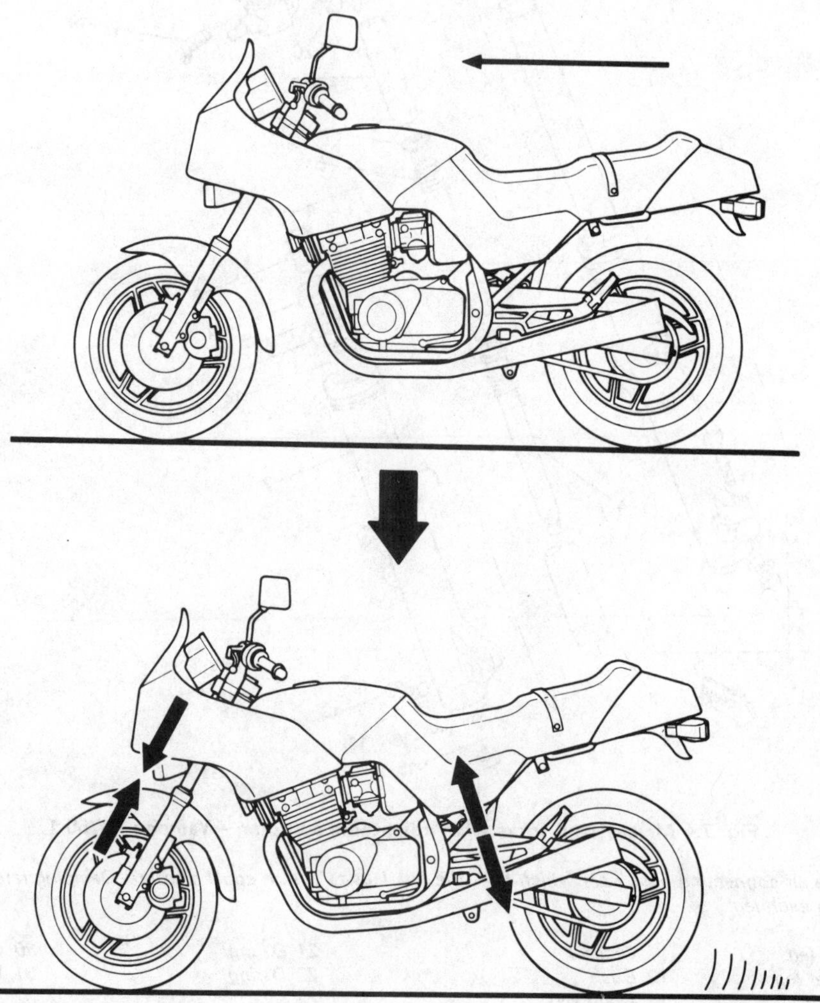

Fig. 7.6 Weight transfer during braking

*When the brakes are applied, forward momentum shifts the machine's centre of mass forward. This compresses the front suspension and causes the rear to lift. Much of the available suspension movement is lost.*

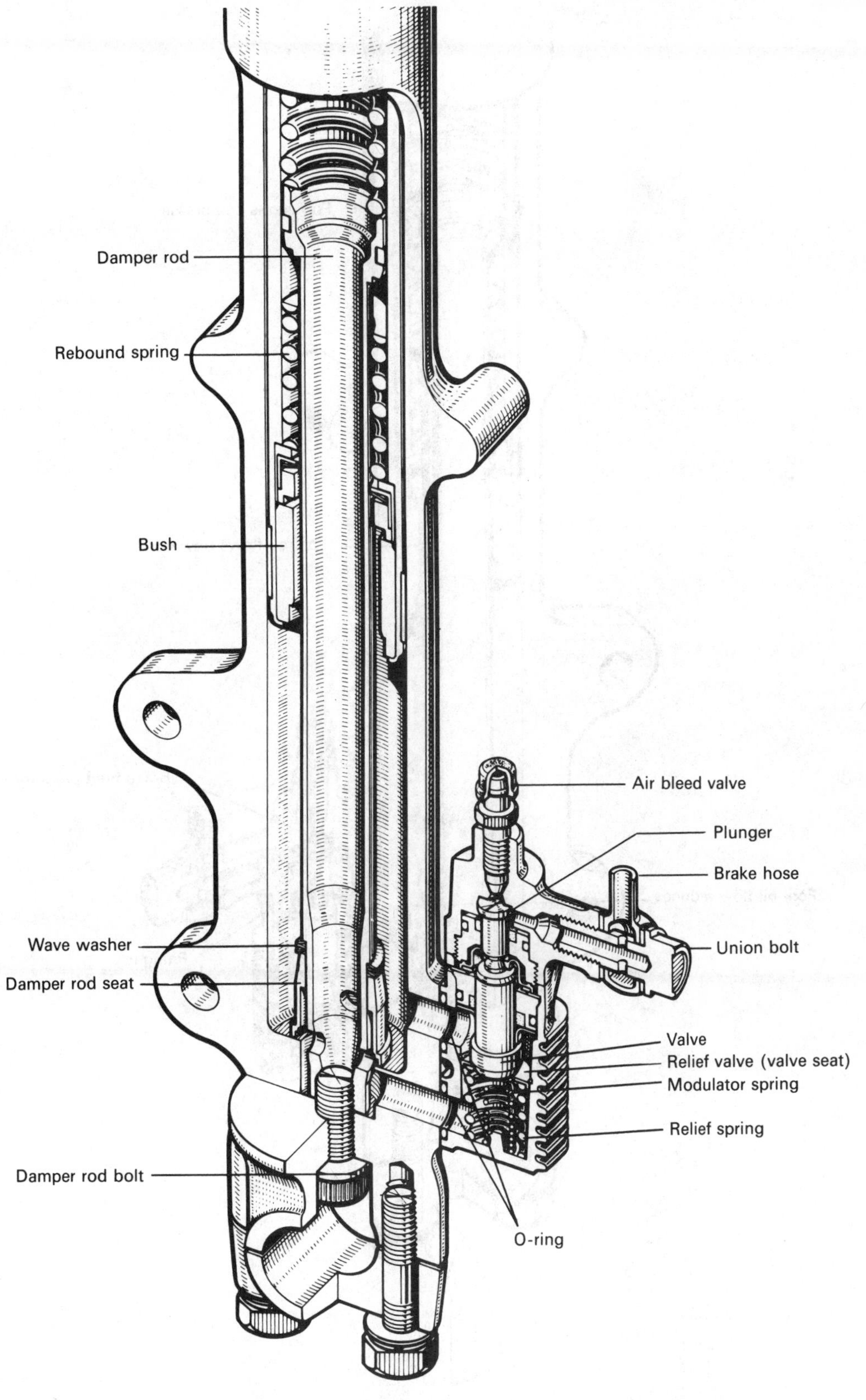


**Fig. 7.7 Suzuki GSX550 fork showing anti-dive unit**

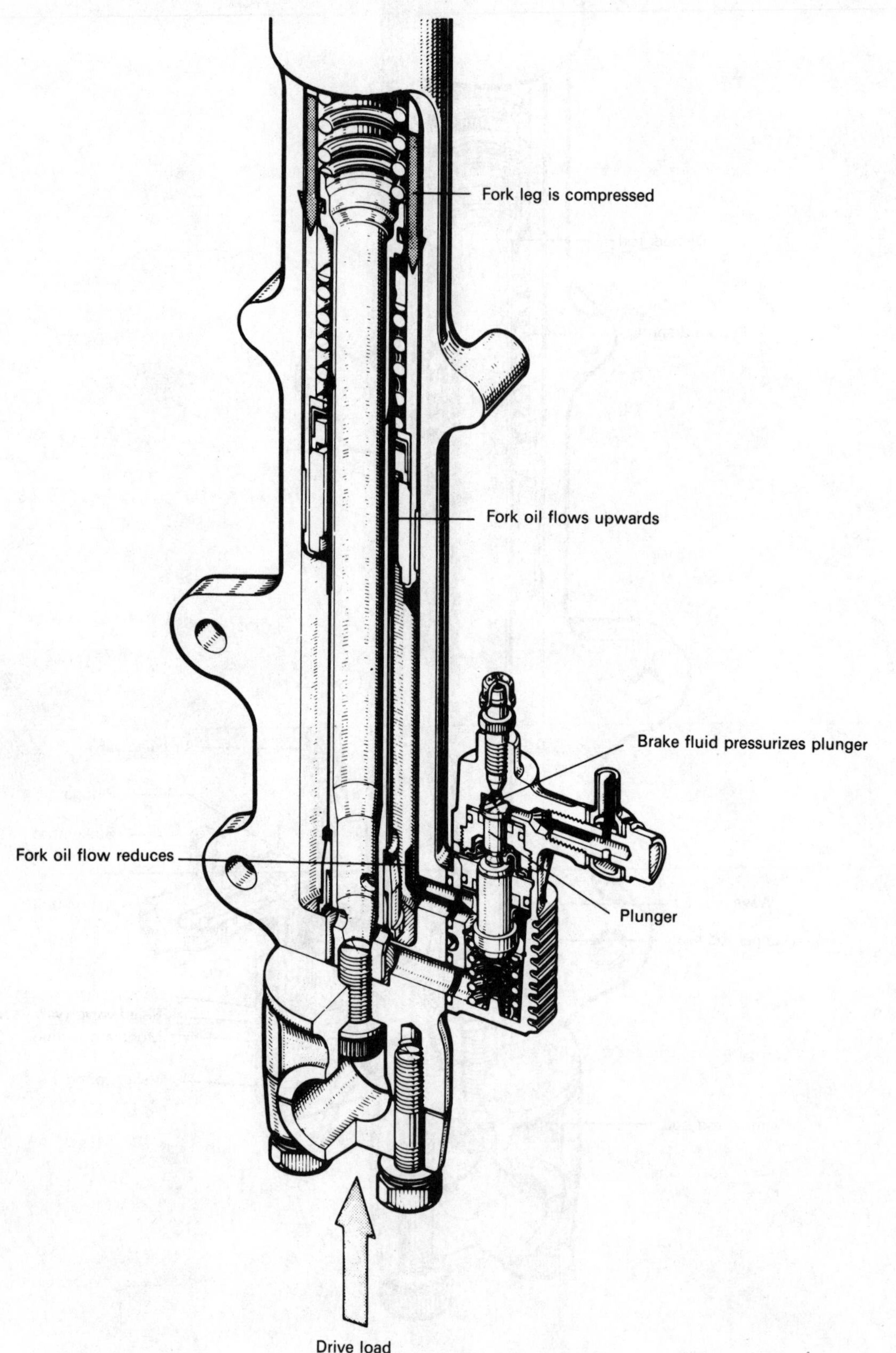


**Fig. 7.8 Anti-dive unit operation during braking**

*When the front brake is applied, hydraulic pressure pushes down the plunger. This in turn restricts the flow of damping oil, stiffening the fork to resist the normal pitching motion.*

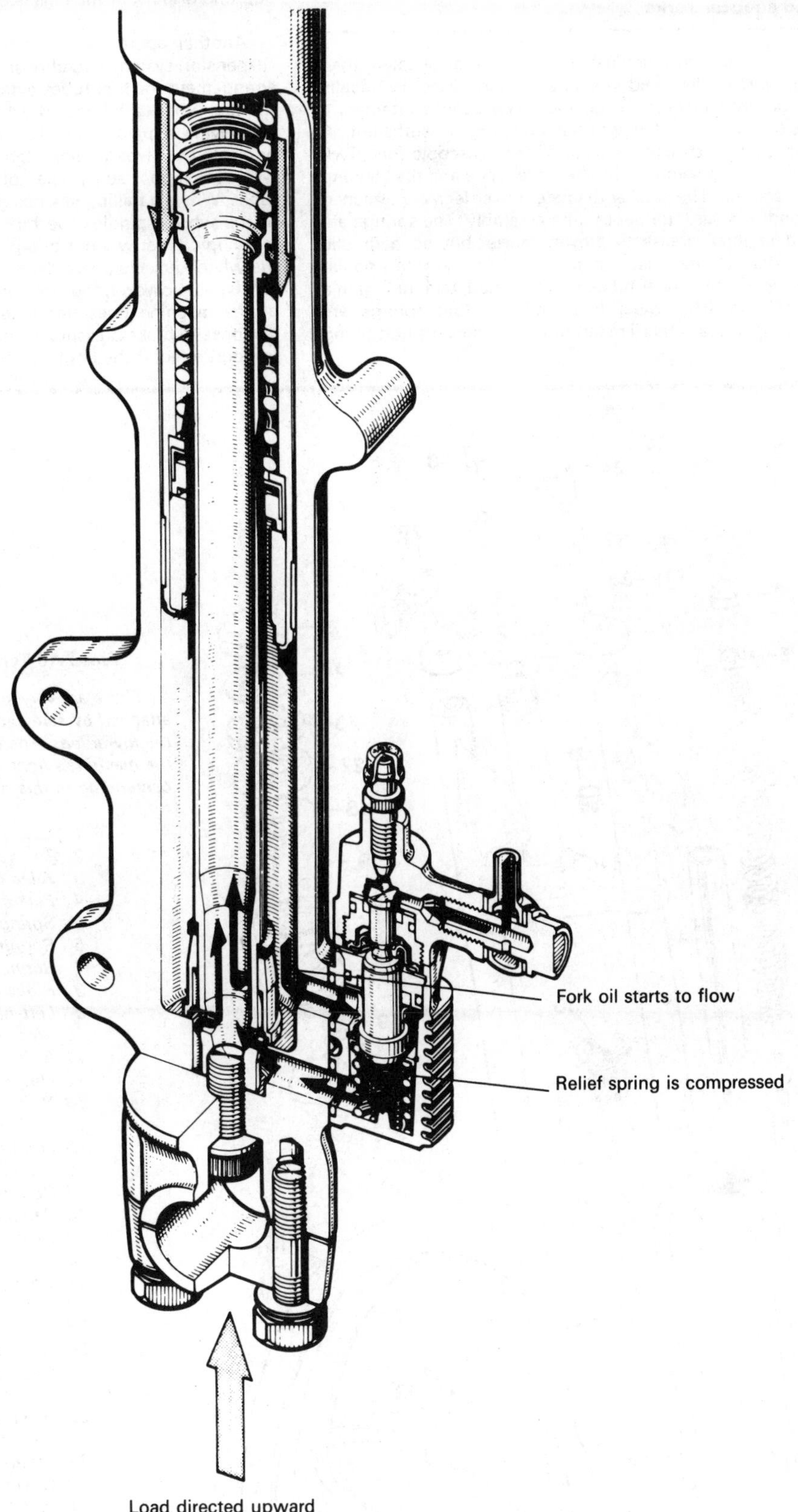


**Fig. 7.9 Anti-dive unit relief valve operation**

*If the machine encounters a bump while the anti-dive unit is in operation it is necessary to allow normal fork action to occur. This is achieved by fitting a relief valve which will open under sudden pressure to bypass the restricted anti-dive damping.*

## 4 Moped and scooter forks

Moped and scooter forks are generally less sophisticated than those fitted to motorcycles, and the arrangement used is usually chosen on the grounds of cost. Given the lower speeds attained, a simple suspension system, often without damping, is sufficient. A good proportion of mopeds employ a simplified telescopic fork. Two upper tubes, built as an assembly with the lower yoke and the steering stem, house the springs. The smaller diameter lower legs are attached to the springs and fit inside the upper tube assembly. The springs are normally coated in thick grease to prevent noise, but no hydraulic damping is provided. On models with small wheels, like the popular scooter-styled mopeds, the upper tubes are shortened, terminating in a long steering column. The lower legs and the fork springs are shortened to suit, giving a rather limited travel. To prevent bottoming out, one or both of the legs is often fitted with a conical rubber bump stop.

Another approach to building a lightweight and low cost front suspension system is to choose a leading or trailing link type. With this arrangement the fork tubes extend to within a few inches of the wheel spindle, where a fabricated extension projects backwards or forwards to provide a pivot point for the two suspension links. At the end opposite the pivot the links carry the wheel spindle, and the machine's weight is supported by a pair of coil springs extending up into the fork tubes. Where a trailing link design is chosen (with the link pivot in front of the wheel spindle) the fork behaves in much the same way as a telescopic type; when a bump is encountered or the brake is applied the wheel deflects upwards, moving through a small arc. With leading link types, however, the behaviour under braking is different; the front of the machine does not tend to dive and in some cases rises in response to brake pressure. Given the lack of damping this can be used to good effect if the angle of the links is chosen with care.

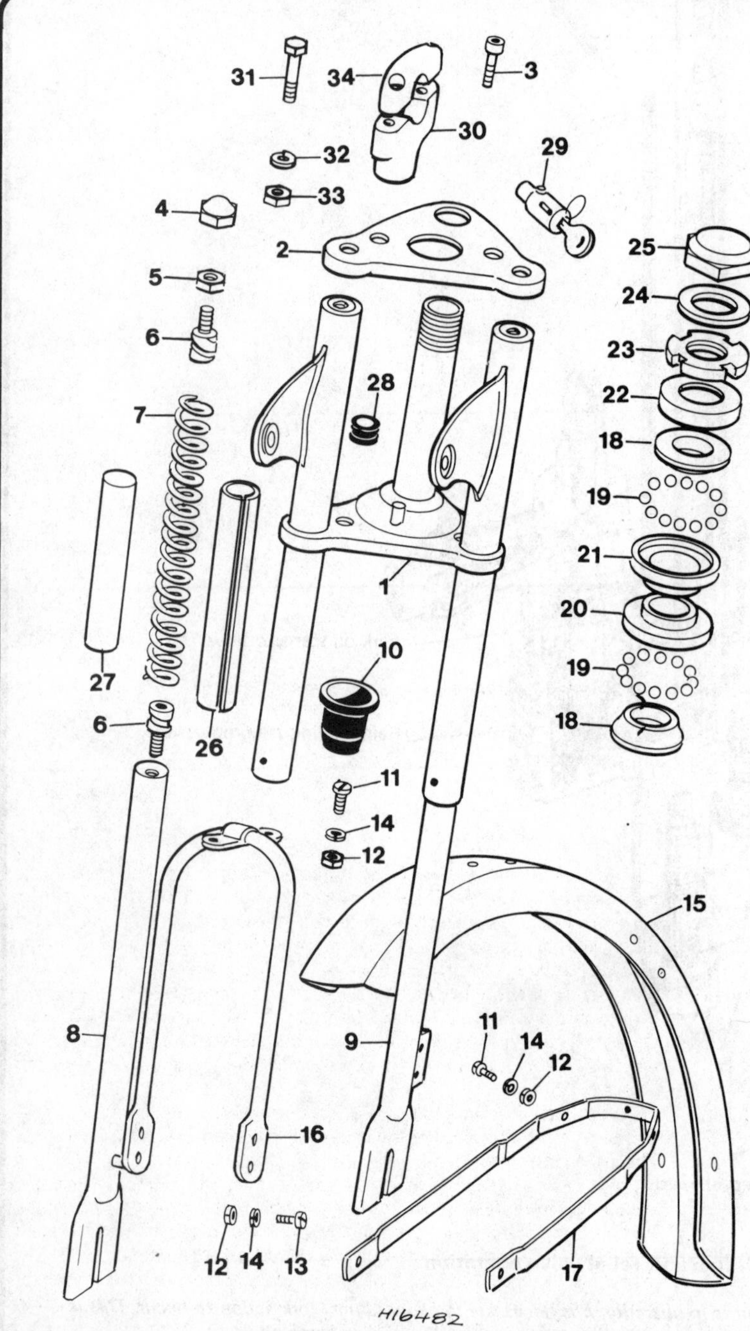


**Fig. 7.10 Typical undamped moped forks**

*These are very simple telescopic forks using springs attached by screwed plugs to the lower yoke tubes and the lower legs. There is no provision for damping, but the machine's light weight and low speed are not too demanding in this respect.*

*1 Lower yoke*
*2 Top yoke*
*3 Allen bolt*
*4 Fork cap nut*
*5 Spring anchor nut*
*6 Spring seat*
*7 Spring*
*8 Right-hand lower leg*
*9 Left-hand lower leg*
*10 Sleeve*
*11 Bolt*
*12 Nut*
*13 Bolt*
*14 Spring washer*
*15 Front mudguard*
*16 Top mudguard brace*
*17 Bottom mudguard brace*
*18 Bearing cone*
*19 Bearings*
*20 Lower bearing cup*
*21 Upper bearing cup*
*22 Dust cover*
*23 Adjusting nut*
*24 Washer*
*25 Steering stem nut*
*26 Plastic insert spacer*
*27 Damper insert spacer*
*28 Grommet*
*29 Steering lock*
*30 Lower handlebar clamp*
*31 Bolt*
*32 Spring washer*
*33 Nut*
*34 Upper handlebar clamp*

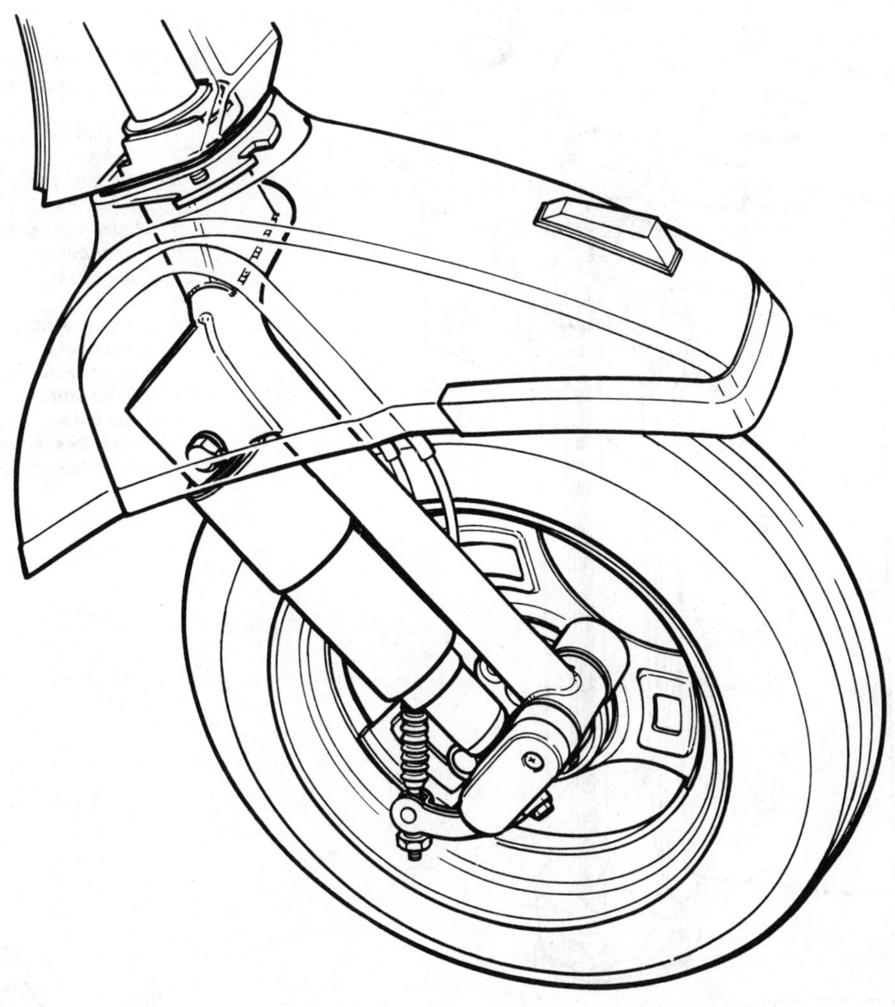

**Fig. 7.11 Single-sided trailing link suspension**

*This arrangement was pioneered by Vespa, and has recently been adopted by Suzuki on their CS125 model. Its single suspension unit offers a reasonable performance and the advantage of simple wheel changes.*

## 5 Steering head design

At the front of the frame is a tubular lug in which the steering stem is carried on bearings to allow the front wheel to be steered. On a typical motorcycle the steering head assembly comprises the tubular steering head, upper and lower bearings and the upper and lower fork yokes. The lower yoke incorporates the steering stem; a short shaft extending up from the centre which passes through the bearings. The upper yoke fits over the top of the steering stem, and both yokes include holes and pinch bolts to clamp the fork stanchions rigidly in place.

The steering head is set at an angle, and this means that the forks extend forward of the steering head, rather than vertically downwards. This angle is known as the 'rake' of the forks. The rake angle determines an important feature of the steering geometry; trail. This can be calculated by drawing a line through the steering head to the ground (rake). If a vertical line is now drawn through the wheel spindle axis to the ground, where the tyre touches the road surface, it will be noted that this contact path lies some way behind the rake axis. This difference is known as the trail of the fork, and is responsible for the self-centring, or 'castor' action.

Without some degree of castor, the front wheel would flutter uncontrollably, and this is easily seen in the behaviour of the castors on supermarket shopping trolleys. If on the other hand the rake angle were too great, the steering would be impossibly heavy, so the correct angle must be chosen carefully. In the case of a trials machine, the angle is deliberately shallow to permit easy and light steering. This is essential on a trials machine where obstacles must be negotiated with precision. On a fast road bike it is more important to have stable steering which is not easily deflected by road surface irregularities, so a greater degree of trail is required.

Most machines employ cup-and-cone steering head races. These comprise a number of steel balls carried between two bearing tracks. The tracks are formed between the cup and cone of each race in a slightly conical plane, and this ensures that the bearing balls are equally loaded whilst allowing the assembly to be adjusted to remove free play. On some larger machines, taper roller races are used instead to ensure a more robust steering head arrangement. These are designed to work under a slight preload to prevent any risk of unwanted free play. Whichever type is used it is essential that any free play is carefully adjusted out. This is because it would be much magnified at the wheel end of the fork, producing sloppy and imprecise steering.

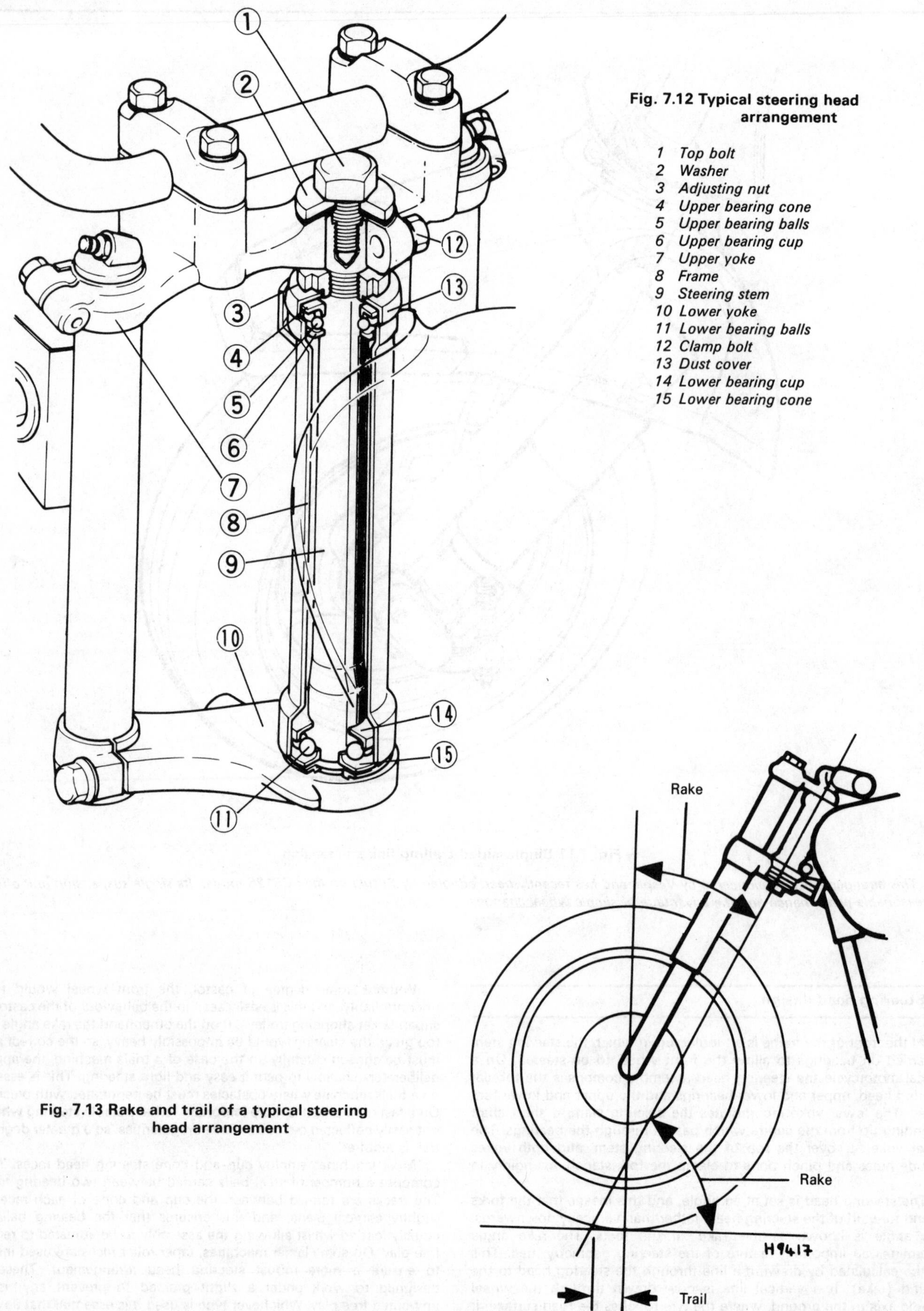


**Fig. 7.12 Typical steering head arrangement**

*1 Top bolt*
*2 Washer*
*3 Adjusting nut*
*4 Upper bearing cone*
*5 Upper bearing balls*
*6 Upper bearing cup*
*7 Upper yoke*
*8 Frame*
*9 Steering stem*
*10 Lower yoke*
*11 Lower bearing balls*
*12 Clamp bolt*
*13 Dust cover*
*14 Lower bearing cup*
*15 Lower bearing cone*

**Fig. 7.13 Rake and trail of a typical steering head arrangement**

# Chapter 8 Frame designs and types

**Contents**



## 1 Introduction

It is the frame's job to locate and support the engine, transmission, suspension and ancillaries. To do this effectively it must be both light and rigid, and it is these two factors which have governed frame designs since the very first motorcycles appeared. Without adequate strength and rigidity in the frame, the resulting flexing between the front and rear wheels can be mildly disconcerting or downright dangerous. Not only can a poor frame make the machine difficult or unpleasant to ride, it can detract from the benefits of the best engine; enforcing a wary riding style which would leave the model outclassed by more sophisticated rivals. There have been countless examples of this in racing, where over the years machines with superior frames but poor engines have triumphed over rivals with superior engines and dubious chassis.

In the commercial world of road-going machines there are other factors which govern the type of frame eventually chosen for a particular model, and in this context cost and fashion have almost as much significance as the frame's actual performance. What is undeniable is the fact that a well-engineered frame can transform almost any machine. The attention to detail that is possible only with small production runs (and the resulting high costs) explains why after-market frame kits continue in popularity. It is in the rather rarified specialist areas occupied by the racing frame manufacturers, and the road frame equivalents like Bimota and Harris, that the blend of instinct, science and craftsmanship are most evident.

## 2 Tubular steel frames

The majority of motorcycle frames, and many moped frames are constructed from steel tubing. This is a popular material for this purpose, combining strength and light weight. It is also fairly easy to work with, and as such is equally suited to specially built one-off frames and to mass produced versions. The usual choice of material is a thin-walled seamless steel tubing, chosen for its stiffness whilst keeping the overall weight of the frame to a minimum. Round section tubing offers resistance to bending in any direction, and thus has been the traditional choice of the frame designer.

Whatever the design technique and materials chosen, the object is always the same. The frame must be able to support the front and rear wheels positively and rigidly, with no appreciable twisting or warping between the two. If the wheels are able to twist out of exact alignment due to a weakness in the frame design, any attempt at precision in the wheels or suspension components is wasted; a good frame is of fundamental importance in obtaining good chassis performance. Of equal importance is the way in which the engine/transmission unit is mounted. The frame must hold this securely, despite the twisting forces imposed by the engine during acceleration. In many designs the frame performs a valuable role in minimising the effects of engine vibration. Finally, the frame must provide the necessary attachment points for the seat, fuel tank, side panels, electrical components and any other ancillary parts.

The traditional approach to tubular frame design is based on triangulation, and this is well illustrated in the standard bicycle frame. This is commonly known as a diamond frame by virtue of its shape, but it will also be noted that the diamond shape is divided into two triangles by a tube running between the saddle and the pedal crank area. This gives the diamond great strength and rigidity, each tube being effectively braced against bending. The same approach is employed in motorcycle and moped frame designs, though there must be allowances made for the accommodation of engine units, and so the triangulation is sometimes incomplete or modified.

The majority of frames are of the cradle type, where the frame tubes form a cradle below the engine unit. The engine sits inside this cradle area and is bolted to the frame via brackets and lugs. On larger and more powerful machines the cradle and top tubes are paired for greater tortional strength, and this results in a duplex cradle frame. In the case of the cradle frame, the engine/transmission assembly is a passive element and merely sits inside the frame loop(s). It is possible, however, to employ the engine itself as a structural element of the frame, provided that the engine was designed with this in mind. This has the benefits of reducing the weight of the frame by eliminating all unnecessary areas, and of allowing the engine unit to be mounted as low as possible to give a low centre of gravity.

The problem of accommodating a bulky multi-cylinder engine unit has in the past become so great that the designer was obliged to resort to fitting the frame around an engine unit, and then attempting to make good any weaknesses by bracing the suspect areas. This has produced some motorcycle chassis which were fairly disastrous. The problem is not so great on more recent designs, chassis design technology having moved on to the point where a good chassis can be built despite the awkwardness of the engine unit.

In recent years the design of frames has become far more exact, often with the assistance of CAD (computer aided design) techniques. These allow a prototype frame to be 'built' on the computer screen, and then subjected to various loading and vibration simulations. As a result, the frame geometry can be developed well in advance of the physical prototype stage. Using these techniques it soon became evident that most of the tubes in the frame needed to be much stronger in one plane than the other. As a result, square or rectangular section tubing can be used to provide added rigidity where needed, and to reduce unnecessary weight where loadings were light. Frames using this type of tubing first appeared on the race track, many using aircraft quality high tensile aluminium alloy tubing. Road-going versions soon appeared, though using more robust and less expensive steel tubing.

Fig. 8.1 The bicycle frame showing simple triangulation

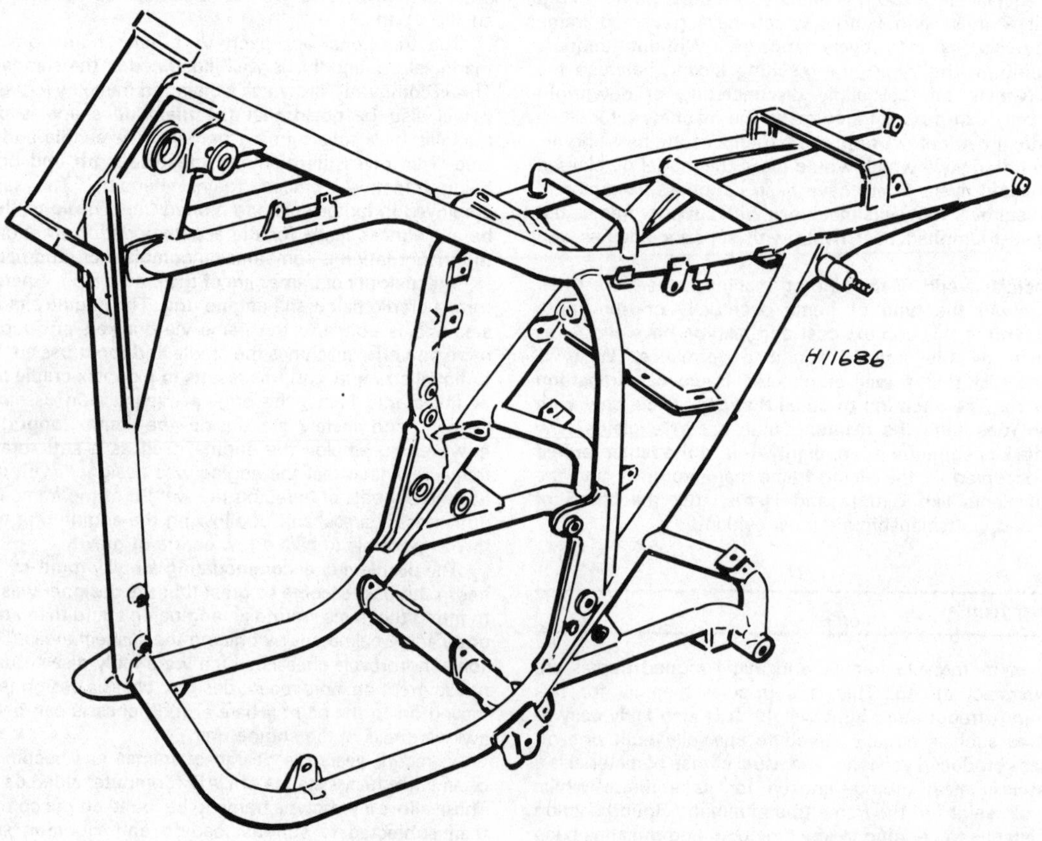


Fig. 8.2 A cradle frame

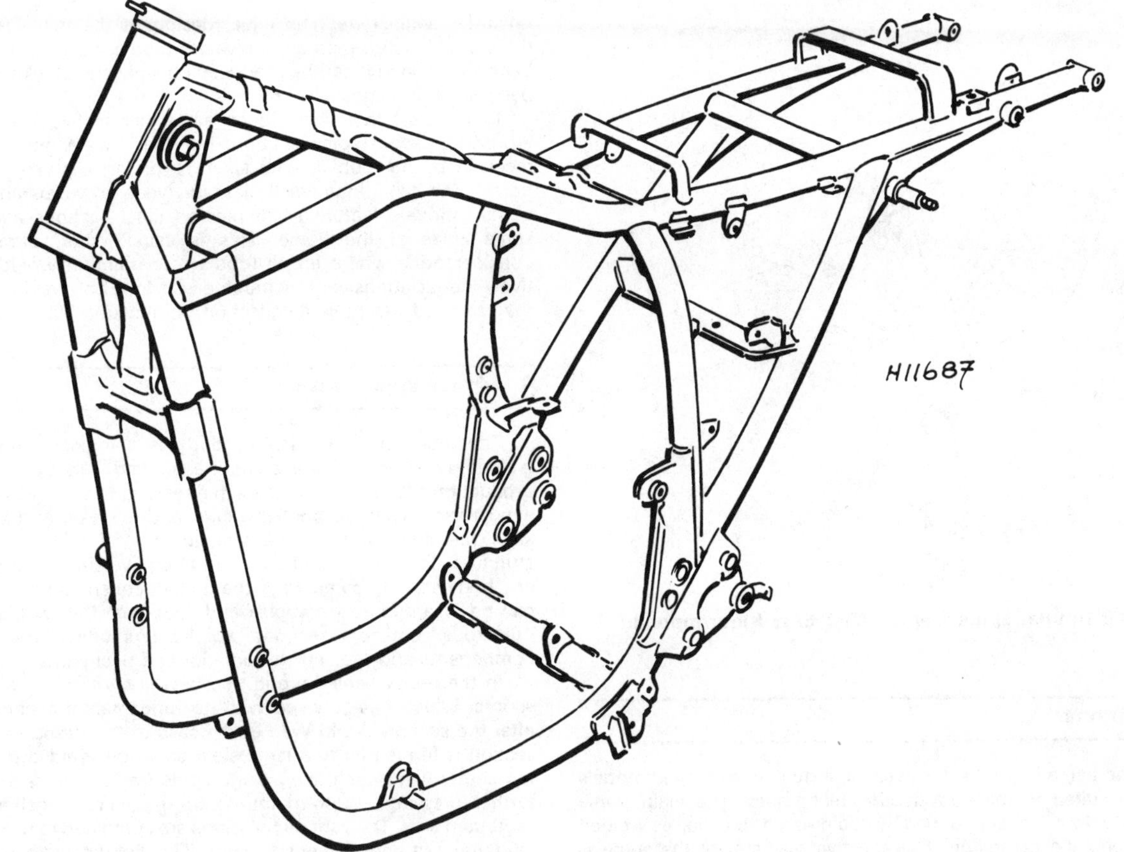


Fig. 8.3 A duplex cradle frame

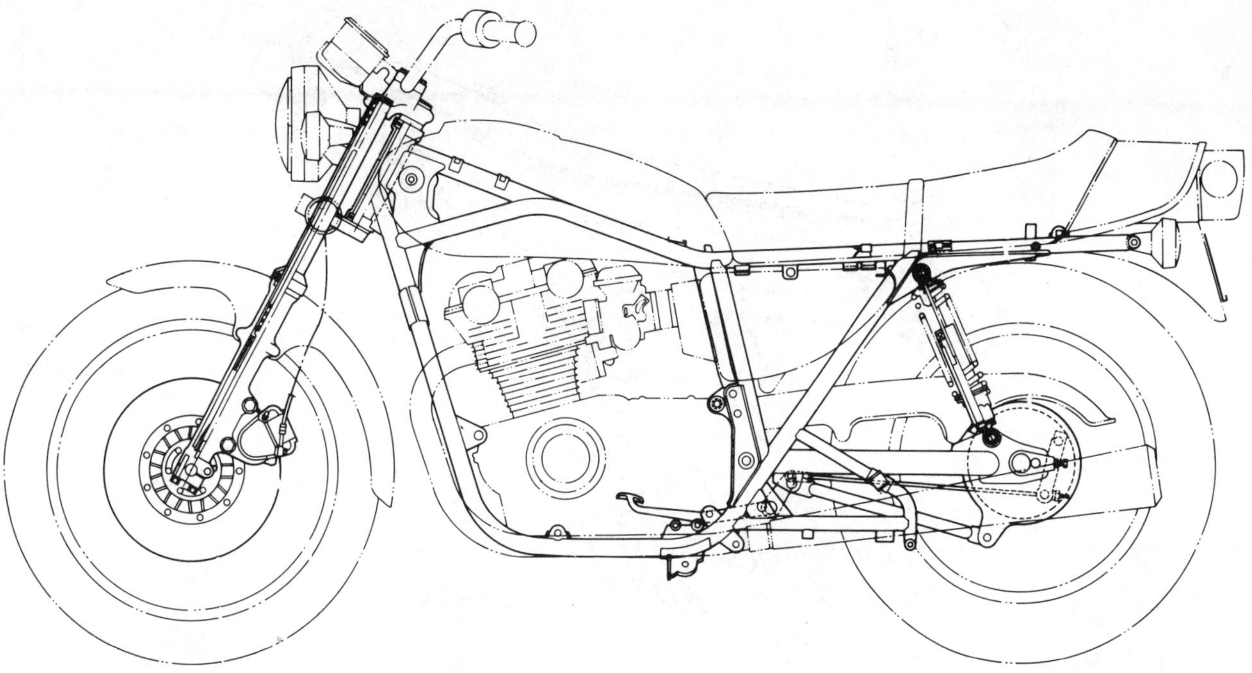

Fig. 8.4 Side view of a typical motorcycle frame showing engine and suspension location points

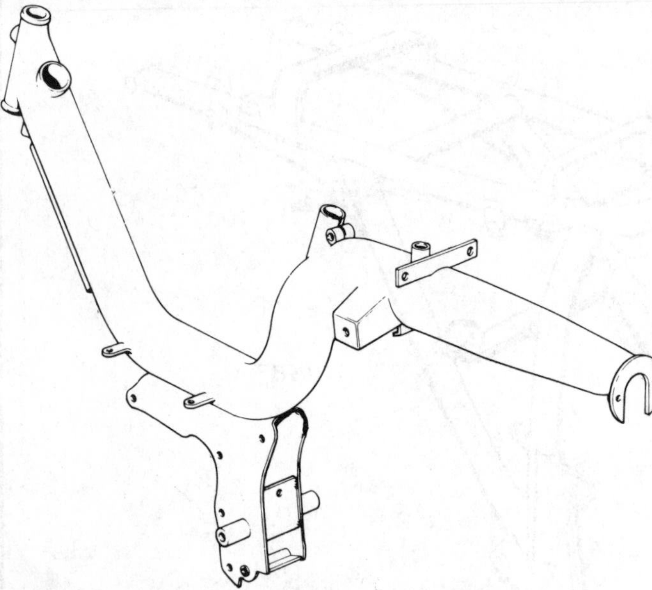

Fig. 8.5 Tubular spine frame – NVT Easy Rider moped

## 3 Spine frames

The spine frame is used extensively on a number of moped models and is well suited to mass production techniques. The main frame section is usually a T-shape formed by two pressed steel halves welded together along the centreline. The effective diameter of the spine is quite large, providing good resistance against twisting. In addition, the spine can be used to form or to house such things as the fuel tank, toolbox, air filter and the electrical fittings, to produce a clean and uncluttered machine. The initial design of the frame is often more difficult to finalise than an equivalent tubular version, but once it has been established it can be produced cheaply and quickly from the two basic steel pressings.

In the past there have been a number of larger machines built around a central spine section, but these were not generally well received by the public, who seem to prefer a 'proper' tubular steel frame. The technique itself has survived, however, and almost all current models feature small pressed steel sections and gussets in some areas of the frame. This is usually due to manufacturing considerations where an all-tubular construction would be prohibitively labour intensive; it is much easier to robot-weld a hybrid frame than to hand-assemble a collection of individual tubes.

## 4 Monocoque chassis

The monocoque chassis or body is a logical extension of the welded pressings of the spine frame, and can be found on few production machines. It is the same technique that has been adopted almost exclusively on post-war cars, and relies on a number of sheet steel pressings welded together to form a stiff and lightweight structure. This provides the structural equivalent of a frame and also any bodywork. In some ways the unitary construction of a car's body can be regarded as a complex and very large thin-walled 'tube' with numerous cut-out sections to accommodate the mechanical components and the vehicle's interior and occupants.

In the two-wheeled world, the best known example is the Vespa scooter which has survived with no fundamental changes since just after the second World War. In the case of the Vespa, the main body section is formed by two large steel pressings welded together along the centre line, much like a large spine frame. This is extended with further pressings to form the steering column, legshields and the footboard area. The various pressings are combined to give a fairly light structure, but with immense rigidity. The alternative approach, using a tubular frame clad with steel body panels, would be both weaker and heavier, and in practice the only non-structural panels are items like the side panels and the front mudguard.

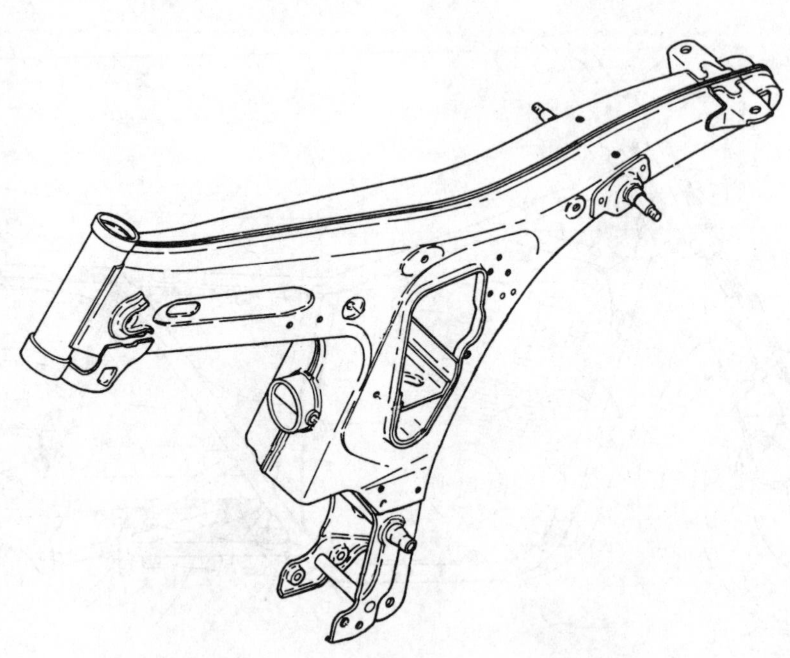

Fig. 8.6 Typical fabricated spine frame – Yamaha YB100

*The T-shaped frame is made up from two sheet steel pressings welded together along the centre line. The designs allows the battery, air filter and other minor components to be housed inside the frame.*

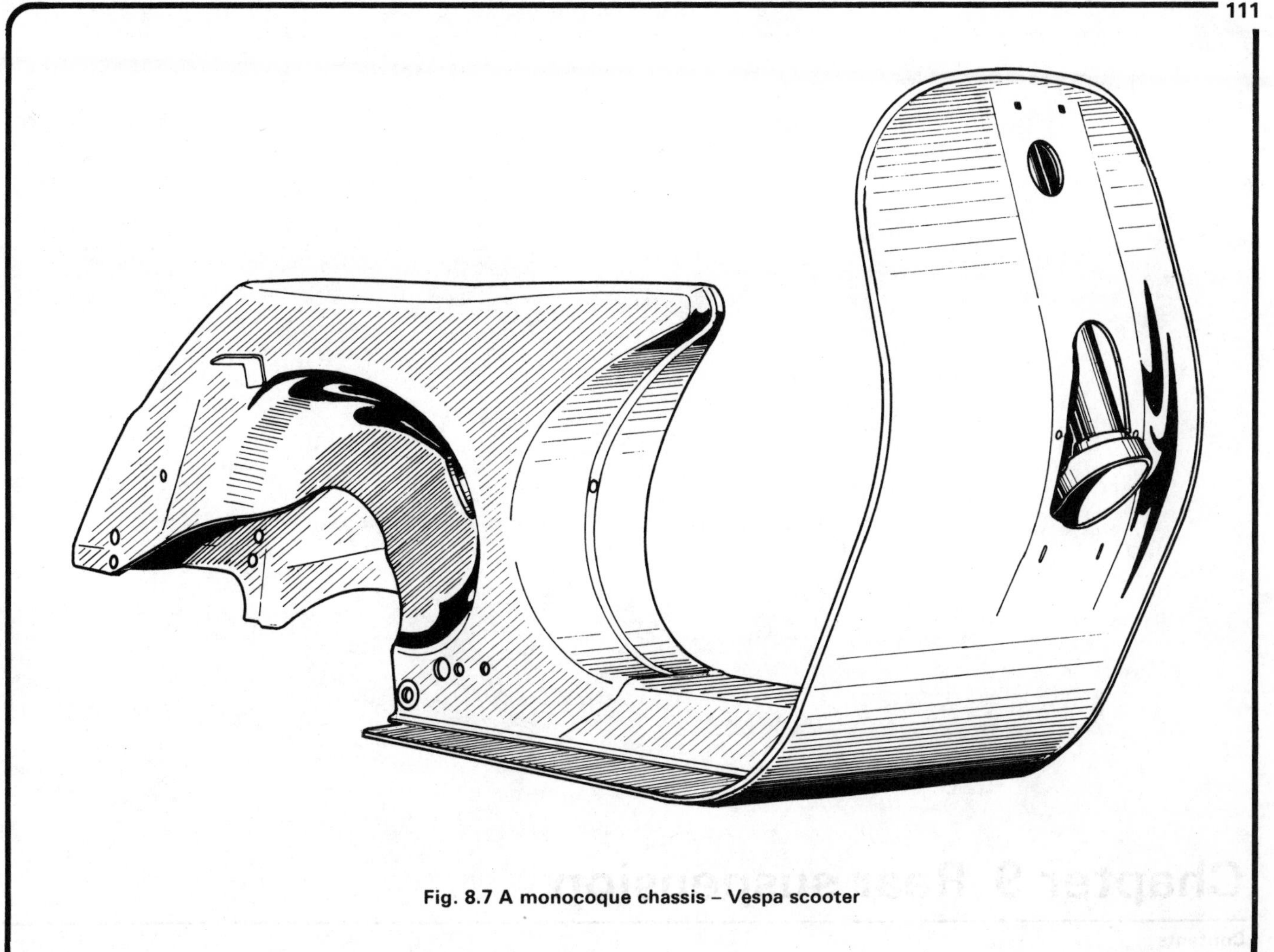

**Fig. 8.7 A monocoque chassis – Vespa scooter**

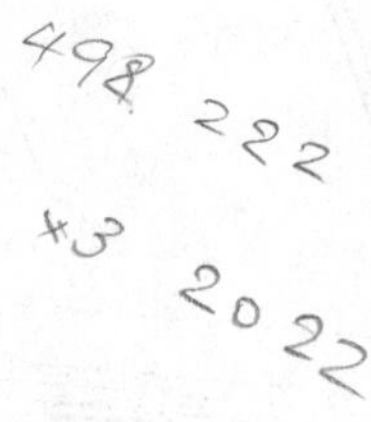


# Chapter 9 Rear suspension

## Contents



## 1 Introduction

Rear suspension first appeared relatively late on in the motorcycle's history. Whilst the need for front suspension became very evident at speeds above about 20 mph, it was far less crucial at the rear. For decades, girder forks were teamed with a rigid frame, the worst of the bumps being tamed by the fitting of a well-sprung single saddle. Any pillion passenger was obliged to endure a rudimentary pad lodged above the rear mudguard, and thus the majority of the shocks transmitted up through the rear wheel. After the second World War the lack of rear suspension soon became a problem on racing machines; as speeds grew steadily higher, so did the amount of time the rear wheel spent off the road surface. This meant that the absence of springing was beginning to impose a limitation on the overall performance of the machines, and thus the spring frame was born.

The earliest version of rear springing was the adoption of the plunger unit. This was little more than a vertical spring unit set at the rear of the frame in place of the earlier fixed fork ends. Though undamped, the plunger frames did allow a measure of comfort and rear wheel control, and they were soon widely used on road models. The real breakthrough was the adoption of the pivoted rear fork, or swinging arm. This eliminated the main drawback of the plunger system; the tendency for the wheel to twist in relation to the frame because of the lack of interconnection between each fork end. The swinging arm soon became universal, and remains a popular choice to this day. A variation of the swinging arm, the cantilever, was soon developed. This was generally ignored in favour of the swinging arm, but has recently found favour as a result of the introduction of rising-rate suspension systems. In this Chapter we will be looking at the swinging arm arrangement and at some of the more sophisticated designs.

## 2 The swinging arm

The swinging arm (or pivoted rear fork) has been in widespread use for well over three decades now, and it is unlikely to be completely replaced by the current rising rate systems for some years yet. On chain drive machines the U-shaped fork is mounted on a pivot shaft and bushes, close to the gearbox output shaft. It is normally attached to the frame at this point, though some designs have seen it pivoted from the engine/gearbox unit. The reason for this is to ensure that the chain tension is kept even throughout the fork's full range of movement. If the pivot is located very far behind the output shaft, the effective distance between the wheel spindle and output shaft varies as the fork moves, and so chain tension cannot be maintained. In the case of shaft drive machines, this is not so crucial, but a universal joint must be fitted at the swinging arm pivot axis to allow movement.

Where chain drive is employed it is necessary to provide some sort of adjustment to correct for chain stretch. This is accomplished by moving the rear wheel spindle forward or backwards in relation to the output shaft. Normally, this is done by having slotted fork ends, though some manufacturers prefer to mount the swinging arm pivot in eccentric blocks. These can then be rotated to provide chain tension adjustment whilst ensuring that the rear wheel alignment is maintained. The need for adjustment does not arise with shaft drive systems, which are simpler in this respect.

The swinging arm ends are connected to the frame by way of a pair of suspension units. These vary considerably in complexity, but normally feature a coil spring fitted around an oil filled damper unit. An eye at each end of the unit is used to attach it to the frame and swinging arm.

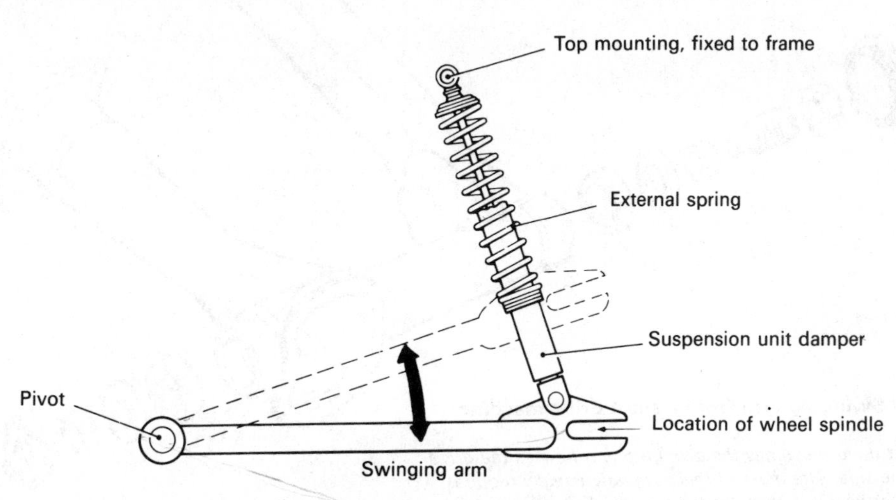


**Fig. 9.1 A swinging arm unit**

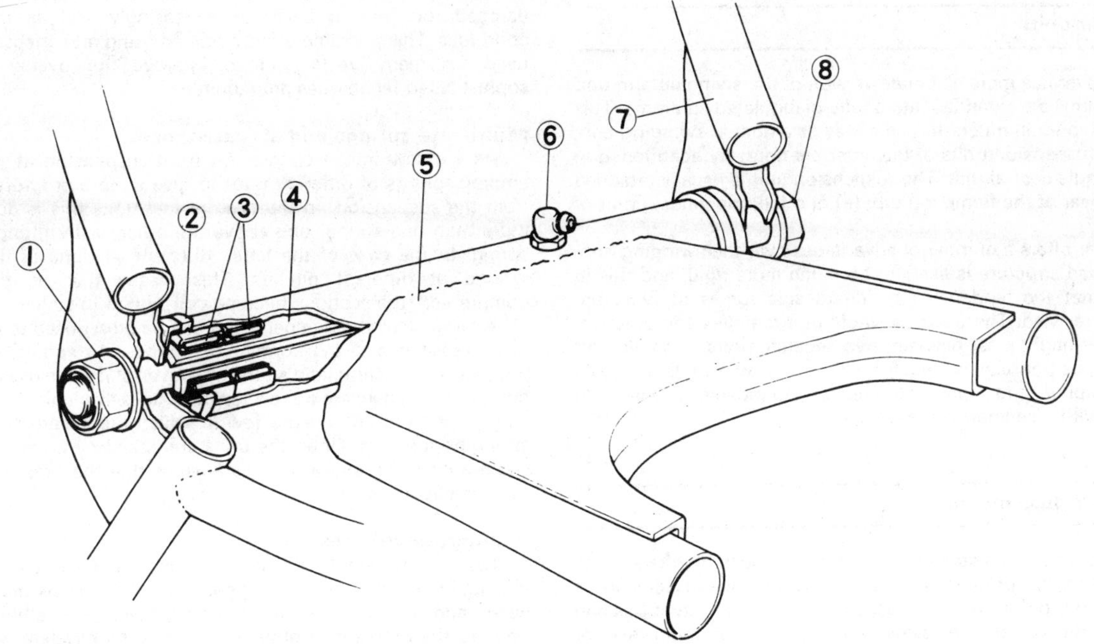


**Fig. 9.2 Section through a swinging arm pivot**

*In this example, needle roller bearings are used. Many other models use plain bushes, whilst some machines use taper roller bearings.*

*1 Nut*
*2 Sealing caps*
*3 Bearings/bushes*
*4 Inner sleeve*
*5 Swinging arm*
*6 Grease nipple*
*7 Frame*
*8 Pivot shaft*

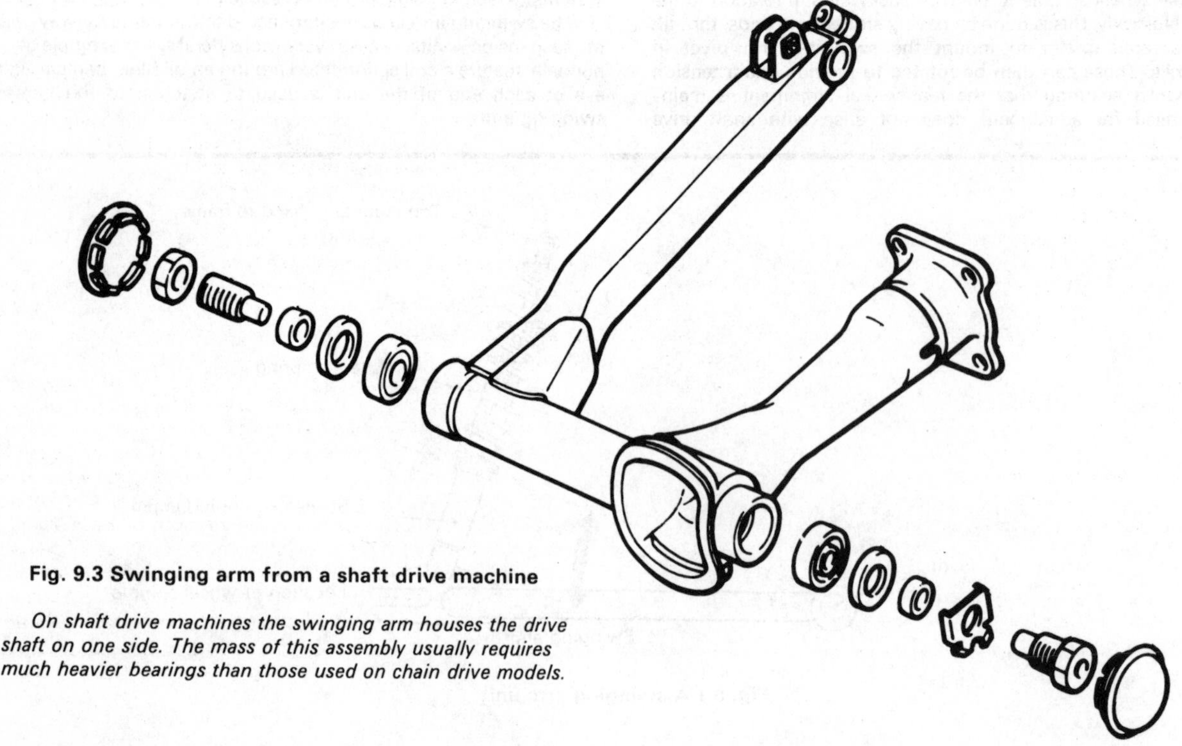

**Fig. 9.3 Swinging arm from a shaft drive machine**

*On shaft drive machines the swinging arm houses the drive shaft on one side. The mass of this assembly usually requires much heavier bearings than those used on chain drive models.*

## 3 Cantilever units

The cantilever is a more elaborate version of the swinging arm unit in which the arms are extended into a fully triangulated subframe. This assembly is pivoted in much the same way as a normal swinging arm, but the twin suspension units of the latter are normally abandoned in favour of a single central unit. The suspension unit is usually attached between the rear of the frame top tube(s) and the uppermost point of the subframe.

A cantilever offers a number of advantages over the swinging arm. The triangulated structure is likely to be much more rigid, and this in turn means that the tendency for side to side forces to twist the assembly are resisted. The use of a single unit removes any potential imbalance that might exist between two separate units. A single unit fitted in this position can be much bulkier than twin units, so more complex damping and springing can be employed, possibly in conjunction with a separate air reservoir.

## 4 Rising rate suspension

Just as the front forks benefit from some arrangement whereby the spring rate can be progressively increased as the suspension is compressed, so too does the rear suspension. To some extent this can be achieved in much the same way, by fitting multi-rate or progressively-wound springs, or by including air or some other gas as a supplementary springing medium. These modifications do work, and are often incorporated in suspension units (see below).

### Inclined suspension units

With a normal twin unit arrangement, a single rising rate effect can be obtained by inclining the units in relation to the swinging arm. If the units are fitted at right angles to the swinging arm, the amount of rear wheel travel is roughly proportional to the amount of suspension unit travel. If the front upper mounting is moved forward, leaving the unit at a steeper angle to the swinging arm, the initial wheel movement takes up very little unit movement, but this relationship becomes more proportional as the angle between the unit and the arm gets greater. The result of this is that the initial wheel movement is softly sprung and damped, but that it becomes increasingly stiff as the deflection continues. This principle offers a limited rising rate effect and has been used for many years, but to improve the overall range more sophisticated techniques are required.

### Multi-rate springs and air assistance

As we saw in the chapter on front suspension, it is possible to employ springs of different rates to give a more progressive response from the suspension. In the case of rear units this is done by fitting more than one spring, one above the other, or by fitting a multi-rate spring. In the case of the latter, different sections of the spring are wound at different pitches. This means that as the spring is compressed, the sections become coil-bound in stages.

Alternatively, the damper insert can be pressurised to give a degree of air assistance to the normal coil springs. Air springing is naturally progressive in action, and so the effective spring rate rises as the unit is compressed. There are quite a few machines available with air-assisted rear suspension and even a few in which the air pressure is the sole springing medium. Often the units are linked by a pressure hose and share a common air valve. This ensures that the pressure in the two units is equalised.

### Rising rate linkages

Rising rate single-shock rear suspension systems have been making increasingly frequent appearances on the new models in recent years, and represent the mechanical answer (if a rather complicated one) to the problem of obtaining a rising rate system with sufficient range to cover all possible operating conditions. This is particularly true of off-road machines, but it also applies to road models.

The various systems currently in use differ widely in appearance, but do the same job in practice. In each case the effect described above for inclined suspension units is used, but the range of the effect is greatly increased through the use of a bell crank or similar linkage. To understand the workings of a typical system, let us look in detail at Suzuki's Full Floater suspension. Other systems operate in a similar fashion, the difference between them being mainly for copyright and patent reasons.

The Suzuki arrangement is based around a single, vertically-mounted suspension unit located just in front of the rear wheel. The unit passes through a U-shaped cut-out at the front of the swinging arm, and is located at its lower end to a bracket just to the rear of the swinging arm pivot. At the top of the unit, it is attached to the front end of a specially-shaped bell crank via a pivot arrangement. Just to the rear of this point, and slightly below it, is the bell crank pivot by which it is attached to the frame. At the rear of the bell crank is a third pivot, this time connected to the tie-rods which run down to the swinging arm at a point just behind the suspension unit. The overall arrangement is difficult to visualise from a verbal description, so it is suggested the accompanying line drawings are studied to get a clearer understanding of the position of each part.

To understand how the system works it should be noted that as the swinging arm is deflected upwards, the suspension unit is pushed up at the lower mounting. At the same time, the rods force the bell crank to pivot at its frame mounting, so the front end moves down, compressing the unit from both ends. The rising rate effect is introduced by the shape of the bell crank and the relative positions of its three pivot points. At rest, the angle formed between the tie-rods, the tie rod pivots and the bell crank frame pivot is about 90°, whilst the angle between the suspension unit, its top mount and the bell crank pivot is roughly half this. This means in practice that the maximum amount of leverage exists between the swinging arm and the suspension unit, so the initial movement is relatively easy; the suspension unit deflecting a small amount in response to a large movement at the rear wheel.

As the swinging arm approaches its maximum deflection, however, these angles are changed quite drastically. The original right angle at between the tie-rods and the bell crank has become much more acute, whilst the suspension unit to bell crank angle is approaching 90°. This means that the leverage exerted by the swinging arm has become far less, and the movement of the unit must be greater for a corresponding movement at the wheel. The overall effect is that the spring rate increases steadily as the swinging arm moves further upwards, and with it the damping effect. This is more useful than changing the spring rate alone, giving much better control at the rear wheel. If possible, it is suggested that the effect of this or any similar rising rate system is observed on a motorcycle so that the changing leverage can be more easily studied.

The advantages of a full rising rate arrangement are clear when compared to the fixed rate of a simple twin-unit arrangement, but care must be taken not to make the assumption that all single-shock systems are of the rising rate type. Yamaha's original Pro-Link suspension, for example, used a simple connection between the cantilever and the suspension unit, and this meant that any rising rate effect was dependent on the progressively-wound spring and nitrogen pressure inside the unit. It is almost inevitable that full rising rate systems will become a common feature on most new machines, but it should also be noted that they are not without disadvantages. Apart from the practical problems of siting the suspension unit where it does not obstruct some other component, and where it can still be cooled by the airflow past the machine, there is the question of wear. With three or more extra pivot points in the suspension, the build-up of play in the various bushes will eventually cause sloppy suspension movement. Another problem involves the question of keeping road dirt and water out of the pivots; not an easy job given their vulnerable location.

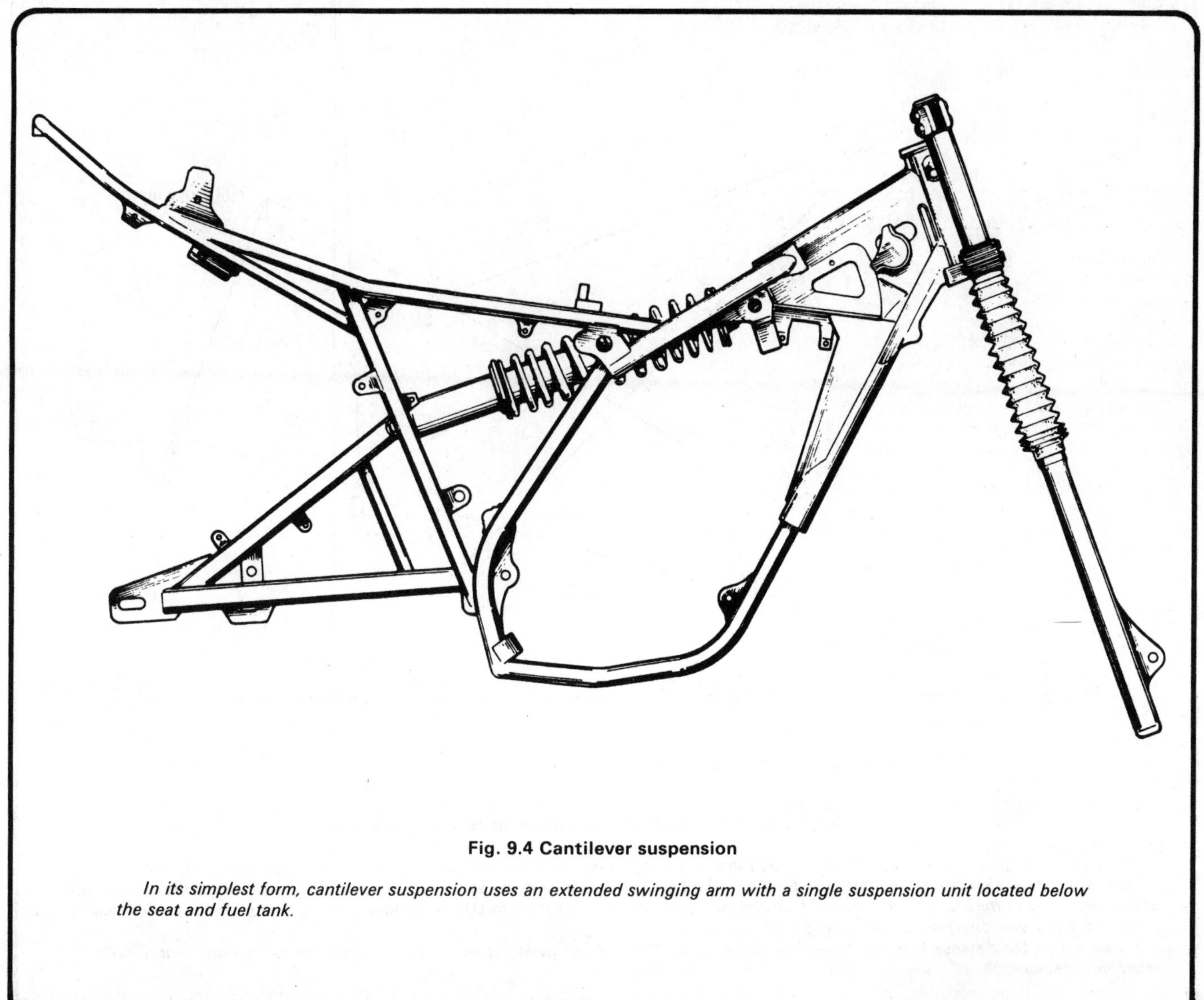

**Fig. 9.4 Cantilever suspension**

*In its simplest form, cantilever suspension uses an extended swinging arm with a single suspension unit located below the seat and fuel tank.*

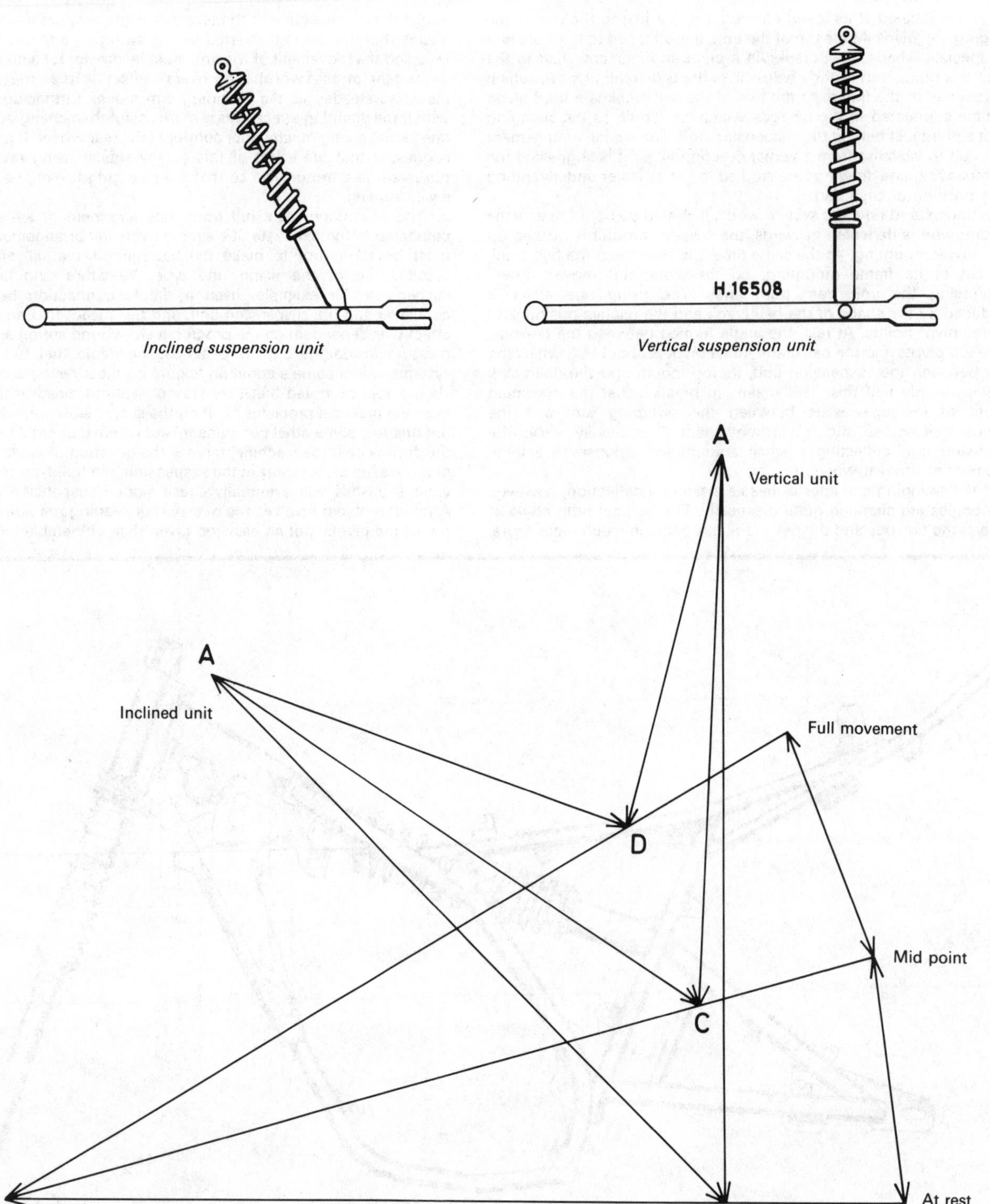


**Fig. 9.5 Rising rate effect from inclined suspension units**

*When the swinging arm is at rest the suspension unit length (A to B) is exactly the same for the inclined and vertical unit. As the swinging arm moves upwards and consequently the suspension unit becomes compressed the amount of compression of the vertical unit is greater than that of the inclined unit (A to C). At full swinging arm movement (A to D) the amount of compression of the vertical unit is progressively greater than that of the inclined unit.*

*In each case the distance from the 'at rest' to mid point positions of the swinging arm is exactly the same as the mid point to full movement positions.*

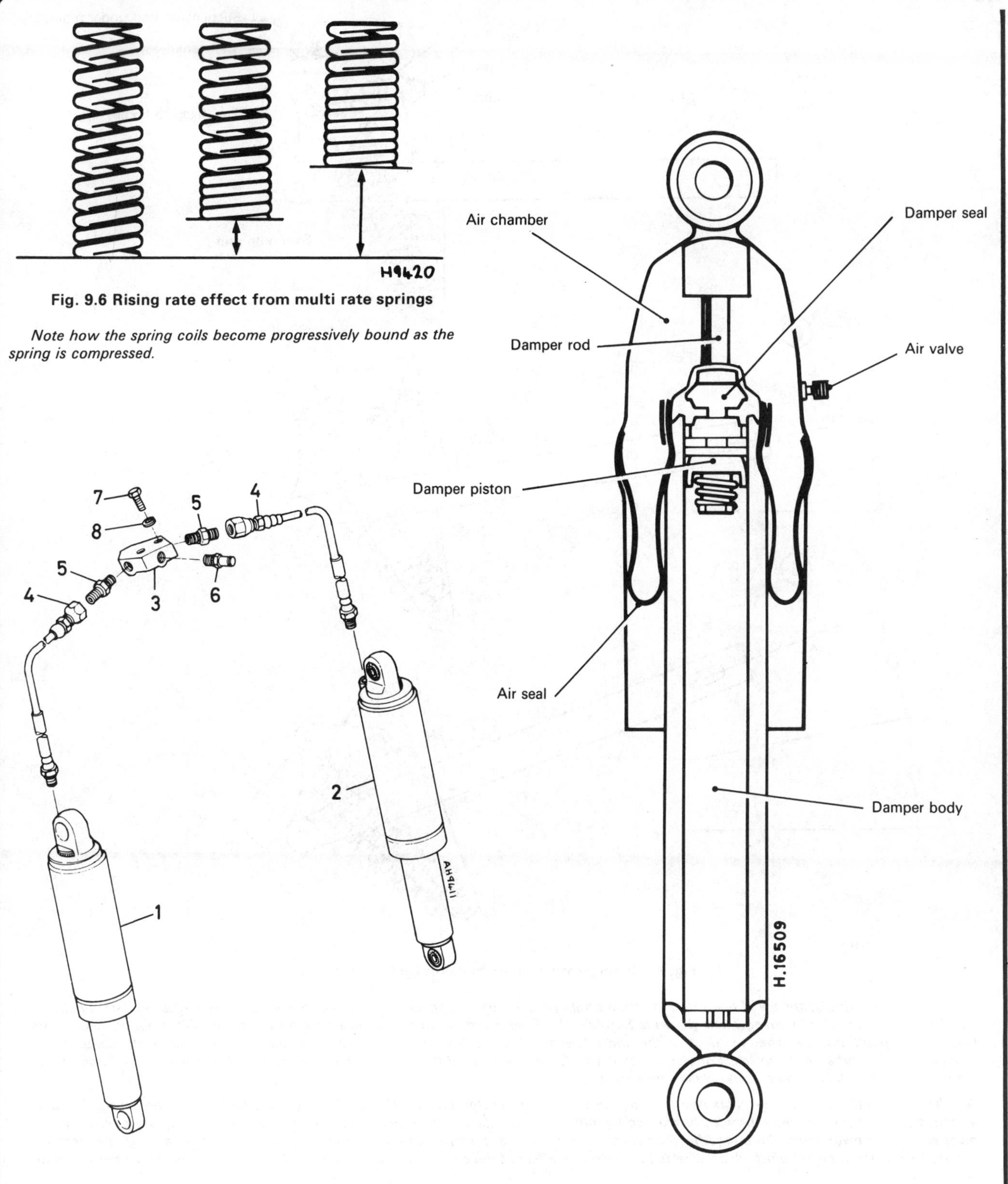


**Fig. 9.6 Rising rate effect from multi rate springs**

*Note how the spring coils become progressively bound as the spring is compressed.*

**Fig. 9.7 Linked air-assisted rear suspension units**

*Where twin units are fitted, they are usually linked by a pressure hose to ensure equal pressure in the two.*

1. *Left-hand suspension unit*
2. *Right-hand suspension unit*
3. *Air valve union*
4. *Air hoses*
5. *Connector*
6. *Air valve*
7. *Mounting bolt*
8. *Spring washer*

**Fig. 9.8 Air rear suspension unit**

*With this type of unit a gas, usually nitrogen, is the sole springing medium*

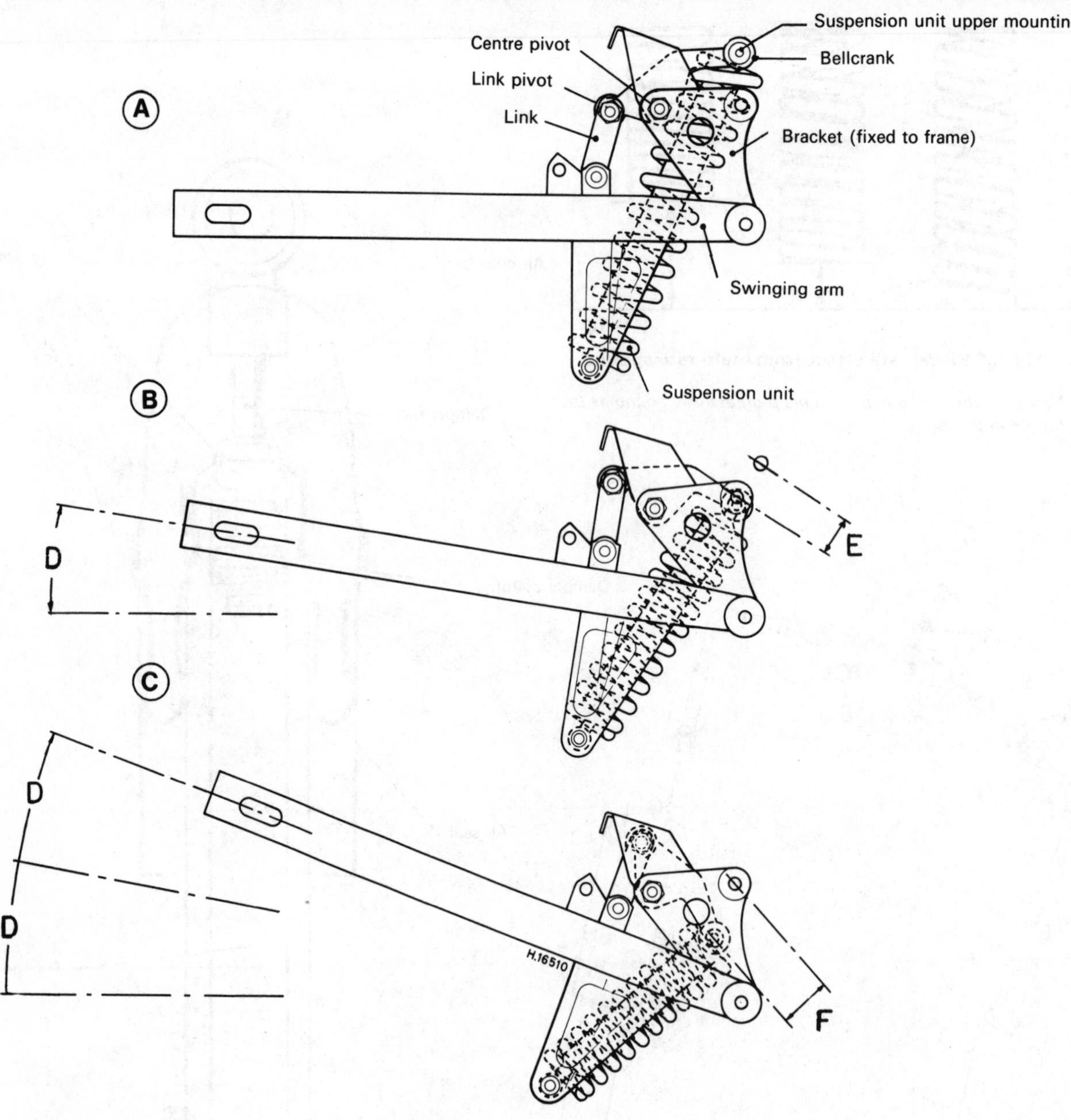


**Fig. 9.9 Rising-rate rear suspension system operation**

*The accompanying sequence of line drawings shows the operation of a rising-rate suspension system in three stages; at rest, at half travel and at full travel. The arrangement shown is Suzuki's Full Floater system, so called because the suspension unit is not attached to the frame at any point, but is allowed to "float" within the suspension linkage. The relative movement of the linkage components has been exaggerated somewhat in the interests of clarity, and it should be remembered that the rising rate effect operates progressively throughout the range of wheel travel; there are no clearly-defined stages.*

**A** *Here we see the major components of the "Full Floater" rear suspension system. The single most important item is the bellcrank, shown in dotted lines where it would otherwise be masked by other components. It will be noted that the bellcrank has three pivot points, the link pivot and centre pivot being closer together than are the centre pivot and suspension unit upper mounting. It is the changing relationship between these three pivot points which creates the rising rate effect at the suspension unit in response to linear movement of the swinging arm.*

**B** *If the swinging arm is moved through a fixed distance (D), movement is transmitted through the link to the link pivot of the bellcrank. The centre pivot of the bellcrank is fixed in relation to the frame, so the bellcrank pivots at this point, pushing the top of the suspension unit downwards by a small amount (E).*

**C** *If we move the swinging arm further, but through the same distance (D) as shown above, the bellcrank again turns about the centre pivot, pushing the top of the suspension unit downwards. In this position, however, the altered geometry of the bellcrank causes the suspension unit to be compressed further than it was in the previous stage – compare (E) and (F). It will be seen that as the swinging arm deflects further it must compress the suspension unit by a proportionally greater amount. In practice this means that the initial travel of the rear wheel is softly sprung and damped, allowing it to follow closely any surface irregularities. Over more drastic bumps the system offers progressively greater resistance and is thus able to cope with a wide variety of surfaces.*

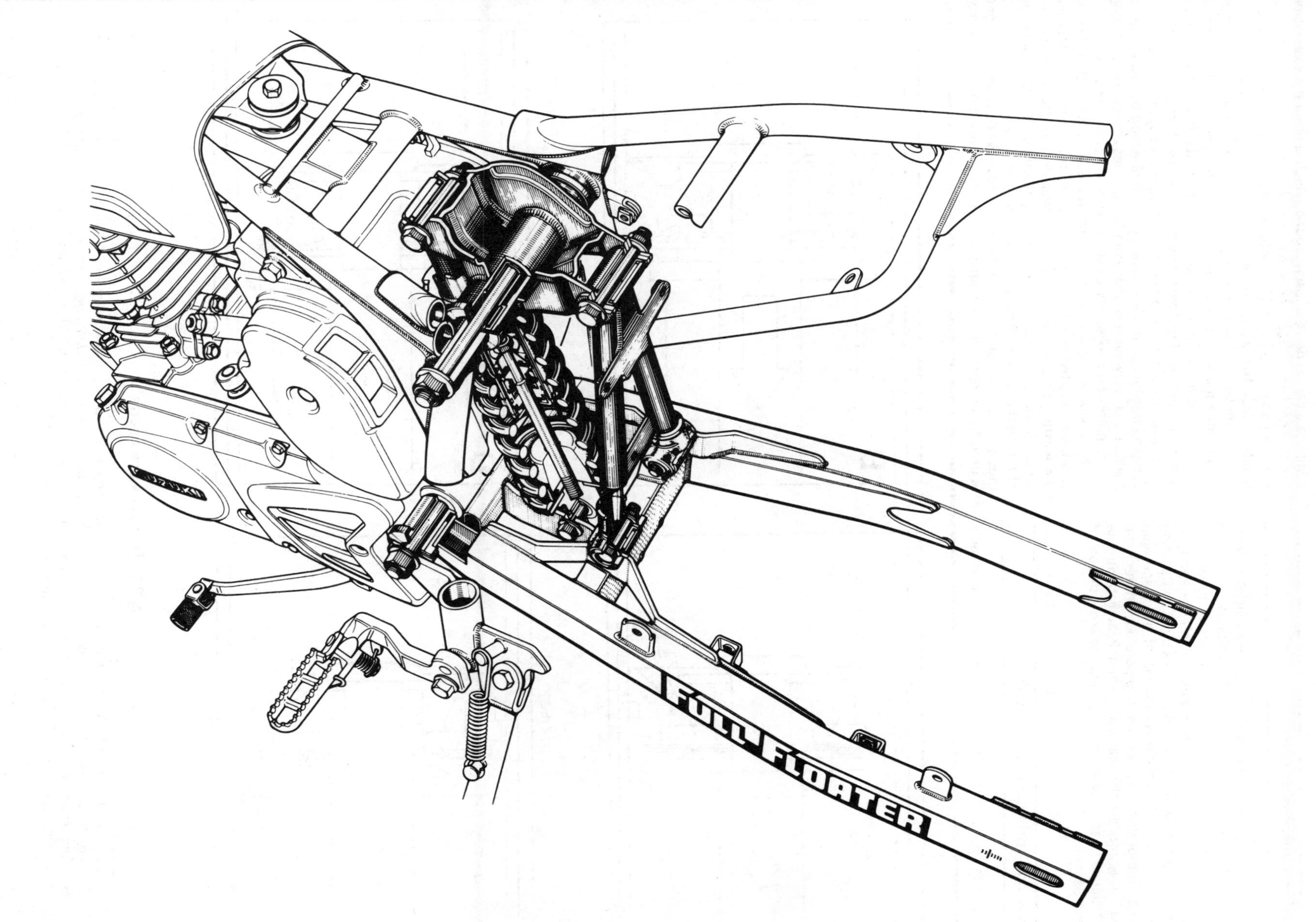


Fig. 9.10 Suzuki "Full Floater" suspension as fitted to the DR125 model

## 5 Undamped rear suspension units

The level of sophistication of the rear suspension unit(s) reflects the type of machine on which they are fitted. On a simple moped, for example, the units often consist of a concentric pair of tubes with mounting lugs at each end, around (or inside) which the spring is fitted. Like the front suspension on machines of this type, no damping is provided. On larger machines more is required of the suspension system, so some form of damping must be incorporated. On the more expensive and larger models the rear units often feature multi-rate springs, air assistance or adjustable damping, and these are discussed in the following Sections.

## 6 Oil-damped coil-spring suspension units

On many small to medium size machines the rear suspension units comprise a sealed damper insert around which is fitted the suspension spring. The damper body takes the form of a tube in which the damper rod and piston move through a light oil. As with the front suspension, the damping effect is minimal during compression, and this allows the wheel to deflect readily when it encounters a bump in the road surface. During the extension stroke the effect is much higher, and this prevents the wheel from pattering over surface irregularities. In its simplest form, damping is achieved by forcing oil through a small hole in the piston, but this means that the damping effect is similar in both directions. The damping rate can be made different in each direction by incorporating a simple one-way valve so that extra bleed holes are uncovered during the compression stroke only to allow relatively easy movement.

A popular valve arrangement employs one or more thin flexible washers supported at their inner and outer edges. During compression, the washer distorts under hydraulic pressure from the damping oil, which flows past the outer edge. On the rebound stroke, the inner edge of the washer opens offering a more restricted passage for the oil and thus a greater damping effect. Where two valve washers are fitted, one is used for compression damping and the other for rebound damping.

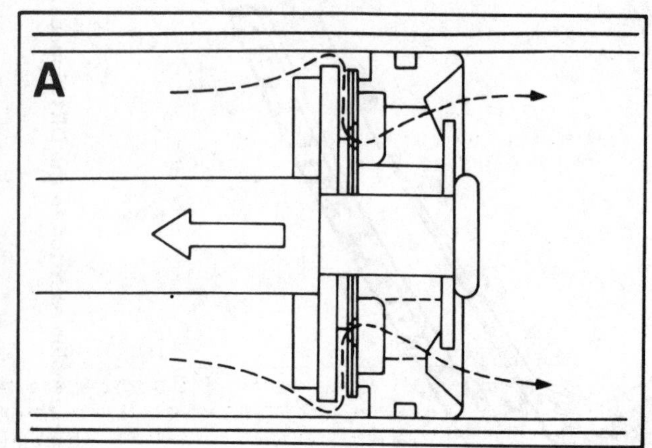


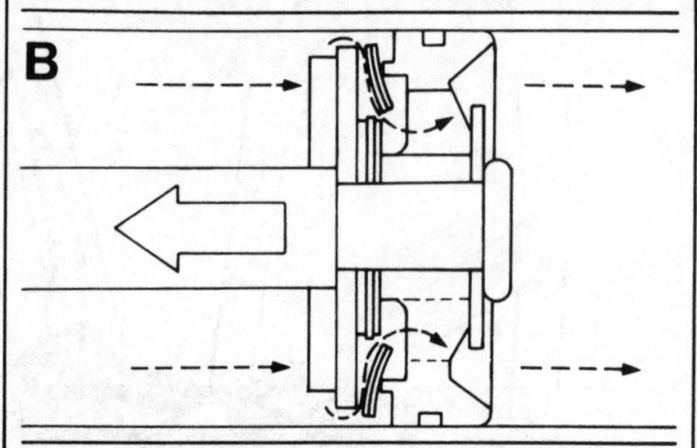


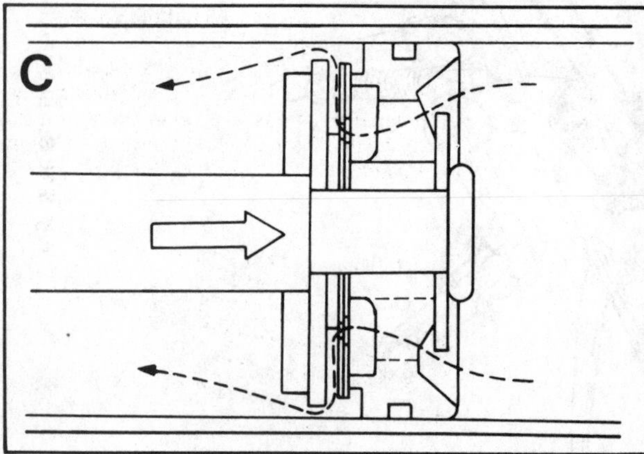


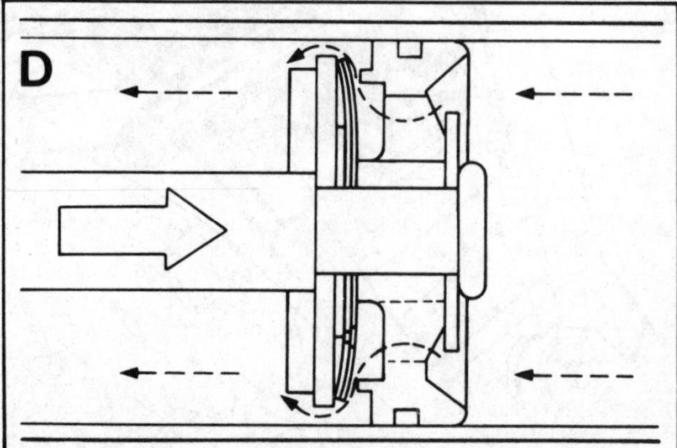


**Fig. 9.11 Damper valve operation**

*In this De Carbon type unit a variable damping rate is obtained by using a thin spring steel washer which can deform under pressure. In drawing (A) the damping oil flows through a conventional fixed orifice to give compression damping. If the rate of compression increases, the washer will deform as shown in (B). A similar pattern occurs during rebound damping; in (C) the oil flows through the fixed orifice, whilst in (D) the washer has deformed to allow faster response.*

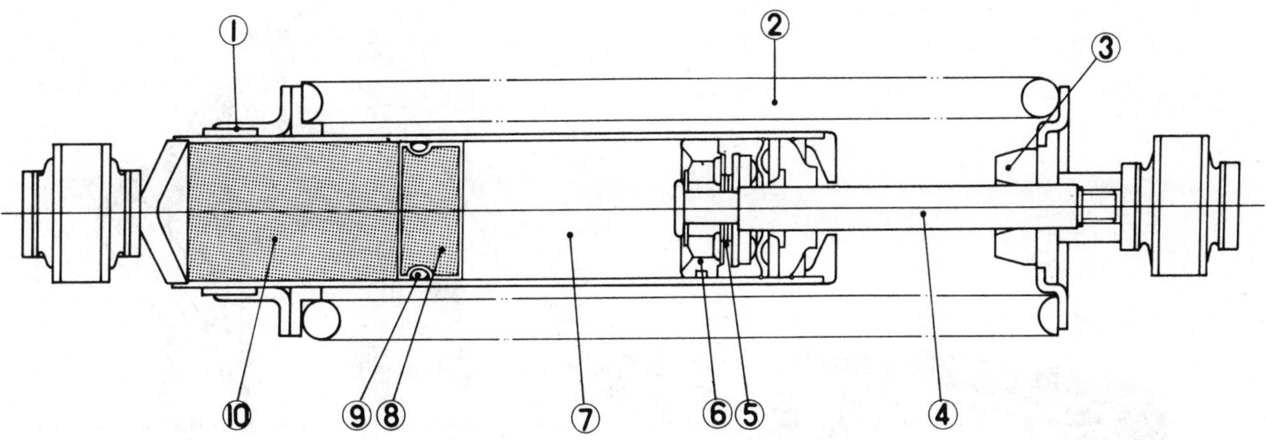


**Fig. 9.12 Gas-filled damper unit**

*Gas under pressure is contained at one end of the unit, separated from the damping oil by a floating piston (8).*

*1 Preload adjuster*
*2 Spring*
*3 Rubber bump stop*
*4 Damper rod*
*5 Valve*
*6 Piston*
*7 Oil chamber*
*8 Free piston*
*9 O-ring*
*10 Gas chamber*

## 7 Gas-filled suspension units

Under hard use, the problem of cavitation in the damping oil can cause the damping effect to be diminished. Cavitation occurs when the damper piston is moving faster than the oil is able to cope with. The oil is unable to flow through the valve quickly enough, so cavities of air appear in the stream of oil. As has been noted earlier, gas makes a poor damping medium; it can be compressed or decompressed quite easily, so the damper will 'fade' and allow the unit to bounce.

The obvious solution would seem to be to fill the damper completely with oil, thus excluding the air which causes cavitation. The problem is that dampers get hot during use as a result of the friction of the oil passing through the valves at high pressure and the repeated compression of any air present. This means that the oil will expand and contract depending on its operating temperature, and so there must be some provision to allow for this. One method is to replace the air space above the oil with a series of sealed bladders, usually containing nitrogen as an inert gas. Expansion can still take place, but the cavitation problem is avoided because there is no direct contact between the oil and gas.

Later arrangements have contained nitrogen or air under pressure above the oil, but separated from it by a floating piston. More recently, remote reservoir designs have become popular. In the case of these units there is a reservoir of oil attached to the unit and connected to it by a passage or by a flexible pressure hose. A piston or bladder in the reservoir allows the unit to be pressurised as in the above example. The damper itself contains only oil, so the heat build-up is greatly reduced. Any expansion of the oil is catered for by the reservoir. Many of these units have an external air valve to allow the reservoir to be pressurised. This should not be confused with air-sprung or air-assisted suspension units; the air in a remote reservoir type serves only to prevent the cavitation of the damping oil.

## 8 Spring preload adjustment

All but the simplest types of suspension units feature some sort of spring preload adjustment. This allows the initial spring rate to be varied to cope with the additional loadings imposed by a passenger or luggage. It should be noted that it does not alter the rate throughout the unit's range; it simply determines the point at which the spring begins to compress. Without this adjustment, a heavily laden machine might have used up half of its travel when static, and this would probably cause the suspension to bottom out over relatively small bumps. Conversely, if the preload is too high, all but the biggest bumps will be transmitted directly to the frame and rider.

The usual method of preload adjustment is provided by a cam ring which can be turned with a C-spanner to the desired position. Most units have three or five preload positions. On other units, the lower spring seat is threaded onto the damper body, and thus can be screwed up or down to the correct setting.

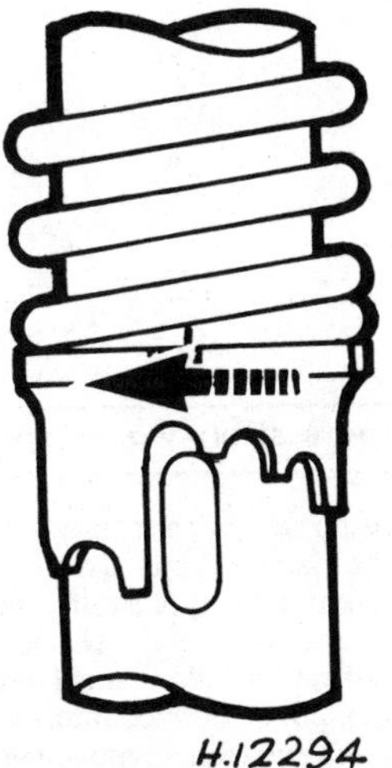


**Fig. 9.13 Spring preload adjuster**

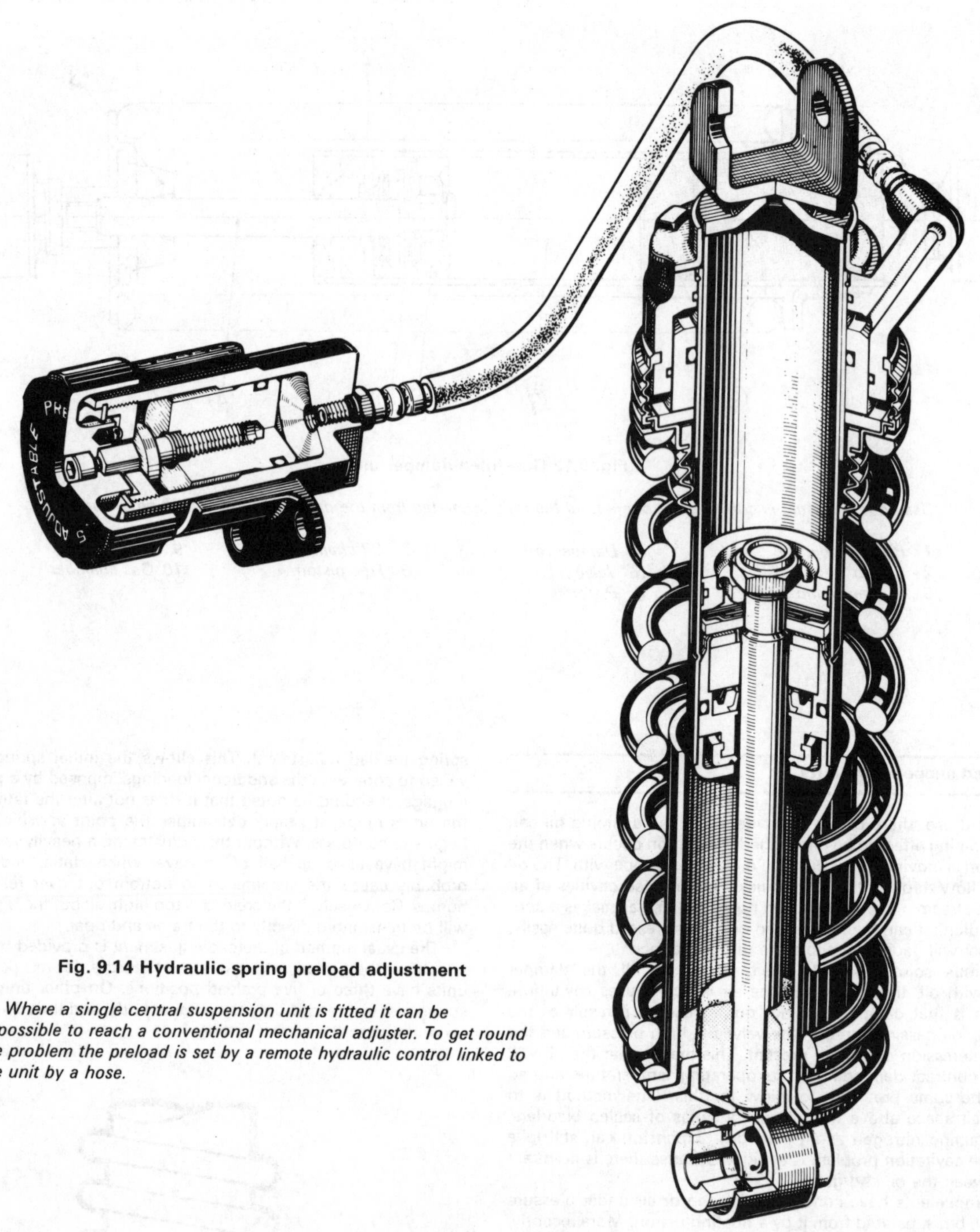


**Fig. 9.14 Hydraulic spring preload adjustment**

*Where a single central suspension unit is fitted it can be impossible to reach a conventional mechanical adjuster. To get round the problem the preload is set by a remote hydraulic control linked to the unit by a hose.*

## 9 Multiple and progressively-wound springs

Some degree of rising rate effect can be obtained by fitting more than one spring to the damper body. These are normally fitted one above the other, each spring being of a different rate. During the initial suspension movement, the softer of the two springs compresses quite easily, allowing the wheel to follow small irregularities in the road surface. When a larger bump is encountered, the soft spring soon becomes coil-bound, and subsequent movement is then controlled by the stiffer spring. This arrangement gives only a limited rising rate effect, and is divided into two distinct stages. Despite this, it offers a finer degree of wheel control than is possible with a single spring.

Progressively-wound springs, like those used in some telescopic fork legs, are designed to become coil bound in a progressive manner from one end. As successive coils come into contact, the effective rate of the spring increases, Like the multiple spring units, this means that the springing becomes harder as the wheel travel increases, but the effect is more progressive than would be the case with two separate springs.

## 10 Air assisted and air suspension units

With the simplest versions of this type of unit, the standard coil spring is supplemented by internal air pressure to give a rising spring rate. The spring provides a basic (relatively soft) spring rate, but as deflection increases the rising air or gas pressure comes into play. The units normally have a valve through which air pressure can be set using a pump or air line. The volume of air in the units is small, so to maintain equal pressure in twin units, the two are often linked by a pressure hose.

The logical extension of the above is to dispense with the coil spring entirely, leaving air pressure as the sole springing medium. Until recently units of this type were available only as rather expensive after-market items, but some of the larger Japanese tourers now fit full air suspension as standard. In its most developed form, the machine carries an on-board compressor which allows the spring rate to be raised or lowered while riding. This type of unit works very well indeed, its only real drawback being the initial expense and complexity of a full compressor-based installation.

## 11 Adjustable damping

An increasing number of the more exotic units now provide adjustable damping rates. The damping effect is controlled from an external dial which controls the damper valve opening via a control rod. This arrangement is an ideal complement to an air assisted unit, because various combinations of air pressure and damper settings can provide numerous overall suspension rates to cope with a wide variety of conditions and loadings. The only problem is that the settings must be made manually. Given that road surface variations occur constantly during a journey, the ideal combination of spring and damping rates cannot be maintained exactly. The answer to this problem is to arrange both to be automatically adjusted according to the suspension movement, and it is this which has encouraged the development of the numerous mechanical rising-rate systems discussed above.

# Chapter 10 The electrical system

## Contents



## 1 Introduction

Every motorcycle, moped or scooter is equipped with some sort of electrical system. In the case of a moped this may be very basic, sufficient only to provide direct lighting and a horn. At the other extreme there is the modern large capacity motorcycle, featuring a wealth of electrical equipment and often using fairly advanced microprocessor-based warning circuits and instrumentation.

As in previous Chapters, we will be concentrating on the basic layout of various electrical systems, and on how the various bits and pieces work. There will be minimal discussion of the niceties of electrical theory; there are plenty of reference books on this subject for those who wish to know more, especially the Motorcycle Electrical Manual, another book in the Haynes Motorcycle Owners Workshop Manual series.

## 2 The electrical circuit

Most people will have some idea about a basic electrical circuit. An ordinary hand torch provides a good illustration, so if you have any doubts, buy a torch battery, a bulb and a piece of wire and make up the arrangement shown in the accompanying diagram. This shows the basic elements of a simple circuit, and has the added bonus of being a useful way of checking switches and bulbs on your own machine, should the need arise. The battery used is one of the flat 4.5 volt types with spring terminals and is easy to connect up by soldering the leads to them. The crocodile clips shown are useful for test connections and can be bought from most electrical or motor accessory shops, but they are not essential.

To make up the battery and bulb circuit, cut two lengths of wire about two feet long, and one about 3-4 inches long, and strip about one inch of insulation from the ends. If you have a soldering iron, proceed as follows, or alternatively ask someone to do this for you. Tin the bared ends of the wires, the battery terminals and the side of the bulb. Solder the short wire between the base of the bulb and one battery terminal. Solder the first long lead to the remaining battery terminal, then connect the final lead to the side of the bulb. If you touch the free ends of the long leads together, the bulb should now light up. To make a neater job, tape the bulb onto the side of the battery and fit a crocodile clip to the end of each lead.

Every electrical circuit on your motorcycle uses the same basic layout as this test circuit, but with a few detail changes. For a start, there is often just one wire running to a particular component. This is because the steel frame of the machine is used to replace the remaining wire, and thus is common to all circuits. It is known as 'earth' in the UK, or 'ground' in the US. If the machine has a battery, and thus a direct current electrical system, the battery terminal connected to the frame determines the polarity of the earth. In most cases the negative (-) terminal is connected to the frame, and the machine is then said to have a negative earth system. If you switch on a light, the power flows from the positive (+) battery terminal, through the wiring and switch to the bulb, returning through the frame to the negative (-) terminal. On some, mainly older, machines a positive (+) earth system was used, but this is uncommon today.

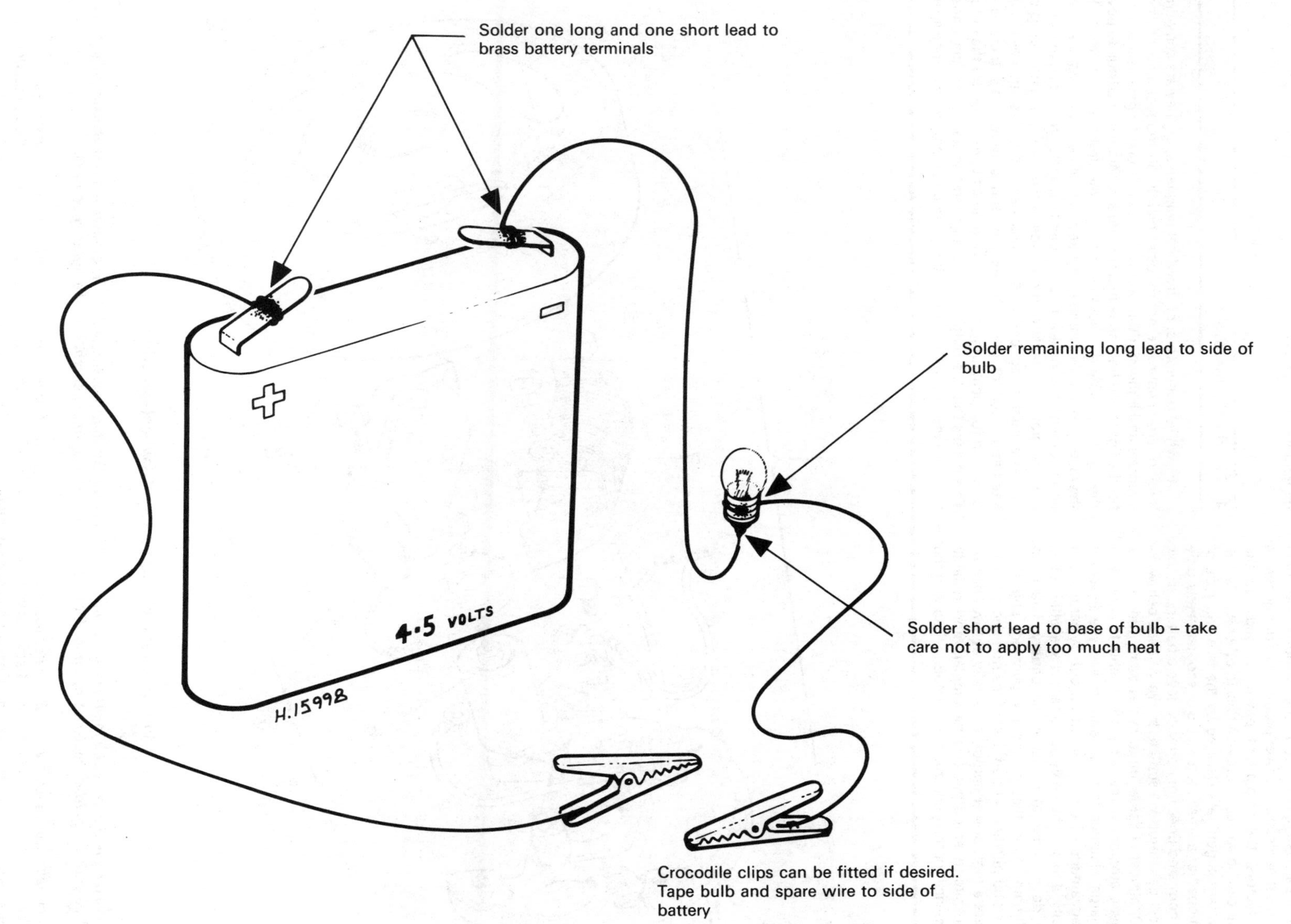
Solder one long and one short lead to brass battery terminals
Solder remaining long lead to side of bulb
4·5 VOLTS
H.15998
Solder short lead to base of bulb – take care not to apply too much heat
Crocodile clips can be fitted if desired. Tape bulb and spare wire to side of battery

Fig. 10.1 A simple test circuit

## 3 Generating power

On all motor vehicles, a proportion of the power from the engine is converted into electrical energy to run the various electrical components. The amount of electrical power produced in the system is dependent on two factors; the amount of power needed and the amount of power that can be spared to provide this. In other words, the complexity of the system is generally decided by the size and type of machine. A simple moped or a small motorcycle or scooter needs only basic lighting and a horn, and does not normally have a battery. In this case a simple flywheel generator will suffice, as we will see below.

Until about 1960, almost all larger motorcycles were fitted with a direct current (dc) generator, or dynamo. These were able to cope with the demands of a large electrical system, and, unlike the flywheel generator, had the advantage of direct current output. A battery can only store dc electricity, and so when only ac current is available, it has to be converted to dc in order to recharge the battery. The main drawback of the dynamo was that it was complicated, and thus expensive to produce and needing a good deal of maintenance. It was also unable to provide a high power output, especially at low speeds.

The alternator, despite its ac output, is a far simpler, more reliable and more powerful device for the generation of electricity than was the dynamo. For this reason it has more or less replaced the latter on all modern machines. The dynamo survives on many post-war British machines and on recent CZ and MZ models, but with due apologies to owners of these machines we will confine our attention to ac generators from here on.

## 4 Flywheel generators

Flywheel generators, or 'flywheel magnetos' as they are sometimes known, are simple alternators used mainly on mopeds and on some scooters and lightweight motorcycles. In addition to generating power for the lights and horn they incorporate a separate source coil to power the ignition system, and occasionally the ignition coil itself. The flywheel generator comprises a fixed baseplate known as the stator, and a rotating flywheel with permanent magnets embedded in its outer rim. The stator is attached to one side of the crankcase and carries one or more generating coils. Machines using this system have a full alternating current electrical system, and consequently there is no provision for rectifying (converting to direct current, or dc) the output. This means that the output from the generating coil is carefully chosen to match the demands of the lighting circuit at maximum engine speed.

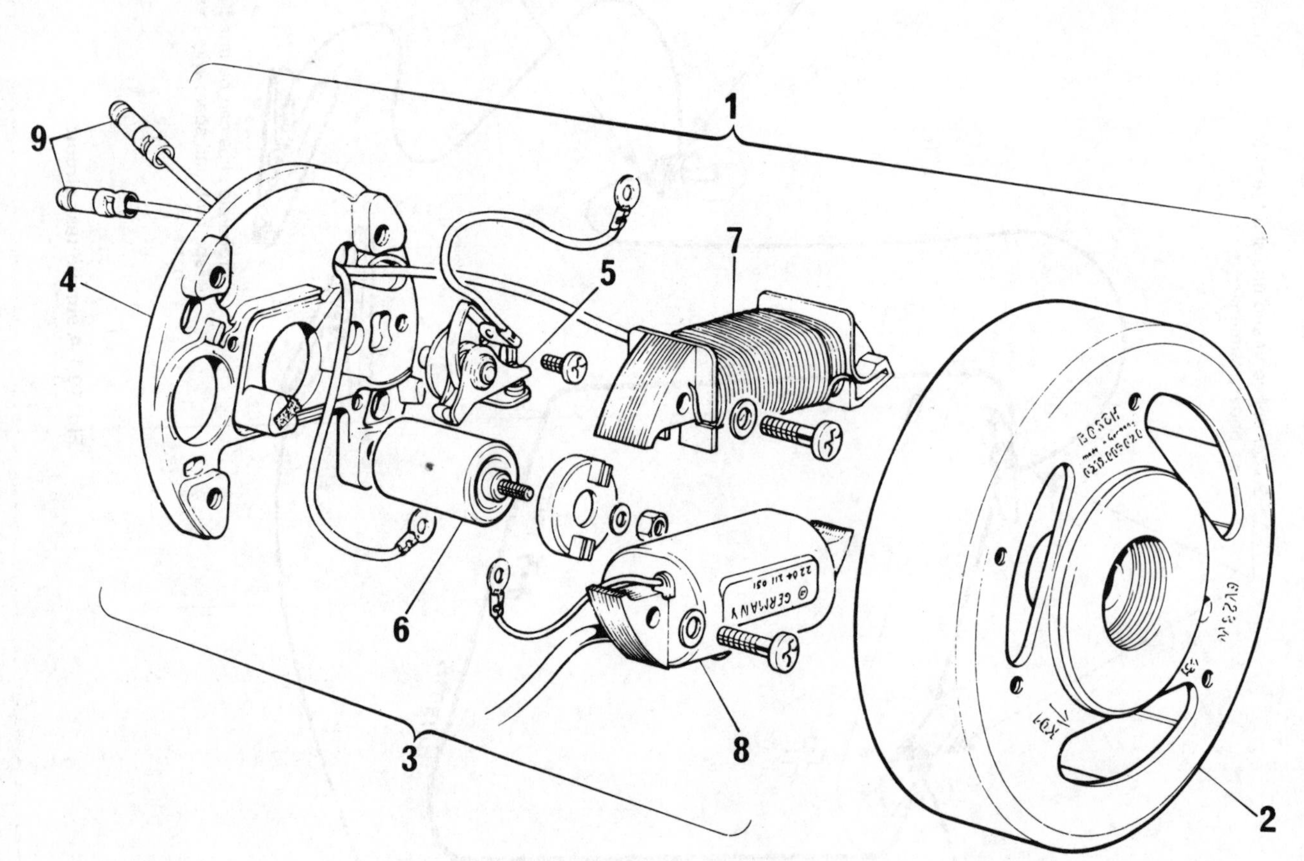


**Fig. 10.2 Typical moped-type flywheel generator**

*Note that in this example the generator includes the ignition coil as part of the stator assembly (8). On other machines an external coil may be used, in which case this would be replaced by an ignition source coil, similar in appearance to the lighting coil (7).*

*1 Flywheel generator assembly complete*
*2 Flywheel rotor*
*3 Stator assembly*
*4 Stator plate*
*5 Contact breaker assembly*
*6 Condenser (capacitor)*
*7 Lighting coil*
*8 Ignition coil*
*9 Bullet terminals*

Power is generated by induction, a principle discussed in the ignition Chapter. To recap briefly, if a wire is passed through a magnetic field, a current is induced in the wire. This flows in one direction as the field builds up, and then reverses as the field decays. In a generator, the field is created by the permanent magnets which sweep past the wire, which is wound into coils to maximise the effect. As each of the magnets passes the coil the current flows first one way, and then the other, hence the term alternating current, or 'ac' for short.

When the machine's lighting system is turned off, the coil is earthed, and no current flows around the lighting circuit. When the lights are switched on the current is obliged to flow through the bulbs in the head and tail lamps, lighting them. At low engine speeds, the power output is limited and the lights will tend to be rather dim. There is also a noticeable flickering as the current alternates rapidly back and forth through a 'dead point'. As the engine speed rises, so too does the output of the generator, but only to a certain level due to what is known as the "terminal voltage" of a particular generator. We need not go into this aspect too deeply here; suffice it to say that the internal losses of the coils means that the output curve gradually tails off after a certain engine speed, and this makes the generator more or less self-regulating. In practice this means that the lights become brighter, and the flickering effect is no longer noticeable.

## 5 Flywheel generator/battery systems

The simple flywheel generator system described above works well enough for most purposes, but if it is wished to fit turn signals, for example, it is no longer adequate. This is mostly because conventional turn signal relays are designed for dc operation from a stable power supply. To get round this problem, many manufacturers fit a hybrid system, where the necessary power for the turn signals is derived from a separate generating coil. The output from this coil is fed through a rectifier, in the form of a single diode, to a small battery. This is then used to supply the turn signals and also parking lights if these are fitted. The rest of the lighting system is supplied directly from the generator and is ac.

The rectifier, as mentioned above, is a single diode encapsulated in a resin block. The diode acts as a one-way valve, allowing current to flow in one direction only. This means that half the output is lost as the diode clips away one side of the output wave, and this gives the system its name; half-wave rectification. Whilst this is not an efficient way to use the coil's output, it is simple, cheap and adequate for the purpose. The system is most often found on the more luxurious mopeds and on small trail bikes where low weight is an important factor.

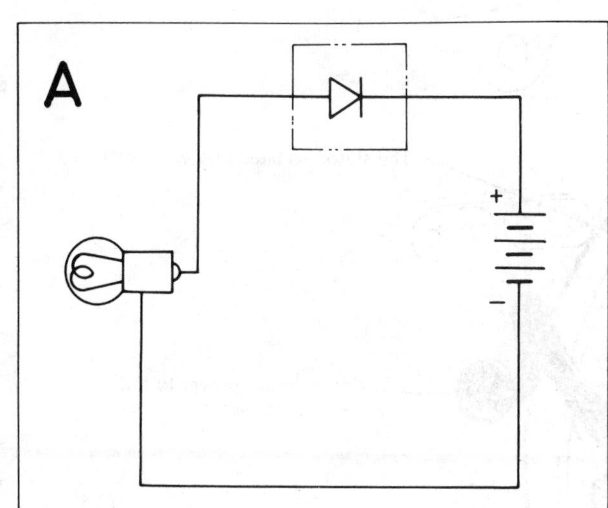


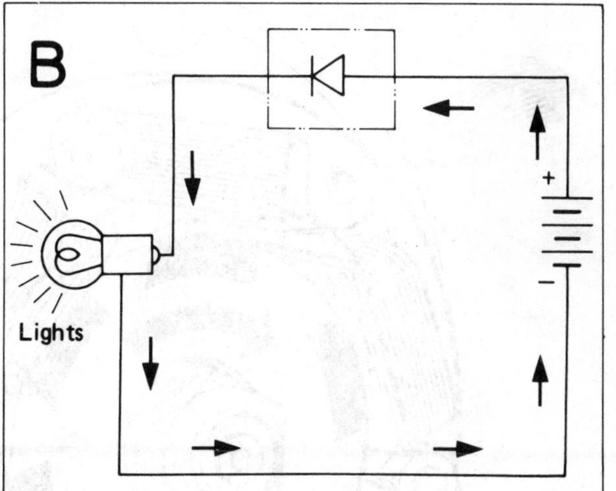


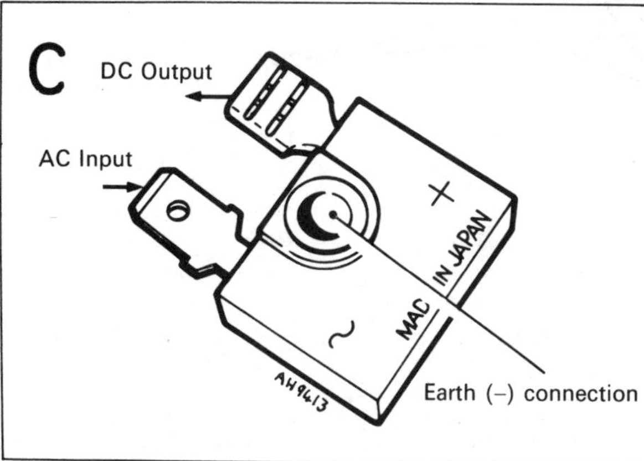


**Fig. 10.3 How a silicon rectifier (diode) works**

**A** *If we connect a silicon rectifier as shown, the current flow from the positive terminal (+) to the negative terminal is blocked, and the lamp does not light.*

**B** *If we turn the rectifier round, current can now flow, and the bulb is lit.*

*If we replace the battery in the above circuit with an alternator the output will attempt to flow first in one direction and then the other. The one-way flow through the diode means that alternate cycles will be blocked, leaving half the output flowing in one direction only. Because half the output wave is lost this is known as half-wave rectification.*

**C** *This is what most simple half-wave silicon rectifiers look like. The small resin-encapsulated unit is bolted to the frame, often below the seat or side panels.*

## 6 Alternator systems: single phase types

A full alternator system is used on all larger machines where a battery is used to supply the entire electrical system. The alternator itself is like a heavy-duty flywheel generator. In its simplest form, an 'internal permanent magnet single phase alternator' is used. This unwieldy term can be unravelled as follows: The rotor consists of a drum-shaped unit keyed to the end of the crankshaft. Embedded in the alloy casting are (normally) six permanent magnets, and these are visible in the form of their laminated pole tips. Fitted around the rotor is the stator assembly comprising six generating coils mounted on a stator. The latter often takes the form of laminated iron rings, and the whole assembly is sometimes encapsulated in resin for protection.

By using much more powerful magnets in the rotor, and bigger coils positioned OUTSIDE the rotor, a lot more power can be obtained. In the early days of alternators, this was controlled by switching combinations of coils in or out to suit the demands of the system, and as such the system was only very roughly regulated. The more important requirement was that the output be converted to direct current (dc) so that a battery could be used. The single diode rectifier described above is a simple device, but as we saw it wastes half the output. Given that the object of the alternator is to produce a lot more power, we cannot afford to lose half of it, and so a more sophisticated rectifier is required.

The answer to the problem is the bridge, or full-wave rectifier. This device comprises four diodes connected in such a way that the output from the rectifier is dc, irrespective of the changing phases of the alternator. The accompanying diagram shows this process more clearly than a verbal description, and should be studied before reading further. Physically, the bridge rectifier is a small, heavily finned device which is bolted to a sound earth point on the frame. The finning (or heatsink) allows the heat generated in the device to be dispersed by the airflow past the machine, and by conduction to the frame. The use of a full-wave rectifier makes a lot of difference to the final output of the alternator. In the case of a half-wave (single diode) device, only about 37% of the unrectified current is available. With full-wave rectification, this figure rises to about 63%.

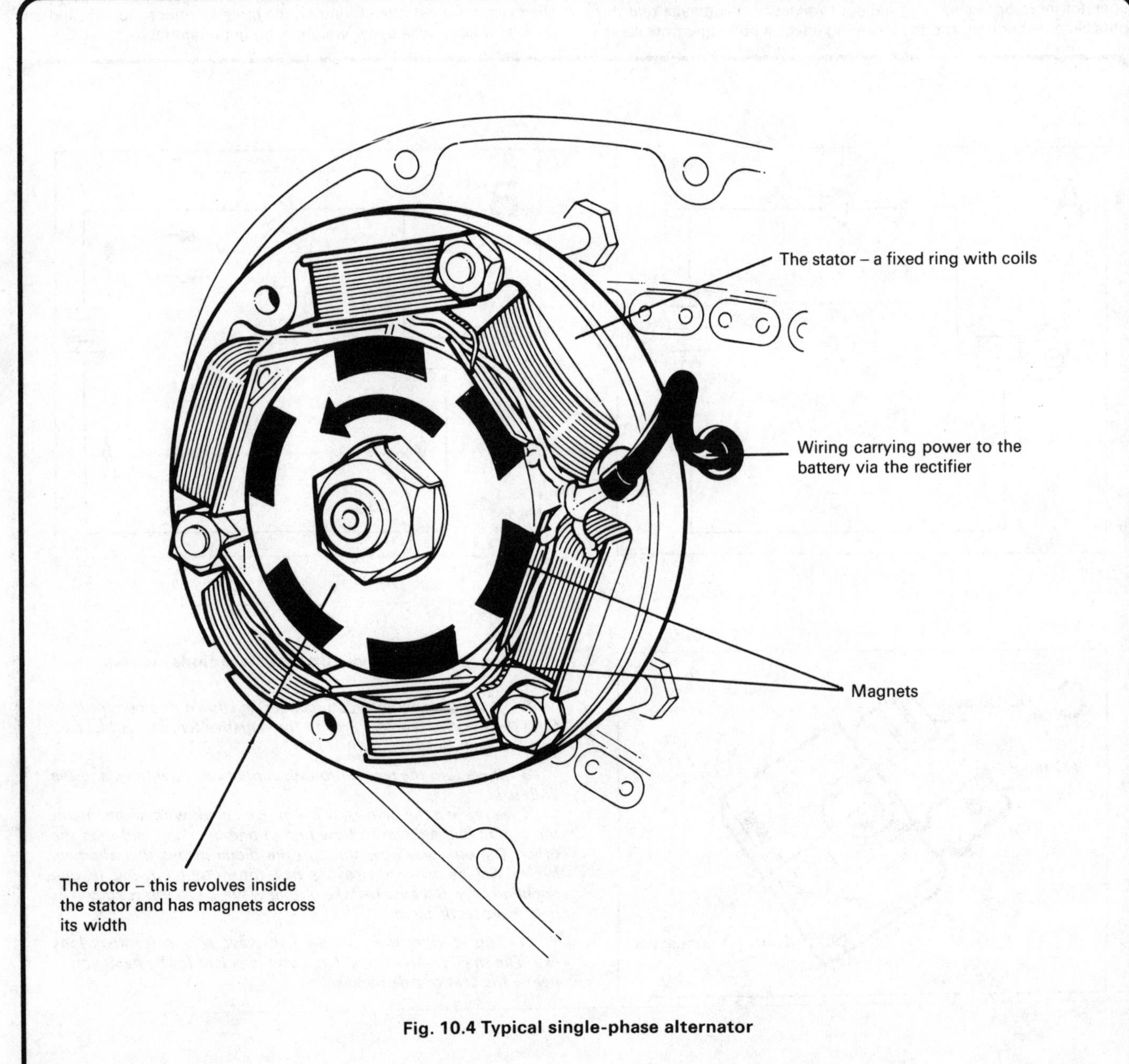


Fig. 10.4 Typical single-phase alternator

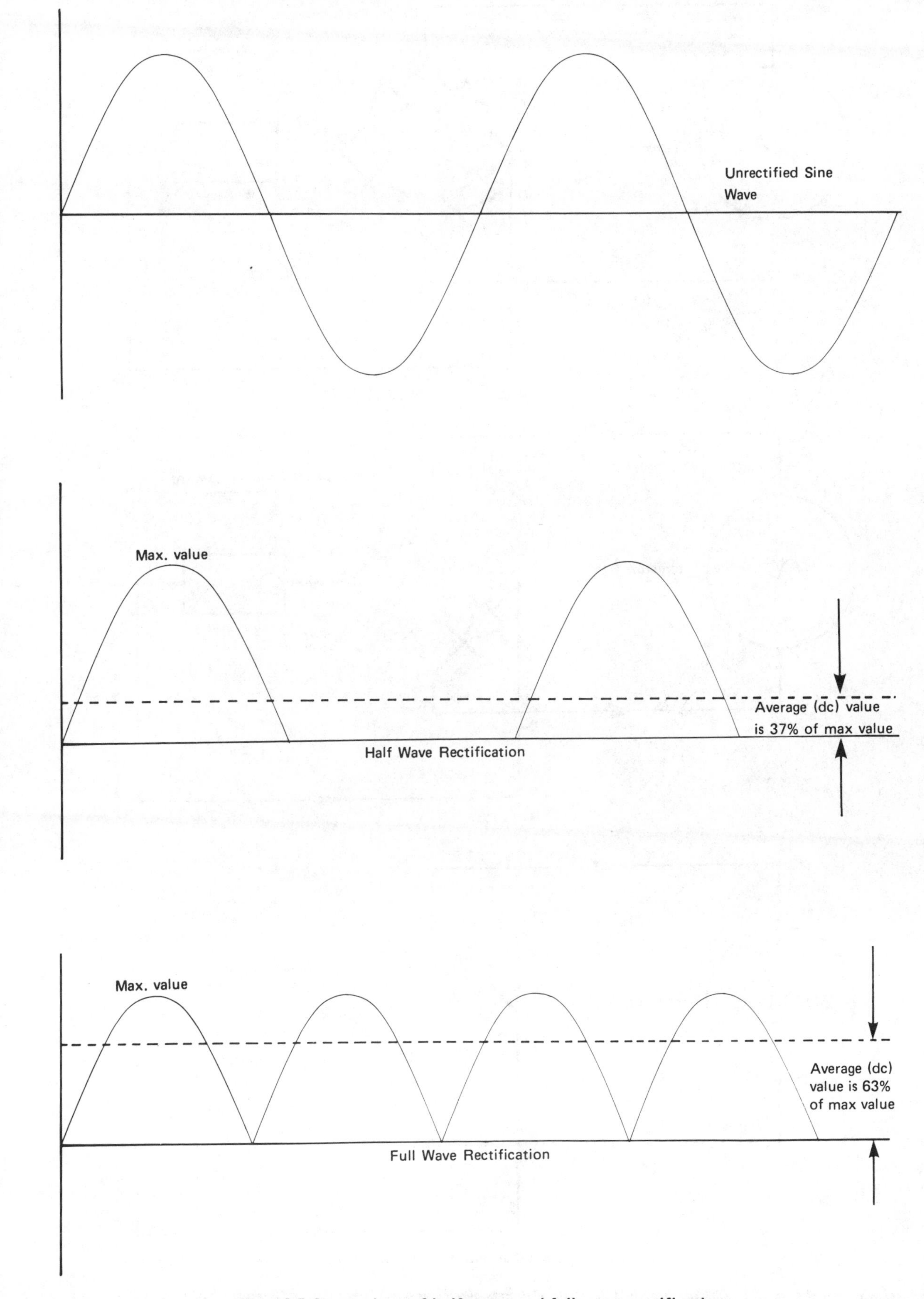


**Fig. 10.5 Comparison of half-wave and full-wave rectification**

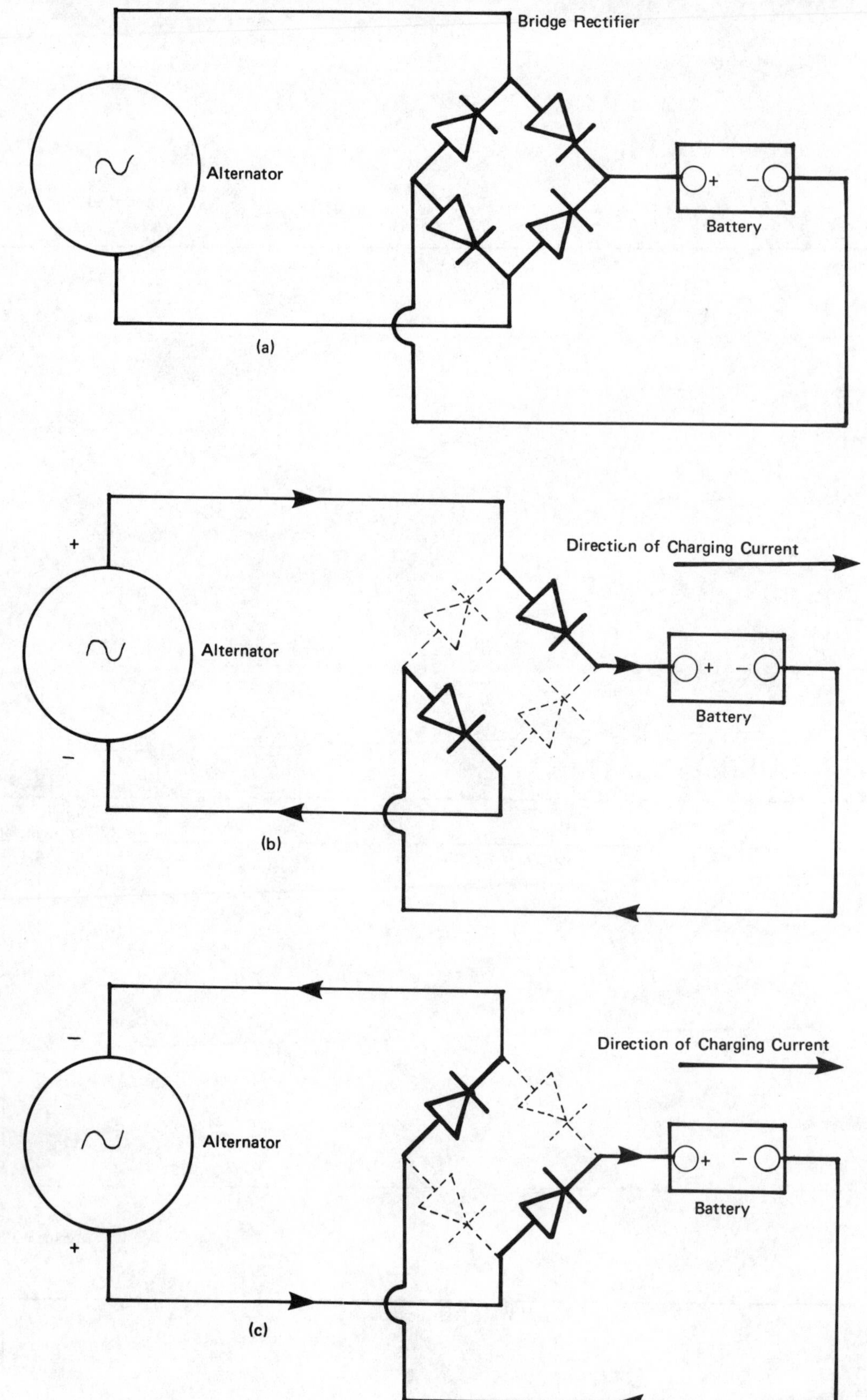


**Fig. 10.6 How a full wave rectifier works**

*The full wave rectifier circuit (a). Note how first one pair of diodes allow current to pass (b) and then the opposite pair (c) so that the direction of current remains the same.*

## 7 The zener diode and electronic voltage regulators

With the demand on the electrical system continuing to rise as machines become more sophisticated, the method of controlling the alternator by switching its coils in and out soon proved inadequate. In the case of machines using Lucas alternators, the introduction of the zener diode allowed the simple, single phase alternator to be run at 12 volts, rather than six, and almost doubled its output. A zener diode works in the same way as the pressure relief valve in a lubrication system. As the voltage in the system rises with the engine speed the zener becomes conductive (at about 14 volts). The excess power is dumped to earth, and the system is thus regulated. As the system voltage drops as a result of the lights being switched on, the zener ceases to conduct and full power is applied to the system until it reaches 14 volts once more.

On most Japanese machines fitted with single phase alternators, an electronic regulator unit was used. This takes the form of a sealed electronic unit controlled by a zener diode in conjunction with a thyristor, or alternately by a pair of thyristors and an integrated circuit device which monitors the ac voltage. These devices differ from the basic zener diode type in that they are sensitive to battery voltage. The way in which the units work varies according to the manufacturer. The regulator is normally built as a unit together with the rectifier.

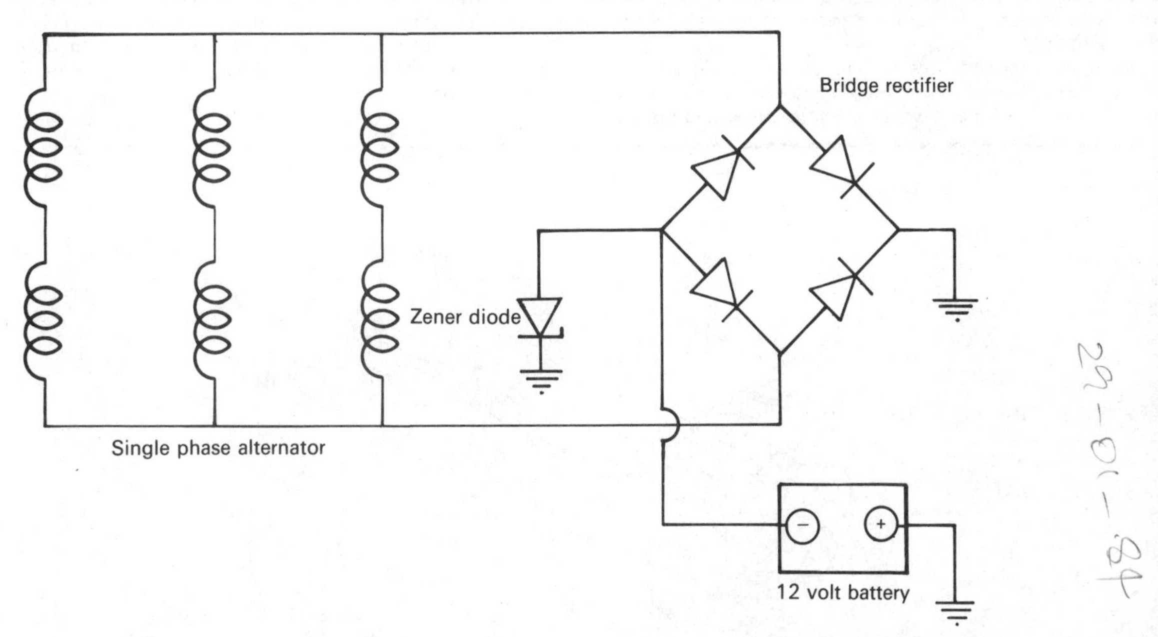


**Fig. 10.7 Basic single-phase alternator circuit showing full-wave rectifier and voltage regulation by Zener diode**

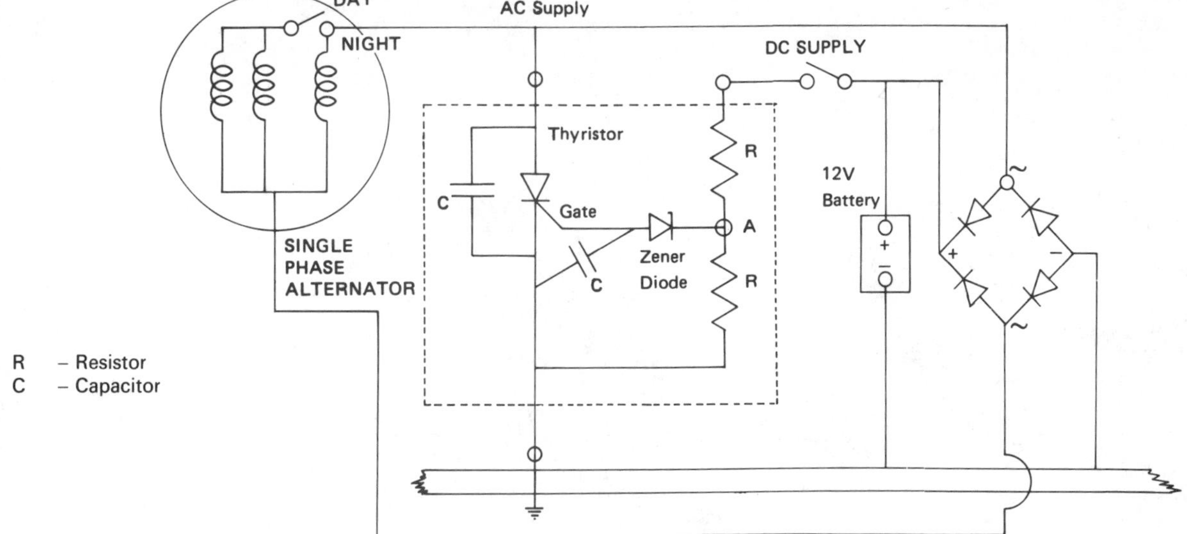


**Fig. 10.8 Single phase alternator circuit showing full-wave rectifier and electronic voltage regulator**

*The dotted line encloses the voltage regulator components. In practice these are built into a sealed unit mounted on the frame.*

## 8 Alternator systems: three phase types

The final development of the motorcycle alternator is the change to three phase operation, rather than the previous single phase types. This was brought about largely by the adoption of electric starters as standard equipment on most medium to large capacity models. Electric starting uses a huge amount of power from the battery – several hundred amps as the starter engages, a lot when compared to the 5 amps or so used by a headlamp bulb. Although this demand is only short lived, it is essential that the battery is brought back up to full charge quickly. On some early (single phase) electric start systems, the starter motor power was of necessity kept low so that the charging system could keep up with the demand on the battery. The result was that it was necessary to 'help' the electric starter using the kickstart on cold mornings.

Without going into the technicalities in great detail, the single phase alternator produces its output in the form of a sine wave, much the same as that of the flywheel generator. By wiring the stator coils in a different pattern, three overlapping output waves, or phases, can be obtained. These are spaced at 120° intervals, and in this way the output is much smoother and more consistent. This and physical considerations allow a much higher output to be obtained from a unit of a given size.

A permanent magnet three phase alternator often looks very much like a heavy duty flywheel generator. The stator takes the form of a ring with the generating coils arranged radially around its outer edge. The rotor runs outside the coils, with its magnetic poles embedded in the alloy rotor casting.

Other three phase alternator units use electromagnets in place of the permanent magnets so far discussed. The rotor consists of a central core upon which is wound a single excitor coil. Around this is fitted the two-claw pole assemblies in which alternate magnetic polarity is induced. The rotor is normally fed by the battery to start with, until the output rises sufficiently for the unit to become self-generating, though on some types, residual magnetism in the poles is sufficient to get the process going.

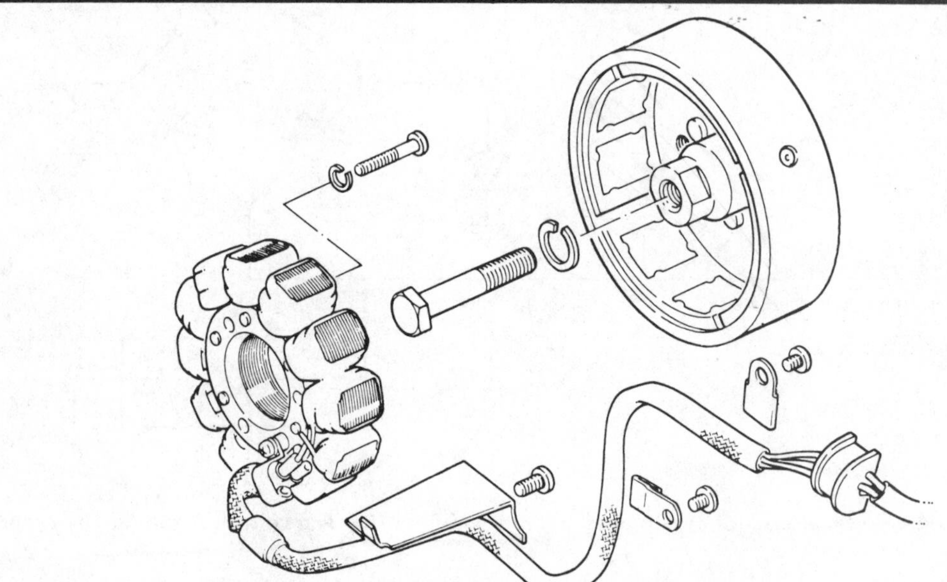

Fig. 10.9 Permanent magnet three-phase alternator

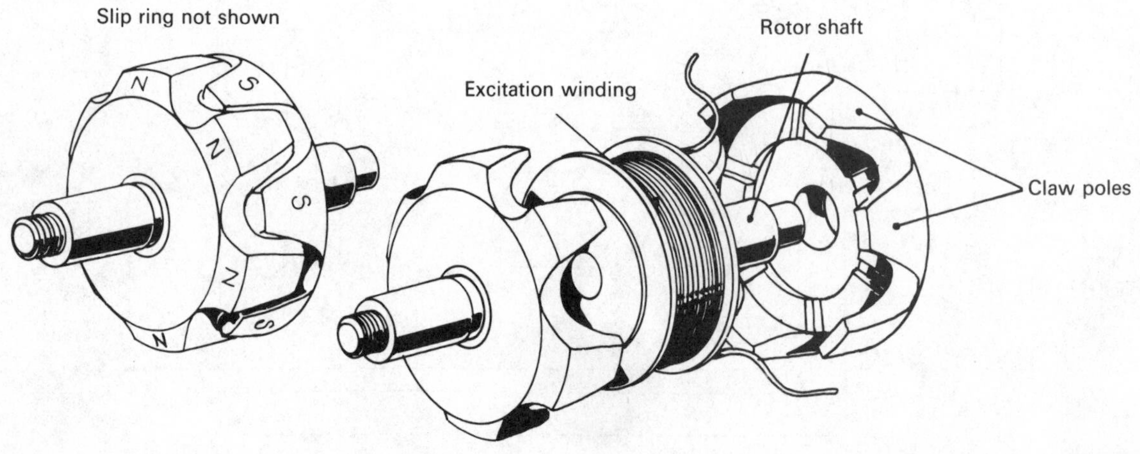


Fig. 10.10 Claw pole (electromagnetic) three-phase alternator

## 9 Three phrase rectifiers and regulators

As might be expected, a three phase rectifier is a good deal more complex than a single phase type. In practice, six diodes are used in place of four to achieve full-wave rectification of the three phases. Each phase, or wave is rectified separately, giving six output 'ripples' rather than the two found in single phase types. The resulting dc output is much smoother and more powerful.

With an electromagnetic three phase unit it is possible to regulate the output voltage quite easily and precisely. The regulator unit senses the output voltage, and when it reaches a predetermined level, cuts the dc supply to the rotor. This in turn reduces the alternator ac output, and the voltage is thus stabilised at this level. The earlier type of three phase regulator works electromechanically. In a typical regulator, an electromagnetic coil is connected to the dc output and is used to operate switch contacts. As the voltage rises, the coil opens a pair of contacts, and this switches the dc current through a resistance. The supply to the rotor is thus reduced, and this in turn reduces the output. If the voltage rises still further, a second connection is made in which the rotor is earthed completely. This cuts off the output completely until the system voltage drops to a safe level.

On more recent models, the electromechanical voltage regulator has been replaced by various electronic equivalents. These use thyristors to shunt excess current to earth, either from one phase or from all three. Like the single phase equivalent, these regulator units usually appear in the form of a resin-encapsulated unit.

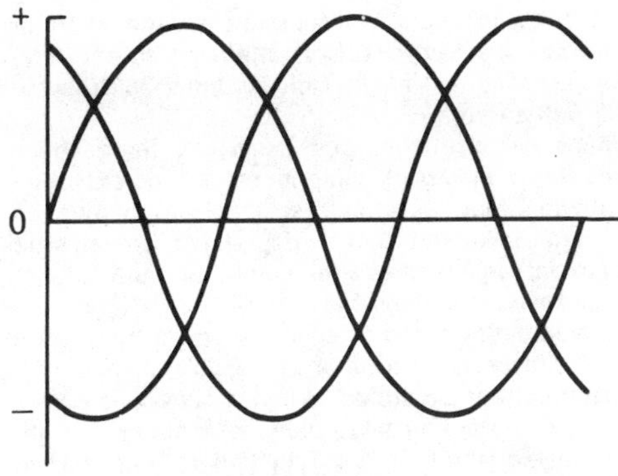


**Fig. 10.11 The overlapping output waves from a three phase alternator**

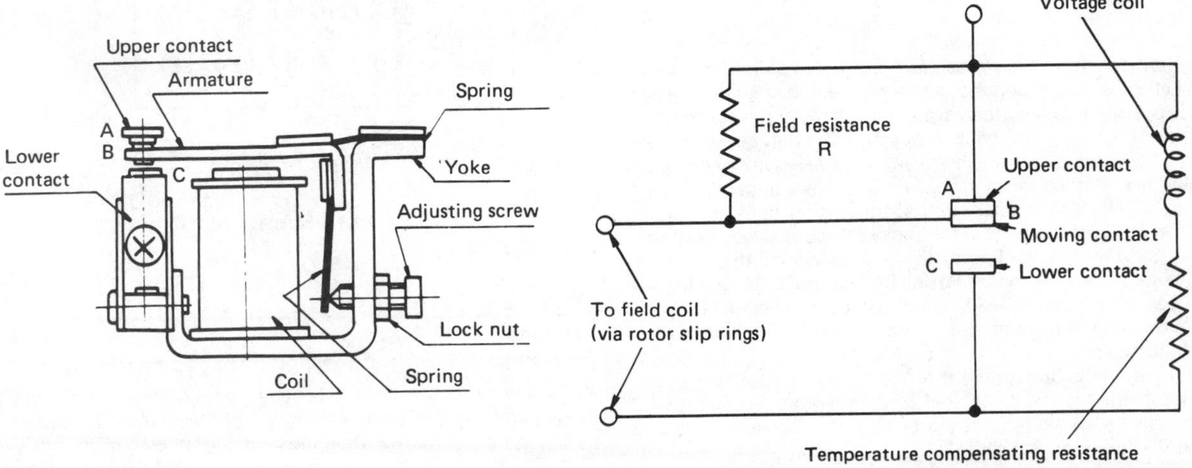


**Fig. 10.12 Electro-mechanical regulator unit**

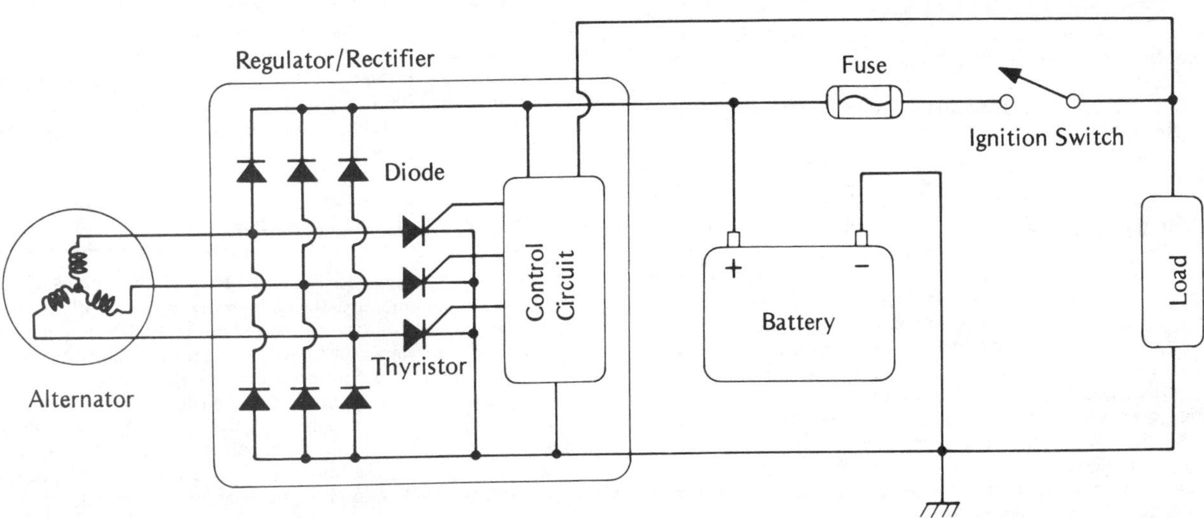


**Fig. 10.13 Three-phase charging circuit showing the regulator/rectifier unit**

## 10 Batteries

In the preceding Sections we have looked at the various methods of generating electricity. If we go back to the simple moped electrical system with direct lighting, there is no need to store electrical power because the electrical requirements are so basic that an ac supply will suffice. A bulb, for example, will function whether the current flows through it in one direction or rapidly alternates to and fro. The same applies to the horn; it may vary in pitch according to the system output, but it works well enough.

As soon as we ask more of the system, things become more complicated. Some electrical components are polarity sensitive and thus require a dc supply. In some cases, this supply must be kept at a constant voltage, irrespective of engine speed, and this necessitates rectification to dc, regulation to a set voltage, and ultimately, some way of storing a reserve of power.

The lead/acid battery used on almost every motorcycle represents a way of storing power in the form of a reversible chemical reaction; the electricity itself cannot be stored. When a current is passed into the battery, a chemical reaction takes place, stopping when the reaction becomes exhausted (the battery is fully charged) or the current stops flowing. Given the opportunity, the reaction will reverse and current will flow out of the battery. In this way the battery offers a reserve of electrical power which will keep the system going even when the generator output is less than that required by the system. For example, it will allow the headlamp to maintain its output when the engine is idling or not running, and will permit an electric starter motor to be used.

The battery consists of a plastic casing, divided up into compartments called cells. Each cell houses a number of separate plates connected together in alternating layers. The plates are made from an antimony-lead compound in the form of a grid, the holes in which are filled with a lead oxide paste. Chemically inert separators and glass fibre matting are fitted between each plate to prevent physical contact between them. The cell is filled with a conducting liquid called an electrolyte which in the case of a lead/acid battery is dilute sulphuric acid. When a current is applied to the two terminals, the resulting chemical reaction converts the lead oxide of the positive plate into lead peroxide, leaving a spongy lead layer in the negative plate. If the current is stopped, the reaction ceases, but if we now connect a load such as a bulb, the reaction will reverse. This causes current to flow out of the cell, lighting the bulb until the reaction becomes exhausted and the cell is discharged, or 'flat'. Each cell produces a voltage of about 2.2 volts, so to obtain six volts from the battery, three cells are used, a twelve volt version requiring six cells.

It is not surprising that the capacity of the battery is dependent on the size of its cells; the bigger the battery, the more it can store. This is usually given as the number of amperes available per hour from a battery discharged over a ten hour period, and is expressed as ampere-hours, or Ah. This means that a 12 Ah battery would be able to supply 1.2 A for ten hours. If the discharge rate were higher – say 2.4 hours, the battery would not be able to cope as well, and would probably be fully discharged before the expected five hours had elapsed.

The lead acid battery is used almost universally on all motor vehicles for the simple reason that it is the best type available for this application at the moment. It has been in use for decades, and will continue to be used until a better type can be found – a line of research being pursued vigorously in almost every country in the world. As this might suggest, the lead acid battery is not without its problems. For a start it is heavy and bulky, neither of which are particularly welcome features for motorcycle use. It does not cope well with heavy charging or discharging. This is because it causes the plates to heat up, and if this becomes excessive they will disintegrate. This means that the battery is being sorely tried every time the starter is used. It will cope with this treatment, but only just. It is also a surprisingly fragile item, and is easily damaged by excessive vibration. This can dislodge the lead sulphate from the plates. The resulting debris at the bottom of each cell can then cause internal shorting. For a combination of the above reasons, coupled with a good measure of neglect and abuse, the battery on any motorcycle has a limited life. If maintained properly, this may average about three years or so, but it is shortened drastically through neglect and damage.

As a final note on batteries, remember that in addition to the damage that you can inflict on it, it can inflict damage on you if you fail to take care when working on or near it. The sulphuric acid it contains is highly corrosive, and will attack skin, eyes, clothing, paintwork and just about everything else it comes into contact with. If you accidentally spill or splash the electrolyte, wash the affected area immediately with copious quantities of water. If the electrolyte enters the eyes, flush them with water and get urgent medical help.

When charging batteries, ALWAYS remove them from the machine to avoid any risk of damage to the alternator. Check that the charger is connected correctly, and avoid charging at a higher rate than that specified. Where no charge rate is given, charge at about 1/10th of the rated capacity. This means that a 12 Ah battery should be charged at 1.2 A maximum. ON NO ACCOUNT 'fast charge' the battery; it will probably damage it, and may even cause it to explode.

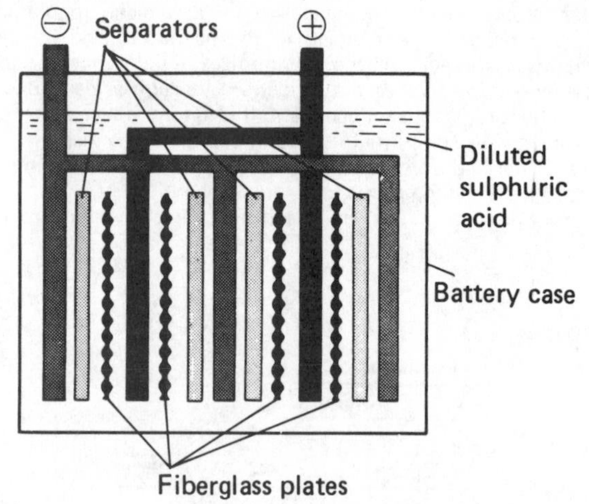


Fig. 10.14 Battery construction

## 11 Lighting systems

Every motor vehicle has its compliment of lamps and bulbs, and the resulting system forms the main part of the machine's electrical circuit. Each lamp has its own circuit, and this is essentially similar to the simple circuit described at the beginning of the Chapter. In many cases this may not be clear from studying the machine's wiring diagram, and the circuit becomes more complicated where some warning lamp circuits are concerned. Some of these are controlled from two sensors or switches, and the circuit may look rather obscure at first. The various electrical bits and pieces are connected by a network of electrical cables and connectors. The various wires are bundled together for convenience, the result being a wiring loom or harness. On most machines this can be seen better if you remove the seat, side panels and the fuel tank. Where the wires emerge from the harness it will be noted that they are colour-coded. This is done to make fault finding easier, and not for appearance.

## 12 Bulbs: tungsten filament types

Bulbs produce light by allowing an electrical current to flow through a very thin wire, usually made from tungsten, called a filament. The resistance of the filament causes heat to build up until it glows white hot and thus gives off light. To fit a lot of filament into a small space it is wound into a tight coil, and this also increases the heating effect in this area. If the filament were heated in air it would simply burn up and break. This is caused by the presence of oxygen, so the problem is avoided by putting the filament in a sealed glass envelope and surrounding it with an inert gas at low pressure. Add to this the brass cap to which the ends of the filament are connected, and you have a bulb.

The wattage, and thus the brightness of the bulb is determined by the thickness of the wire and the number of turns in the filament coils, and this allows bulbs of various types to be made to suit different purposes. Some bulbs do more than one job – the stop/tail lamp for example, and these have two separate filaments of two different wattages. The same applies to the headlamp bulb, but the second filament has a special role in this case. In the headlamp, the filaments are very carefully positioned so that on main beam the light is focussed by the reflector into a narrow beam. This is further directed by the fluted patterns of the glass front of the headlamp unit to illuminate the road ahead. When dip beam is selected, the main filament goes out and the second filament is lit. This is positioned so that the light is deflected downwards and to one side to avoid dazzling oncoming traffic.

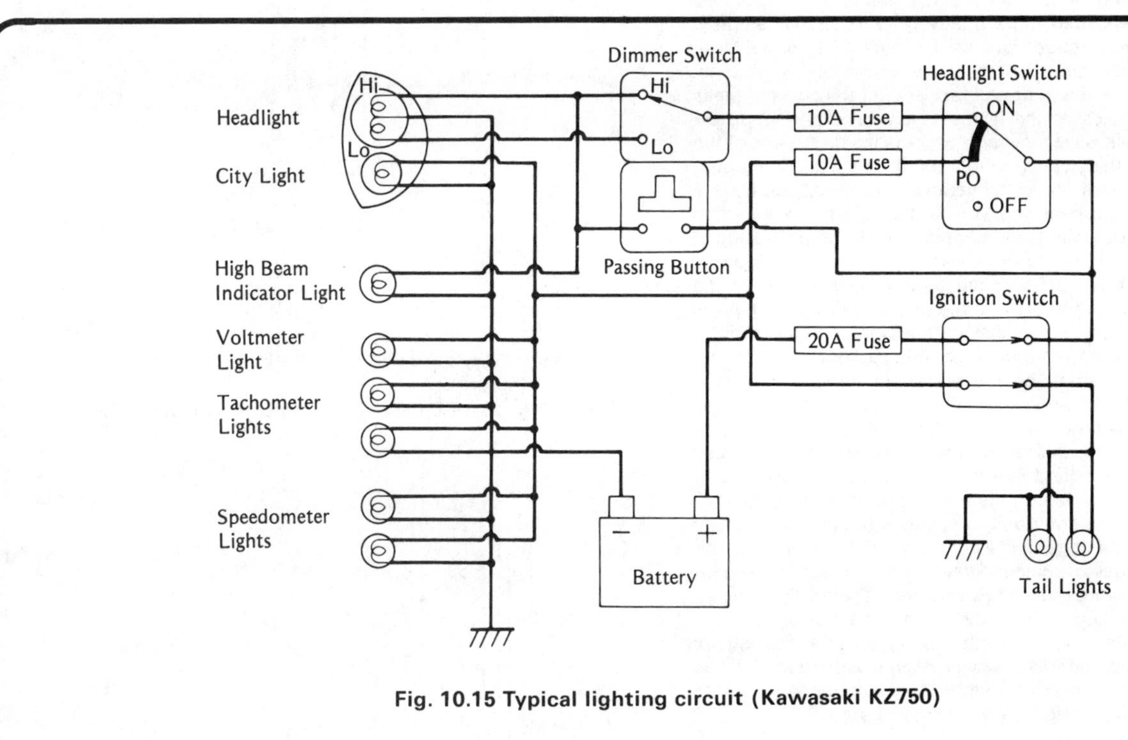


Fig. 10.15 Typical lighting circuit (Kawasaki KZ750)

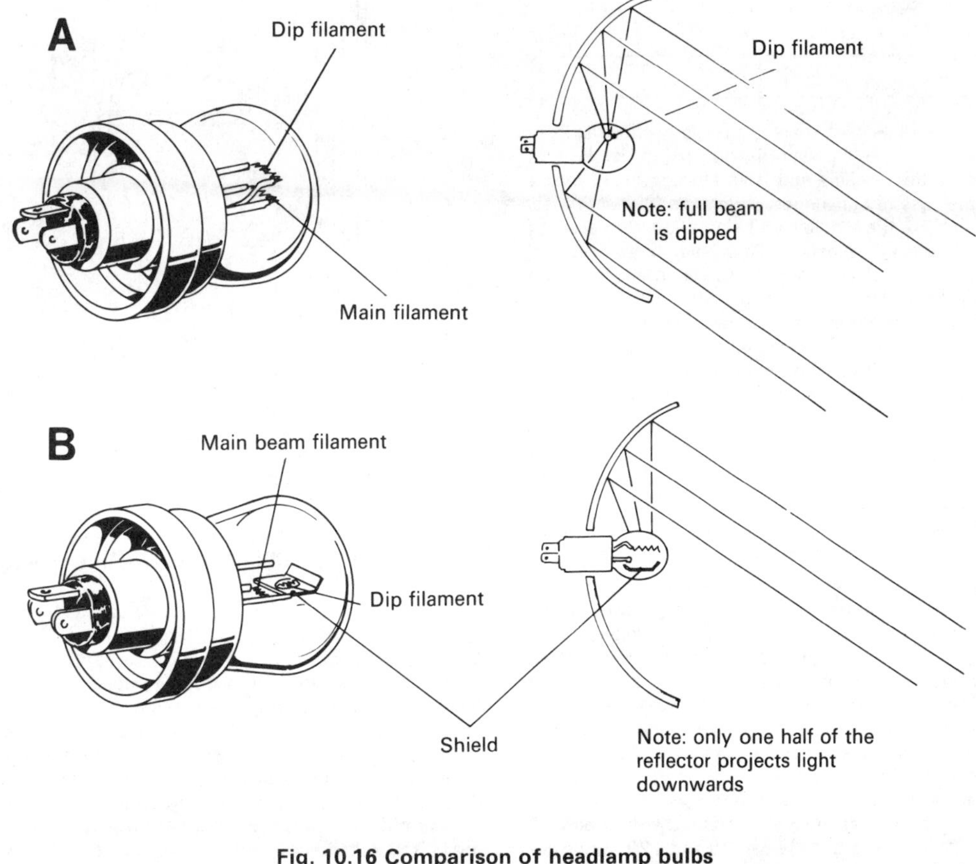


Fig. 10.16 Comparison of headlamp bulbs

*A Offset dip filament*   *B Shield dip filament*

## 13 Bulbs: quartz halogen types

A conventional tungsten filament bulb has limitations which prevent it running above a certain operating temperature. This is determined by the way that the filament material evaporates, eventually becoming deposited on the relatively cool glass envelope. If the filament temperature is raised significantly beyond its normal level, this process is speeded up; the envelope becomes increasingly blackened, causing heat to build up still further until the element melts and breaks. In dramatic cases the filament may be evaporated very rapidly, forming a metallic silvery coating over the inside surface of the glass. Bulb failure of this type is often found with direct lighting systems where the failure of one bulb overloads the remainder, usually at high engine speeds. So next time you find a bulb that appears to have been silvered, you will know that it failed through sudden overloading, rather than by the filament fracturing due to vibration.

If a gas of the halogen group, such as iodine, is added to the envelope, it prevents the evaporation of the filament. What happens is that the evaporating tungsten combines with the halogen gas to form tungsten halide. This compound will then diffuse back towards the filament instead of depositing on the envelope. As it reaches the filament area, it breaks down once more, and a circulation is maintained. The process requires careful control of the temperatures inside the envelope, and for this reason the envelope is made smaller and of heat-resisting quartz glass. The resulting bulb runs much hotter, and thus much brighter than a conventional tungsten filament type.

The so-called quartz halogen bulb provides a brighter and whiter light output for a given wattage than a conventional bulb, but is much more sensitive to changes of temperature. In particular, if its running temperature is lower than normal, the service life is drastically reduced, so voltage drop due to corrosion in the wiring and connectors can cause problems. Another point worth noting is that the quartz envelope is easily etched and marked by acids in perspiration. For this reason the envelope must never be handled. If it is touched, it should be carefully cleaned whilst cold, using methylated spirit.

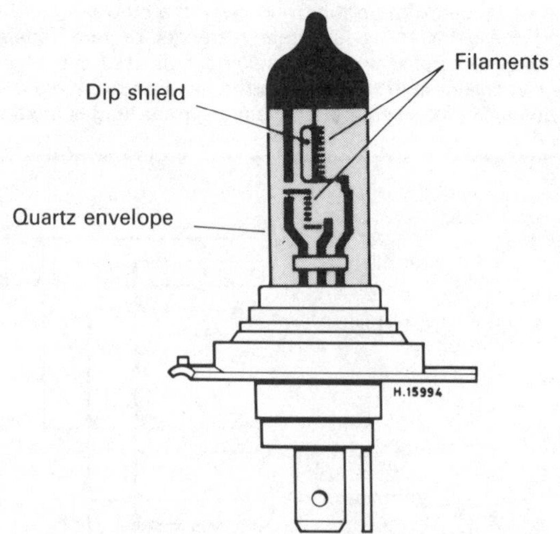


Fig. 10.17 Quartz halogen bulb construction

## 14 Sealed beam units

Some models produced in recent years, particularly those sold in the US, have been fitted with sealed beam headlamps. In this type of headlamp, the separate reflector, lens and bulb are combined into a single sealed unit. In the case of conventional tungsten filament types, the bulb envelope is omitted, the whole unit being filled with an inert gas at low pressure to do this job. Where a quartz halogen unit is used, the separate quartz envelope is retained to maintain filament temperature at the required level.

The sealed beam unit offers a number of advantages, the main one being that there is no possibility of corrosion of the reflector or misalignment of the bulb filaments. The main drawback is that the whole unit must be renewed in the event of a filament failing, and this is rather more expensive than renewing a bulb.

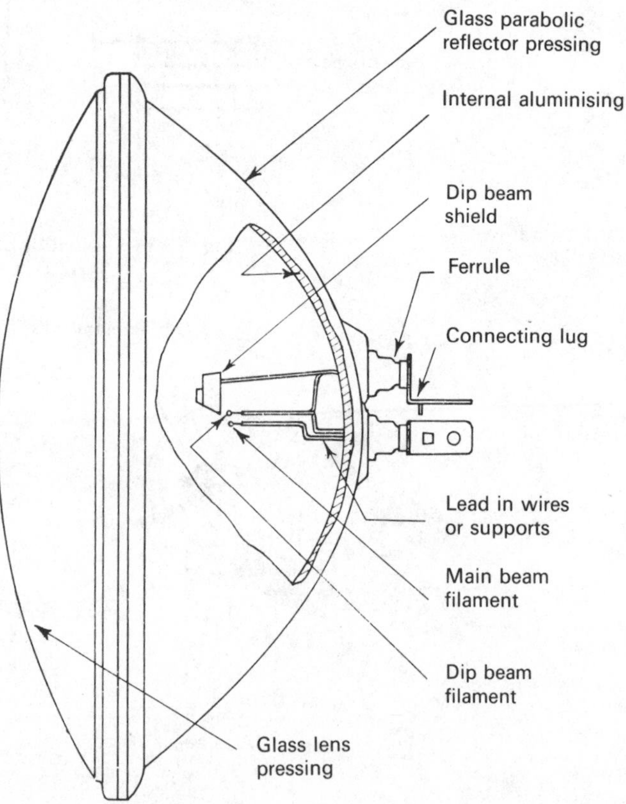


Fig. 10.18 Sealed beam unit construction

## 15 Turn signal systems

With the exception of some mopeds, almost every new machine sold is equipped with turn signals. On some larger and more sophisticated models, a separate switch allows all four lamps to be flashed simultaneously as a hazard warning. The system comprises two pairs of lamps, a turn signal relay or 'flasher unit', and a three-way switch to control it. The lamps are usually mounted on stalks which position them well out from the centre line of the machine; this makes the direction of the intended turn clear to other road users. Each lamp is fitted with an amber coloured lens to avoid confusion with any of the other lamps on the vehicle. The relay is a device which switches either pair of lamps on and off at regular intervals. In the UK, the relevant traffic laws require the flash rate to be between 60 and 120 cycles per minute, and this frequency is almost universal throughout the world. The handlebar switch has a left and right position with a central 'off' setting.

### Capacitor relays

Most systems are controlled by a capacitor type relay. The relay unit takes the form of a cylindrical aluminium alloy canister with two spade, or Lucar, terminals at the base. Inside the canister is the capacitor, the solenoid assembly and contacts, and a small resistor. The relay solenoid has two sets of windings; the voltage coil comprising several thousand turns of thin wire and connected across the supply, whilst the current coil has a few hundred turns of thicker wire, is wound on top of the voltage coil and is connected in series with the supply.

When the ignition switch is on and the turn signal switch is at its central 'off' position, current flows through the voltage coil and charges the capacitor. If the switch is moved to the left or right position, current now flows through the current coil, the warning lamp and the turn signal lamps, to earth. This small current is enough to light the warning lamp, but not the two turn signal lamps at this stage. The current flow through the current coil produces a magnetic field which attracts the armature to the core, opening the contacts. This cuts off the supply to the relay, but the capacitor now discharges through the windings to keep the contacts open and to light the turn signal lamps. Once the capacitor is discharged (its capacity determines the duration of each flash) the contacts close again.

Until the capacitor is recharged, the current flows in opposite directions in the two sets of windings. This means that the magnetic flux is inhibited and the contacts remain closed, with the turn signal lamps lit by battery current. As the capacitor nears full charge, the current flowing through the current coil ceases and the contacts open once more. This switches off the supply to the relay and the turn signal lamps, and the cycle now repeats. The working of the capacitor relay may seem rather complicated, but it is designed to take in its stride the voltage fluctuations and the effects of vibration which might otherwise affect the flash rate. By using a capacitor to control the effective timing of the relay, these variations are avoided.

**Bimetal relays**

A popular alternative to the capacitor relay relies on the use of two bimetal strips to control its operation. A bimetal strip consists of two dissimilar metals (usually brass and steel) fused together into a thin strip. If heat is applied to the strip the differing rates of expansion of the two metals cause the strip to bend to one side. In a bimetal relay, the two strips are mounted slightly apart and carry the relay contacts at their free ends. The voltage coil strip is wound with numerous turns of resistance heating wire, and this coil is connected at one end to the contact, and at the other to the common terminal. The current coil strip is wound with fewer turns of heating wire, again with one end of the coil attached to the contact and the other to the common lamp terminal.

When the turn signal switch is operated, current flows through the voltage coil, which heats up and begins to bend its bimetal strip. As the contacts close, the turn signal lamps are lit and current ceases to flow in the voltage coil, flowing instead through the current coil. As the first strip cools and begins to bend back, the second strip is heated and bends away. This separates the two contacts, turning off the lamps. The sequence now repeats until the turn signal switch is reset.

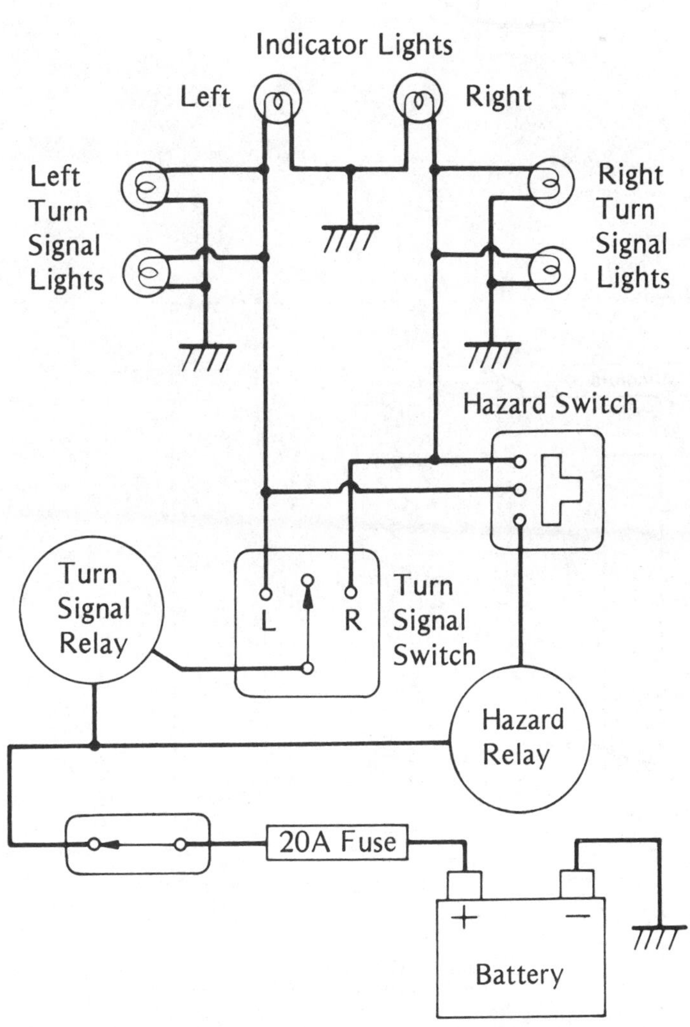


**Fig. 10.19 Turn signal circuit**

*In this example a second relay is used to flash all four lamps simultaneously for hazard warning purposes.*

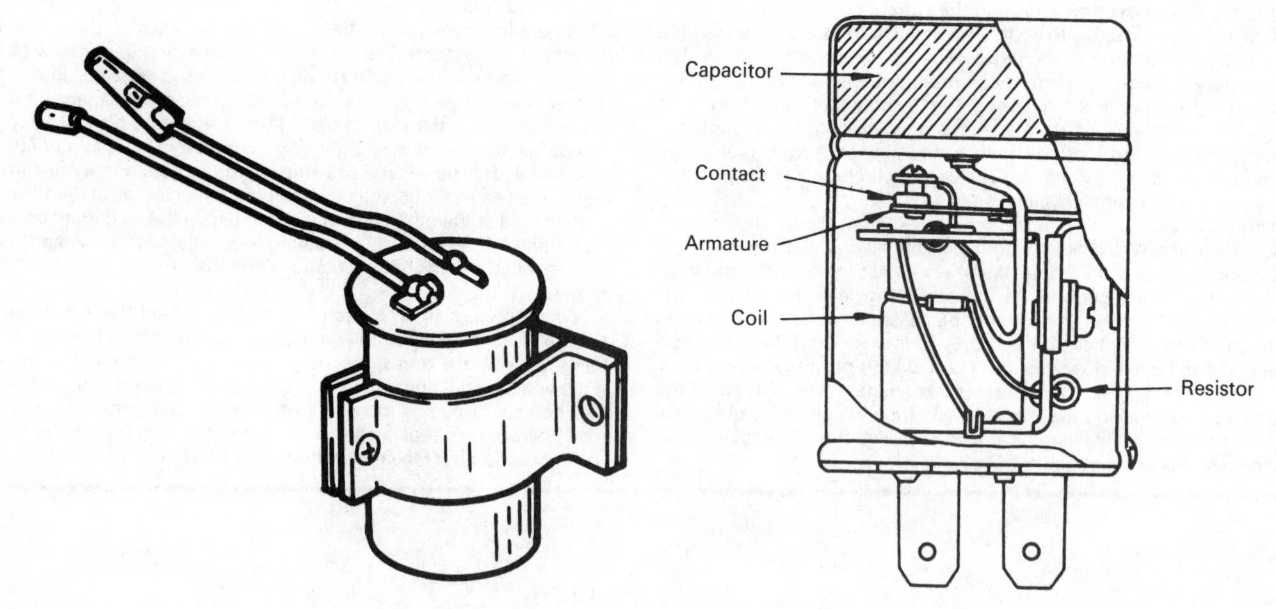


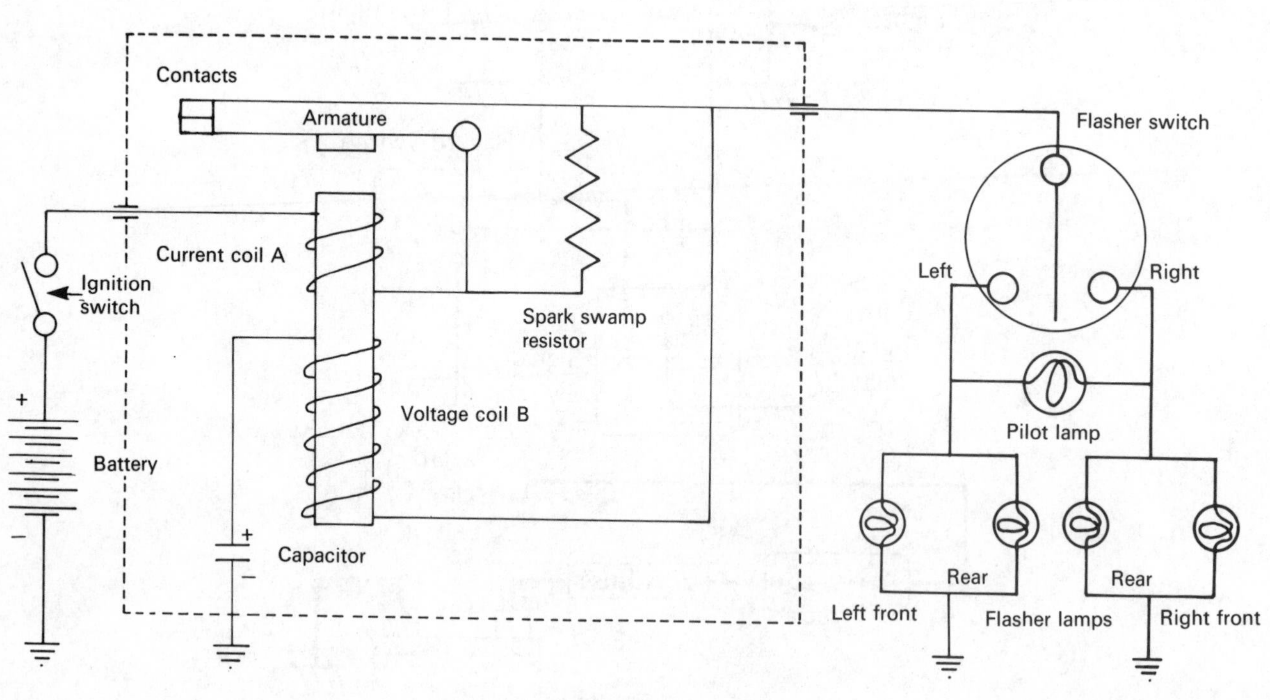


**Fig. 10.20 Capacitor-type relay and circuit**

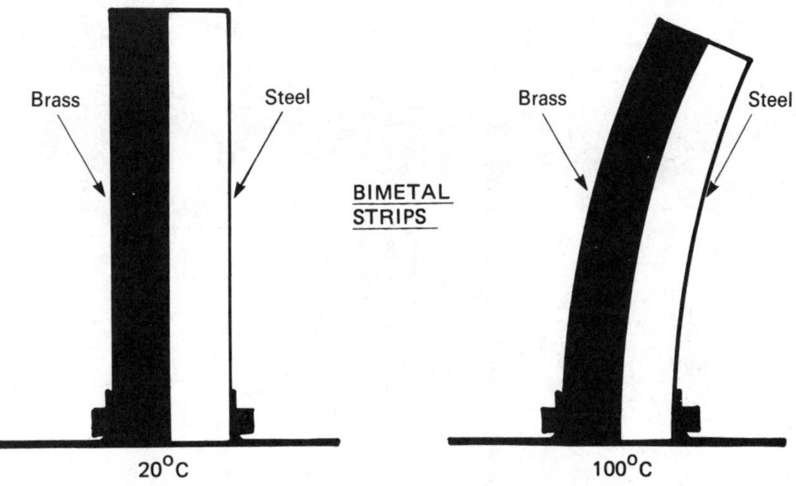


*Brass expands more than steel when the temperature is raised*

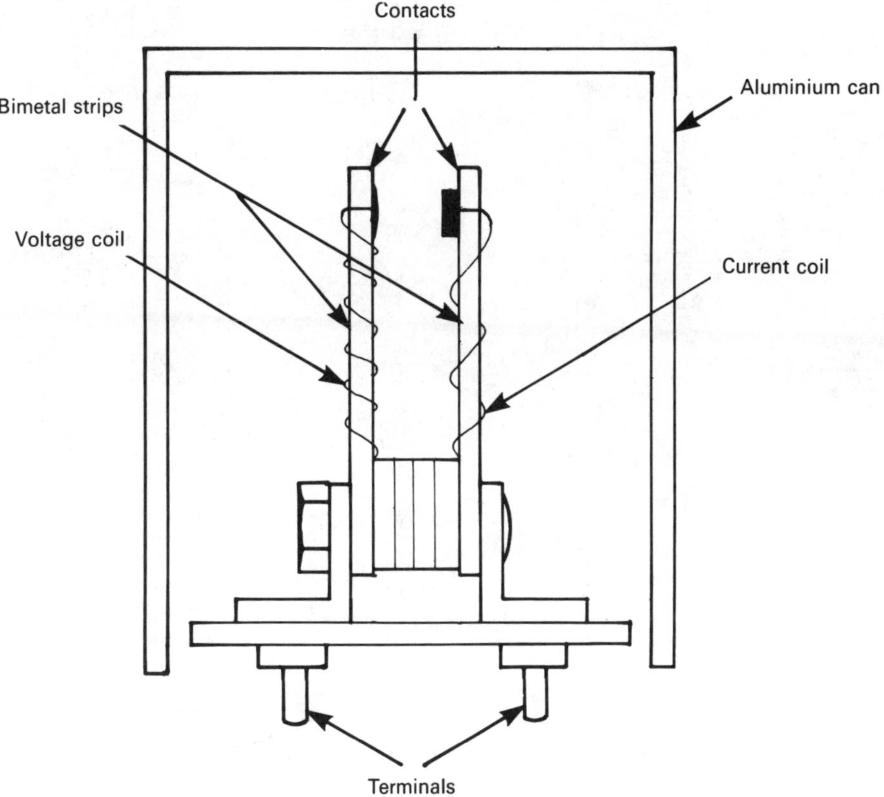


**Fig. 10.21 Principle and construction of bimetal relay**

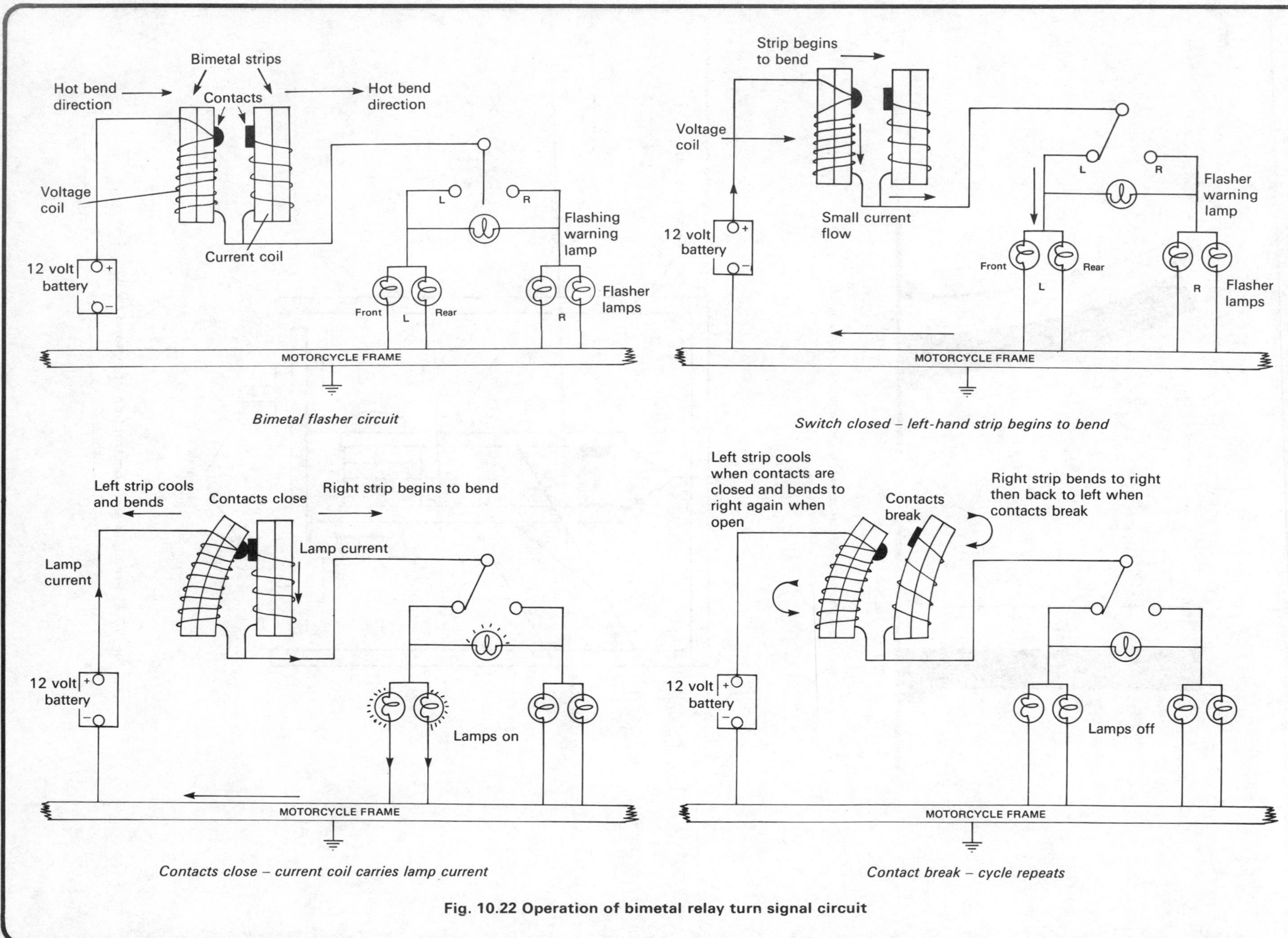


*Bimetal flasher circuit*

*Switch closed – left-hand strip begins to bend*

*Contacts close – current coil carries lamp current*

*Contact break – cycle repeats*

**Fig. 10.22 Operation of bimetal relay turn signal circuit**

## 16 Self-cancelling turn signals

For many years the majority of cars have been equipped with self-cancelling turn signals. These are controlled by a small cam attached to the steering column; as the steering wheel returns to the straight ahead position after negotiating the turning, the turn signal control is tripped back to the off position. This frees the driver from having to remember to cancel the turn signals after each manoeuvre. If self-cancelling turn signals are useful to the car driver, then they would be even more of an asset to the motorcyclist, whose hands and feet tend to be more than adequately employed with the more important controls when negotiating road junctions.

Unfortunately, the simple cam-operated arrangement used on cars cannot be implemented on a motorcycle. This is because the steering stem moves surprisingly little during normal riding (it is worth looking at this when riding through a few bends) and so is not suitable as a control for a self-cancelling system. The obvious approach is to employ some sort of timer circuit to cancel the turn signals after a predetermined amount of time has elapsed. This works fine for overtaking, or for turns where it is not necessary to wait for traffic. If the rider is obliged to wait, it would result in the system switching off before it was required to do so.

To get round this problem, a second control is added which measures the distance travelled. This takes the form of a sensor built into the speedometer head and working in the same way as the pickup coil in an electronic ignition system. The signal pulses are 'counted' by the timer circuit, which will keep the turn signals operating until the specified time and distance have been covered. In this way, when overtaking on a straight road, the distance will have been covered way before the timer has elapsed. Conversely, when waiting at a road junction the timer will rest, leaving the system running until the correct distance has elapsed. In addition, the rider has the option to override the self-cancelling system and switch the turn signals off manually.

## 17 Horns

Most machines are fitted as standard with an electromagnetic horn unit. This works on the basis of an electromagnetic coil mounted in a circular case, the armature of which is connected to a diaphragm. When the horn button is pressed, the armature is pulled towards the solenoid core, and the attached moving contact breaks the circuit. The diaphragm returns the armature to its original position, the contacts close, and the cycle is repeated many times each second. At the front of the diaphragm is a tone disc, which is designed to vibrate at a much higher frequency than the diaphragm. The resulting sound includes both high and low frequencies and is thus more audible than would be the diaphragm alone. A variation of the above is the windtone horn which uses a spiral trumpet section to modify the sound produced by the diaphragm assembly.

Air horns are often fitted as an accessory and can be an invaluable aid to safety in heavy traffic. (Most motorcyclists will be painfully aware that both they and their machine seem to be entirely invisible to the average car driver). They are powered from a remote compressor which forces air at high pressure through the trumpet-shaped horn. At the back of the horn is a pressure chamber, the outlet of which is closed by a flexible diaphragm. As the pressure rises in the chamber, the diaphragm opens and releases a pulse of air, and then closes until the pressure builds up once more. This cycle repeats many times each second, resulting in a penetrating note from the horn trumpet. There are versions of the air horn which are operated from an aerosol can of compressed carbon dioxide; useful where the machine's electrical system is not capable of providing enough power to drive a compressor.

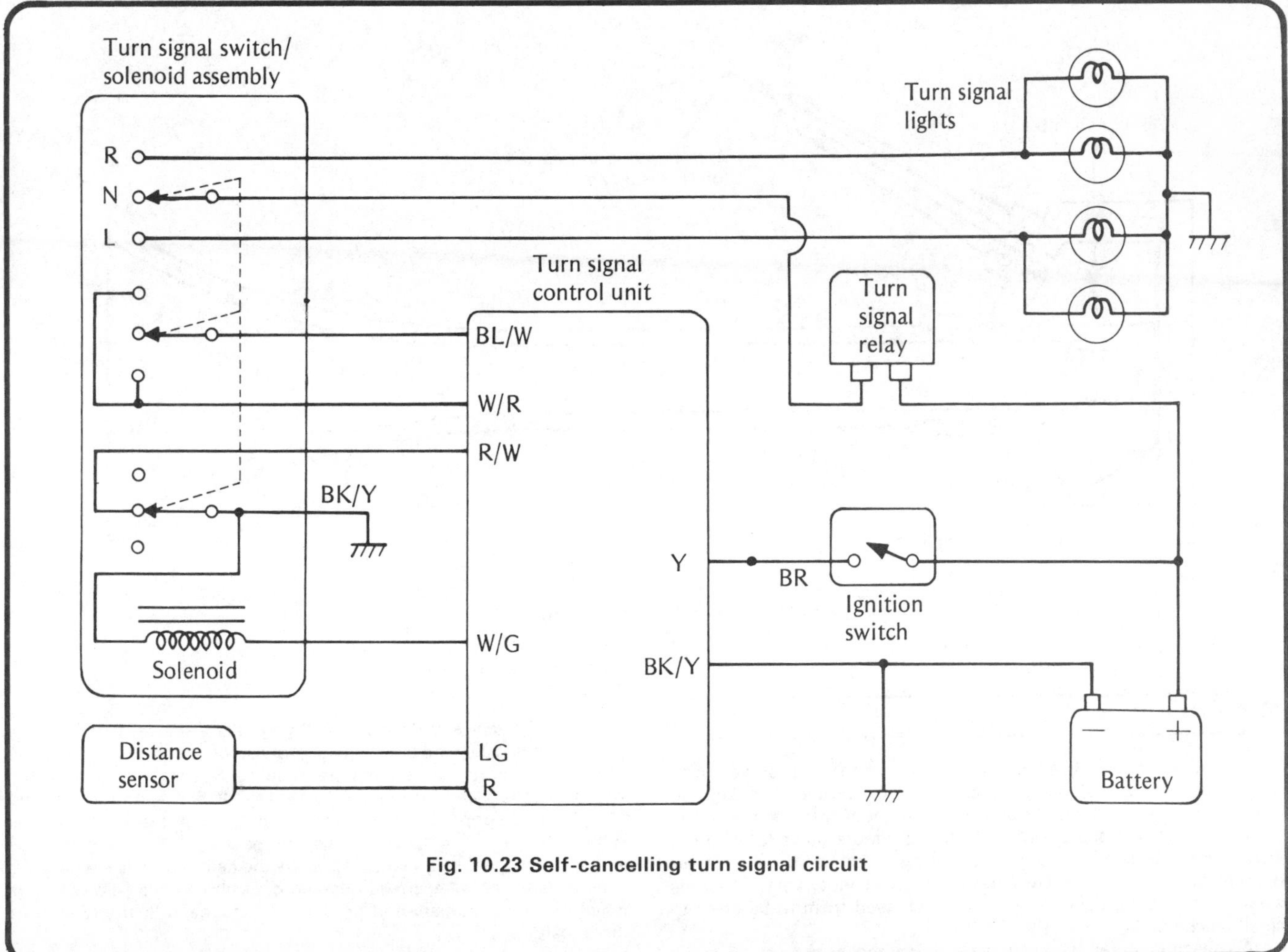


Fig. 10.23 Self-cancelling turn signal circuit

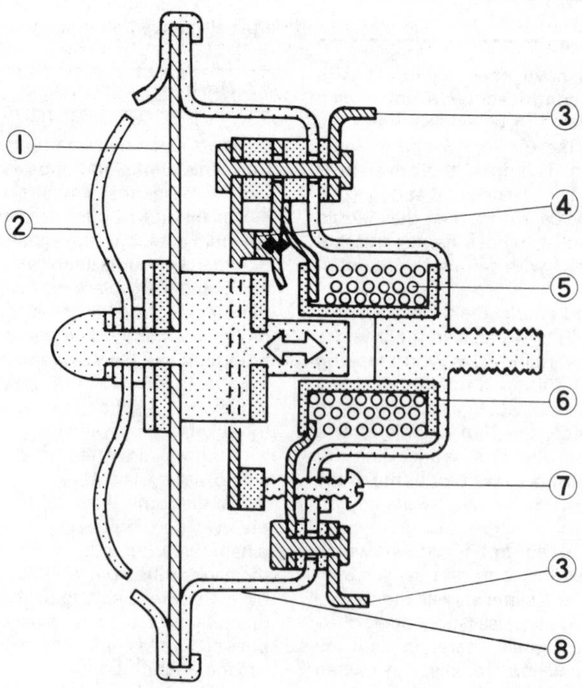


Fig. 10.24 Section through a tone-disc horn

1 *Diaphragm*
2 *Tone disc*
3 *Terminal*
4 *Contacts*
5 *Coil*
6 *Insulator*
7 *Adjusting screw*
8 *Housing*

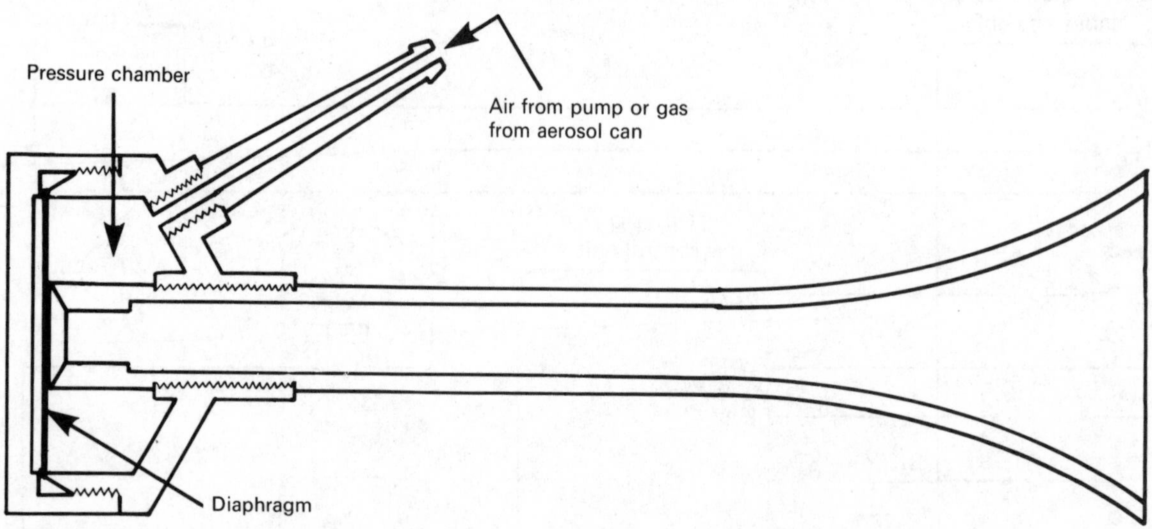


Fig. 10.25 Section through an air horn

## 18 Starter motors

The adoption of the alternator in place of the less powerful dc generators (dynamos) allowed the use of electric starting on motorcycles. About twenty years ago, very few machines were so equipped, but with the advent of larger and more powerful engines, kick starting became a major undertaking, encouraging the development of an alternative. Over the years starter motors have become smaller and more efficient, and this has allowed them to be fitted to small machines.

An electric motor works in very much the same way as a dc generator (in fact any dc motor will generate electrical power if it is spun mechanically, and any dc generator can be run as a motor). At the heart of the motor is the armature, a series of coils built around the rotating central shaft. At one end is a drum-shaped section composed of numerous copper segments separated by mica insulators. This is known as the commutator, and its purpose is to allow power to be applied to successive armature coils, via the carbon brushes which rub against its surface. Attached to the motor casing are the field windings which remain stationary and produce the magnetic field which turns the armature.

Without going into too much detail of the theory involved, the motor works by using the magnetic field generated by the field coils to push away the adjacent set of armature windings. As the armature turns in response to this pressure, the brushes apply power to the next pair of commutator segments, and thus the next set of armature windings repeat the process. As the speed of rotation increases, the motor begins to generate its own internal power (called back-emf) in opposition to the supply. This effectively limits the speed of the motor, but gives it high initial torque characteristics; ideal for the purpose of cranking the engine.

To use the motor for starting purposes it must be connected to the crankshaft in such a way that once the engine starts, the connection can be broken to avoid damage to the starter motor. This is most often done by incorporating some sort of clutch in the starter drive train. The most popular type uses spring loaded rollers set on an inclined ramp in relation to the plain shaft section being driven. When the starter motor begins to turn, the rollers (aided by the springs) move down their ramps and wedge against the shaft section. When the engine starts and the shaft section begins to turn faster that the motor, the rollers run back up into their ramp cutouts, disconnecting the drive. Both the rollers and the shaft section are ground smooth and case-hardened, and with adequate lubrication, wear takes place very slowly despite the high loadings imposed on these components.

A few machines use a car-type pre-engaged starter as an alternative to the roller clutch arrangement described above. With this system, the starter electromagnetic coil (of which more below) is fitted on the outside of the starter motor casing and is used to throw a drive pinion into mesh with the crankshaft before the motor begins to turn. When the engine begins to run faster than the starter motor, the drive pinion is forced out of engagement down a spiral thread in the armature end, and this protects the motor from damage.

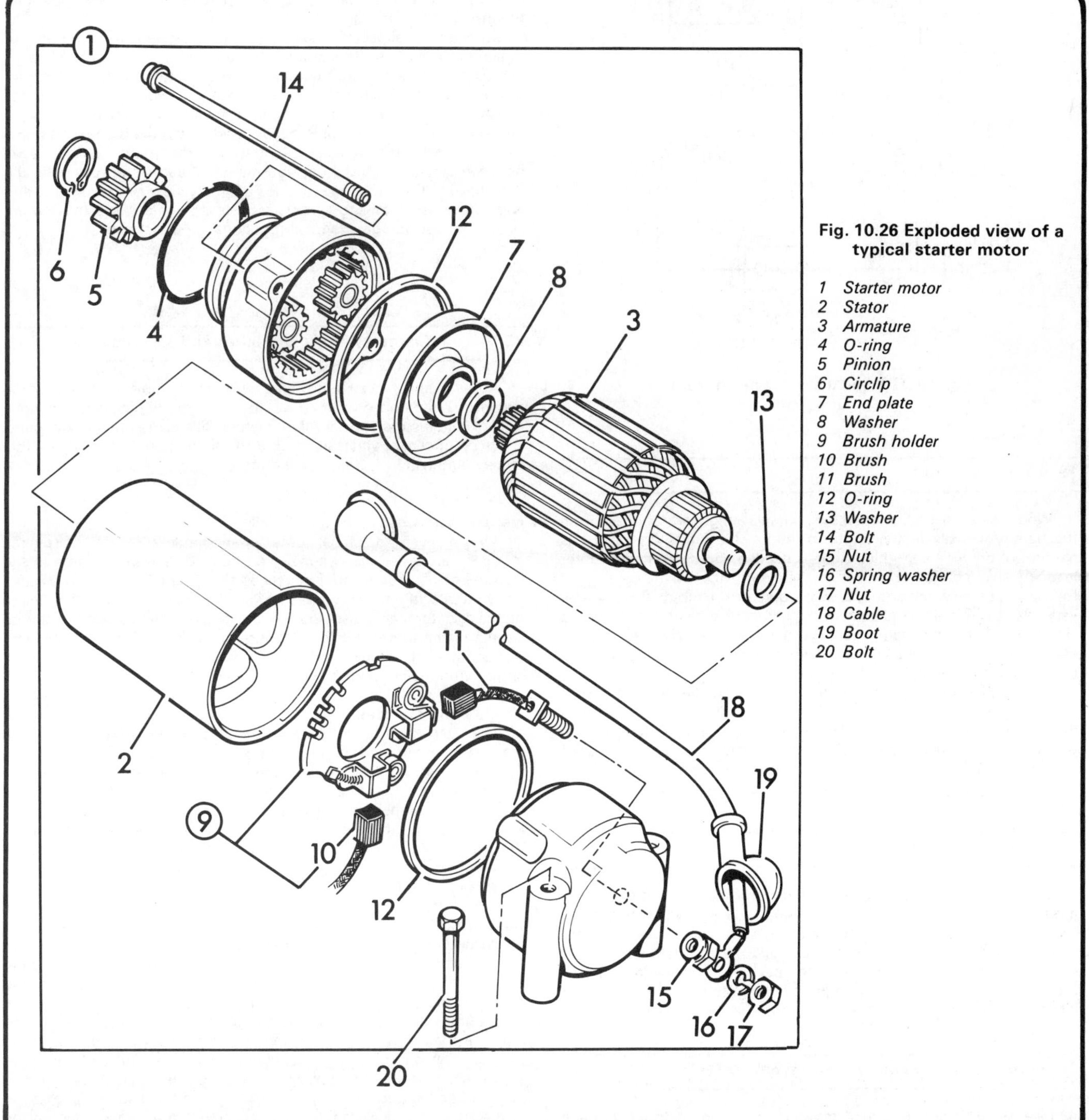


**Fig. 10.26 Exploded view of a typical starter motor**

*1 Starter motor*
*2 Stator*
*3 Armature*
*4 O-ring*
*5 Pinion*
*6 Circlip*
*7 End plate*
*8 Washer*
*9 Brush holder*
*10 Brush*
*11 Brush*
*12 O-ring*
*13 Washer*
*14 Bolt*
*15 Nut*
*16 Spring washer*
*17 Nut*
*18 Cable*
*19 Boot*
*20 Bolt*

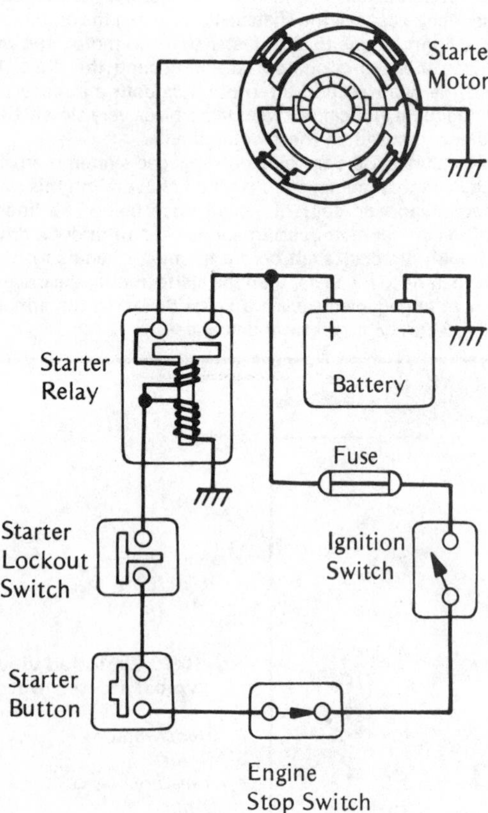


**Fig. 10.27 Typical starter motor circuit**

## 19 Starter solenoids

When the starter is first operated, it draws a high initial current from the battery; usually in the region of about 300 amps. To carry this amount of power a very thick cable is needed and if the starter motor lead on any motorcycle or car is examined this will be evident. It follows that the switch contacts which operate the motor must also be very heavy. If normal handlebar switch contacts were used they would simply overheat and melt when the starter button was pressed. To avoid this, the motor is switched indirectly via an electromagnetic coil or solenoid switch, often called a starter relay.

Pressing the starter button supplies power to the relay windings. The relay armature is energised, drawing only a light current, and thus not overloading the contacts. This closes the heavy starter contacts which supply power to the starter motor. The heavy current used does not require a fuse in the starter circuit for protection, so the thick starter motor lead runs directly to the appropriate battery terminal.

## 20 The starter-dynamo

Given the similarity between the starter motor and the dc generator, it is not too surprising that the two units have been amalgamated into a single dual-purpose device, the starter dynamo. These units are not common on current machines, but have been fitted to a few lightweight two-stroke engines in the past. Their main drawback is that they cannot produce a high cranking force, and are rather inefficient as generators, and so have never been widely used.

## 21 Instrumentation and warning systems

Like almost every aspect of motorcycle design, instruments have become increasingly sophisticated in recent years. The basic mechanical speedometer has been supplemented by a variety of extra instruments, usually electronically-operated. These include tachometers, voltmeters, ammeters, clocks and fuel gauges. The array of warning lamps has also grown over the years and most current models are fitted with a comprehensive display indicating the status and general condition of the machine. The level of sophistication is, naturally enough, dependent on the type of machine. At one extreme there are the simpler mopeds with a speedometer and one or two warning lamps, whilst some of the larger capacity machines are equipped with complicated microprocessor-based instrument systems.

In some of the latter arrangements, the instruments are interconnected via a central 'black box' which monitors all aspects of the engine and electrical functions while the machine is being ridden, and carries out a comprehensive self-checking sequence each time the engine is started. Information is gathered from a variety of switches and sensors and any fault is displayed by warning lamps or in some cases, on a liquid crystal display (lcd) panel and/or a meter built into the instrument console.

As might be expected, the more complex systems use a number of sealed units, and are thus difficult to deal with in the event of a fault. The usual approach in these cases is to substitute new components for those that are suspect until the fault is isolated, though the construction of the control circuits is invariably such that repair is impracticable. Another problem that besets the professional and home mechanic alike is the wide variation in monitoring systems, even between similar models from one manufacturer. As an example, the Yamaha XJ 650/750 range features a wide variety of instruments and warning systems on the various models. In some cases these differ even where seemingly identical functions are performed.

## 22 Warning lamp systems: switches and sensors

A wide variety of switches and sensors are employed to check the status or condition of the various parts of the engine and electrical system, and also to control safety features like starter interlock circuits. The type of sensor varies according to its function, but most are little more than switches. Some of the more common types are discussed below.

### Neutral switches

Almost every machine, other than single-speed or automatic mopeds, has a neutral switch which controls a warning lamp in the instrument panel. On most machines the switch is a simple contact screwed into the transmission casing. When neutral is selected, a cam on the selector mechanism touches the contact. This allows the neutral warning lamp to be earthed, allowing it to light up. On machines with starter interlock circuits, the neutral switch is used to prevent the engine from being started unless the machine is in neutral.

### Brake lamp switches

The main function of these switches is, of course, to operate the brake lamp when the front or rear brakes are applied. On some models, however, the switches are connected to a computer monitor system which give the rider warning if the stop lamp bulb has failed. Front brake lamp switches are usually small plunger-type units fitted into the lever stock, though on some models a pressure switch is operated by the front brake hydraulic system. The rear brake switch is usually operated via a spring from the rear brake pedal, and is adjustable to allow for pedal height and brake free play adjustments.

### Side stand switch

A good proportion of the more expensive models are equipped with a side stand switch, connected either to a warning lamp or to a safety interlock circuit. In its latter role, the switch is either connected to the starter solenoid so that the engine cannot be started until the stand has been retracted, or it is used in conjunction with the neutral switch to stop the engine if a gear is selected with the stand down. In each case the intention is to prevent the machine being ridden off with the stand down, this being a common cause of accidents when the stand digs into the road surface at the first left-hand bend. On some systems the side stand switch is wired in conjunction with a relay mounted on the frame.

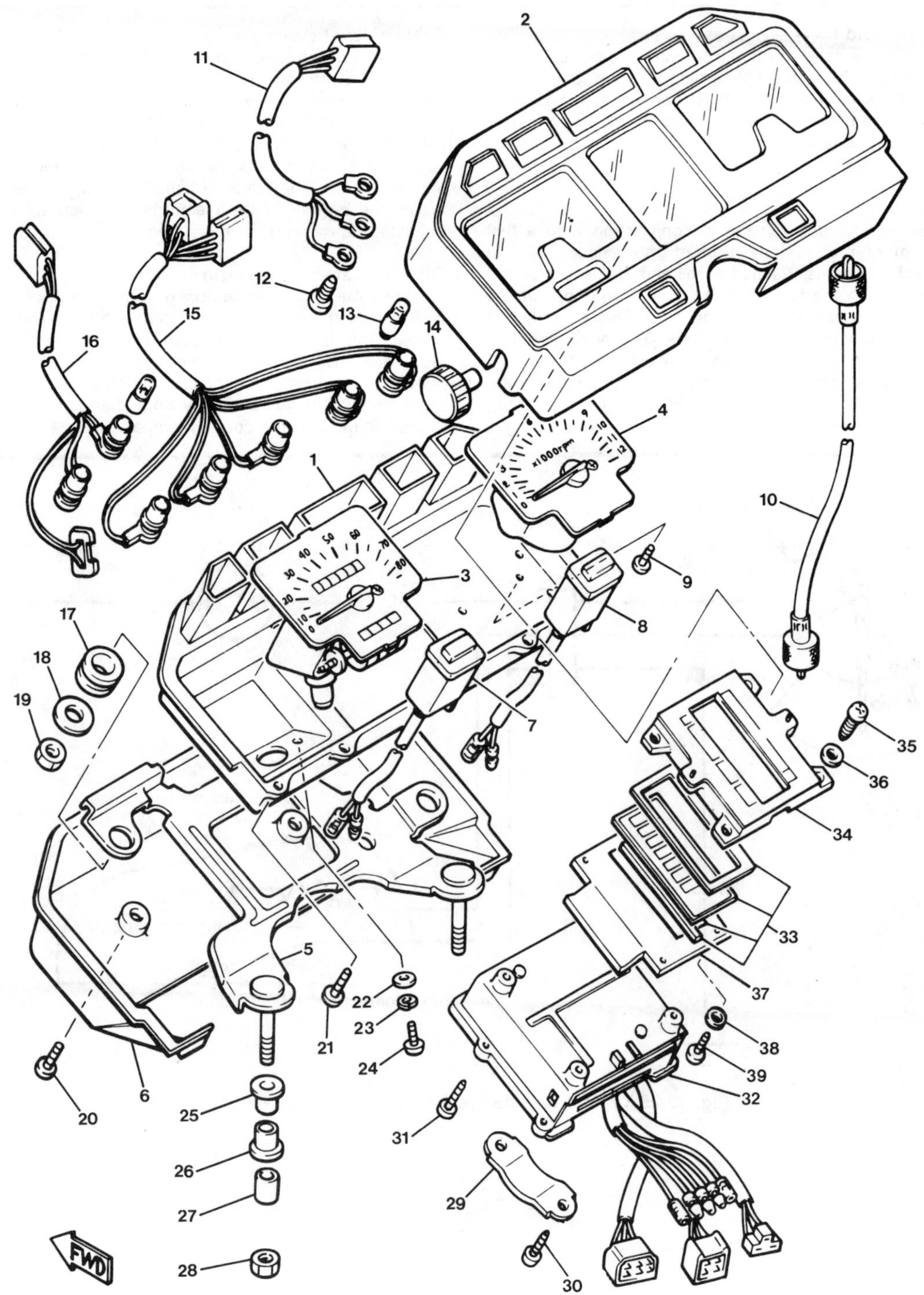


**Fig. 10.28 Instrument console – Yamaha XJ750**

*Note the row of warning lamps across the top of the panel, and also the LCD monitor panel between the speedometer and tachometer.*

*1 Instrument housing*
*2 Instrument cover*
*3 Speedometer*
*4 Tachometer*
*5 Mounting bracket*
*6 Instrument lower cover*
*7 Control switch*
*8 Control switch*
*9 Screw and washer*
*10 Speedometer drive cable*
*11 Wiring harness*
*12 Screw*
*13 Bulb*
*14 Reset knob*
*15 Bulb holder assembly*
*16 Bulb holder assembly*
*17 Grommet*
*18 Washer*
*19 Nut*
*20 Screw*
*21 Screw*
*22 Washer*
*23 Spring washer*
*24 Screw*
*25 Damping rubber*
*26 Damping rubber*
*27 Spacer*
*28 Nut*
*29 Bracket*
*30 Screw*
*31 Screw*
*32 Computer monitor unit*
*33 Computer monitor panel*
*34 Panel cover*
*35 Screw*
*36 Washer*
*37 Backing plate*
*38 Washer*
*39 Screw*

### Fuel, oil and brake fluid level switches

These are float-type switches designed to warn of low fuel, oil or hydraulic fluid level by lighting the appropriate warning lamp in the instrument panel. The switch has one fixed contact and a moving contact fitted to the base of the float. As the level drops, the contacts close, earthing the warning lamp.

### Fixed level senders

A float-operated sender unit is used in conjunction with a fuel gauge to give a more precise indication of the amount of fuel remaining in the tank. A float is attached to the end of a wire arm and moves up and down with the fuel level. As it does so it operates a variable resistance known as a rheostat. This comprises a number of turns of resistance wire wound round a flat former. The moving contact blade sweeps along the windings, thus determining the overall resistance in the circuit. This is measured by the gauge meter mechanism which can then be calibrated to show the corresponding fuel level.

### Battery level switches

These are normally used in conjunction with a computer monitor circuit to warn of low electrolyte level in the battery, and are particularly useful where the battery is awkwardly located and thus difficult to check visually. A lead electrode is fitted to one of the battery cells, and when in contact with the electrolyte produces a reference supply of about 9 volts. As long as this voltage is detected by the microprocessor, the warning lamp remains off, but if the level drops below the bottom of the electrode, the warning lamp comes on to indicate that topping up is required.

### Oil and water temperature senders

Some machines are equipped with oil temperature gauges which warn when the engine temperature reaches a dangerous level. The sender unit is a device known as a thermocouple which has a resistance that varies according to its temperature. The sender is connected to a meter mechanism which indicates the temperature on the instrument panel. On water-cooled engines a similar arrangement is used to monitor the coolant temperature.

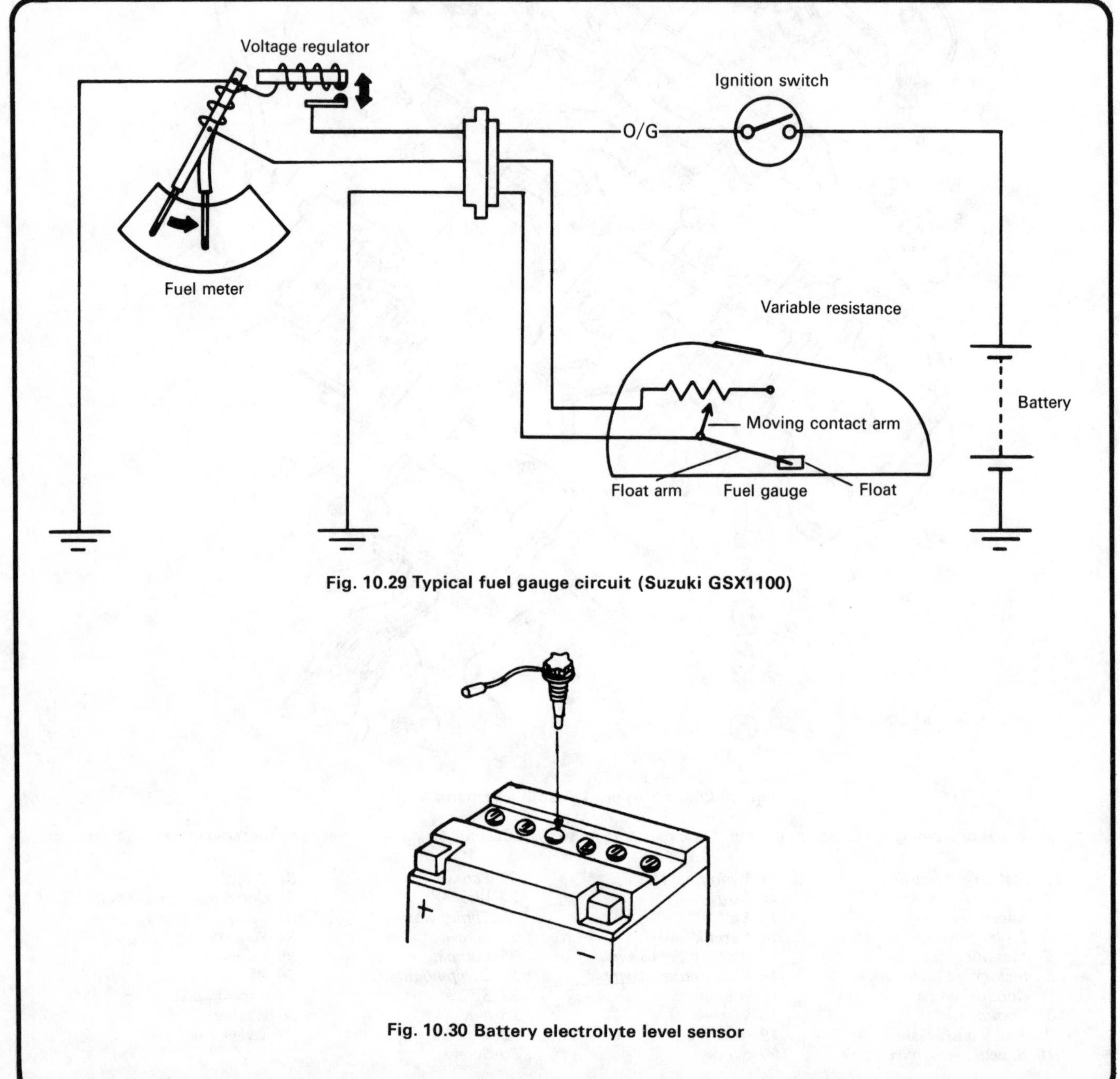


Fig. 10.29 Typical fuel gauge circuit (Suzuki GSX1100)

Fig. 10.30 Battery electrolyte level sensor

## 23 Control switches

The various electrical systems are controlled from the main switch (ignition switch) in conjunction with switch clusters on each end of the handlebar. The design of the latter varies considerably according to the make and model of the machine, but in general the various switches are of the momentary, or non-latching push-button type (the starter, horn and headlamp flasher buttons) and either lever or rocker type switches for the lights and turn signals. The action of the latter can make a machine pleasant or nightmarish to ride at night, as can the positioning or even the shape of the various switches.

The main requirement is that the switch action should be positive and easy to feel through gloved hands. Most current models have switchgear which is at worst tolerable, but many earlier designs were either vague and annoying to use, or in some cases positively dangerous. Early Italian switches gained a well-deserved reputation for poor action and quality, and with one notorious and widely used switch it was very easy indeed to turn the light off completely when attempting to operate the adjacent dip switch. Fortunately, this type of switch is no longer used, but there are still examples where otherwise good switch clusters are ruined by bad positioning of their levers. A common problem is the turn signal switch which on many machines does not have a sufficiently clear centre 'off' position. A little careful design can avoid this problem, a good example being Yamaha's excellent design where the switch lever is pushed to one side to switch the turn signals on. The lever then returns to the centre position, and the turn signals are cancelled by pushing the switch towards the handlebar.

Problems are sometimes experienced with switches which could easily be avoided with a little maintenance. Most switch problems are due to corrosion of the contacts, and this is often caused by water getting into the switch in bad weather. The switches (and the various wiring connectors on the machine) can be made virtually impervious to water by packing them with silicone grease. Given the cost of renewing a switch cluster in the event of total failure, this is well worth doing; it is not normally possible to purchase the individual switches. In emergencies, the electrical system can usually be restored after swamping with water by spraying it with a silicone-based maintenance aerosol spray, such as WD40 or similar.

## 24 The wiring harness and connectors

As has been mentioned earlier in this Chapter, the various electrical components are connected by a network of wires bound together to form a harness or loom. The size of each wire is determined by the current it must carry, thus the majority of the wires on the machine are fairly thin and flexible. A few wires, such as earth cables and the starter motor leads are very much heavier. Each wire consists of numerous fine strands of copper covered with a flexible plastic insulator sheathing. The same job could be done with a single, thick conductor, but this would make the wire rather stiff and inflexible. The insulator is coloured to permit individual identification. To cover a large number of leads, most have a base colour with a contrasting stripe, or 'tracer' line running along its length.

At various points along the harness, leads are connected to other leads or to electrical components. On earlier machines this was done using individual Lucar (spade) or bullet (cylindrical) connectors, but on more recent models much better multi-way block connectors are used. These are usually handed to ensure that they can only be connected in the correct position, and there is little risk of connecting things wrongly.

On many of the larger machines, the complexity of the electrical system has necessitated the interconnection of some of the circuits to keep the wiring to manageable proportions. This can lead to backfeeding between circuits, so to prevent this, diodes are sometimes included in the harness to act as 'one way valves'. The diodes are sometimes soldered into the harness itself and so may not be visible. In other cases, a small encapsulated diode block is plugged into the system via a two pin block connector.

# English/American terminology

Because this book has been written in England, British English component names, phrases and spellings have been used throughout. American English usage is quite often different and whereas normally no confusion should occur, a list of equivalent terminology is given below.

| English | American | English | American |
|---|---|---|---|
| Air filter | Air cleaner | Mudguard | Fender |
| Alignment (headlamp) | Aim | Number plate | License plate |
| Allen screw/key | Socket screw/wrench | Output or layshaft | Countershaft |
| Anticlockwise | Counterclockwise | Panniers | Side cases |
| Bottom/top gear | Low/high gear | Paraffin | Kerosene |
| Bottom/top yoke | Bottom/top triple clamp | Petrol | Gasoline |
| Bush | Bushing | Petrol/fuel tank | Gas tank |
| Carburettor | Carburetor | Pinking | Pinging |
| Catch | Latch | Rear suspension unit | Rear shock absorber |
| Circlip | Snap ring | Rocker cover | Valve cover |
| Clutch drum | Clutch housing | Selector | Shifter |
| Dip switch | Dimmer switch | Self-locking pliers | Vise-grips |
| Disulphide | Disulfide | Side or parking lamp | Parking or auxiliary light |
| Dynamo | DC generator | Side or prop stand | Kick stand |
| Earth | Ground | Silencer | Muffler |
| End float | End play | Spanner | Wrench |
| Engineer's blue | Machinist's dye | Split pin | Cotter pin |
| Exhaust pipe | Header | Stanchion | Tube |
| Fault diagnosis | Trouble shooting | Sulphuric | Sulfuric |
| Float chamber | Float bowl | Sump | Oil pan |
| Footrest | Footpeg | Swinging arm | Swingarm |
| Fuel/petrol tap | Petcock | Tab washer | Lock washer |
| Gaiter | Boot | Top box | Trunk |
| Gearbox | Transmission | Two/four stroke | Two/four cycle |
| Gearchange | Shift | Tyre | Tire |
| Gudgeon pin | Wrist/piston pin | Valve collar | Valve retainer |
| Indicator | Turn signal | Valve collets | Valve cotters |
| Inlet | Intake | Vice | Vise |
| Input shaft or mainshaft | Mainshaft | Wheel spindle | Axle |
| Kickstart | Kickstarter | White spirit | Stoddard solvent |
| Lower leg | Slider | Windscreen | Winshield |

# Glossary of technical terminology

## A

**Accelerator pump** A carburettor device for temporarily increasing the amount of fuel delivered (i.e. for richening the mixture) so as to improve acceleration.

**Aeration** Mixing of air and (usually) oil to form an undesirably frothy mixture.

**Air filter** Usually a paper, fabric, felt or gauze element through which the engine draws its air, and intended to trap wear-creating particles of abrasive mixture.

**Air-fuel ratio** Proportions in which air and fuel are mixed to form a combustible gas.

**Alternating current** Electricity varying in polarity and potential (voltage), reversing direction regularly. The kind generated in an alternator (which see). Abbreviated to a.c. (Compare with **direct current**).

**Alternator** A generator of alternating current (a.c.) electricity. Often does not have brush gear. (see **alternating current**)

**Anode** The positive pole in a direct current situation (Compare wth **cathode**).

**Arc weld** To join material by the use of a heavy electric current so that an arc is struck to generate heat.

**Argon arc** To electrically weld material using a shield of inert argon gas to avoid oxidation of the parent metal. Often used in the welding of aluminium.

**Armature** That part of an electrical apparatus such as a solenoid, dynamo or magnet, which comprises the electrical windings in which a current flow or a magnetic field is generated or excited. (See **magnet**).

**Aspect ratio** With a tyre, the ratio of the section's depth to its width. Old tyres had an aspect ratio of 100% (as fat as they were deep) but modern motorcycle tyres are flatter with an aspect ratio of say 80%.

## B

**Belt drive** Drive by a belt, originally often of rubber-fabric composition, but today may incorporate terylene or nylon and have a toothed construction.

**Bevel gear** Gear with slanted teeth, a pair of such gears turning the drive through ninety degrees.

**Big-end** The larger of two bearings of a connecting rod and the one mounted on the crankpin.

**Bi-metallic** Made of two metals.

**Blow-back** Mixture blown back out of the carburettor against the normal direction of air flow into an engine.

**Bobweight** A countershaft weight on a crankshaft offsetting piston and con-rod mass.

**Bore** Diameter of a cylinder. Slang for the cylinder itself. In some senses, the surface of a hole.

**Bore: stroke ratio** The ratio of cylinder diameter to stroke. When these are equal the engine is said to be square (which see). May be given as a ratio or a percentage.

**Boss** A raised area on a component, the thickness being provided for more strength.

## C

**Calipers** Leg-like measuring instrument (pair of), hinged in the middle and used to gauge gaps, bores or external sizes. In brakes, the component spanning the disc and carrying one or two pistons and pads. (See **swing caliper**).

**Cam follower** A component with intimate contact against the camshaft (which see) so as to take up the cam's eccentricity in a non-destructive manner, transmitting the resultant linear (or non-linear) motion to the rest of the valve gear. Followers may have flat or curved feet, sometimes fitted with rollers.

**Camplate** A flat (or slightly bowed) plate in which are formed slots in which pegs may move for converting complete rotary motion into a sliding mode for the operation of, say, control gear (such as selector forks for controlling gearbox ratio choice).

**Camshaft** A rotary shaft equipped with lobes (which see) for converting rotary into linear movement, generally for the operation of valve gear in poppet valve engines.

**Cantilever** A bracketing arrangement notable for its overhang and absence of support at one end. Some sub-frames are cantilever.

**Capacitor** Strictly, a condenser (which see). But, by convention, often one of considerably larger capacity than a normal condenser and able to perform a smoothing role in battery-less current generation.

**Carburettor** Mechanism for mixing air and fuel to form a combustible mixture and (ideally) automatically correcting for speed, load and other variables.

**Catalyst** An ingredient present in trace quantities in glass fibre mixes to bring about setting. Not to be confused with accelerator, which controls the rate of setting.

**Cathode** The negative pole in a direct current situation. Sometimes spelt kathode. (Compare with **anode**).

**Centre of gravity** The point from which a mass could be suspended so that it would be in 'all round balance' and would remain in any attitude in which it was placed. The 'centre of its mass' so to say.

**Centrifugal** To be thrown outwards. A force. The opposite – the tending inwards – is centripetal.

**Clearance volume** The space inside the combustion chamber when the piston is at the top of its stroke, and extending half way up the sparking plug threads. Sometimes called the trapped volume.

**Clutch** A device for engaging or disengaging the engine from the driving wheel and (except for some specialised applications or in historic form) so designed that connection may be engaged smoothly and progressively at any time.

**Coefficient** The reduction of a characteristic to a numeral value and related to basic units (e.g. per degree Celsius).

**Collet** A ring-shaped device, usually divided into two segments, for wedging a component on to a rod, shaft, spindle etc. Especially to be found on valve and suspension units to enable the spring retainer to lock itself against the valve stem or damper rod.

**Commutator** Part of a rotating armature (which see), against which the pick-up brushes rub, so that electricity generated in the spinning armature may be collected in the proper cyclic manner for delivery to the main circuitry.

**Compression** Squeeze smaller, particularly a fresh charge of mixture in the cylinder by the rising piston.

**Compression ratio** The extent to which the contents of the cylinder are squeezed by the rising piston. The ratio of the swept volume (cubic capacity) plus the clearance volume (cylinder head space) in relation to the clearance volume alone (which see).

**Concave** Curved inwards. Hollow or cave-like. Opposite to convex (which see).

**Concentric** Tending to a common centre. Also a proprietary name of an Amal carburettor in which the float chamber is concentric with the mixing chamber's main jet, thus reducing mixture errors caused by swirl.

**Condenser** Electrical device able to store electricity and particularly to release it very rapidly. Can assist in the control of arcing in a make-and-break system. Properly called a capacitor.

**Con-rod or connecting rod** The rod in a reciprocating engine connecting the piston to the crankshaft via big and small ends (which see).

**Constant rate** A spring is this when each increment in load produces an equal change in length. (Contrast with **multi-rate** and **progressive rate**).

**Contact breaker** Abbreviated to c.b. An electrical switch designed to permit a field-producing current to flow in an HT coil and then to abruptly cut the current so that the rapid inward collapse of the magnetic flux produces a strong, high voltage current in the secondary windings.

**Convoluted** Coiled, sinuous. Convoluted hose is alternately tapered and expanded along its length.

**Coupling gears** Gears that couple two crankshafts together

**Cradle** A support, usually designed to embrace components. A type of frame in which the bottom tubes embrace the power unit.

**Crankcases** The structurally-strong chamber in which is carried the crankshaft (which see). The singular and plural forms are used indiscriminately as, in much motorcycle design, this component is made in two non-mirror images to form a pair.

**Crankshaft** A contrivance, using the principle of the eccentric (crank) for converting the reciprocating-piston engine's linear power pulse into rotary motion.

**Cross-ply** Form of tyre construction, almost universal in motorcycling, in which the wraps of fabric in the tyre carcase are laid over each other diagonally instead of radially. (see **radial ply**).

**Cross valve** A rotary valve placed above the cylinder and handling exhaust as well as inlet gases on the four-stroke cycle. Permits high compression ratios with a good resistance to detonation and yields excellent fuel consumption.

**Crownwheel** The larger of the two gear wheels in the reduction (or final drive) pair at the axle of a shaft-drive motorcycle. The smaller is called the pinion.

**Cruciform** Cross-shaped.

**Cush drive** A shock-absorbing type of transmission system, often involving rubber.

**Cush hub** A rear wheel, provided at the hub with a means of separating wheel from sprocket in respect of transmission shocks.

**Cycle** Slang term for C.E.I. thread favoured by the cycle industry as it is easily rolled rather than cut. Has close pitched fine threads usually 26 t.p.i. in small sizes and 20 t.p.i. in the larger.

**Cylinder** A parallel-sided circular cavity, usually containing a piston.

**Cylinder head** End piece closing of the blind end of a cylinder.

## D

**Damper** A device for controlling and perhaps eliminating unwanted movement. In suspension systems, for quickly arresting oscillations, and for absorbing unwanted energy to release it as heat.

**Decarbonise** To remove accumulated carbon and other deposits from the combustion chamber, inlet tract and exhaust system.

**Decompressor** A small, manually-operated valve on a two-stroke to release above-piston compression. Used to stop the engine and also, on a trials machine, as an aid to descending steep hills. (Compare with **valve lifter**).

**Deflector crown** A raised part or hump on the piston crown of some two-strokes to deflect the incoming fresh charge away from the exhaust port.

**Density** Solidity or heaviness. Also the ratio of the substance in question's mass to that of an equal volume of pure water, and termed relative density or specific gravity. (see latter).

**Depression** A concavity, say in a panel. Also an engine term for the amount of partial vacuum in the inlet manifold, measured in pounds per square inch at atmospheric pressure or in inches of barometric mercury.

**Desmodromic** A method of operating poppet valves so that they are positively closed as well as opened. Cams, and sometimes rockers and fingers, are often used. Supplementary return valve springs may or may not be featured. The purpose is to maintain full control at high rpm, with savage valve events also specified.

**Detent (spring or plunger** A mechanical device to lock a movement and in particular the selector system of a gearbox.

**Detonation** Explosion of mixture in the combustion chamber, instead of controlled burning. May cause a tinkling noise under an open throttle. Intensely destructive. May be confined to the end gases only or may involve the whole charge.

**Diode** An electrical device which allows a current to flow in one direction only. Often used as a simple rectifier on mopeds etc. See zener diode.

**Direct current** Electricity of constant polarity (direction) which may or may not fluctuate in potential (voltage). The kind of electricity produced in a dynamo or stored in a battery. Abbreviated to d.c. (Compare with **alternating current** and **alternator**).

**Displacement** The amount of volume displaced by the piston of an engine on rising from its lowest position to its highest. In some cases may be marginally different from the cubic capacity calculated from the bore and the crankshaft's eccentricity (throw).

**Distillation** The process of boiling a liquid and then condensing the vapour to yield a pure form of that liquid.

**Dog** A projection from a moving part, mating with another dog or a slot, on another part, so that the two components may be locked together or left free of each other. Much used in gearboxes to connect pinions or a pinion to a shaft.

**Downdraught** Downward inclination of the induction tract, usually the carburettor too.

**Drum brake** One with a rotating chamber (of drum shape) attached to a wheel and inside which are placed stationary pieces of friction material which may be forced outwards against the inner periphery of the chamber to retard motion.

**Dry liner** Cylinder liner not in contact with water (see **liner**).

**Dry sump** Four-stroke lubrication system in which the oil is carried in a separate container and not in the sump. Drainage into the sump is removed by a scavenge pump so that the sump is kept dry.

**Duplex** Two. A duplex frame has two front down tubes. A duplex chain has two rows of rollers (a simple chain has but one).

**Dwell** That period of rotation of a valve or contact-breaker cam in which events, as it were, stand still.

**Dykes ring** A piston ring of 'L' section, the long upright in contact with the cylinder wall and the base of the 'L' inserted in the narrowed groove in the piston. The purpose is to get the top ring as close to the piston crown as possible to protect the top land.

**Dynamic** Moving, in action – the opposite of lifeless or static (which see).

**Dynamo** A generator of direct current (d.c.) electricity.

## E

**Earth** The grounded pole of a battery. A connection to earth (or ground). By definition, of zero potential (voltage).

**Eccentric** Not central. An offset pin used to drive or be driven.

**Electrode** A conductor with an end, from that end being taken the electricity.

**Electrolyte** The liquid in a battery, usually an acid but sometimes an alkali.

**Electro-magnet** A magnet, strongly excited by an electric current, used to create a local field by means of flowing the current in windings. Has the quality of losing virtually all magnetism (which see) practically instantaneously the moment the current flow ceases.

**Energy transfer** A system of ignition in which closed contact-breaker points allow energy to build up in the alternator windings, point opening resulting in a rush of current to an external ht coil which transforms its low voltage into high voltage for the sparking plug. Correct ignition timing is vital to spark strength.

**Expander ring** An auxiliary ring, inserted behind a scraper ring, and intended to raise ring-to-wall pressure to the desired value (see scraper ring).

## F

**Ferrous** Iron. (Steel is, of course, an iron).

**Filament** Electrical resistance wire incandescing (glowing) when made to pass an adequately heavy current and thus yielding light.

**Finning** A thin but wide plate-like projection, usually arranged in multiples, and generally functioning for the dissipation of heat. Fins are sometimes used for strengthening and often for appearance.

**Flat head** An engine with a flat cylinder head instead of curved internal contours. The valve arrangement may be sv or ohv.

**Flat top** Piston with a flat top, in contrast to one with a concave (hollow) or convex (domed) crown.

**Flat twin (or four)** An engine with horizontally-opposed cylinders and having a flat configuration (also called a pancake).

**Float** A buoyant object in, say, a carburettor, used to operate another component such as a fuel-admission needle. Also used in a fuel gauge.

**Float chamber** A carburettor component used to stabilise the fuel level regardless of the head of fuel supplied by gravity flow from an overhead tank or by a pump. It uses a float to operate a cut-off valve.

**Float needle** The needle part of the fuel cut-off and admission valve in a carburettor float chamber (which see). It works in conjunction with a float to raise it against a needle seat.

**Flywheel** A rotating mass of considerable weight and radius, used to smooth out power impulses and to store energy to assist clutch engagement 'nicety'. It is also an aid to idling, low-speed running when in gear, and delays changing down on hills.

**Free play** Clearance in a mechanism, say, a clutch control, introduced to avoid any destructive tightness.

**Friction** The resistance set up in two bodies moving relatively to each other. (Compare with **stiction**).

**Fulcrum** The point (or sometimes edge, where line contact is involved) about which a leverage system pivots. (See **lever**).

**Full-wave** Half of the wave of alternating current is positive and half negative. Full-wave means from maximum plus to maximum minus, or 'all of the electricity'. But half-wave is from either maximum to just the neutral mid-point. (See **rectifier**)

## G

**Gaiter** A tubular, usually corrugated and always flexible, shroud round a sliding or otherwise moving joint, and used for protection of working components and/or for appearance.

**Gassing** The giving-off of gas from the cells of a battery due to excessive charging. Explosive hydrogen-oxygen mixture is released. Gassing does not commence prior to the achievement of full charge. Also flooding of an engine with fuel so that it ceases to run or fails to start because of a hopelessly rich mixture.

**Gas weld** To join material with the aid of heat from gaseous combustion. In the workshop, acetylene and oxygen are frequently employed, though propane and compressed air is now much used in industry.

**Gear** A component, often circular, with projections for the positive transmission of movement to a companion gear which may, or may not be, of the same shape and size.

**Gearbox** An assembly containing the transmission components used in varying the ratio of the gearing. Even when this is effected by short chains and sprockets, and other methods of ratio variation, the term gearbox is still used.

**Gear ratio** The ratio of turning speeds of any pair of gears or sprockets being the arithmetical product of the number of their teeth. Particularly the total drive ratio of each set of gears in a gearbox or the overally transmission ratio(s) of a vehicle.

**Grease** A stabilised mixture of a metallic soap and a lubricating oil. Lime (calcium) and lithium are both used as base soaps.

**Gudgeon pin** The pin, usually made of hardened steel, linking the piston to the small end of the connecting rod. Possibly the most high stressed bearing of an engine.

## H

**Hairpin** A type of spring, once much used for valve gear, shaped like a hairpin (but sometimes with one or more coils at the 'closed' end).

**Halogen lighting** See quartz iodide. The filament regeneration cycle at work in a quartz iodine lamp will, in fact, function with other halogen gases of which bromine is also coming into commercial usage.

**Heat sink** The ability of, say, a brake drum to store heat until it can later be shed.

**Helicoil** Proprietary system of strengthening female threads formed in weak metal by making a rude thread of a special form and lining it with a tough wire insert that itself forms the true thread. Also used for reclaiming stripped threads (in holes only).

**Hertz** A measurement of frequency. A Hertz is a movement of one cycle per second. For large values, the Kilo-Hertz is a convenient unit, being 1000 cycles per second.

**High tensile** Material of high tensile (or 'stretch' strength). Tough.

**Homogeneous** Thoroughly mixed. The same all through. Applied to fuel/air mixture.

**Honing** Achieving a good finish and precision control of size, to better than one ten thousandth part of an inch is, say, cylinders, by a slowly-proceeding abrasion process. Similar to grinding, but done slowly.

**Horizontally-opposed** A type of engine in which the cylinders are opposite to each other with the crankshaft in between.

**Hub** The centre part of a wheel, sometimes called a nave.

**Hub centre steering** Motorcycle steering modified to car practice so that the lock to lock axis lies within the hub itself.

**Hydrocarbon** Hydrogen and carbon compound forming the basis of all lubricants and oils formed from crude oil.

**Hydrometer** A device for measuring the specific gravity (S.G.) of a liquid, and of battery acid in particular so to assess the state of charge. It consists of a small float giving a reading against its containing glass cylinder's graduations, liquid being raised into the cylinder by means of a squeeze bulb.

**Hygroscopic** Water absorbing. (Silica Gel is a commonly-used, extremely hygroscopic substance).

**Hypoid oil** An extreme-pressure oil formulated to stand up to severe and unique conditions in hypoid transmission gears.

## I

**Idler** Gear interposed between two others to avoid using overlarge proper gears. An idler does not alter the ratio between the proper gears.

**Impeller** A powered device used to impel coolant through an engine and radiator to assist natural thermo-syphon action (which see). Usually a rotary, vane-type pump.

**Incombustible** Unburnable. The opposite of combustible.

**Inertia** The property of matter by which it wants to continue at rest, or in motion, without change of direction or velocity (See **momentum**).

**Injector** Equipment for squirting. Used for both fuel and oil. Also the proprietary name of the Wal Phillips fuel injector, a system of metering fuel to a petrol engine using gravity supply, a rotary variable jet and a throttle butterfly.

**Insulator** Substance or component for handicapping the transfer of heat or entirely preventing the transmission of electricity.

**Interference fit** Two parts so sized that the inner is slightly larger than the outer. When forced together they jam in place, grasping each other to obstruct separation.

**In-unit** Engine and gearbox, manufactured as separate components, but fastened together to form one whole. (Compare with **unit**).

**Isolastic** Proprietary name registered by Norton-Villiers for a frame in which the engine, transmission and rear wheel are isolated in respect of their vibration by means of rubber mountings.

## J

**Jet** A hole through which passes air, petrol or oil, the size determining the quantity.

**Jockey** A wheel placed between the centres of a belt or chain, engaging with one run of it, and used to adjust tension.

## K

**Kickstarter** A crank, operated by foot, for starting an engine.

**Kilovolt** One thousand volts, abbreviated to Kv.

**Kinetic energy** The energy of motion, and not that of position.

## L

**Land** The raised portion between two grooves. However, the 'raised' part may not actually be proud of the main material but merely superior to the 'lower' section(s).

**Latent heat** The amount of heat input needed to change a solid to its liquid state, or a liquid to a gas, without change of temperature. A fuel with a high latent heat, such as methanol, has a considerable cooling effect on an engine.

**Layshaft** A gearbox shaft parallel to the mainshaft and carrying the laygears with which the mainshaft gears mesh to achieve ratio change.

**Leading link** A form of front suspension using a pivoting link – approximately horizontal – with the axle in front of the pivot. In the short link the pivot is reasonably close to the axle. In the long link design the pivot is behind the wheel. The same distinctions apply to the trailing link (which see) but are rarely applied.

**Leading shoe** A brake shoe which has its cam end 'reached' by any given spot on a revolving brake drum before that spot gets to the shoe's pivot end. (Compare with **trailing shoe**).

**Lean out** Found on sidecar outfits. The machine's steering head is leant out of the vertical (the top away from the sidecar) to combat road camber.

**Liner** A detachable insert in a component used either to reduce size or to provide a better working surface or to restore one. (see **sleeve**).

**Lines of force** The imaginary lines tracing out the pattern of a magnetic system and 'along which magnetism flows'. Shown by placing a card over a magnet, sprinkling on it some iron filings, and tapping the card. (See **magnetism**).

**Live** The pole of a battery other than the earth one. A lead carrying current 'above' ground potential. (See **earth**).

**Lobe** The total part of a cam that is eccentric to its centre, the part not on the base circle.

**Long reach** Sparking plug term for a plug hole of three-quarters-inch depth. (See **reach** and compare with **short reach**).

**Long stroke** Undersquare (which see), but to a significant degree. (See also **bore:stroke ratio**).

**Lubricant** A substance interposed between rubbing surfaces to decrease friction. Friction cannot be eliminated entirely and so-called frictionless bearings do not exist.

## M

**Magnetism** A force invested in magnetic situations or substances, having the quality of attraction and repulsion depending on polarity, and of some similarity to electricity.

**Magneto** A self-contained ignition spark generating instrument featuring primary and secondary (ht) windings and requiring no external power source. Ones with fixed magnets are called rotating armature magnetos (or just magnetos); those of the fixed winding sort are called either rotating magnet or polar-inductor magnetos.

**Main bearing** The principal bearing(s) on which a component is carried but usually reserved exclusively for the crankshaft.

**Mainshaft** A principal shaft, as in an engine or a gearbox.

**Master cylinder** The operator end of an hydraulic control system, so called because (on cars) it operates several slave cylinders (which see). A large piston, in a cylinder, is depressed manually to expel fluid down a pipe(s) to the slave cylinder(s).

**Megaphone** An outwardly tapering chamber in which exhaust gas expands, sometimes fitted with a small reverse cone (which see). The original purpose was to extend a plain pipe rearward without altering its effective length. Later it was found that a megaphone could increase power if blended with other engine characteristics such as valve timing.

**Mesh** The closeness of fit of the teeth of gears and similar articles. Also the grid-like formation, often woven if made from fabric, but sometimes made of metal or moulded from plastic; mesh then refers to the closeness of the weave as in tight mesh and loose mesh.

**Mixing chamber** That part of a carburettor distinct from the float chamber both in function and layout and in which the air and the fuel mix as they meet. (See **concentric**).

**Momentum** The desire of a moving object to continue in motion. (See **Inertia**).

**Monobloc** Made in one. Also a proprietary name used by Amal (and then taking a capital M) to differentiate a carburettor featuring mixing and float chambers formed in one piece from an earlier layout in which these items were separate.

**Monograde oil** An oil, the viscosity of which falls within the limits set for a single SAE number. (See **multigrade, viscosity** and **SAE.** Compare with **straight oil**).

**Multigrade oil** An oil the viscosity and temperature characteristics of which are such that the low and high temperature viscosities fall within the limits of different SAE numbers. (See **Viscosity, SAE** and **monograde**).

**Multi-rate** A spring which changes length unequally for equal increments of load. (Contrast with **constant rate** and **progressive rate**).

## N

**Needle roller** A roller, usually of hardened steel, having its length greatly superior to its diameter.

**Negative earth** Connecting the negative or minus pole of the battery to earth.

**Non-ferrous** Not iron.

## O

**Octane** A measure of the knock resistance of a fuel on a scale of zero to 100 with higher values extrapolated. Most British petrol lies in the band 92 to 101, the larger the number, the more knock resistant the fuel.

**Odometer** A mileage recorder.

**OHC** Abbreviation for overhead camshaft (which see).

**OHV** Abbreviation for overhead valve (which see).

**Oilbath** Invariably for a chain and intended to provide lubrication by partial submergence, as well as to protect from dirt.

**Oil cooling** The use of oil as a cooling medium to transfer heat from a hot component to the environment (atmosphere or even a cooler part of the machinery).

**Oil thrower** A specially-shaped ring or plate designed to throw oil away from a protected site. May take the form of a reverse scroll (which see).

**Oldham coupling** A tongue and groove sliding joint, much used for vertical shafts (which see), having the ability to handle modest amounts of misalignment of shafts.

**Otto cycle** The cycle of operation of an engine featuring charge compression as a prime element, and invariably applied to four-stroke engines only.

**Overhead valve** A four-stroke engine with the poppet valves in the cylinder head and not at the side of the cylinder (side valve). Abbreviated to ohv.

**Overhead cam** An ohv four-stroke with the cams mounted in or on the cylinder head.

**Overlap** The duration of crankshaft rotation during which the inlet and exhaust valve are open at the same time. Equally split overlap means the inlet opens as much before TDC as the exhaust closes after.

**Over-square** Bore greater than the stroke (see **short stroke**).

## P

**Pawl** A catch to mesh with a ratchet wheel, usually to prevent reverse motion.

**Periphery** Round the outside. Circumference.

**Permanent magnet** A magnet made of very retentive steel alloy which holds its magnetism well, in contrast to soft iron and electro-magnets (which see).

**Petroil** Lubricant system for two-strokes using oil mixed with the petrol prior to the petroil mixture's admission to the carburettor.

**Petroleum jelly** A semi-solid formed mainly from a wax but having a high oil content and refined from crude petroleum. Often used on battery terminals.

**Phosphor bronze** An alloy of copper and tin plus a trace of phosphorus, having excellent bearing qualities, e.g. small-end bushes.

**Pinion** In transmission terms, strictly the smaller of a pair of gears but colloquially any gear. The larger gear (or sprocket) is termed the wheel.

**Pinking** Detonation (which see). A tinkling noise from an overloaded engine.

**Piston** A moving plunger in a cylinder, intended to seal the cylinder and to accept or deliver thrust.

**Piston boss** The material below the piston crown (and also joined to the skirt) which carries the gudgeon pin.

**Pitch** The nominal distance between two specified points such as gear teeth, spring coils or chain rollers.

**Planetary** A system of gears in which two or more wheels orbit round a central sun wheel. Found in some transmission systems.

**Plug cap** A cover over the top of a sparking plug fulfilling several purposes such as neatness, protection, a convenient method of attaching the H.T. lead, and for incorporating the legally-required suppressor (which see).

**Plug lead** The wire carrying the high tension current from the spark creation apparatus to the sparking plug. Such a wire is very heavily insulated. In some cases the actual wire conductor is replaced by graphited cord (in slang, string H.T. leads).

**Plunger pump** An oil pump consisting of a reciprocating plunger in a chamber, and provided with ports.

**Pneumatic** Utilising or pertaining to air or another gas. Nitrogen is sometimes used instead of compressed air to inflate tyres.

**Polycarbonate** A lightweight, rigid yet resilient, shock-absorbing plastic, easily moulded and therefore chosen for the shells of safety helmets.

**Poppet valve** One which pops open and shut and in its crudest form like a disc on the end of a rod, the rod guiding and the disc opening or closing an associated hole.

**Porous** Permitting the passage of gas or liquid through the interstices in the 'structure' of the material. The opposite is impermeable.

**Port** Strictly, a hole or opening but now also applied to the passageway leading to the actual window.

**Positive earth** Connecting the positive or plus pole of the battery to earth.

**Power band** The band of rpm in which the engine produces really useful power in contrast to the speeds outside of it in which disproportionately much less power is available.

**Pre-ignition** Auto-ignition taking place before the desired moment and happening, not by sparking, but by incandescence. Invariably extremely damaging.

**Pre-load** Compression applied to a spring, even when it is at its maximum permitted length. Not in a free state. Suspension springs are often pre-loaded and all valve springs must be.

**Pressure** The exerting of a pushing force. Expressed in Britain as pounds per square inch.

**Pre-unit** Engine and gearbox as separate entities and produced prior to a later but similar design featuring the two built as a whole and single unit.

**Primary chain** That joining engine to gearbox, being the first chain the power passes through on its way to the tyre.

**Primary current** The low voltage current (also called low tension or L.T.) in an ignition circuit. That handled by the contact-breaker (which see).

**Primary gears** The pair of gears connecting engine to gearbox and providing the primary (or first) reduction.

**Printed circuit** A route for electricity to flow impressed on to insulating material, instead of actual wires being used to join the terminals involved. Very often, the circuit is, in fact, printed.

**Progressive rate** A spring that builds up resistance to deflection as the load in it increases (see **Constant rate** as **Multi-rate**).

**P.S.I.** Abbreviation for pounds per square inch, a unit of pressure.

**P.T.F.E.** Abbreviation for poly-tetra-fluoro-ethylene, a very low friction plastic often used for bushes.

**Pump** Slang term concerning hydraulics. Several rapid

applications of the operating lever or pedal 'overcharges' the system so that sponginess or lost movement is temporarily overcome by excessive master cylinder action sending more than the proper amount of fluid down the slave cylinder feed pipe.

**Pushrod** A stout rod used to transmit a push as in clutch or valve operation.

## Q

**Quadrant** A selector piece, usually provided with gear-like teeth for driving purposes, and strictly occupying a fourth part of a circle (namely 90°). Found in kickstarters and gearchange mechanisms and often without any suggestion of a quarter part.

**Quartz iodide** A type of incandescent filament light bulb utilising a reversible action based on quartz glass and iodine gas whereby material evaporated from the filament is later returned to the filament. The higher temperatures thereby possible (which would destroy an ordinary tungsten lamp) produce high outputs.

**Quill** A tube-like component, often tapering, generally used for oil injection into a rotating crankshaft.

## R

**Radial ply** Form of tyre construction, only occasionally used in motorcycling in which the wraps of fabric in the tyre carcase are laid over each other radially (or bandage fashion), and not diagonally. (See **cross-ply**.)

**Radiator** Device for losing heat. An input via a cooling fluid is transferred to the atmosphere via a large surface area.

**Rake** The slope of the stanchions of front forks relative to the vertical. Also the slope of the steering head column in some usages.

**Ratchet** A wheel or quadrant with inclined or castellated teeth into which a pawl can notch to prevent reverse movement or to achieve one-way drive with an over-running capacity as in a kickstarter.

**Ratio** The proportion of one thing to another, in terms of quantity. Often reduced to a comparison against unity (one) as a base figure. (See **gear ratio** and **compression ratio**).

**Reach** The depth or height or length to which something extends. Particularly used in conjunction with the effective depth of sparking plug holes (See **long reach** and **short reach**).

**Rebore** A cylinder equipped with a new working surface by removing a worn one. Such a bore is, of course, always therefore larger.

**Rebound** A bouncing back, particularly of suspension or of spring-controlled poppet valves.

**Reciprocate** Backwards and forwards. A reciprocating engine has a piston that goes 'to and fro', coming to a standstill at each reversal.

**Reciprocating weight** The mass of parts that reciprocate. In the case of a piston and con-rod assembly, all of the piston, ring and gudgeon pin mass, plus half of the mass of the rod as determined by laying the rod horizontal and weighing the small-end eye, the big-end being free to pivot on a 'frictionless' mount placed away from the balance pin.

**Recoil** The bouncing backwards, towards its static position, of a spring as it asserts itself.

**Rectifier** Electrical device passing current in one direction only (and thus a wave), used to convert alternating current into direct current. Rectifiers may be of full-wave or half-wave types.

**Recuperation** Hydraulic term for the action which goes on when a column of fluid is returned to the slave-cylinders.

**Reed valves** A two-stroke valve functioning like a reed with pressure itself causing the 'flap' to open or close. Capable of working at extremely high speeds.

**Relay** An operational device to reduce the load on switchgear and/or cabling. The relay functions as the main current-carrying switch while the control switch is nothing more than a trigger carrying a tiny current. Relays may be used to switch heavy currents for horns and headlamps.

**Reverse flow** Control of the fresh charge into the two-stroke combustion space by oblique and upward angling of the transfer ports, so directing the new charge that it drives the burnt gases out before it.

**Rim** The edge, margin or periphery. In the case of a wheel, the part that carries the tyre.

**Ring flutter** Literally, flutter of a piston ring in its groove. Taper rings suffer less from this than conventional rings.

**Rivet** A headed pin of which the unheaded end is subsequently clenched over so as to fasten components together which it sandwiches between its ends.

**Rocker** A device pivoting between its ends and transmitting a push on one end in the opposite direction at the other. Rockers can also handle pulling forces. Some rockers (e.g. in some valve gear) lack the true rocking action and are pivoted at one end and so do not reverse motion.

**Rocking couple** The tendency of some kinds of reciprocating engine to generate a rocking effect on the machine.

**Roller bearing** One containing rollers as the support medium, and not balls. The rollers run in specially-prepared tracks and may be kept clear of each other by a cage. Rollers are usually of hardened steel.

**Rotary** Capable of rotation. Spinning. An engine, the principal components of which spin instead of reciprocate.

**Rotary valve** A valve for two-stroke or four-stroke which, by rotation, opens and closes gas passageways at the appropriate times and usually disc, conical or cylindrical in shape. Normally found on inlet systems.

**Runout** Wobble. Out of truth. Total runout is the full measurement from one extreme to the other. Sometimes referred to as total indicator reading. Confusion occurs when runout is measured from the midpoint which is, of course, half the total runout.

## S

**S.A.E.** Abbreviation for Society of Automotive Engineers. S.A.E. numbers form a system for classifying lubricating oils into viscosity ranges at prescribed temperatures.

**Scavenge** To clear away, particularly exhaust gas from the cylinder and oil from a dry sump (which see).

**Schnurle** Loop scavenging with the attendant flat top (or deflectorless) piston. The incoming charge via the transfer port loops up the cylinder, across the head, and down towards the exhaust port, propelling burnt gas residues before it.

**Schrader** A proprietary air valve for an inner tube (see valve core).

**Seat angle** The angle at which valve seats are formed, usually 45° but sometimes 30°, the latter giving greater effective open gap at low lifts. In some engines the valve face angle is up to one degree smaller than that of the seat for manufacturing and bedding-in reasons.

**Secondary current** That flowing, at high voltage (or **high tension, H.T.** which see), in the multi-turn windings, in the plug lead, and across the plug points. Could be of the order of 20,000 volts, though usually less.

**Security bolt** A reinforced rubber pad, put inside a tyre, and pulled down on to the tyre beads (by an external nut on its bolt) so as to hold the cover in position on the rim. If the cover moves during acceleration or braking, it may otherwise wrench the inner tube's valve enough to cause a puncture.

**Seizure** A binding together through pressure, temperature or lack of lubrication, and often all three. Also called freezing up.

**Selector fork** A forked-shaped prong, mating with the track of a gearbox pinion or dog, for the purpose of sliding that component from side to side, under the instructions of the camplate or cam drum, so as to change ratio.

**Semi-conductor** Material passing electricity freely in one direction but not at all in the other.

**Serrated washer** A washer which is made with tiny 'teeth' round the rim. Also called shakeproof. An internal shakeproof has a regular outer edge and the 'teeth' on the inside.

**Shim** A piece of very thin tough metal used to adjust the position or effective thickness of a component during assembly.

**Shock absorber** A mechanical or rubber device for ironing out minute irregularities in power delivery to smooth the transmission of power. Also, on a three-wheeler, an alternative term for a suspension damper.

**Shoe** A rigid component able to press against another, sometimes, as in many brake shoes, being faced with a friction material.

**Short reach** Sparking plug term for a plug hole of half-inch depth. (See **reach** and compare with **long reach**).

**Short stroke** Oversquare (which see) but to a significant degree. (See also **bore:stroke ratio**).

**Siamese** Two joined into one, particularly two exhaust pipes joining together and entering a common silencer.

**Side valve** An engine having its valve gear at the side of the cylinder and not overhead. Some designs place the valves at the front or rear but these are still called side valves.

**Sidewall** The part of a tyre between the bead and the tread. On this part is moulded the maker's name, sizing etc.

**Silencer** Device to quieten. Normally applied to the exhaust side of an engine, but inlet silencers also exist.

**Silentbloc** A proprietary part consisting of a rubber insert bonded to metal to provide shock-insulating support.

**Silicon** Next to oxygen, the most abundant element (such as sand), and a valuable ingredient in aluminium alloys.

**Silver solder** One containing a high proportion of silver and having a moderate melting point, good capillary migration, and giving a strong joint.

**Single leading shoe** A brake with only one shoe leading and the other trailing, a very common type. Abbreviated to 1LS or SLS.

**Sintered metal** Finely divided metal powder subject to immense pressure (and sometimes heated) in a mould, producing an article with a porous structure and so accurately sized and shaped that little or no machining is required. Sintered metal usually holds oil like a sponge.

**Skimming** Machining operation involving the removal of the minimum amount of metal for the purpose of straightening or flattening. Operations involving stock removal are often erroneously called skimming.

**Skirt** A hanging down. On a piston that part below the gudgeon pin and ring belt areas.

**Slave cylinder** The equipment end of an hydraulic control system (e.g. brake or clutch end). A small piston in a cylinder is forced outward by hydraulic pressure and so operates the equipment concerned. (Compare with master cylinder).

**Sleeve** Much as liner (which see) but more in the sense of restoration of size.

**Slider** A part that moves up and down. On tele forks, the moving bottom leg, which slides on the fixed stanchion (which see).

**Small-end** The smaller bearing of the two on a connecting rod (which see) and through which the piston is attached. Usually fitted with a plain bearing or a needle-roller assembly.

**Solenoid** An electrical operating device consisting of a soft iron core drawn into an electro-magnetic field by magnetic suction, the displacing core being able to push on or pull at some mechanism it is desired to operate by remote control.

**Sparking plug** Device for arcing an electric current, as a spark, between two electrodes inserted in the combustion space, so as to initiate burning, the entire assembly being detachable and mounted in a threaded hole.

**Specific gravity** The density or 'weight' of a substance compared with an equal volume of pure water as unity (1.0). Thus common steel is 7.830 and ice 0.918.

**Spindle** The fixed rod about which an article turns or perhaps swings in an arc.

**Spine** Backbone. A spine-type frame consists of and derives all its strength from its upper member (though the engine unit may also play some minor role).

**Splayed head** A cylinder head of a four-stroke twin having its inlet and/or exhaust ports boldly angled to each other in plan view. The 'opposite' of the parallel conditions of port routing.

**Spoke** A wire rod, hooked at one end and threaded at the other, uniting a wheel rim to the hub. A sturdy, integral part of a wheel, joining centre to periphery.

**Sprag** A jamming device.

**Spring** A deformable component used to permit a movement but to provide a positive return. Springing mediums may be metal, rubber or even gas.

**Sprocket** Toothed wheel used in chain drive.

**Stainless steel** A tough durable steel that does not rust and is highly stain resistant. Usually incorporates at least 25 percent of the alloying metal, chromium. The 18/8 Austenitic grade is non-magnetic and totally resistant to salt water. The S80 Ferritic is magnetic and partly salt resistant, but extremely stubborn to machine.

**Stanchion** A strong, rigid, structural member. In a telescopic fork, that tubular part attached to the fork crowns and on which travels the moving slider (which see).

**Steering head** The top of the front forks of a motorcycle.

**Stem** A narrow, lengthy projection from the main body of a component.

**Stiction** Initial resistance to movement. When once overcome, the item moves more readily. Mainly used in respect of suspension systems. Not to be confused with friction – a rubbing resistance – stiction exists only when movement is absent.

**Stoichometric** Air: fuel ratio calculated in accordance with the pure mathematics of molecular exchanges. An engine cruising will run a little weaker than this and under power a bit richer.

**Stove enamel** A painted finish hardened and dried by heat, extremely durable and possessing a high gloss. In slang, called stoving.

**Straight oil** A mineral oil without additives (See **Monograde**).

**Stroke** The linear travel of a component. In a reciprocating engine, the distance between the highest and lowest points of the piston. Usually, it is numerically twice the crankshaft throw though many piston engines exist where this is marginally untrue.

**Stud** A rod threaded at both ends (but not necessarily with the same threads or even having the same diameters). Usually screwed into one component, there to become a permanent or semi-permanent fixture, for another component to be nutted up to it.

**Subframe** The rear part of a motorcycle frame which carries the seat and upper abutments for the suspension. However, if the frame proper is extended rearward or so designed to fill this function, there is no subframe.

**Sulphuric acid** A strongly corrosive liquid, acid in nature, used in a lead battery. It is a registered poison.

**Sump** A well, hollow or reservoir. Sumps of engines may be oilholding (wet) or scavenged free of draining-down oil (dry).

**Supercharger** A rotating pump for increasing the quantity of mixture delivered to an engine. In slang, a blower.

**Suppressor** An electrical resistance of 5 to 15 thousand ohms value inserted into the H.T. side of an ignition system to suppress interference with TV and radio reception in houses. Also, a resistance, perhaps of one ohm, placed in series in the L.T. circuit or across a dynamo to eliminate interference in a receiver carried on the same vehicle.

**Surging** A wave-like action in the centre of a spring, often destructive.

**Swept volume** The volume of an engine as swept by the piston.

**Swing caliper** A kind of brake caliper featuring only one moving piston and obtaining compensation between the two pads by its whole body being free to swing about the disc. Otherwise calipers are fixed.

**Swinging arm** A radius arm which sweeps out an arc and used to carry the wheel mounted in its free end to provide suspension. An arm, strictly is one-sided though general usage has resulted in a swinging fork also being called, erroneously, a swinging arm.

**Swirl** Rotary or swirling motion given to a charge mixture as it enters the cylinder by offsetting the inlet tract.

**Switch** A device for making or breaking an electrical circuit, often mechanical. However, electrical relays are but semi-mechanical and perform switching functions as can solid state devices which have no moving parts at all.

**Synthetic** A paint based on artificial materials and not on organic ones such as cellulose. Half-hour synthetic is a trade term for such a paint, on which further work may be done in 30 minutes.

## T

**Taper** A narrowing width along the length.

**Taper pin** A tapered pin of metal driven through two or more components until it jams in the hole thus locking all together.

**Taper roller** A hardened steel roller, being tapered instead of cylindrical, and able to take heavy axial ('lengthways') as well as radial loads.

**Tachometer** Rev-counter or tacho. An instrument for measuring engine rpm.

**Tappet** A reciprocating cylinder placed between a cam and a valve stem or pushrod to absorb wiping loads and functioning as a cam follower (which see). May have provision for valve clearance adjustment.

**Telescopic** Two tubes, one fitting snugly inside the other, which are able to slide in and out like a telescope. Such form an effective front suspension (slang: tele) which may or may not feature hydraulic damping.

**Terminal** Literally an end. The fitting to which an electrical connection is made. On a battery usually called terminal post.

**Thermal efficiency** The ratio of useful work available from an engine to the heat supplied from the fuel in question. Values vary from 10 percent for a steam engine, through 35 percent for a petrol motor, to 45 percent for a high-speed diesel.

**Thermo-syphon** Natural cooling, utilising the fact that two columns of liquid at different temperatures possess natural circulation because the hotter weighs less on account of its lower density. Thus the hot engine must be lowermost and the cool radiator must be sited at a higher level (see **impeller**).

**Thermostat** A controlling device changing operational conditions according to temperature rise or fall. It may take the form of a rod or strip producing more or less push according to how much distortion is created by its heat. Frequently used to control the temperature of engine coolant so stabilising engine temperature.

**Throttle** A variable impediment in the inlet tract, designed to provide control of power output by limiting the amount of fresh mixture induced. Literally, a throttling.

**Throw** The amount the crankshaft is eccentric from the crankshaft's rotational centre and, in a conventional engine, equal to half the stroke.

**Throwback** The tendency of a 'suddenly' compressed spring to throw back beyond the position it should assume had the load been applied infinitely gently.

**Thrust face** A working surface of a piston, bearing, shim etc, which takes the thrust and any rubbing action. The 'active' face in contrast to the 'passive' one.

**Timing** The opening and closing points of valves and breathers, and in the moment of ignition. Usually recorded in degrees of crankshaft rotation or in linear piston movement in millimetres or inches, in relation to dead centre positions.

**Timing chain** The chain driving the valve gear and/or ignition equipment.

**Timing clearance** The use of extra clearance to the valves for timing purposes only, so as to give unambiguous indication of the opening and closing points. Some 20 thou is often used.

**Timing gears** Those involved in driving the valve mechanism and/or ignition equipment.

**Timing light** Electrical device, featuring a bulb, which gives visual indication of the moment the ignition equipment makes its spark, and used for ignition timing in the workshop.

**Toe-in** The turning inwards of a sidecar wheel so that it points slightly across the bows of the outfit. Intended to combat the slewing effect created by an offset driving wheel. But note that some racing outfits feature toe-out, the reverse.

**Tolerance** Permissible variation in manufacturing limits. Do not confuse with clearance.

**Tongue** A narrow projection, for example in an Oldham coupling (which see).

**Tooth** An accurately shaped projection on a component so that, in conjunction with others, motion may be positively transmitted from one toothed component to another. Gears, sprockets and racks may all have teeth.

**Toothed belt** A flexible belt, used for driving overhead camshafts, superchargers etc, which has a toothlike formation on it able to engage positively with matching pulleys. Also called a cogged belt.

**Torque** A twisting force, measured in pound feet, tending to cause rotation.

**Torque converter** Device, such as a gearbox, for varying the relative speeds of input and output shafts, thus varying the torque (which see) but not the power.

**Torsion** Twist or turning.

**Torsion bar** A spring in the form of a rod deriving its springiness from being twisted along its length.

**Total loss** A system of lubrication in which the oil is lost after its one and only delivery to the working surfaces. Thus two-stroke oiling is total loss.

**Track** The distance apart, measured sideways, of two wheels, as the rear and sidecar wheels of an outfit. (See wheelbase).

**Trail** The castor action of a steerable front wheel, causing it to take up a natural straight ahead position during running. With positive trail, the centre of the contact path of the tyre lies to the rear of the projected line of the steering head. With negative trail, used in sidecar racing, there is a reverse condition.

**Trailing link** A form of front suspension using a pivoting link – approximately horizontal – with the axle behind the pivot. (See **leading link**).

**Trailing shoe** A brake shoe of the opposite kind to a leading shoe (which see).

**Transfer port** The port (or passageway) through which the fresh mixture, in a two-stroke, is transferred from below the piston to above the piston.

**Transistor** An electrical device with zero warm-up time which magnifies the strength of a small input signal provided it is also supplied with a 'bulk' supply of current to draw on. Used in transistorised ignition systems (which see).

**Transistorised ignition** A system in which all switching is done by transistorised circuiting and a magnet plus magnet detector produces the triggering instead of contact-breaker points. (see **transistor**).

**Tread** The part of a tyre intended to grip on the road. A plain tread or treadless tyre has no pattern on it.

**Triangulation** Achieving rigidity and stiffness by making a structure triangular or introducing triangles into it. A triangle cannot be collapsed without bending one of its sides whereas a square, say, can – it then being said to lozenge.

**Trickle charger** A small, mains-powered charger used to boost a battery. Provision is often made for 6 and 12 volt charging and sometimes for varying the rate (amperage). If 1/2 to 2 amps is delivered, this is said to be a trickle. More is categorised as a fast rate of charging.

**Triplex** Three. A triplex chain has three rows of rollers (see also **duplex**).

**Trunnion** A component permitting the marriage of pivoting and linear movement. Found often in plunger oil pump drives and in some forms of three-wheeler suspension.

**Tufnol** Proprietary material used for timing gears and a resin reinforced fabric.

**Tungsten** A rare metal used as an alloy with tough steels and as an electric filament in a conventional light bulb. The term tungsten lighting is deliberately used to distinguish it from halogen (which see).

**Turbulence** Agitation in a liquid or gas and especially in the fresh charge inside a cylinder. Adequate turbulence may assist good combustion.

**Twirl** A twirling motion given to a charge entering a cylinder. Also called swirl.

**Twistgrip** Rotary throttle control on the right handlebar, operated by twisting. But twistgrip ignition controls on the left handlebar also exist.

**Two leading shoe** A brake possessing two leading shoes. A normal brake has but one. Abbreviated to 2LS.

**Two-stroke** An operating cycle for an internal combustion engine, devised in 1880 by Sir Douglas Clerk, in which combustion takes place on every ascent of the piston, that is the cycle is complete in two strokes of the piston (see four-stroke).

## U

**Undersquare** Stroke greater than the bore (see **long-stroke**).

**Unit** Engine and gearbox manufactured as one single unit and not capable of being separated.

**Unsprung weight** That part of the suspension which lies the road side of the springs and partially the weight thereof.

## V

**Valve bounce** A poppet valve crashed on to its seat too hard for the spring to hold it down on that seat.

**Valve cap** Either the safety or dust cap on a tyre valve, or the now rare hardened and loose cap on the end of an inlet or exhaust valve protecting the valve from wear when struck by the rocker.

**Valve core** A detachable inner half to a valve in a pneumatic tyre, mating with a seat formed integrally in the valve body formed as part of the tube.

**Valve lifter** A manually-operated lever to raise a four-stroke's exhaust valve off its seat independently of the normal operating mechanism. Used to make the engine easy to kick over, to help an electric starter, to stop the engine, and on a trials machine, to assist in the descent of steep hills (compare with **decompressor**).

**Valve seat** That part of a valve, or the part of the cylinder head against which it seats, which contacts the matching part. Much usage centres on the cylinder head half rather than the valve itself. Many seats are renewable. Some seats are formed in other components (e.g. side valve barrels).

**Variable transmission** A system of gearing which adjusts itself, within limits, to load and speed, and without steps. Also called stepless or infinitely variable.

**Vee belt** A flexible belt, usually of rubber and canvas, having a vee-like section.

**Vee engine** A motor with its cylinder axes arranged, not in parallel, but in vee formation.

**Velocity** Speed, gait, rate of movement.

**Venturi** A narrowing down of a gas passage intended to cause a pressure reduction. Found in carburettors and used to create the suction needed to lift fuel from a jet.

**Vernier gauge** A parallel jawed sliding caliper able to measure to precision exactitude by a vernier system.

**Vibration** Shaking. The higher the frequency, the faster the vibration.

**V.I. Improver** Viscosity index improver. An oil additive helping an oil to keep its viscosity (thickness) as it thins out when heated. (See **viscosity and multi-grade**).

**Viscosity** Thickness. Indicated by an S.A.E. number. The higher the numerical figure the thicker (or more viscous) the fluid.

**Viscosity index** The rate of change of viscosity with temperature. A low V.I. means a small temperature change produces a large change in viscosity. A typical quality straight mineral oil might have a V.I. of 95 and a multigrade (with its concomitant V.I. improver) could have a value of 120. (see **viscosity**).

**Volt** Unit of electrical pressure or tension.

**Voltmeter** Electrical instrument for measuring voltage.

**Volume** Space occupied by gas or liquid, usually measured in cubic centimetres and abbreviated to cc, cl or $cm^3$.

**Vortex** A whirling of gas or liquid, the rotation creating a central cavity.

**Vulcanising** Hot curing of a repair to a rubber article such as a tube. The basic process was discovered by Charles Goodyear of Massachusetts, in 1839.

## W

**Wankel** A type of engine, invented by Felix Wankel, containing an inner rotor in a specially shaped chamber and which, in its usual form, possesses three compression and combustion spaces to each rotor.

**Washer** A piece of material, often steel and circular, used to spread the load over a larger area and to absorb the scouring action of the nut, bolt head or screw. It may also have a sealing role to play. The hole pierced is invariably circular.

**Watercooling** Indirect transmission of heat from a rejection surface to the atmosphere, water being used as an intermediate carrier (See **radiator**).

**Water pump** See impeller and thermo-syphon.

**Watt** Unit of electrical 'size' and the product of volts multiplied by amperes.

**Wave** A cyclic variation in direction, polarity and/or intensity in electrical current. In gas, a cyclic variation in pressure, often with reference to the speed of sound.

**Weld** To join materials by heat and sometimes by pressure. Metals and plastics are two groups of material commonly welded.

**Wet liner** A liner inserted into a cylinder block so that cooling water has direct contact with the liner for much of the liner's area. (See **liner**).

**Wet sump** An engine lubrication system, sometimes called car-type, in which the oil is carried in a tray below the crankshaft. Such engines rely on gravity drainage of circulated oil and need no return pump. (Compare with **dry sump**).

**Wheelbase** The distance, measured lengthwise, between the centres of front and rear wheels. Not to be confused with track.

**Windings** Coils of wire for generating a magnetic field in which electricity is generated, and wound in an orderly manner round a former or coil.

**Woodruff key** Slip of metal fitting simultaneously into grooves in a shaft and in a component thereon, for location. Often supposed, erroneously, to be able to drive.

## X

**Xenon** An inert gas naturally present in the air in small quantities and in its radioactive form sometimes used for air-leak detection in pressurised vessels such as tyres.

## Y

**Yoke** A component that connects two or more others.

## Z

**Zener diode** An electrical component allowing a controlled leak to earth above a specified voltage, surplus current appearing as heat. It prevents overcharging with an alternator system.

# HAYNES MOTORCYCLE OWNERS WORKSHOP MANUALS

| | No |
|---|---|
| **BMW** | |
| Twins | **249** |
| K100 & 75 | **1373** |
| **BSA** | |
| ● Bantam | **117** |
| ● Unit Singles | **127** |
| ● A7 & A10 Twins | **121** |
| ● A50 & A65 Twins | **155** |
| *Rocket 3 – see Triumph Trident* | |
| **BULTACO** | |
| Competition Bikes | **219** |
| **CZ** | |
| 125 & 175 Singles | **185** |
| **GARELLI** | |
| Mopeds | **189** |
| **HARLEY DAVIDSON** | |
| Sportsters | **702** |
| Glides | **703** |
| **HONDA** | |
| ● Four Stroke Mopeds | **317** |
| ● SS50 Sports Mopeds | **167** |
| PA50 Camino | **644** |
| ● NC50 & NA50 Express | **453** |
| SH50 City Express | **1597** |
| ● NB, ND, NP & NS50 Melody | **622** |
| NE & NB50 Vision | **1278** |
| MB, MBX, MT, MTX50 | **731** |
| C50 LA Automatic | **1334** |
| C50, C70 & C90 | **324** |
| ATC70, 90, 110, 185 & 200 | **565** |
| XR75 Dirt Bikes | **287** |
| ● XL/XR 80-200 2-valve Models | **566** |
| ● CB/CL100 & 125 Singles | **188** |
| ● CB100N & CB125N | **569** |
| H100 & H100S Singles | **734** |
| ● CB/CD125T & CM125C Twins | **571** |
| CG125 | **433** |
| ● CB125, 160, 175, 200 & CD175 Twins | **067** |
| MBX/MTX125 & MTX200 | **1132** |
| ● CD/CM185, 200T & CM250C 2-valve Twins | **572** |
| ATC250R (US) | **798** |
| ● XL/XR 250 & 500 | **567** |
| ● CB250RS Singles | **732** |
| ● CB250T, CB400 T & A Twins | **429** |
| ● CB250 & CB400N Super Dreams | **540** |
| ● CB400 & CB550 Fours | **262** |
| ● 500 & 450 Twins | **211** |
| ● CX/GL500 & 650 V-Twins | **442** |
| ● CBX550 Four | **940** |
| CB650 Fours | **665** |
| ● CB750 sohc Four | **131** |
| Sabre (VF750S) & Magna V-Fours (US) | **820** |
| ● CB750 & CB900 dohc Fours | **535** |
| ● GL1000 Gold Wing | **309** |
| GL1100 Gold Wing | **669** |
| **KAWASAKI** | |
| AE/AR50 & 80 | **1007** |
| KC, KE & KH100 | **1371** |
| AR125 | **1006** |
| 250, 350 & 400 Triples | **134** |
| 400 & 440 Twins | **281** |
| 400, 500 & 550 Fours | **910** |
| ● 500 & 750 3 cyl Models | **325** |
| ● ZX600 Fours | **1780** |
| 650 Four | **373** |
| 750 Air-cooled Fours | **574** |
| 900 & 1000 Fours | **222** |
| ZX900, 1000 & 1100 Liquid-cooled Fours | **1681** |
| **MOBYLETTE** | |
| Mopeds | **258** |
| **MOTO GUZZI** | |
| 750, 850 & 1000 V-Twins | **339** |
| **MZ** | |
| ● TS125 | **1270** |
| ● ES, ETS, TS150 & 250 | **253** |
| ETZ Models | **1680** |
| **NORTON** | |
| ● 500, 600, 650 & 750 Twins | **187** |
| ● Commando | **125** |
| **NVT** | |
| (BSA) Easy Rider Mopeds | **457** |
| **PUCH** | |
| Maxi Mopeds | **107** |
| Sports Mopeds | **318** |
| **SUZUKI** | |
| ● A50P, A50 and AS50 | **328** |
| CL50 Love | **1084** |
| ● CS50 & 80 Roadie | **941** |
| ● FZ50 Suzy | **575** |
| ● FR50, 70 & 80 | **801** |
| GT, ZR & TS50 | **799** |
| TS50 X | **1599** |
| ● Trail Bikes ('71 to '79) | **218** |
| ● Air-cooled Trail bikes ('79 to '89) | **797** |
| A100 | **434** |
| GP100 & 125 Singles | **576** |
| GS & DR125 Singles | **888** |
| GT125 & 185 Twins | **301** |
| ● 250 & 350 Twins | **120** |
| ● GT250X7, GT200X5 & SB200 Twins | **469** |
| ● GS/GSX250, 400 & 450 Twins | **736** |
| ● GS550 & 750 Fours | **363** |
| ● GS/GSX550 4-valve Fours | **1133** |
| ● GT750 Three Cylinder Models | **302** |
| ● GS850 Fours | **536** |
| GS1000 Four | **484** |
| ● GSX/GS1000, 1100 & 1150 4-valve Fours | **737** |
| **TOMOS** | |
| A3K, A3M, A3MS & A3ML Mopeds | **1062** |
| **TRIUMPH** | |
| ● Tiger Cub & Terrier | **414** |
| ● 350 & 500 Unit Twins | **137** |
| ● Pre-Unit Twins | **251** |
| ● 650 & 750 2-valve Unit Twins | **122** |
| Trident & BSA Rocket 3 | **136** |
| **VESPA** | |
| P/PX125, 150 & 200 Scooters | **707** |
| ● Scooters ('59 to '78) | **126** |
| Ciao & Bravo Mopeds | **374** |
| **YAMAHA** | |
| FS1E, FS1 & FS1M | **166** |
| ● RD50 & 80 | **1255** |
| ● V50, V75, V80 & V90 | **332** |
| ● SA50 Passola | **733** |
| DT50 & 80 Trail bikes | **800** |
| T80 Townmate | **1247** |
| YB100 Singles | **474** |
| ● 100, 125 & 175 Trail bikes | **210** |
| RS/RXS100 & 125 Singles | **331** |
| ● RD125 Twins | **327** |
| ● RD & DT125LC | **887** |
| TZR125 & DT125R | **1655** |
| ● TY50, 80, 125 & 175 | **464** |
| ● 250 & 350 Twins | **040** |
| ● XS250, 360 & 400 sohc Twins | **378** |
| 250, 360 & 400 Trail Bikes | **263** |
| ● RD250 & 350LC Twins | **803** |
| RD350 YPVS Twins | **1158** |
| ● RD400 Twin | **333** |
| ● 500 Twin | **308** |
| ● XT, TT & SR500 | **342** |
| ● XZ550 Vision V-Twins | **821** |
| ● 650 Twins | **341** |
| ● XJ650 & 750 Fours | **738** |
| ●Yamaha XS750 & 850 Triples | **340** |
| ● Yamaha XV750, XV920 & TR1 V-Twins | **802** |
| XS1100 Four | **483** |
| **MOTORCYCLING DIY** | |
| Motorcycle Basics Manual | 1083 |
| Motorcycle Carburettor Manual | 603 |
| Motorcycle Electrical Manual | 446 |
| Motorcycle Workshop Practice Manual | 1454 |

# Index

## A



## B



## C



## D

## E



## F



## G



## H



## I



## L



## M

## O



## P



## R



## S



## T



## V



## W



## Z